S0-BDP-110

WORLD VIEWS:

Multicultural Literature for Critical Writers, Readers, and Thinkers

Patricia A. Richard-Amato

California State University,
Los Angeles

THOMSON

™

HEINLE

Australia Canada Mexico Singapore Spain United Kingdom United States

THOMSON

HEINLE

World Views:

Multicultural Literature for Critical Writers, Readers, and Thinkers

Patricia Richard-Amato

Vice President & Publisher: *Stanley J. Galek*

Editorial Director: *Erik Gunderson*
Market Development Directors: *Bruno Paul, Jonathan Boggs*
Production Service Coordinator: *Maryellen Eschmann-Killeen*
Associate Editor: *Ken Pratt*
Associate Market Development Director: *Mary Sutton*
Manufacturing Coordinator: *Mary Beth Hennebury*

Developmental Editor: *Heide Kaldenbach-Montemayor*
Managing Developmental Editor: *Amy Lawler*
Photo/Video Specialist: *Jonathan Stark*
Interior Designer: *PC&F, Inc.*
Cover Designer: *J Cosloy Design*

Printed in the United States of America
4 5 6 7 8 9 10   06 05 04 03 02

For more information contact Heinle, 25 Thomson Place, Boston,
MA 02210 USA, or you can visit our Internet site at
http://www.heinle.com

For permission to use material from this text or product contact us:
Tel   1-800-730-2214
Fax   1-800-730-2215
Web   www.thomsonrights.com

ISBN: 0-15-506565-3

For my sister,
Wendy Abbott Hansen

Text Credits

Three Days to See
from THREE DAYS TO SEE by Helen Keller.
Copyright © 1993 by Helen Keller. Used by
permission of Doubleday, a division of
Bantam Doubleday Dell Publishing Group,
Inc.

Unit IV

Poem from "To America"
by James Weldon Johnson. Reprinted from
Black Voices © 1968 by Abraham
Chapman. A Mentor Book by Penguin
Books.

The Lottery
"The Lottery" from THE LOTTERY AND
OTHER STORIES by Shirley Jackson.
Copyright © 1948, 1949 by Shirley Jackson,
and copyright renewed © 1976, 1977 by
Lawrence Hyman, Barry Hyman, Mrs.
Sarah Webster and Mrs. Joanne Schnurer.
Reprinted by permission of Farrar, Straus
& Giroux, Inc.

The Most Dangerous Game
"The Most Dangerous Game" by Richard
Connell. Copyright © by Richard Connell.
Copyright renewed © 1952 by Louise Fox
Connell. All rights reserved. Reprinted by
permission of Brandt & Brandt Literary
Agents, Inc.

All God's Children Need Traveling Shoes
From ALL GOD'S CHILDREN NEED
TRAVELING SHOES by Maya Angelou.
Copyright © 1986 by Maya Angelou.
Reprinted by permission of Random House,
Inc.

The Man Who Liked Dickens
From HANDFUL OF DUST by Evelyn
Waugh. Copyright 1934, © renewed 1962
by Evelyn Waugh. By permission of Little,
Brown and Company.

An American Slave
from "An American Slave" by Frederick
Douglass. From NARRATIVE OF THE LIFE
OF FREDERICK DOUGLASS, AN
AMERICAN SLAVE < WRITTEN BY
HIMSELF: Anti-Slavery office, 1945. New
York: Signet Paperback, 1968. Cambridge:
Harvard University Press, 1960.

Unit V

The Peace of Wild Things
from OPENINGS. Copyright © 1968 and
renewed 1996 by Wendell Berry, reprinted
by permission of Harcourt, Brace & Co.

Anbody Home?
from "Anybody Home?" by William
Saroyan. Reprinted from I Used to Believe I
Had Forever—Now I'm Not So Sure by
William Saroyan © 1968 by William
Saroyan.

One More Adventure
From THE COURAGE TO GROW OLD by
Philip L. Berman, editor. Copyright © 1989
by the Center for the Study of
Contemporary Belief. Reprinted by
permission of Ballantine books, a Division
of Random House, Inc.

An Interview with Arturo Madrid
From BILL MOYERS: A WORLD OF IDEAS
by Bill Moyers. Copyright © 1989 by Public
Affairs Television, Inc. Used by permission
of Doubleday, a division of Bantam
Doubleday Dell Publishing Group, Inc.

Shalom, Salaam, Peace: Views of Three
Leaders
From "Shalom, Salaam, Peace: Views of
Three Leaders" speeches by William
Jefferson Clinton, Yitzhak Rabin, and
Yassar Arafat as published on September
14, 1993 in the Los Angeles Times.
Copyright © 1993, Los Angeles Times.
Reprinted by permission.

The Creative Process
"The Creative Process" is excerpted from
CREATIVE AMERICA published by Ridge
Press, 1962. Collected in THE PRICE OF
THE TICKET (St. Martin's, 1985). Reprinted
by arrangement with the James Baldwin
Estate.

Acknowledgments

I am very grateful to the following instructors and professors on college and university campuses who carefully read and commented on the materials:

Alan Ainsworth, Houston Community College
Tracy Carrick, San Francisco State University
Ida Ferdman, Glendale Community College
Lisa Gonsalves, UMASS Boston
Deanne Harper, Northeastern University
Mary Lynn Holes-Gehrett, Clovis Community College
Jennifer Hurd, Harding University
Bill Lamb, Johnson County Community College
Fran Lozano, Gavilan College
Patricia Malinowski, Finger Lakes Community College
Lynne Mazadoorian, Central Connecticut State University
Melissa Mentzer, Central Connecticut State University
Katherine Ploeger, Modesto Junior College and California State University at Stanislaus
Jennifer Reed, UMASS Boston
Marion Von Nostrand, Northeastern University

I am particularly indebted to Heinle and Heinle Publishers and Ken Pratt for seeing the merits of this project and for encouraging me to pursue it and to Heide Kaldenbach-Montemayor for her very thoughtful and intelligent editorial assistance and many other contributions. I also want to thank Maryellen Eschmann Killeen for her expertise and patience as she and her staff successfully guided the book through production. In addition, many thanks to Elaine Hall, the team editor, who coordinated efforts to get the book in its final form. Appreciation goes to Rebecca Oxford and Robin Scarcella, who recognized the book's unique purpose to begin with, and to Kenneth Mattsson, whose guidance helped it through its initial stages. Special thanks are also in order to Beth Burch and Sue Gould for sharing their ideas and a few of their favorite pieces of literature with me and to Elizabeth MacKey, Marjorie Sussman, and the many anonymous readers who gave me wonderful suggestions in the early stages of this project. And, of course, to my husband Jay, whose patience and love enabled me to complete it.

Introduction

An Overview

World Views: Multicultural Literature for Critical Readers, Writers, and Thinkers presents a unique combination of multicultural literature representing a variety of cultures and points of view. Students will not only find their own views represented, but also the views of others.

The book acknowledges that all students bring a range of experiences and abilities to the classroom. Self-accessing features such as glossaries and a quick reference for writers provide resources to encourage independent, yet supported learning. Class time can be best spent on discussion, short-term projects and on other activities intended to interest, motivate, and challenge. From journal writing and information mapping to interviewing and researching both in the library and online, learners will find activities suited to their preferred learning styles. The suggested activities will help students build skills in the areas of critical thinking, predicting, synthesizing, analyzing, and other skill areas that will be important to them throughout their lives.

The book's twenty-five multicultural readings have been selected to invoke powerful writing and discussion. They are grouped into five universal themes:

- Caring for Ourselves and Others
- Wanting to Understand and to Be Understood
- Breaking Through to Success
- Illusion vs. Reality
- Looking Ahead

The selections include essays, biographical sketches, stories, drama, and poetry. The readings and their accompanying activities are organized according to difficulty. Sample graphic devices are provided in the early units, but, by the end, students are required to create their own.

Focus on Critical Thinking and the Creation of Meaning

Each theme begins with a thought-provoking photo and quotes from the readings contained therein. A prereading activity asks students to relate to the theme and make predictions about the content of some of the selections in the unit based on the quotes and on the information given in the introduction to the unit. The following sections encourage critical thinking and, at the same time, aid students in creating the meaning:

Before You Read requires that readers draw from their prior knowledge and experience. Students are asked to react to questions and hypothetical situations in their journals (notebooks purchased for this purpose).

Questions for Reflection/Discussion allow students to work with partners, in groups, or individually as they discuss the motives of the characters, the meaning of the selection, and/or the images invoked by the author's words. Was the author successful in getting across the intended meaning? Did the characters act in responsible ways in pursuing their goals? Did the author's use of language add to the reading's effectiveness?

Exploring Other Sources encourages students to go beyond the textbook to resources in the library and the community, as well as on the Web.

Synthesis Through Writing addresses the needs of all learners, regardless of learning preferences. It allows students to synthesize what they have learned with their own experiences and those of others at home and in the surrounding environment.

Making Connections brings together the more global ideas addressed by the unit overall. Here students critically compare the way authors have treated the theme, making connections across readings.

World Views Online

Using World Views Online (http://worldviews.wadsworth.com), students will gain important computer research skills and experience with the World Wide Web. This site, specifically designed to accompany the book, links the text's themes to online research opportunities and additional interactive resources. A section on **How to Use the World Wide Web** can be found on page xxi. It is designed to give students enough direction to begin their independent online investigations with or without the guidance of the instructor.

Self-Help Features

As they progress through the text, students are expected to become increasingly more independent as readers, writers, and thinkers. However, they will need a few self-help tools along the way. Below are the features provided within the book to give support when needed:

A Quick Reference for Writers This concise guide provides help with the most common writing problems. Clear explanations and examples allow students to avoid and/or easily correct frequently made errors in their own writing. Included are problems having to do with subject-verb agreement, forming complete sentences, article and other modifier use, choosing the right words, and parallel construction.

Strategies for Reading, Writing, and Vocabulary Building Strategies for reading, writing, and vocabulary building are listed for quick reference. They offer many clues to what good readers and writers do while they are participating in these important processes. Just by knowing a few strategies, students can dramatically increase their abilities to perform in the critical skill areas.

Vocabulary Glossaries at the bottoms of the pages provide assistance with unfamiliar words when that assistance is most needed—while the students are reading. Many of the definitions have been adapted from the *Newbury House Dictionary of America English*. In these glossaries, the student will find clear definitions, contextual clues, pronunciation guidance, and prefix, suffix, and root definitions where beneficial.

Cultural Notes Cultural notes at the bottoms of the pages help readers to better understand terms such as the "Dalai Lama" or "Phi Beta Kappa," when they encounter them in their reading.

Reading for Enrichment This section ends each unit. It offers further readings related to the theme. Titles of books, additional stories and essays, poetry, etc. are annotated for the reader.

Contents

UNIT 1 *Caring for Ourselves and Others*

Two rivals realize the humanity of the other in a situation in which
one of them faces almost certain death.

The oldest son of Chinese immigrants must decide whether
or not to put his own needs over those of his family.

Two young people from the Laguna Pueblo in New Mexico are thrown
together in the same household and become "brothers" as they struggle
with a less-than-sensitive world.

R. Mugo Gatheru tells of his own dependence upon his American friends
who try to keep him from being sent home to an unknown fate.

A Mexican-American youth struggles to find out who he
is as he discovers the bicultural nature of his identity.

UNIT 2 *Wanting to Understand and to Be Understood*

UNIT 3 *Breaking Through to Success*

UNIT 4 *Illusion Versus Reality*

UNIT 5 *Looking Ahead*

Rhetorical Contents

Note: Several titles are listed in more than one category.

Cause-and-Effect Analysis

Shalom, Salaam, Peace—Views of Three Leaders
Different Words, Different Worlds [excerpt]
Voices in the Mirror [excerpt]
Back to Bachimba
An American Slave [excerpt]
This Earth Is Sacred

Classification

Different Words, Different Worlds [excerpt]
Anybody Home? [excerpt]
Back to Bachimba
Brain's Use of Shortcuts Can Be a Route to Bias [excerpt]
An Interview with Arturo Madrid [excerpt]

Comparison

Double Face
Brain's Use of Shortcuts Can Be a Route to Bias [excerpt]
An Interview with Arturo Madrid [excerpt]
Different Words, Different Worlds [excerpt]
An American Slave [excerpt]
Shalom, Salaam, Peace—Views of Three Leaders
All God's Children Need Traveling Shoes [excerpt]

Definition

Anybody Home? [excerpt]
Different Words, Different Worlds [excerpt]
Brain's Use of Shortcuts Can Be a Route to Bias [excerpt]
An Interview with Arturo Madrid [excerpt]
The Creative Process
Voices in the Mirror [excerpt]
Bach to Bachimba
An American Slave [excerpt]

Description

Ceremony [excerpt]
The Lottery
Three Days to See

Persuasion

Process Analysis

Strategies for Reading, Writing, and Vocabulary Building

Reading

1. Try to predict the content of the materials (look the text over; think about the title/subtitles; notice the pictures—if there are any). Try to imagine what you might learn from the text.

2. Question yourself as you read (What is the author trying to say here? How does it relate to what you already know? What does it have to do with what the author has just said? What might come next?).

3. Do not stop reading each time you find an unfamiliar word or phrase (the meaning may come as you read further).

4. Mark the important ideas with a pencil, pen, or highlighter. You may want to return to them later.

5. If a word seems critical but the meaning is not coming clear as you read further, check the glossary or look in a dictionary (the *Newbury House Dictionary of American English* is a good one to use).

6. Make a note of any parts you did not understand; you can return later and reread for better understanding. (Are the parts you did not understand at first, more clear to you now? If not, perhaps they will be made clear through discussion with others.)

Writing

1. Find out as much as you can about your topic using sources in the library and/or on the Internet. What do you already know about your subject?

2. Brainstorm for ideas (discuss with peers, your instructor, family members, and others in the school or in your community).

3. Consider who you are writing for. Who is your audience?

4. Make a plan; map out or cluster your ideas.

5. Think about the structures you are using but do not let them interfere with what you want to say.

6. Begin writing (do not worry about making mistakes); let your ideas flow.

7. Think of writing as a process through which the product develops gradually.

8. Consult frequently with peers, your instructor, etc.

9. Rewrite and consult as many times as necessary.

10. Develop your paragraphs with examples, fact, and/or other supporting details. Avoid using a series of short, choppy paragraphs or paragraphs that are too long.

11. Share your written products with others.

Vocabulary Building

1. Make your own word bank or dictionary, using only those vocabulary words that you think will be useful to you. You may want to create a computer data base in which to store your words.

2. Group your new words into logical categories.

3. Use semantic maps or clustering to show relationships.

4. Try to focus on the units (or chunks) of meaning rather than only on individual words. Notice if other words are often grouped with your vocabulary item.

5. Check with various dictionaries as necessary.

6. Use the new words and phrases in your own contexts.

How to Use the World Wide Web

To some, the World Wide Web is like an instant library of free resources; to others, it is a confusing maze of information that is unreliable and hard to get at. Both views are correct, yet, with the right kind of search strategies, the Web can provide quick and helpful information. To successfully search the Web, you will need to think carefully about what you want and how to go about getting it. Below you will find some helpful suggestions.

The Web is one part of the Internet. It is commonly thought of as the visual element, providing viewers with text, graphics, sound, video, and 3D images. Browsers are software programs (such as Netscape Navigator and Microsoft Explorer) that allow users to view the contents of the Web and to travel to places there with the click of a button. As you search the Web, you will find that some pages provide information and that others simply provide a list of links.

How to Begin Searching

Come to the worldviews homepage (http://worldviews.wadsworth.com) to begin your search for information relating to the book. At this site you will find additional information regarding search engines, search strategies, additional information on authors, topics, themes, etc.

Your search of a specific topic can begin by pointing your browser to a search engine. There are many search engines available today such as Alta Vista, InfoSeek, and Yahoo that will help you narrow your investigation and find your needed information. Each engine searches through the Web, looking for the ideas and key words you type into its search box. Searches can generate thousands of related sites and may provide many sites that have nothing to do with your subject. It helps to use words that are specific, but still general enough to obtain the information you seek. For example: a search for "Ferrari" will return much more specific results than a search for "sports cars." If your search yields too few suggestions, try using words that are similar in meaning to your original key words.

Search Tips

Each search engine that you use provides information for focusing your research. Many engines provide "Search Tips" or "Help" buttons. Here are a few tips:

Broaden your search before you narrow it; search for ideas and concepts instead of just keywords.

Use more than one word in your search to broaden and gain important information for a further, more refined search.

Use the " + " (plus) sign for words that your results MUST contain. For example: "native + american + author."

Placing quotation marks around groups of words tells the engine to find these words only when they appear together. As an example, "rolling stones" will bring information about the rock group, not about stones that are rolling.

Choose your search word carefully, using unique, specific terms. For example: "narrative writing" instead of "writing" will result in fewer, more focused results.

You can learn a lot by scanning search results. If you're close to finding your information, you may simply need to refine your search once more.

Places to Find Information

Government information services and newspapers are great places to begin your search for information. Most of the newspapers offer an opportunity to search their archives for articles and topics.

Library of Congress	http://www.loc.gov
US Census Bureau	http://www.census.gov
US Government documents and publications	http://www.fedworld.gov
Boston Globe	http://www.boston.com/globe
CNN	http://www.cnn.com
Los Angeles Times	http://www.latimes.com
New York Times	http://www.nytimes.com
USA Today	http://www.usatoday.com
Washington Post	http://www.washingtonpost.com

Evaluating Your Findings

Examine the sources. Who wrote the information you found? Is the author credible in the field in which he or she is providing information? Are there full citations that can be verified? Are the author's sources reliable? Does the source give you the information you need to link you to other relevant sites? Government sources (.gov) and education sources (.edu) can generally be trusted to provide reliable information. Companies (.com) also can provide excellent information and research tools. The worldviews homepage suggests specific sites to which you can travel for various kinds of information.

http://worldviews.wadsworth.com

Come to the worldviews homepage to begin your search for information regarding the information and authors found within this text. At this site you will find additional information regarding search engines, search strategies, additional information regarding the author of a piece within the text, additional information regarding the subject or theme of the reading, and any additional writings by the many featured authors in *World Views*.

Damn the Chinese custom. He was an American. He had a right to leave the family and pursue his own happiness.

—Monfoon Leong
from "Number One Son"

. . . In time of danger and need, they were reaching out to each other, their feelings put aside.

—James W. Ryan
from "Last Jump"

"Give them hell, Mugo. We are with you." This gave me real strength, and I even began to enjoy the struggle.

—R. Mugo Gatheru
from "Child of Two Worlds"

He Ain't Heavy . . . He's My Brother

—Bob Russell
from a song by the same title, 1969

The road is long, with many a winding turn,
that leads us to who knows where, who knows where.
But I'm strong, strong enough to carry him;
He ain't heavy... He's my brother.

So on we go; his welfare is my concern.
No burden is he to bear. We'll get there.
For I know he would not encumber me;
He ain't heavy... He's my brother.

If I'm laden at all, I'm laden with sadness
that every one's heart isn't filled with the gladness
of love for one another.
It's a long, long road, from which there is no return.
While we're on our way to there, why not share?
And the load doesn't weigh me down at all;
He ain't heavy... He's my Brother.

CARING FOR OURSELVES AND OTHERS

Introduction

The world is a different place for those who see themselves and others as part of one big human family. Whether we see each other as brothers or sisters or as aunts, uncles, or cousins doesn't really matter. What matters is that we have empathy for other people, no matter what their skin color, language, and traditions. Within the United States exists a rich mixture of ethnic groups from around the world—European Americans, African Americans, Korean Americans, Mexican Americans, and Vietnamese Americans, to name a few. All of these groups bring to the society their own talents, skills, knowledge, values, lifestyles, traditions, languages, and much more. But many find themselves needing to overcome the same obstacles that have challenged citizens throughout history. These include poverty, lack of opportunity, racism, and xenophobia (the fear of strangers or foreigners). Others have not had the education necessary to "make it" in the competitive job market in which they find themselves.

An Overview

In this unit we are introduced to several people, both fictional and real, who have done something to make the world a better place. Not all the persons included here purposely set out with this goal in mind. Some of them were inadvertently thrown into situations that brought out what was "human" in them. Others attempted to help, but sometimes with only limited success.

The first selection is an excerpt from James W. Ryan's "Last Jump." In this story two rivals realize the humanity of each other in a situation where one of them faces almost certain death. Next comes "Number One Son" by Monfoon Leong. Here the author introduces us to the oldest son of Chinese immigrants. Upon his father's death, the son must decide whether to take on the traditional responsibilities for the family or to put his own needs first. Following this is an excerpt from *Ceremony*, a novel by Leslie Marmon Silko. In this selection, two young people thrown together in the same household become "brothers" as they struggle with a less-than-sensitive world. Next is the excerpt from *Child of Two Worlds: A Kikuyu's Story*, by R. Mugo Gatheru. In this autobiographical sketch, the author tells of his dependence upon the goodwill of his fellow classmates and others at Lincoln University in Pennsylvania who try to keep him from being sent home to an unknown fate. And last is "Back to Bachimba" by Enrique "Hank" López. His story is based on his own experience of finding out who he is in relation to others. Here we see how deeply Enrique's roots are established as he discovers the bicultural nature of his identity.

Thinking Critically About the Theme

The quotes beginning this unit come from the selections you will be reading. Think about the quotes in relation to the Unit 1 theme, Caring for Ourselves and Others. Choose one or two to write about in your journal. Predict what might happen in the selection, based on the quote you chose and on the overview you just read.

Now look back at the song, "He Ain't Heavy . . . He's My Brother." How does it relate to the theme? Write your response in your journal. Do you like the song? Why or why not?

Last Jump [excerpt]

James W. Ryan

Brotherhood can be found sometimes in the most unlikely places. "Last Jump" presents a vivid example of how two long-time rivals overcome their animosity toward one another when one of their lives is threatened. The main character, Johnny Welcome, is a United States paratrooper. He had survived the Korean War only to find himself facing one more battle for his life. Now that he is at the end of his career, all he wants to do is finish his time with the Airborne and go back to Boston to marry his fiancée, Sally. Here he is, making his last jump, as though he needs to prove himself one more time.

Before You Read

Think of a time when you felt you had to prove yourself either physically or mentally. What were the circumstances? Were you successful? What happened? In a small group, share your experience or write about it in your journal.

*W*elcome had counted only, "One thousand . . . two thous . . ." when he heard the parachute risers zing past his ears. He braced himself. It was coming now—the opening shock! His falling body would have zoomed from a speed of about 100 miles per hour to absolute zero when the main chute burst open. It was like running into a stone wall in midair. He cringed° involuntarily,° awaiting the imaginary crash.

With his eyes still shut, he realized instantly that something had gone wrong. Welcome had jumped forty-seven times. And always he had crashed into that invisible stone wall by now. *How had he missed it?* Opening shock time had passed.

His next thought was that his main chute had failed to open and he was plummeting° to earth like a wingless stone. Yet, the thought was dispelled° immediately when he recalled the sounds of the chute's zinging by his ears.

VOCABULARY

cringed: Shrank backward, as though in fear.
involuntarily: Not of one's own free will.
plummeting (plum-it-ing): Moving straight down.
dispelled: Gotten rid of (*dis-* means away here; *-pel* means push).

His eyes snapped open. *What was happening?* He felt as if he were being hauled upstream against powerful water currents. He saw his boot toes pointed straight up in the sky.

In his bewilderment, he realized that he was flat on his back, rushing horizontally through the sky. Currents of air buffeted° and whipped his neck and shoulders. Hands seemed to reach out of the sky in repeated attempts to wrest° his helmet from his head. Other hands, more powerful, more cruel, beat steadily on his arms and legs.

He twisted slightly, trying to flip over. He caught a glimpse of the earth's varied-colored squares and oddly shaped shadows. Between his toes, far to the rear where the sky and the dark November earth appeared to touch, he saw white splotches. Many of them were spread on the ground. His buddies were already landing.

Then the truth struck him. He sought to scream but his cry was stifled by the powerful air currents. *Why did it have to happen to him? Why on his last jump? If only he could have gone backward in Time. He'd never have made the last jump. He could have said his wounds ached.*

But he hadn't. He had to be airborne all the way. Right to the end. Now he was hung up. Hung up on a C-46. Flying through the sky like a hooked fish.

It couldn't be denied. Not the way he was streaming through the sky with the air smashing against his aching body like a runaway mountain stream.

Strange sounds pounded in his ears. *Did he hear a voice calling? How could that be? Was he cracking up?* But there it was again. He heard shouts.

The shouts came from the C-46. Somebody was calling to him on the bullhorn. If only he could hear. *Oh, for a moment of silence.*

Calling on every possible bit of willpower to soothe his reason and collect his wits, he figured for the time being that he was not going to get clobbered. He found comfort in the old paratrooper joke that no one got hurt or killed until he hit the ground.

VOCABULARY
buffeted: Hit repeatedly (*buf-* refers to a sharp blow). ". . . whipped his neck and shoulders" is a
 clue.
wrest: Force.

He had to stay cool and think. Sure he was afraid. That was nothing new for him. But he had to suppress° his fears long enough for his brain to function and to figure out a plan of action. He was alive and if he remained cool, he would stay alive.

OK, now what? he asked himself. There he was, flat out on his back, zipping through the sky at about 110 miles per hour. The C-46 undoubtedly had climbed up to 1,500 feet or so, maybe even higher to give the pilot maneuvering room. He had to do something. For all he knew, the pilot might have fuel for only a few minutes.

He imagined the C-46 landing with himself still attached to the tail. He shuddered, feeling shaken and sick. He immediately tried to erase the mental picture from his imagination.

"Stop it!" he screamed into the wind. He had to wipe such thoughts from his mind. There had to be a way out of his predicament. He considered shaking the chute free of the tail wing. But how? He would have to roll over on his stomach first to see what was going on.

He tried to flip over. The air currents snapped him sharply on his back. He winced° as the helmet jump strap bit into his neck. The helmet would have to go.

He slid his hands up his field jacket to the buckle beneath his right ear. The air currents lashed at his hands.

"C'mon," he cried angrily. "C'mon! Move!" His fingers let off, tired and buffeted. The strap remained fastened. He had pulled the strap skintight and looped it around several times, as he usually did, to keep the helmet from spinning off when his chute opened.

He chided° himself for always doing everything by the book. Couldn't he just this once have left the end of the strap loose? *Hold on!* he warned. *This was getting him nowhere. He'd leave the helmet on. Let the strap cut into his neck. What could that possibly be compared to his landing still hung up on the tail wing?*

He felt the panic rising again. *All right, relax! Hold on!* But what was he going to do? He didn't want to die dangling on the end of an airplane.

VOCABULARY

suppress: To hold down (*sup-* means down; *-pres-* means to press).
winced: Made a twisted facial expression of pain. ". . . as the helmet jump strap bit into his neck" is a clue.
chided: Criticized. ". . . for always doing everything by the book" is a clue.

He ordered himself to stop that talk. He had been in tough spots before. All he had to do was take it easy. The solution would come to him. But not if he panicked. He had to think. He should try to roll over again. Maybe he could see what they were doing in the plane.

He remembered that Riley was the jumpmaster. He groaned. Riley, he was sure, was not about to break his back to help Johnny Welcome. Luck was against him. Riley hated him. Riley would let him dangle helplessly in the sky.

"Devil take Riley!" he gasped. He didn't need his help. An image of Riley's deeply tanned face rose before his eyes. The face glared fiercely at him.

"Forget Riley!" he urged his aching body. He had to come up with a solution. There wasn't much time. He had to get going. Just like when his squad was clobbered in Korea and he had been the sole survivor. He had lived then because he kept his head. He would work this out too.

Welcome took a series of short rapid breaths, steeled his body and then twisted violently. He spun about in his chute harness and found himself staring at the earth. The air currents battered his face. He squinted to catch a glimpse of the full impact of his situation. The immensity° of it hit him like a punch in the belly. For a few seconds he was certain he was going to pass out.

His partially opened main chute was tangled over the outer edge of the C-46's tail wing. Sections of the chute fluttered like paper strips in the face of a big electric fan. The lines stretched tautly° from the edge of the chute back to the risers fastened to his empty backpack. He was hung up in the sky some fifteen feet behind and at an angle from the plane's tail section.

He thought that he might be able to shake the chute loose from the wing. But the idea was quickly rejected. He never would be able to gain any slack. The rushing air currents and prop blast clearly held the chute glue-tight against the wing's edge.

He caught a glimpse out of his battered eyes of someone gesturing to him from the door of the C-46—some twenty feet forward from the tail section. He dropped his head to catch his

---

VOCABULARY

immensity: The state of being very large (*im*- means not; *-mens-* refers to being measurable).
tautly: Tightly, with no slack.

breath and then forced his head up for another look. It was Riley! The first sergeant was practically hanging out of the open door. He was down on his knees, with one arm working at something outside.

Welcome had to keep dropping and raising his head to see what Riley was up to. Riley's actions flickered before him in a series of shadowy tableaus.°

The next series of blurred glimpses of Riley showed him down on his stomach in the doorway. Riley was clutching a long wooden pole. It seemed to have a crook at the extreme end.

Welcome saw broken flashes of the pole as it edged toward the tail section. Ever closer and closer it moved. But, oh, so slowly. Then it seemed to stop.

Welcome jerked up his head for a look back at the door. He saw Riley inching even further out of the open door. Within the darkened interior of the aircraft, he thought he saw one of the airmen hanging onto Riley's boots.

He called in vain against the powerful wind for Riley to be careful. He was sure Riley was going to fall out of the C-46. The irony° of the situation instantly became obvious to him. *Neither had any use for the other. And yet, in time of danger and need, they were reaching out to each other, their feelings put aside.*

He could see that Riley was fighting to slide the hook out and away from the fuselage° along the edge of the tail wing to try and reach the chute. Welcome's despair hit a new low. It wasn't going to work. The prop blast kept slamming the pole back against the fuselage.

Then to Welcome's astonishment, Riley inched even farther out from the doorway of the aircraft. "Don't, you fool!" he cried out, his voice unheard in the roar of the engines and air currents. The force of the air rushing into Welcome's open mouth nearly took his breath away.

He looked up again just as Riley made one last desperate lunge with the hook to snare the chute. Half of Riley's body popped out of the plane like a field-green jack-in-the box. In the next instant, the turbulence whipped the pole right out of Riley's hands. It zipped past Welcome like a missile in search of a prime target.

VOCABULARY

tableaus: Scenes in a play during which the actors stand still, holding their positions.
irony: When things turn out the opposite of what one might expect.
fuselage: The main body of an airplane that contains the crew, the passengers, and the cargo.

Welcome ducked his head and spun around in his harness. When he recovered the strength to twist around again, it was to see Riley struggling to grab the side of the open door. Riley's right hand shot out and missed. His face was strained and his neck distorted, as though Riley was instantly and vividly aware of the price of his failure.

Caught by the full impact of the prop blast, Riley flung out both arms and plunged from the aircraft. To save himself, the plane's crew chief released his grip on Riley's boots. Riley's arms and legs vainly flailed° the air, seeking something, anything, to grasp. But there was nothing but yielding, unfriendly sky. Welcome swung out his arms, his fingers opened and spread. Riley missed them by a good three feet. In Riley's upturned features, Welcome saw nothing but horror.

Then Riley flashed down like a stricken trapeze artist who has missed his partner's outstretched hands. His mouth was wide open, but whatever sounds came out were muffled by the irate° air and lost in the sky.

Then Welcome remembered that Riley had been wearing a freefall chute. It was mandatory° for a jumpmaster. *Maybe Riley had used it. Why wouldn't he? Riley was a veteran jumper.*

As this thought flashed through his fevered mind, he suddenly was buffeted violently about and sent spinning crazily around like a top. For a moment he thought the plane was about to land. Again he almost passed out. Yet he refused to believe that the C-46 could be so low on fuel.

What was the pilot doing? Welcome tossed about the sky like a puppet. *The fly-boys would kill him,* he thought. He spun one way and then the reverse.

The gorge° rose in his throat. Then he realized that the pilot of the C-46 was trying to shake loose his chute. *The pilot's desperate aerobatics° meant the aircraft was running low on fuel after all.* The C-46's gyrations° obviously weren't going to fling him loose. Sergeant Welcome was still on his own.

VOCABULARY

flailed: Waved about.
irate: Angry (*ira-* means anger or ire).
mandatory: Required. A "mandate" is a requirement.
gorge: a narrow passage carved through rock by a river.
aerobatics: The fancy turns and loops made by an airplane.
gyrations: Going around in circles.

Now he was rushing through the sky on a fairly even keel.° The pilot had stopped his frantic maneuverings. Welcome found himself gradually unraveling. And then he was flat out on his back once more, careening° tumultuously° through the sky.

A voice called to him. It was the crew chief on the bullhorn. But he couldn't understand him. If only the pilot would cut down his engines. Didn't the fly-boys realize he couldn't possibly hear them above the roar of those two powerful engines?

As though in reply to his question, the incessant° throbbing of the engines rapidly diminished to about half what it had been. The pilot apparently was feathering° one of his engines.

Welcome exerted all his strength to twist about in his harness. He groaned from the effort. His helmet strap knifed into his raw neck. He grimaced° and looked up toward the C-46's open door.

"Jumper! Jumper in the air!"

Welcome glimpsed the crew chief. His thin pale face appeared anxious and perplexed.° Welcome tried to wave, but could only muster a weak fanning motion toward the plane.

The crew chief's voice boomed out through the bullhorn: "We're going to land. We have no choice. Our fuel is about done. Sorry, fellow."

Welcome's heart jumped! "They're going to kill me!" he cried. "They'll kill me for sure!"

The crew chief bellowed:° "We are going down now. Sorry. Nothing we can do. Runway is covered with foam. Might soften your landing. Pilot will bring the aircraft to a stop as quickly as possible. Good luck!"

"Good luck! Good luck!" Welcome repeated, as though in a stupor.° He was shaken from his daze as the C-46's engines erupted into a deep roar. The prop blast° again struck him with its full intensity, flinging him over on his back. His bruised chin slammed into his chest and his forehead whacked the reserve chute. Tears gathered in his eyes.

VOCABULARY

even keel: Here it means steady or balanced.
careening: Moving fast without control.
tumultuously: In a disorderly way. "Tumult" is a disturbance or uprising.
incessant: Never ending or ceasing (*in-* means not; *-ces-* means cease).
feathering: Here it means adjusting.
grimaced: Twisted the face, as though in pain.
perplexed: Puzzled.
bellowed: Roared loudly.
stupor: The state of being mentally asleep. "He was shaken from his daze . . ." is a clue.
prop blast: The rush of air from an airplane's propeller in flight.

Last Jump

He thought of Sally and how much he wanted to go home. He couldn't believe it was going to end like this after Korea and everything else he had been through. It wasn't fair. Why had he been singled out?

The C-46 was beginning to descend. The prop blast was hitting him higher up on his shoulders. The toes of his boots rose slowly above the level of his eyes.

If only he could pass out, he thought. Then he wouldn't feel anything. Whatever you feel won't last more than a split second anyway, he retorted° angrily. The moment he slammed down on that runway at 80 to 90 miles per hour, it would be over. He could forget going home, forget Sally and college and all his other hopes and plans.

The enormity° of that conclusion hit him with near-paralyzing force. He didn't want to die. No, then he had better think of something mighty fast. Where were his brains?

Welcome sensed his fear lessening. It was being replaced by an innate° craftiness as death waited only a few minutes away on the runway of the Fort Campbell field. This new-found cunning° was familiar to him. An extra something he had inherited from a long line of Welcomes. He had been infused° with the same sense of craftiness when his squad had been ambushed in Korea and he had fought his way back singlehanded to "C" Company.

He had pulled it off then. He could do it again. Right now.

OK, he thought. *But what are you going to do? Where's the action? That ground must be coming up awful fast. You'd better get going!*

Welcome became alert to the panic suffusing° his body and clenched his fist, determined to fight it off. He swung his arms and revolved his shoulders. He caught several glimpses of the earth. Its great flatness seemed to be rising up to smash him. Out of the corner of his eye he spotted a section of the concrete runway on the horizon.

They must be dropping fast. Probably down to about 800 feet or so. He urged himself to action. If only he could get out of his

---

VOCABULARY
retorted: Returned in kind.
enormity: Something outrageously excessive. ". . . hit him with near-paralyzing force" is a clue.
innate: Inborn. "An extra something he had inherited . . ." is a clue.
cunning: Shrewd cleverness.
infused: Filled.
suffusing: Here it means going into.

harness. "Great," he retorted cynically. "Then what—fall right to the ground?" But if he could unstrap his reserve chute, grasp it in one hand and bang his quick-release box with the other, he should fall right out of the straps. Then all he would have to do was grab for the reserve-chute handle with his free hand.

He thought it might be possible. Might just work. But again he was overwhelmed by the massive odds against. it. The shock of the chute opening would tear it right out of his hand, even though he wouldn't be falling as fast as when he had jumped from the plane.

He prodded° himself to try it. He had nothing to lose. Even now he detected the odor of red Kentucky clay and scrub pine. They were dropping, dropping. The C-46's engines seemed to be cutting out.

For another second Welcome relaxed helplessly in his harness. He dragged along in a forlorn manner behind the C-46 like a drogue° bag for target-shooting pilots. He felt a wave of indifference and euphoria° wash over him. Why fight it? Why not just accept it? It would soon be over. Even now they must be at about 500-feet elevation and lining up on the runway.

"No!" he growled to himself. He had never quit before. Not in jump school at Benning.[1] Not in combat. He had only his knife then and had won out.

He cursed himself for a fool. His knife! He had only had his knife. And yet he had made it back through the enemy lines. How dumb could he be! His knife, of course. The same beautiful sheath knife° he had bought years before when he was a Scout.

The knife would save him. It would free him from his predicament.

His right hand was already searching frantically for the knife. It wasn't on his belt. "Where is it?" he shouted angrily. *Stop it! Think. Just think. Remember. Where did you put it? Hurry!* His mind was a frenzy of conflicting thoughts like an overworked computer, the mental tape selecting and rejecting information in hundredths of seconds.

VOCABULARY
prodded: Urged.
drogue: Here it means a small parachute used to slow down a plane.
euphoria: Extreme happiness.
sheath knife: A knife with a fixed blade that fits into a case (a sheath).

CULTURAL NOTES
[1] Benning refers to Fort Benning in Georgia.

He had it. In his right boot. His remaining strength fast ebbing,° he arched his body painfully to reach down and grab the knife. It was tucked into the top of his boot. If he could just get his fingertips over the handle, he would be able to pull it free.

Welcome groaned. A stabbing pain shot through his right thigh. The leg still hurt where the grenade shards° had ripped it three months earlier.

"Forget the pain!" he cried "Get the knife." His fingers crept along the heavy cloth of his jump pants. He slowly forced his leg up against the punishing wind currents.

"C'mon!" he urged himself. "Just a little bit more. C'mon now! Another inch." Flat out on his back, he could see the top of the knife glistening only half an inch from his straining fingertips.

He lunged, hardly knowing if he had the strength left to succeed. His fingers closed over the steel knob, clenched it securely; then he raised his shoulder to slip it free.

Now the smells of the earth filled his nostrils. He had to hurry! He brought the knife up near his chest and gained a full grasp on the handle. Quickly he reached up behind his helmet for one set of risers and grabbed it. The blade severed it smoothly.

Pain laced his arched back while he grabbed for the other set of risers. His clawing fingers found it and he reached with his knife to cut it. A scream broke from his lips. To relieve the scorching agony in his back and arms, he had to drop his hands.

Mustering up° the reserves of his courage, he grasped once more for the final set of risers, which led to the shroud lines° streaming back to the hooked chute. Grabbing it with his left hand, he slashed at it with his knife. He missed. Quickly tried again.

Make it good, he prayed. That sky big enough to open his chute had to be there. He needed about 150 to 200 feet to give the reserve chute time to open.

VOCABULARY
ebbing: Fading away.
shards: Broken pieces.
mustering up: Bringing together.
shroud lines: Cords that suspend the harness of a parachute from the canopy.

The scything° knife hit the risers and slashed through. Almost instantly the roar of the plan engines began to diminish. He sensed his body starting to arch and fall vertically toward the earth. His head dropped backwards. His boots rose upwards. He was falling free—plunging to earth. He caught a glimpse of the ground. Then of the runway. It was coming up swiftly, a whirling black-and-gray-and-red monstrosity preparing to smash him.

Not today, he vowed. He dropped his knife and grabbed for the handle of the reserve chute. It came away in his hand. A sharp popping noise exploded in his ears. The small pilot chute had snapped out of the reserve chute. As he hurtled toward the ground, the pilot chute caught the air, opened and whipped out the neat folds of the reserve chute.

"Open! Open!" he cried. The great folds of silk fluttered in the sky, gushing in an orderly manner out of the chute pack. One panel caught the air. Then another. With a blinding burst of whiteness that filled the sky, the reserve chute blossomed completely.

Sergeant Welcome slammed to a jarring halt 60 feet above the runway. His mind for a few seconds was a merciful cipher;° his body one painful bruise.

The pain was still out of contact with the nerve ends of his consciousness. *For now he was alive.* That thought dominated all others as his heels slammed four inches into the clay soil just five feet off the concrete runway.

He rolled over on his thigh and took another big portion of the landing impact on his back. His head ricocheted° off the ground. Stunned, he heard, as though at a great distance, the chute collapsing with a drawn-out sigh over him. Its silk folds felt cool and comforting as they settled on him.

Sounds of motor vehicles and whining sirens rushed toward him. Doors slammed. He felt the earth tremble from the pounding of running feet. Hands snatched at the folds of the chute, seeking to uncover him.

VOCABULARY

scything: Cutting like a scythe, which is a long handle and knife with a curved blade for cutting tall grass.

cipher: Here it means almost not existing.

ricocheted (rĭk-ō-shād): Rebounded. ". . . off the ground" is a clue.

Last Jump   **13**

One voice calling to him sounded familiar. Puzzled, he wrinkled his forehead. Then he recognized it. Once he would have sworn that he couldn't have cared less if he never heard that voice again. But now the voice rang in his ears like that of a long-lost brother safely home. He heard the obvious concern in the voice.

"OK, Welcome, you're blinking your eyes, so you must be alive. That sure was a long jump. Longest ever. Now how about getting back on your feet?"

Johnny Welcome reached up to grasp the hand offered him. He smiled softly. "You sure are a sight to behold, Sergeant Riley. Just lovely. The most beautiful trooper I ever saw."

QUESTIONS FOR REFLECTION/DISCUSSION

1. The author, in his attempt to make Welcome's jump real, uses many appeals to the senses involving sight, sound, taste, smell, and touch. For example, "Currents of air buffeted and whipped his neck and shoulders" (p. 4) appeals to the sense of touch. The sense of sight is appealed to in "He caught a glimpse of the earth's varied-colored squares and oddly shaped shadows" (p. 4).

   Work with a partner to find other examples of appeals to the senses. Use these categories: sight, sound, touch, smell, and taste. There may be a category for which you can find no examples.

   Was the author successful in making the story seem real to you? Why or why not?

2. Tell about Welcome's predicament. What went wrong?

3. When something turns out to be the opposite of what we expect, we call it *irony*. Explain the irony in this story. Was more than one irony involved?

4. Think about the way Welcome perceives his relationship with Riley, the jumpmaster. How is it possible that "Neither had any use for the other. And yet, in time of danger and need, they were reaching out to each other, their feelings put aside" (p. 7)? Why do you think this happened? Does this phenomenon happen often in life? Discuss these questions with a small group. Share the group's conclusions with your class.

5. Why did Welcome's fear lessen as he began to think about what he "had inherited from a long line of Welcomes" (p. 10)? Is it possible to "inherit" what he thinks he received from his predecessors?.

6. On page 11, Welcome relaxes helplessly in his harness as he is being dragged along by the C-46. He becomes indifferent to his situation and even goes into a temporary state of euphoria. Do you think this relaxed state, as pleasant as it was, hindered his chances for survival? Explain. Are there other life-and-death situations in which similar states may be dangerous? Think, for example, of a person who is in freezing weather with no shelter. Or of someone who may be drowning.

7. This selection contains several comparisons called similes. *Similes* are figures of speech in which two things are compared using the words "like" or "as." Explain the comparison in the following similes:

    ". . . he was plummeting to earth *like* a wingless stone" (p. 3).

    ". . . the air smashing against his aching body *like* a runaway mountain stream" (p. 4).

    "It [the pole] zipped past Welcome *like* a missile in search of a prime target" (p. 7).

Find other examples of similes in the story. Do you think the author's use of simile is effective? Why or why not?

EXPLORING OTHER SOURCES

In the library and/or on the Internet, find out as much as you can about the Korean War. Try to find information about American troops and their role in the confrontation. Key words in your search might include "Korea," or "Korean War." If you need assistance, ask your instructor or the librarian for help. Share what you learn with a small group. Point your browser to http://worldviews.wadsworth.com for links to information on the Korean War.

SYNTHESIS THROUGH WRITING

1. In your journal, write about an experience in your life or in the life of someone you know in which an "enemy" turned into a friend because of circumstances.

2. Write your own story in which someone faces almost certain death. If appropriate, make irony a key element. You can use this story as a model, if you wish. Include appeals to the senses to make your story seem real. You also may want to try your hand at using simile. Refer to the writing strategies on page xix.

3. Write an informative essay about the Korean War. Use the information you gathered in the previous section, Exploring Other Sources, to develop it. You may want to include the events leading up to the war, a description of the war, how the war ended, and the war's results. See page xix for writing strategies, if needed. You may first want to create a graphic organizer such as the following one.

EVENTS LEADING TO THE WAR:
DESCRIPTION OF THE WAR:
HOW THE WAR ENDED:
THE RESULTS OF THE WAR:

Number One Son

Monfoon Leong

In this story we are introduced to the first-born son of a Chinese-American family. When his father dies, he experiences a mixture of negative as well as positive feelings toward the father and toward the whole situation in which he now finds himself. He must make a critical decision. Should he take his traditional place at the head of the family now that his father is dead? Or should he instead remain in school and let others take on responsibility for the family? The decision is a painful one to make, especially now that he is in the United States where children are usually not expected to take on such responsibilities, especially while still so young.

Before You Read

Think about a decision you may have made concerning your needs versus the needs of others close to you. Did you have small children or were you expecting a child at the time? Did you have elderly parents to think about or a spouse who was dependent on you? What things did you consider in making your decision? What eventually happened? Write about it in your journal.

 n a few minutes Ming would be home. Slumped in his seat, he glared out of the window as the suburban bus jerked and shook its way through the downtown traffic. The usual hurrying shoppers pushed along, arms filled with packages. The usual harried° policemen watched over the intersections. The usual drivers inched through the crowds to make their turns. All were preoccupied° with the business of the shopping for Christmas.

Ming wondered, and reproached° himself even as he wondered, if he really cared any more than those strangers did that his father had died. This father of his had been little more than an old man with iron-gray hair that he saw occasionally on his Sunday trips home. Then it was nearly always only, "Hello, Pa," answered by an almost inaudible° grunt as the old man hurried in from the restaurant to spend his two-hour rest period in bed. The dishwashing was bad for his rheumatism,° Ming had heard him say many times, but you had to work when there were six children and a woman to feed. Really, there were only five since Ming was out working a houseboy, but Ming had never corrected him. Now he was dead.

Ming braced himself against the window ledge as the bus turned a corner and headed toward Chinatown. He wondered if Mrs. Warner would be able to take care of the house and the twins without him.

The twins, a pair of hellions,° were only eight, but they were nearly as tall as Ming, and he was fifteen. He had planned to

---

VOCABULARY
harried: Made angry repeatedly.
preoccupied: Having the mind already fixed on something (*pre-* means before).
reproached: Blamed. The next words in the sentence are a clue.
inaudible: Not able to be heard (*in-* means not; *-aud-* refers to hearing).
rheumatism: (room′ mă tism): A painful condition of the muscles and joints in the body.
hellions: Uncontrollably wild persons; usually used when referring to misbehaving children.

teach them to play football. There was always a time right after school before he had to start helping with the preparation of dinner. He saw again the three square boxes already under their Christmas tree. Two helmets and a football, probably. He caught himself wishing that his father could buy him a football helmet and he shut the Warners from his mind. His father could never buy him anything. He should be grieving, but all he could feel was a harsh resentment against the man who had been hardly aware of his existence and who had just left him with a family to support.

He deposited a dime in the coin box and got off the bus to walk the one block to his home. Passing the two "hotels" just around the corner from his home, he couldn't resist glancing up at the second story windows. A woman sat at one of them, the hard beauty of her much too heavily made up face apparent even through the curtains. Catching Ming's glance, she winked at him. He jerked his eyes quickly back to the street, walked a little faster, and turned the corner.

A half dozen of the neighborhood boys were playing football in the street. They stopped their playing to let a car go by and saw Ming.

One of the boys yelled, "Come on—" but stopped short when one of the others whispered fiercely into his ear. Ming raised his hand in greeting, but said nothing. They very carefully ignored him and started playing again.

"Home" for Ming was in a long, one-story building running the entire length of the block. Set at regular intervals° in the once-whitewashed plaster wall that faced the street were screen doors, each flanked° by a large, screened window. Most of the screens were brown with rust and sagging gently in their frames. Ming stopped at the third door from the corner and pulled it open. He stepped directly into his front room, for the heavy inner door was open.

The entire family was in the small room. He knew that his mother must have gathered them together to await his coming. On the worn, faded couch that squatted in front of the window sat his brothers, the three youngest of the family. All three

VOCABULARY
intervals: Here it means spaces between objects (*inter-* means between).
flanked: Placed beside.

turned identically serious faces toward him as he walked in, faces whose subdued° quality was strained and unfamiliar, almost ludicrous.° The younger of his sisters, sitting near the end of the couch in a straight-backed chair with her thin, brown legs wrapped around those of the chair, looked as if she were about to burst into tears. The other was seated with their mother opposite the boys. She held her mother's hand in both of hers and was looking anxiously up into her face.

His mother's eyes were dull with a lifeless opaqueness,° their lids red and puffy. Her fleshless cheeks were tightly drawn, her lips set in a line of resignation.° Ming wanted to run to his mother, to throw his arms around her to ease the pain of her grief, but his Chinese childhood and years of working as a houseboy had taught him to restrain° his impulses.° If he did hold her in his arms, he would not know what to say to console° her. He did not know the proper Chinese words. He took a few steps toward her and stood mute° for a few moments, searching for something to say. Then he said quietly and deliberately in his mother's Cantonese dialect,° "Papa . . . when die?"

She opened her mouth, closed it again and swallowed hard, then said hoarsely, "Last night. I wait till morning to call you. Not want to wake up your boss."

Poor mother, Ming thought. Afraid he'd lose his job? The pay wouldn't be enough to take care of the family. He said, "Papa is where now?"

"At funeral parlor. Last night they took him there."

"Did you call doctor?"

"Papa died before he came. Doctor said, heart had something wrong." She paused, then added, "Papa gone now, Ming. You are number one son, now head of family."

VOCABULARY

subdued: Brought under control (*sub-* means under).

ludicrous: Laughable; foolish (*ludi-* refers to silly playfulness).

opaqueness: Here it means something not able to give off or reflect light. "His mother's eyes were dull . . ." is a clue.

resignation: Acceptance of whatever happens without a fight (*re-* here means back; *-signa-* refers to sealing or signing). "Her lips set . . ." is a clue.

restrain: Hold back (*re-* here means back; *-strain-* means to bind).

impulses: Sudden urges.

console: Comfort (*-sole-* here refers to comfort).

mute: Silent. ". . . searching for something to say" is a clue.

dialect: A variety of a language spoken in a certain area (*-lect-* means language). It may differ somewhat in pronunciation, vocabulary, and grammar from other varieties of the language.

She needn't have told Ming that. He had heard often of the old custom. Even his mother was to abide by° his decisions now. He looked around at his brothers and sisters and felt the circle closing in about his life, tying it in chains of traditional responsibility. He felt his jaw tighten.

It was his father who had begotten° this big brood,° his father who could earn barely enough to keep them alive, his father who had left the empty rice bowls for him to fill, his father who had given him nothing. He wanted to curse his father and did not dare. There would be no more school for him. He would have to work full time now to support his father's children. He had been told in school that his I.Q.° was high. What good was a high I.Q. when he would not be able to finish high school, much less even dream of college? Damn the Chinese custom. He was an American. He had the right to leave the family and pursue his own happiness.

"Ming?" The voice at the door was a familiar one.

"Come in, Grandfather Choak," he said, trying to hide the tremor° in his voice.

The door opened with a creak and a short, round man entered. He looked like nothing more or less than a Buddha[1] in an American business suit. Ming had always called the man "Grandfather" although they were not actually related in any way. It was customary because he was of the same clan° as Ming's mother and had come from the same village in China. To Ming, he had always been no less than a real grandfather.

The old man glanced quickly at all the family, but addressed himself only to Ming in his mother's dialect. "Ming," he said very solemnly,° "Your father leave no money. We must get money from friends for funeral. You come with me."

"I must go?" Ming started to turn toward his mother as he said it.

VOCABULARY

abide by: Accept.
begotten: Given birth to. This word is not used very often today.
brood: Family.
I.Q.: A score on a test of intelligence.
tremor: Shaking.
clan: Several families related to each other.
solemnly: Very seriously.

CULTURAL NOTES

[1]*Buddha* was the name given to a very rich man in northern India who gave up his wealth and his family to teach his ideas to others. These ideas served as the basis of Buddhism, an important religion in eastern and central Asia.

"You are head of family," Grandfather Choak said.

Ming started to frame a denial, but under Grandfather Choak's placid° gaze, he stopped himself and said, "Yes, I go with you." He followed the old man to the door, but stopped and said, "My Chinese not very good. I won't know what to say to people."

"I talk for you."

They stopped first at Kwon Kim's herb store. Kwon Kim was weighing out some bear gall for a customer. Ming watched the wizened° old herbalist° behind the counter as he carefully placed a whole gall bladder° on the pan of his balance and peered over his glasses to read the weight. Ming remembered that Kwon Kim had always grumbled when the kids had come in the store to beg for the sweet prunes that were kept in a huge jar on the counter. They were only to be used by his customers to take the bitter taste of his herb teas from their mouths, Kwon Kim had said. The memory of the man's miserliness° made Ming very uneasy and he found himself wishing that Grandfather Choak had decided to start with someone else.

When Kwon Kim had finished with his customer, he turned to Ming and Grandfather Choak. He clucked his tongue and said, "Very sorry your father pass beyond, Ming. Leave big family for you."

Ming strained for the words to reply. Grandfather Choak cleared his throat and said, "Father of Ming leave no money, Kim."

The herbalist cocked his head over to one side for a moment as if to let the statement drain from his ear to his mind. Then, without a word, he pulled out a drawer behind the counter, picked up a bill, and dropped it on the counter, shaking his head and muttering, "Too bad. Too bad."

While Grandfather Choak pulled a pencil and a tablet of rice paper from his coat pocket and started writing some characters in the tablet, Ming stared at the bill on the counter. It was a twenty. And Grandfather Choak had not even asked Kwon Kim for money. Kwon Kim was speaking.

VOCABULARY

placid: Calm.

wizened: Shriveled.

herbalist (er' băl list): A person who grows herbs, which are plants or parts of plants used for seasoning foods and making medicines of various kinds.

gall bladder: The organ in the body that stores bile produced in the liver.

miserliness: The state of being stingy.

"Father of Ming was good father," he said. "Every day I saw him go by carrying bag of cakes for children."

It was true. Ming had forgotten. His father had unfailingly brought home a bag of cakes from the restaurant when he returned for his afternoon nap. But they couldn't live on those cakes now.

He thanked Kwon Kim and followed Grandfather Choak out. The Budda-like man waddled down the street with Ming at his side and turned into a new, self-service grocery. Flaunting° its modernity,° shiny gold letters on the big front window announced, "Chung's Super Market." Grandfather Choak went directly to the well-fed looking young man who was presiding° over the cash register. There was no mistaking the Mr. Chung of "Chung's Super Market."

Before Grandfather Choak had finished telling of the need of Ming's family, Mr. Chung snorted, "Man is fool to have such big family when cannot make enough money for them." He looked hard at Ming. "Young man must face truth about father. He was failure as father and failure as man. Must depend on others even when he is dead. I would be fool to give money."

Ming felt his heart pounding in his throat and choking him and his fists doubled up, ready to lash out at the face with its upper lip curled over white teeth in a self-righteous grimace.° He sucked in his breath with a sob when Grandfather Choak took his arm and said, "Come."

As they turned to go, Chung said, "Wait," rang up a "No Sale" on the register and drew out a five-dollar bill which he tossed on the counter. "Here."

Grandfather Choak picked it up without a word and made a note in his tablet.

"Don't take it, Grandfather Choak," Ming forced out through his clenched teeth.

"Must pay for funeral, Ming." He put a hand on Ming's shoulder before he could say anything more and urged him out of the store.

VOCABULARY

flaunting: Showing off something. ". . . gold letters on the big front window. . ." is a clue.

modernity: Modern state.

presiding: Having control over (pre- means before; -sid- means to sit).

grimace: A twisting of the face as though in pain. ". . . the face with its upper lip curled over white teeth . . ." is a clue.

On the sidewalk, the anger oozed quickly out of Ming, leaving him weighted with a great weariness. He unclenched his fists. "He was right, Grandfather Choak," he said. "My father was a failure."

"Do not talk that way about your father."

"But he was. Family lives in hole in wall, goes without so many things other people have. Mother washes all our clothes with washboard and tub. You know I have worked since I was nine years old." All the resentment of years began to boil out of Ming. He stuttered and stumbled over the words that had to be torn up from his Chinese vocabulary, but they had to come out. "Father had no love for me. Hardly know he had eldest son."

Grandfather Choak again put his hand on Ming's shoulder and stopped him. "Your father did best he could, Ming. Came from China without education, without English. What could he do? Raised fine, healthy family. Loved his children."

Ming's lips squeezed together. "Father loved children? He did not know what love is."

They glared into each other's eyes for a long time. Then Grandfather Choak said gently, "You go home, Ming. Perhaps it will be better if I go see others by self." He patted Ming's arm and waddled off. Ming watched him go up the street, then he turned and started homeward.

From babyhood he had been taught to respect the words of his elders. Always he had had an especially profound° respect for the wisdom of Grandfather Choak, but he felt sure that Grandfather Choak was dead wrong now. Perhaps his father had tried, but trying wasn't enough. He thought of Mr. Warner's home, the football helmets. His father had not given him even the love of a father. And now he was expected to revere° his memory, to take his place, to give up his chance for an education, to struggle and go down as had his father. They had no right to ask it of him.

He was about to pass the Widow Loo without speaking when she gripped his arm. "Ming Kwong!" she said. "How tall you are now." She was a dumpy woman of about forty, several inches

---

VOCABULARY

profound: Very deep.
revere: To show great respect (re- means again; -vere- means respect).

shorter than Ming. The note of surprise dropped from her voice as she continued, "I heard about your father. Am so very sorry. Your father fine man."

She released Ming's arm to fish in a well-worn purse she was carrying. "Many times your father helped me and children. He had little money but much heart." She pulled two crumpled bills from her purse and put them into Ming's hand. "I know he did not leave you much," she said. "Maybe this will help a little."

Ming whispered a "Thank you," and she bustled° away. He looked at the two one-dollar bills in his hand for a long while.

His mother was anxiously waiting at the door for him. "Ming, your father's watch. They took it with them last night. We must get it back."

"Watch? Of what importance is watch? We can get it back at any time."

"No. It is gold watch your father had for many years. Undertakers will keep it. He told me many times that he wanted to give it to you when he was ready to go."

Ming could not believe his father had actually said that, but he said, "OK," then continued in Chinese, "We go now."

The young man in the office of the undertaker greeted them cordially. He listened politely while Ming explained that they had come for the gold watch that his father had been wearing when they had taken him away. The man said that he would check on it and glided into another office. He returned and said with a smile, "I'm sorry, but your father had no watch when he was brought in."

Ming interpreted for his mother. She looked sharply at the man and said to Ming. "He lies. Your father always wore watch. They try to steal it." Only the knowledge that his mother's eyes were filling with tears kept Ming from hurrying her out of the office. He turned to the man, who was listening curiously.

"My mother says that she is sure that he had it on," he said.

"I'm sorry," the man said with a shrug of his shoulders.

The condescension° on the man's face struck deep into Ming and his anger began to rise within him. Did this man think that

---

VOCABULARY

bustled: Hurried away busily.

condescension: Attitude or behavior toward those whom one considers to be of a lower social or economic level (-de- means down; -scen- means to climb).

he was talking to a child? He spoke deliberately, trying to keep the tremor out of his voice. "I suggest that you check on it again."

"But I'm sure it is not here."

Ming used his deepest tones to say, "If the watch isn't found, we will go to the police."

A slight twitch passed over the man's face, but he recovered quickly and said, "Of course, we may have overlooked it. I'll check again." He disappeared into the inner office. It was not long before he strode back in, waving his fist triumphantly. "We did find it in a pocket we had overlooked," he said. He put the watch into Ming's outstretched hand.

Closing his fingers over the watch without looking at it, Ming muttered, "Thank you," and, taking his mother's arm, walked out.

Ming blinked at the sudden wintry sunlight. He stopped with his mother in the shadow of the building and looked at the watch in his hand. It was large and heavy, attached to a massive-looking chain. It must have been many years old for it was of the type whose face was protected by a snap cover. He squeezed down the stem and the cover flipped open. Inside the cover, he saw several words engraved in ornate° script. Squinting his eyes against the brightness he read, "For Ming, my son." His mouth was suddenly dry and he had difficulty swallowing as he tried to moisten it.

His mother was watching him. "Only last year, your father had something put in cover," she said.

Ming couldn't speak. They started walking homeward.

"You are number one son, head of family now, but after funeral, you must go back to Mrs. Warner and to school," his mother said.

"But the family—."

"Many things a woman can do at home to earn money."

"No," Ming said firmly. "I will work and go to night school"

His mother started to say something further, but Ming stopped her with, "Remember, I am number one son, head of family."

He took her arm to help her across the street.

VOCABULARY

ornate: Very fancy or decorative.

QUESTIONS FOR REFLECTION/DISCUSSION

1. Why do you think Ming does not grieve for his dead father? Why does he feel resentment toward him? Does he feel guilty about it? How do you know?

2. Describe the neighborhood in which Ming's family lives. What clues from the reading helped you? How does it compare to the neighborhood in which you live?

3. In reaction to the expectation that he become the head of the family upon his father's death, Ming said, "Damn the Chinese custom. He [Ming] was an American. He had the right to leave the family and pursue his own happiness" (p. 20). For what reasons do you think he reacts this way? Does he feel guilty about challenging this tradition? How do you know? Discuss these questions with a small group. Share the group's conclusions with your class.

4. In the culture you know best, what expectations are placed upon the surviving children when a parent dies? What are the expectations in your own family concerning surviving children?

5. Why do you think Ming did not accept the five-dollar bill he was given by Mr. Chung? Do you think he was right to do this when the family needed the money so desperately?

6. What does Ming learn about his father from others after his father's death? How does he react to what they reveal?

7. Why do you think Grandfather Choak sent Ming home and told him he would collect the money for the family by himself?

8. For what reasons does Ming have a change of heart about taking responsibility for the family? What leads to his decision to work for the family and go to night school? Do you think he made the right choice? Why or why not?

 EXPLORING OTHER SOURCES

In the library and/or on the Internet, find current statistics about students in the country in which you live who drop out of high school for one reason or another. What generally happens to these students? Do many ever finish their education in night school or in some alternative school setting? How do the earnings on the job of those who finish compare with those who do not? What about those who drop out of college or never attend? What happens to them? How do their earnings compare with those who graduate? Key words in your search might include "high school dropouts,"

"college dropouts," "graduates," and "earnings of graduates." To search the Internet, go to World Views Online (http://worldviews.wadsworth.com) for links to information on graduates/nongraduates. Ask your instructor or the librarian for assistance if you need it. Share what you learn with a small group. Then decide as a group what advice you would give Ming about his situation.

Synthesis Through Writing

1. In your journal, extend your prereading entry; write about a decision you made concerning your needs versus the needs of others close to you, such as your own children, siblings, or parents/guardians. How did your decision compare with the one made by Ming? Was your decision a good one? Explain.

2. Write an essay comparing college graduates with non–college graduates. Use the information you gathered in the previous section, Exploring Other Sources, to support your point of view. First divide a piece of paper into two columns (see the following example). Label the first column "College Graduates" and the second "Non–College Graduates." Write the details in the appropriate columns and use this as a guide for writing your essay. Refer also to the writing strategies on page xix.

College Graduates	Non–College Graduates

Ceremony [excerpt]
Leslie Marmon Silko

In this selection we learn about negative attitudes and how they are often revealed in the small things people do and say. And we learn what it means to be a brother, not so much in the global sense, but within the more personal world of the family. The main characters in this story are Rocky and Tayo, both from the Laguna Pueblo in New Mexico. While not blood brothers, they are brothers nevertheless, in the idealized sense of the word. In spite of adversity, they have developed mutual respect and a certain amount of interdependence that become a source of strength for both.

Leslie Marmon Silko is the author of the novel *Ceremony*, from which this reading was taken. She was raised on the Laguna Pueblo[1] Reservation in New Mexico, where she stills lives today with her husband and two children. Her works are grounded in the storytelling tradition of the Pueblo Indians and highlight the chants and other ceremonial features that have been used for generations to bring about cures for diseases and protection from serious illness and potential disaster. Her stories deal with current problems common to Native Americans, including depression, alcoholism, and related stresses. Her characters often seek and find relief in the rich ceremonial traditions associated with Native American culture.

Before You Read

Think of a relationship in which you may have been involved in which you considered the other person to be like a brother or a sister. How did this relationship develop? What eventually happened to it? Think about the positive effects it may have had on your life. Discuss it with a partner or write about it in your journal.

*T*he Army recruiter had taped posters of tanks and marching soldiers around the edge of a folding table. The Government car was parked next to the post office under the flagpole, and he had set up the table next to the car, trying to find shelter from the wind. But the posters were flapping and twisting around, and the brittle edges of the paper were beginning to split and tear. There was a chill in the wind during the last days the sun occupied a summer place in the sky—and something relentless° in the way the wind drove the sand and dust ahead of it. The recruiter was sitting on his folding chair, but he had to keep both hands on his pamphlets° to keep them from scattering. He had been waiting for more people to show up before he began his speech, but Rocky and Tayo and old man Jeff were the only people out in the wind that afternoon.

"Anyone can fight for America," he began, giving special emphasis to "America," "even you boys. In a time of need, anyone can fight for her." A big gust of sand swirled around

---

VOCABULARY
relentless: Steady; unyielding.
pamphlets: (păm flĕts): Small booklets of few pages giving information about some subject of interest. Also called *brochures* or *leaflets*.

CULTURAL NOTES
[1]The Laguna Pueblo is one of several small villages in the southwestern United States in which the dwellings are typically made of adobe, a brick made of clay that has been dried in the sun.

them; Rocky turned his back to it and Tayo covered his face with his hands; old man Jeff went inside the post office. The recruiter paused to rearrange the pamphlets and check the damage the wind had done to the posters. He looked disgusted then, as though he were almost ready to leave. But he went on with his speech.

"Now I know you boys love America as much as we do, but this is your big chance to *show* it!" He stood up then, as he had rehearsed, and looked them in the eye sincerely. He handed them color pamphlets with a man in a khaki° uniform and gold braid on the cover; in the background, behind the figure in the uniform, there was a gold eagle with its wings spread across an American flag.

Rocky read each page of the pamphlet carefully. He looked up at Tayo and his face was serious and proud. Tayo knew right then what Rocky wanted to do. The wind blew harder; a gust caught the pamphlets and swirled them off the card table. They scattered like dry leaves across the ground. The recruiter ran after them with his arms out in front of him as if he were chasing turkeys. Rocky helped him pick them up, and he nodded sharply for Tayo to help too. Rocky talked to the recruiter about the training programs while they shook sand out of the brochures and folded them up again.

"I want to be a pilot." He paused and looked at the recruiter. "You can fly all over the world that way, can't you?"

The recruiter was packing the leaflets into a cardboard box; he didn't look up. "Sure, sure," he said, "you enlist now and you'll be eligible° for everything—pilot training—everything." He folded the legs under the little table and slammed down the lid of the car's trunk. He glanced at his big chrome° wristwatch.

"You men want to sign up?"

Rocky looked at Tayo as if he wanted to ask him something. It was strange to see that expression on his face, because Rocky had always known what he was doing, without asking anyone.

"And my brother," Rocky said, nodding at Tayo. "If we both sign up, can we stay together?"

It was the first time in all the years that Tayo had lived with him that Rocky ever called him "brother." Auntie had always

---

VOCABULARY

khaki (kă kē): A greenish light-brown color.
eligible: Qualified.
chrome (krōm): Chromium, a hard, shiny, steel-gray element.

Ceremony

been careful that Rocky didn't call Tayo "brother," and when other people mistakenly called them brothers, she was quick to correct the error.

"They're not brothers," she'd say, "that's Laura's boy. You know the one." She had a way of saying it, a tone of voice which bitterly told the story, and the disgrace she and the family had suffered. The things Laura had done weren't easily forgotten by the people, but she could maintain a distance between Rocky, who was her pride, and this other, unwanted child. If nobody else ever knew about this distance, she and Tayo did.

He was four years old the night his mother left him there. He didn't remember much: only that she had come after dark and wrapped him in a man's coat—it smelled like a man—and that there were men in the car with them: and she held him all the way, kept him bundled tight and close to her, and he had dozed and listened, half dreaming, their laughter and the sound of a cork squeaking in and out of a bottle. He could not remember if she had fed him, but when they got to Laguna that night, he wasn't hungry and he refused the bread Uncle Josiah offered him. He clung to her because when she left him, he knew she would be gone for a long time. She kissed him on the forehead with whiskey breath, and then pushed him gently into Josiah's arms as she backed out the door. He cried and fought Josiah, trying to follow her, but his uncle held him firmly and told him not to cry because he had a brother now: Rocky would be his brother, and he could stay with them until Christmas. Rocky had been staring at him, but with the mention of Christmas Tayo started crying and kicking the leg of the table. There were tears all over his face and his nose was running.

"Go away," he screamed, "you're not my brother. I don't want no brother!" Tayo covered his ears with his hands and buried his face against Josiah's leg, crying because he knew: this time she wasn't coming back for him. Josiah pulled out his red bandanna handkerchief and wiped Tayo's nose and eyes. He looked at Rocky sternly and then took both of the little boys by the hand. They walked into the back room together, and Josiah showed him the bed that he and Rocky would share for so many years.

When old Grandma and Auntie came home that night from the bingo game at the church, Tayo and Rocky were already in bed. Tayo could tell by the sound of his breathing that Rocky was already asleep. But he lay there in the dark and listened to voices in the kitchen, voices of Josiah and Auntie and the faint voice of old Grandma. He never knew what they said that night, because the voices merged into a hum, like night insects around a lamp; but he thought he could hear Auntie raise her voice and the sounds of pots and pans slamming together on the stove. And years later he learned she did that whenever she was angry.

It was a private understanding between the two of them. When Josiah or old Grandma or Robert [Rocky's brother] was there, the agreement was suspended,° and she pretended to treat him the same as she treated Rocky, but they both knew it was only temporary. When she was alone with the boys, she kept Rocky close to her; while she kneaded° the bread, she gave Rocky little pieces of dough to play with; while she darned socks, she gave him scraps of cloth and a needle and thread to play with. She was careful that Rocky did not share these things with Tayo, that they kept a distance between themselves and him. But she would not let Tayo go outside or play in another room alone. She wanted him close enough to feel excluded, to be aware of the distance between them. The two little boys accepted the distance, but Rocky was never cruel to Tayo. He seemed to know that the narrow silence was reserved only for times when the three of them were alone together. They sensed the difference in her when old Grandma or Josiah was present, and they adjusted without hesitation, keeping their secret.

But after they started school, the edges of the distance softened, and Auntie seldom had the boys to herself any more. They were gone most of the day, and old Grandma was totally blind by then and always there, sitting close to her stove. Rocky was more anxious than Tayo to stay away from the house, to stay after school for sports or to play with friends. It was Rocky who withdrew from her, although only she and Tayo realized it. He did it naturally, like a rabbit leaping away from a shadow suddenly above him.

Tayo and Auntie understood each other very well. Years later Tayo wondered if anyone, even old Grandma or Josiah, ever understood her as well as he did. He learned to listen to the undertones of her voice. Robert and Josiah evaded her; they

---

VOCABULARY

suspended: Here it means put on hold without a decision being made (-pend- means hanging).
kneaded (nē dĭd): To mix something by folding it in over and over with the hands. ". . . the bread [dough]" is a clue.

were deaf to those undertones. In her blindness and old age, old Grandma stubbornly ignored her and heard only what she wanted to hear. Rocky had his own way, with his after-school sports and his girl friends. Only Tayo could hear it, like fingernails scratching against bare rock, her terror at being trapped in one of the oldest ways.

An old sensitivity had descended in her, surviving thousands of years from the oldest times, when the people shared a single clan° name and they told each other who they were; they recounted the actions and words each of their clan had taken, and would take; from before they were born and long after they died, the people shared the same consciousness.° The people had known, with the simple certainty of the world they saw, how everything should be.

But the . . . world had become entangled with European names: the names of the rivers, the hills, the names of the animals and plants—all of creation suddenly had two names: an Indian name and a white name. Christianity separated the people from themselves; it tried to crush the single clan name, encouraging each person to stand alone, because Jesus Christ would save only the individual soul; Jesus Christ was not like the Mother who loved and cared for them as her children, as her family.

The sensitivity remained: the ability to feel what the others were feeling in the belly and chest; words were not necessary, but the messages the people felt were confused now. When Little Sister had started drinking wine and riding in cars with white men and Mexicans, the people could not define their feeling about her, but the people felt something deeper; they were losing her, they were losing part of themselves. The older sister had to act; she had to act for the people, to get this young girl back.

It might have been possible if the girl had not been ashamed of herself. Shamed by what they taught her in school about the deplorable ways of the Indian people; holy missionary white people who wanted only good for the Indians, white people who dedicated their lives to helping the Indians, these people urged her to break away from her home. She was excited to see

---

VOCABULARY

clan: Here it means a part of a tribe having a common ancestor.
consciousness (kŭn' shás nĭs): Here it means the overall sensitivities, perspectives, and attitudes resulting from shared prior knowledge and experience.

that despite the fact she was an Indian, the white men smiled at her from their cars as she walked from the bus stop in Albuquerque back to the Indian School. She smiled and waved; she looked at her own reflection in windows of houses she passed; her dress, her lipstick, her hair—it was all done perfectly, the way the home-ec teacher taught them, exactly like the white girls.

But after she had been with them, she could feel the truth in their fists and in their greedy feeble love-making; but it was a truth which she had no English words for. She hated the people at home when white people talked about their peculiarities°; but she always hated herself more because she still thought about them, because she knew their pain at what she was doing with her life. The feelings of shame, at her own people and at the white people, grew inside her, side by side like monstrous twins that would have to be left in the hills to die. The people wanted her back. Her older sister must bring her back. For the people, it was that simple, and when they failed, the humiliation° fell on all of them; what happened to the girl did not happen to her alone, it happened to all of them.

They focused the anger on the girl and her family, knowing from many years of this conflict that the anger could not be contained by a single person or family, but that it must leak out and soak into the ground under the entire village.

So Auntie had tried desperately to reconcile° the family with the people; the old instinct had always been to gather the feelings and opinions that were scattered through the village, to gather them like willow twigs and tie them into a single prayer bundle that would bring peace to all of them. But now the feelings were twisted, tangled roots, and all the names for the source of this growth were buried under English words, out of reach. And there would be no peace and the people would have no rest until the entanglement° had been unwound to the source.

VOCABULARY

peculiarities: The things that make a person or group of people appear strange or very different.
humiliation: The state of feeling degraded and of low status (*humil-* means humble).
reconcile: Here it means to re-establish a good relationship (*re-* means again; -*concil-* refers to overcoming distrust and bitterness).
entanglement: The state of being twisted together. ". . . had been unwound to the source" is a clue.

He could anticipate her mood by watching her face. She had a special look she gave him when she wanted to talk to him alone. He never forgot the strange excitement he felt when she looked at him that way, and called him aside.

"Nobody will ever tell you this," she said, "but you must hear it so you will understand why things are this way." She was referring to the distance she kept between him and herself. "Your uncle and grandma don't know this story. I couldn't tell them because it would hurt them so much." She swallowed hard to clear the pain from her throat, and his own throat hurt too, because without him there would have not been so much shame and disgrace for the family.

"Poor old Grandma. It would hurt her so much if she ever heard this story." She looked at Tayo and picked a thread off the bottom of her apron. Her mouth was small and tight when she talked to him alone. He sat on a gunny sack full of the corn that Robert and Josiah had dried last year, and when he shifted his weight even slightly, he could hear the hard kernels move. The room was always cool, even in the summertime, and it smelled like the dried apples in flour sacks hanging above them from the rafters. That day he could smell the pale, almost blue clay the old women used for plastering the walls.

"One morning," she said, "before you were born, I got up to go outside, right before sunrise. I knew she had been out all night because I never heard her come in. Anyway, I thought I would walk down toward the river. I just had a feeling, you know. I stood on that sandrock, above the big curve in the river, and there she was, coming down the trail on the other side." She looked at him closely. "I'm only telling you this because she was your mother, and you have to understand." She cleared her throat. "Right as the sun came up, she walked under that big cottonwood tree, and I could see her clearly: she had no clothes on. Nothing. She was completely naked except for her high-heel shoes. She dropped her purse under that tree. Later on some kids found it there and brought it back. It was empty except for a lipstick." Tayo swallowed and took a breath.

"Auntie," he said softly, "what did she look like before I was born?"

She reached behind the pantry curtains and began to rearrange the jars of peaches and apricots on the shelves, and he knew she was finished talking to him. He closed the storeroom door behind him and went to the back room and sat on the bed. He sat for a long time and thought about his mother. There had been a picture of her once, and he had carried the tin frame to bed with him at night, and whispered to it. But one evening, when he carried it with him, there were visitors in the kitchen, and she grabbed it away from him. He cried for it and Josiah came to comfort him; he asked Tayo why he was crying, but just as he was ashamed to tell Josiah about the understanding between him and Auntie, he also could not tell him about the picture; he loved Josiah too much to admit the shame. So he held onto Josiah tightly, and pressed his face into the flannel shirt and smelled woodsmoke and sheep's wool and sweat. He even forgot about the picture except sometimes when he tried to remember how she looked. Then he wished Auntie would give it back to him to keep on top of Josiah's dresser. But he could never bring himself to ask her. That day in the storeroom, when he asked how his mother had looked before he was born, was the closest he'd ever come to mentioning the picture.

"So that's where our mother went.
How can we get down there!"

Hummingbird looked at all the
skinny people.
He felt sorry for them.
He said, "You need a messenger.
Listen, I'll tell you
what to do":

Bring a beautiful pottery jar
painted with parrots and big
flowers.
Mix black mountain dirt
some sweet corn flour
and a little water.

Cover the jar with a
new buckskin
and say this over the jar
and sing this softly
above the jar:
After four days

Ceremony

you will be alive
After four days
you will be alive
After four days
you will be alive
After four days
you will be alive

. . . The Army recruiter looked closely at Tayo's light brown skin and his hazel eyes.

"You guys are brothers?"

Rocky nodded coolly.

"If you say so," the recruiter said. It was beginning to get dark, and he wanted to get back to Albuquerque.

Tayo signed his name after Rocky. He felt light on his feet, happy that he would be with Rocky, traveling the world in the Army, together, as brothers. Rocky patted him on the back, smiling too.

QUESTIONS FOR REFLECTION/DISCUSSION

1. What do the following quotes from the reading tell you about the attitude of the recruiter toward Native Americans in general?
   a. "Anyone can fight for America," he began, giving special emphasis to "America," "even you boys. In a time of need, anyone can fight for her." (p. 28)
   b. "Now I know you boys love America as much as we do, but this is your big chance to *show* it!" (p. 29)

2. How does Tayo's aunt feel about him? How do you know? With a partner, make a list of actions and words that reveal her feelings toward him. What can we learn from this about being a parent or a guardian?

3. Tayo's aunt said, "They're not brothers, that's Laura's boy. You know the one [referring to Laura]" (p. 30). What do these few words reveal about her attitude toward Laura? Why does she seem to like to talk about Laura's past in a negative way?

4. How could it be that Tayo and his aunt "understood each other very well"? In what ways did he understand his aunt better than did all the others?

5. How did the Catholic priest's reaction to Laura's drunkenness and lust differ from the reaction of her own people in general? What cultural differences did this appear to reveal between the Christian white world and the world of Native America? According to your own experience, do you feel these differences were real? Discuss these questions with a partner.

6. Why was it so difficult for her older sister to get Laura back from the unhappy life she was leading? Consider what had happened to Laura in school and in the community around the school. To what extent do you think others have experiences similar to Laura's? In what ways were her reactions typical?

7. Consider the words ". . . knowing . . . that the anger could not be contained by a single person or family, but that it must leak out and soak into the ground under the entire village" (p. 33). Think about the culture you know best. How does it react to those who stray from its teachings? To what extent does the anger focus on the individual who strays and on his or her family? To what extent does the anger "leak out and soak into the ground under the entire village"? Which way is best? Discuss these questions with a small group. Share your conclusions with the class.

8. Tayo's aunt once told him the hurtful story about his mother's walk down toward the river. In addition, she took the picture of his mother away from him and did not offer to return it. Why do you think she did these things?

9. Did the appearance of the Native American chant on page 35 seem strange to you? Why do you think the author placed it there? What significance do you think it has to the story?

10. Why was joining the army with Rocky so important to Tayo? Describe the relationship they seemed to have developed over the years. In what ways was it a very positive relationship?

11. The author uses comparisons extensively, especially similes. We learned earlier that similies are comparisons in which the words "like" or "as" are used. For example, in the excerpt from *Ceremony* we find the words, "They scattered *like* dry leaves across the ground." Here, pamphlets are compared to dry leaves. Notice that the comparisons in this selection usually involve nature. Work with a partner to find similes and other comparisons in the reading. Did the use of these comparisons increase your enjoyment of the selection? If so, in what ways?

EXPLORING OTHER SOURCES

Find other examples of relationships similar to those typically associated with siblings. Your search may involve pieces of literature or your own community environment. Share your examples with a small group. What do these relationships appear to have in common?

SYNTHESIS THROUGH WRITING

1. In your journal, write about a relationship you may have had in which the other person was like a brother or sister. How did this relationship come about? What positive effects did it have on you?

2. In this selection, Rocky was described as the "pride" of the aunt, whereas, Tayo was ". . . this other, unwanted child" (p. 30). Write an essay discussing what you think happens to children who are treated as inferior, for whatever reason, within the family unit. Include how you think children should be treated by their caretakers. Divide your paper into two columns. Label the first "What Happens" and the second "How Children Should Be Treated." Use your graphic organizer to help you develop your paper. Refer to the writing strategies on page xix.

3. Write an essay about sibling-like relationships. You may want to use the examples you gathered in the activity, Exploring Other Sources, to develop your ideas. If necessary, refer to the writing strategies on page xix. Create a graphic organizer such as the following one.

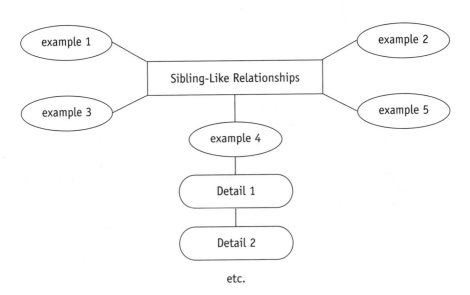

Child of Two Worlds: A Kikuyu's Story [excerpt]

R. Mugo Gatheru

This autobiographical sketch is based upon the author's personal experience in the United States when, as a college student from Kenya, he attended Lincoln University in Pennsylvania. Much to his surprise, he was visited by an agent from the United States Immigration Service. Suspecting what the service was trying to "get at," he became very frightened that he might be deported for something he had not done.

During the time that Mr. Gatheru was in the United States, the Mau Mau in Kenya, made up mostly of members of the Kikuyu tribe, rose up in a bloody rebellion against British rule. However, independence did not become a reality until 1963. The following year, Kenya became a republic and elected Jomo Kenyatta of the Kenya African Union as its president. Interestingly, Mr. Gatheru had served as an assistant newspaper editor for the Kenya African Union before coming to the United States.

Before you Read

Try to imagine what it might feel like to be falsely accused. If you have children or a spouse, how might it affect them? What about your parents or guardians? Talk about it with a partner or write about it in your journal.

 n September 23, 1952, at about 11 A.M., the shadow of Mau Mau fell upon me. I had just finished my English class and was on my way to another class when a white man walked over to my professor and said: "Where is Mr. Gatheru?" The professor pointed me out to him. He walked over to me and showed me a card. It identified him as an agent of the United States Immigration Service. My heart sank. What did this agent want with me? He told me that he had been sent by the Immigration Services from Philadelphia to check on certain facts about my visa. He advised me to go and have my lunch first and to get excused from the rest of my classes for the day because the checking on these facts was going to take a long time. I didn't want any lunch. I said: "Let's start it right now."

I invited him to come to my room in one of the dormitories, and I offered him a seat. He offered me a cigarette. Then he pulled some papers out of his bulky briefcase. I could not help noticing that he had a long list of questions in his hand. I started getting really frightened. My heart was beating furiously. I felt in the pit of my stomach as if I had eaten a big meal that was weighing like a rock inside me. Did all of this mean that now, perhaps, I should never be able to get the higher education for which I had struggled so much?

The agent began to question me as though I were before a grand jury°.

"What's your full name?"

"Reuel John Mugo Gatheru," I replied.

"How did you come to the United States?"

"I came to the United States by way of India and England," I answered.

"Why didn't you come to the United States directly from Kenya instead of going to India?" he asked.

"After I was offered a scholarship at Roosevelt College, I went to the American Consul in Nairobi¹ to seek information about the U.S. student visa. The American Consul advised me that in order to obtain a student visa, I had to get a certificate of good conduct or political clearance from the Kenya Government. I tried to obtain the necessary clearance, but all in vain. Hence, I went to India with a hope that if I did not obtain a U.S. visa, I could further my higher education in India."

"Who financed your trip to India?" he asked.

"My friends and relatives," I replied.

"You seem to have been very active in politics in Kenya. Can you tell me something about your activities in Nairobi?" he asked again.

"Well, first of all I went to Nairobi in 1945. I joined the Medical Research Laboratory as a learner laboratory technician. After some two years I left the Medical Department and joined the Kenya African Union as an assistant editor," I replied.

"What sort of literature were you editing?" he asked.

"A weekly newspaper published by the Kenya African Union," I replied.

"Any other literature?" he asked.

"Not to my knowledge," I replied.

"What was the Kenya African Union?" he asked.

VOCABULARY

grand jury: A jury set up to decide whether or not there is enough evidence to try a person.

CULTURAL NOTES

¹Nairobi is the capital city of Kenya. It is located in the south-central portion of the country.

"A country-wide political organization headed by Jomo Kenyatta whose main purposes were to secure African rights and self-government through constitutional means," I replied.

"Were you a member?" he asked.

"No, I was not a member officially, but there was nothing to prevent me becoming one."

"How could you be an assistant editor without being a member?" he asked.

"I was not compelled° to join, as membership was quite voluntary. But do not think that because of this I did not fully support the union's policy."

"Was the Kenya African Union a communist body?" he asked.

"No it was not," I replied.

"Do you know of communists in Kenya?" he asked.

"No I don't," I replied.

"Is there a Communist Party in Kenya?" he went on.

"No, there is not," I replied.

"What's the population of Kenya?" he demanded.

"About 5,000,000 Africans, 100,000 Asians, and about 33,000 Europeans," I replied.

"Were you then an agitator° for the Kenya African Union?" he insinuated.

"I was not an agitator from the point of view of the Kenya Africans, but the Kenya settlers may have thought me one. After all, even George Washington was an agitator here in your country," I replied.

He laughed appreciatively but said nothing.

"Have you ever carried on any political agitation in the United States, in India, in England?" he asked.

It was now clear to me that he thought that I had some kind of revolutionary aims.

"No," I answered.

I thought that even though my answers were genuine and clear, this man had a preconceived° idea that I was a communist.

VOCABULARY

not compelled: Not forced (com- means together; -pel- means driven).
agitator: Here it means a person who gets others aroused about his or her cause. "It was now clear to me that he thought that I had some kind of revolutionary aims" is a clue.
preconceived: Formed beforehand (pre- means before).

Child of Two Worlds: A Kikuyu's Story

"What form of government would you like to see in Kenya?" he asked.

"A republican type of government," I replied.

"Who are your friends in the United States?" he asked

"They are both white and black," I answered.

"Have you ever addressed or attended a meeting in the United States?" he asked.

"No," I answered.

"How do you support yourself financially?" he asked.

"I have a college scholarship," I answered.

"Are you supposed to perform some duties on completion of your college career, that is, after you have gone back to Kenya?" he asked.

At this I became angry. What kind of 'duties' could he mean? Why was he asking what I'd do when I went back home? Did all of this have something to do with the fact that there were disturbances in Kenya and, if so, what could he want from me?

"What are you major subjects here at Lincoln University?" he asked.

"History and political science," I replied.

"For what degree?" he asked.

"The B.A. degree," I replied.

Why this, I wondered? I still don't know, but it seemed obvious that the investigation had been initiated° from overseas, that some kind of information must have been given to the immigration authorities by someone who knew me back in Nairobi.

The interrogation° lasted from 11:15 A.M. until 2 P.M. The man was friendly in a detached, diplomatic way. I took his cigarettes and smoked them, but I was very angry at some of the questions. In fact, I was angry about the whole procedure. I asked him what was behind all this, and he said it was just a routine matter and that I should not worry. This was hardly the truth as we shall see later.

I reported the matter to Dr. Bond (President of Lincoln University). He was disturbed and worried, but he said, "Just sit

---

VOCABULARY

initiated: Begun (*initia-* means beginning).

interrogation: A formal questioning often in a strong or aggressive way (*inter-* means between; -*roga-* means to ask).

tight and wait." He became very busy. He put everything else aside, including correspondence, and made several long calls to Philadelphia, New York, and Washington. He was thoroughly angry, particularly at those questions with which the immigration agent tried to implicate° me with communism. At that time, American public opinion was very afraid of communism.

On October 20, 1952, only four weeks after my interrogation, the Kenya Government declared a state of emergency; two days later over a hundred leaders and officers of the Kenya African Union were imprisoned, including Jomo Kenyatta. I felt in my inner soul that these events must be connected with my interrogation although the immigration agent had said it only concerned my visa. Why were they concerned about my visa anyhow?

I never broke any immigration regulations, and each time I went to get my student visa renewed, I had no trouble at all. I never tried to hide anything from anybody. Once, I lost my passport and applied to Kenya for another one which they sent through the British Consulate General in Philadelphia. The knew exactly where I was. Everything I did was open and above board.° You can imagine my surprise when on November 5, 1952, six weeks after my interview with the immigration agent (and barely two weeks after the state of emergency had been declared in Kenya), I received a letter from the Immigration Office in Philadelphia which read as follows:

Dear Sir,

Pursuant° to instructions received from the office of the Commissioner of Immigration and Naturalization at Washington, I request that you depart from the United States as soon as possible.

I am obliged° to say that unless such departure is effected° within thirty days, this office will be obliged to take the necessary steps to enforce your departure.

VOCABULARY

implicate: Here it means incriminate or entangle (*im*- means in; -*plica*- here refers to enfolding).
above board: Not hidden. "Everything I did was open . . ." is a clue.
pursuant: In accordance with.
obliged: Obligated or compelled (*ob*- means to; -*lige*- means bind).
effected: Brought about.

What did this mean? What had I done to warrant° this expulsion?° Was it connected with the things happening in Kenya? Did the United States Government think that I had something to do with Mau Mau?

So, amid all my worries about the fate of my people at home, I now had my personal worries. I could hardly believe my eyes when I read the letter. I had struggled along until I had reached my junior year at Lincoln University. The fall term had just begun, and now the United States Immigration Office was telling me to get out. Where was I to go? To Kenya? I would certainly be thrown into a concentration camp° immediately as a former assistant editor of the Kenya African Union newspaper. To Britain? What would I do there? I had no scholarship or means of support.

I wanted to stay in America to prepare myself to serve Kenya after the Mau Mau crisis was over. Now, I faced deportation.° I had come to love Lincoln University and I wanted to get my B.A. degree from there.

I went in haste to Dr. Bond. He read the letter carefully, and I could see that he was getting more annoyed. He took the phone and made a call to Philadelphia. The immigration authorities refused to tell him why I was being ordered out the country. He said he'd never take this lying down. He started to work immediately to set up a committee to defend me.

It was rough. At night I could not sleep. I thought of numerous things as I was tossing around. Why am I suffering this much, I would ask myself? This was the price of my past activities in Kenya.

The students at Lincoln University were my real salvation. I was now a sort of hero, and they all came round and said:"Give them hell, Mugo. We are with you." This gave me real strength, and I even began to enjoy the struggle.

People all over the United States rallied° to my cause, and I fear that sometimes I really felt too important. Even the *New York Times* carried stories on me, and I began to hear that the Kenya papers were writing about the case too. The attempt by

---

VOCABULARY
warrant: Justify or deserve.
expulsion: The state of being forced out (*ex-* means out; *-pul-* refers to pushing).
concentration camp: A place where people are held against their will, usually for political reasons.
deportation: The state of being forced out of a country (*de-* means away; *-port-* means carry).
rallied: Came together for a cause (*-allie-* means to unite).

the immigration authorities to smear me with communism did not stop people from supporting me. The American people were intelligent enough to understand that one did not have to be a communist to appreciate the fact that the Kenya settlers had more arable° land than the Africans or that the living conditions in the Nairobi African locations were appalling! This was just everyday common sense.

My American friends fought so hard to save me from deportation that on February 4, 1953, I received a letter from the immigration authorities to say that:

> . . . as a result of further consideration given to your status under immigration laws, you may ignore letter of this office dated November 5, 1952, requesting you to depart from the United States as soon as possible. In this connection, however, your attention is directed to the fact that your authorized stay in this country will expire on April 30, 1953, and you will be expected to depart by that date.

We had won a partial victory. I had been saved from deportation.

There was one fly in the ointment.° My visa was to run out two months before school closed. What was I to do?

[Mr. Gutheru's lawyer fought to obtain a permanent visa for his client so that he could continue his education, finish graduate school, and earn a living at the same time. He ended up suing the U.S. government. The case was pursued for four years until a settlement was finally reached.]

I am grateful to all my friends who made it possible for me to stay in America and to complete my studies there. I can't forget how scared I sometimes was and how sometimes I felt so much all alone. But I had faith in my lawyer and in my many friends. I knew that if we lost, it would not be because they hadn't tried as hard as they could to save me. This whole experience "made a man out of me." I do not regret it.

VOCABULARY
arable: Fit for planting things.
fly in the ointment: A problem in a basically good situation.

QUESTIONS FOR REFLECTION/DISCUSSION

1. Was the agent from the Immigration Service concerned only with the author's visa during the interrogation? What did he appear to be concerned with? What does he suspect? How do you know?

2. Why was the author angered by the interrogation? What did he fear? Were his fears justified? How do you know?

3. How did the author defend himself while being interrogated? What did he mean when he said ". . . even George Washington was an agitator . . ." (p. 41).

4. Why was Dr. Bond so disturbed and worried about the interrogation?

5. To whom did the author seem to give most of the credit for saving him from deportation? Why?

6. Do you think the experience "made a man out of him" as the author claims? Wasn't he already a "man"? Explain.

7. Have you read about or know of someone who was wrongly accused of doing something forbidden or of being part of a suspected group? How did that person feel? What did that person do? What would you do if you were wrongly accused in this way? Discuss these questions with a partner. Summarize your discussion in your journal.

 EXPLORING OTHER SOURCES

1. In the library and/or on the Internet, find out as much as you can about the Mau Mau uprising in Kenya and the government that eventually arose from it. Which side did the United States support at the time of the uprising, if any? If you need help, ask your instructor or the librarian to assist you. Share what you learn with a small group.

2. Why do you think communism was a factor in the interrogation? Find information about what was happening in the United States at the time concerning communism and why some people in government were obsessed with it. The name Joseph McCarthy (a United States senator) will be a key in your search. Ask your instructor or the librarian to help you, if you need assistance. Discuss your findings with your class and the instructor.

3. Find out as much as you can about immigration laws and what is expected of immigrants in the country in which you live. Use the library and/or the Internet. Key words include "immigration," "immigration laws," and "immigrants." Share your information with a small group.

Synthesis Through Writing

1. In your journal, write about an experience during which you or someone you know was wrongly accused of doing something forbidden or of being part of a suspected group. How did it feel? Were children, a spouse, parents or guardians affected? If so, in what ways? How was the situation handled? Is there a good way to handle such accusations?

2. Write an essay about immigration laws in the country in which you live. How fair are they, in your opinion? Are there any changes you would make in them? Divide a piece of paper into three columns. In the first column, list what you think are the most important immigration laws; in the second, comment on their fairness; and in the third, describe the changes you would make. Use the information you gathered in the Exploring Other Sources activity. Your graphic organizer will help you develop your paper. See additional writing strategies on page xix.

	Immigration Law	How Fair Is It?	Changes I Would Make
1.			
2.			
3.			
etc.			

3. Write an informative essay about one of the following topics:
   a. The Mau Mau uprising in Kenya and the government that eventually arose from it
   b. Joseph McCarthy and his influence on the attitudes of many in the United States toward communism

Use the information you found in the Exploring Other Sources activity to develop your paper. Refer to the writing strategies on page xix. Create your own graphic organizer.

Back to Bachimba

Enrique "Hank" Lopez

Maintaining pride in one's first culture can be an important factor in caring for oneself. In this selection, Enrique "Hank" Lopez, who lived from 1921 to 1985, shares with us some of the personal challenges of living between worlds. Even his name reflects the bicultural nature of his identity. He became the first Mexican American to graduate from Harvard Law School. He was an author, educator, and an activist in the community upon which he never turned his back. His respect for himself and for both his cultures comes through in this touching account of life in his new world.

One important question closely related to this reading involves the extent to which one should try to keep the first culture and the first language and, at the same time, adjust to that which is new. As the author of this selection indicates, it may very well be that this question is not really a matter of choice at all, considering how deeply one's cultural roots are implanted as a child.

A word of caution: The reader might find some of the language used here a bit strong. Perhaps this use of language is due to the depth of the author's feelings concerning his ethnicity and his struggle for identity in a new world.

Before You Read

Think about your own cultural roots. What effect do they have on you now that you are an adult? To what extent can you voluntarily deny them? To what extent can you nurture and develop them? Discuss these questions with a small group and write about your conclusions in your journal.

*P*ocho is ordinarily a derogatory° term in Mexico (to define it succinctly,° a *pocho* is a Mexican slob who has pretensions of being a gringo° sonofabitch°), but I use it in a very special sense. To me that word has come to mean "uprooted Mexican," and that's what I have been all my life. Though my entire upbringing and education took place in the United States, I have never felt completely American, and when I am in Mexico, I sometimes feel like a displaced gringo with a

---

VOCABULARY

derogatory: Showing lack of respect (*de*-means away from). The rest of the sentence is a clue.
succinctly: Briefly and clearly, using only a few words.
gringo: A slang term meaning a white person.
sonofabitch: A phrase used to demean or belittle someone. It means son of a bitch (female dog).

curiously Mexican name—Enrique Preciliano López. One might conclude that I'm either a schizo°-cultural Mexican or a cultured schizoid° American.

In any event, the schizo-ing began a long time ago, when my father and many of Pancho Villa's¹ troops fled across the border to escape the oncoming *federales*° who eventually defeated Villa. My mother and I, traveling across the hot desert plains in a buckboard wagon, joined my father in El Paso, Texas, a few days after his hurried departure. With more and more Villistas° swarming into El Paso every day, it was quickly apparent that jobs would be exceedingly scarce and insecure; so my parents packed our few belongings and we took the first available bus to Denver. My father had hoped to move to Chicago because the name sounded so Mexican, but my mother's meager° savings were hardly enough to buy tickets for Colorado.

There we moved into a ghetto of Spanish-speaking residents who chose to call themselves Spanish Americans and resented the sudden migration of their brethren° from Mexico, whom they sneeringly called *surumatos* (slang for "southerners"). These so-called Spanish Americans claimed direct descent from the original *conquistadores*² of Spain. They also insisted tht they had *never* been Mexicans, since their region of New Spain (later annexed° to the United States) was never a part of Mexico. But what they claimed most vociferously°—and erroneously°—was an absence of Indian ancestry. It made no difference that any objective observer could see by merely looking at them the results of considerble fraternization° between the conquering Spaniards and the Comanche and Navaho women who crossed their paths. Still, these *manitos*, as they were snidely° labeled by

---

VOCABULARY

schizo, schizoid: Having characteristics of someone who is schizophrenic, meaning someone who has withdrawn from reality and lives in a world of the imagination.
federales: The Spanish word for U.S. troops.
Villistas: Refers to the persons admiring Pancho Villa.
meager: Very small. ". . . hardly enough to buy tickets for Colorado. . ." is a clue.
brethren: An old-fashioned term meaning brothers.
annexed: Added to (*a-* means to; *-nex-* means to tie).
vociferously: Loudly with much emphasis (*voci-* means voice).
erroneously: In error.
fraternization: Here it means socializing intimately with each other (*frat-* means brother).
snidely: Sarcastically or with meanness.

CULTURAL NOTES

¹Pancho Villa (1878–1923) was a Mexican revolutionary and folk hero who led guerrilla raids into U.S. Territory in 1915.
²The *conquistadores* were leaders of the sixteenth-century Spanish conquest of Mexico and Peru.

the *surumatos*, stubbornly refused to be identified with Mexico, and would actually fight anyone who called them Mexican. So intense was this intergroup rivalry that the bitterest "race riots" I have ever witnessed—and engaged in—were between the look-alike, talk-alike *surumatos* and *manitos* who lived near Denver's Curtis Park. In retrospect° the harsh conflicts between us were all the more silly and self-defeating when one recalls that we were all lumped together as "spiks" and "greasers" by the Anglo-Saxon community.

Predictably enough, we *surumatos* began huddling together in a sub-neighborhood within the larger ghetto, and it was there that I became painfully aware that my father had been the only private in Pancho Villa's army. Most of my friends were the sons of captains, colonels, majors, and even generals, though a few fathers were admittedly mere sergeants and corporals. My father alone had been a lowly private in that famous Division del Norte.[3] Naturally, I developed a most painful complex, which led me to all sorts of compensatory° fibs. During one brief spell I fancied my father as a member of the dreaded *los dorados*, the "golden ones," who were Villa's favorite henchmen.° (Later I was to learn that my father's cousin, Martin López, was a genuine and quite notorious° *dorado*.) But all my inventions were quickly un-invented by my very own father, who seemed to take a perverse° delight in being Pancho's only private.

No doubt my chagrin° was accentuated° by the fact that Pancho Villa's exploits° were a constant topic of conversation in our household. My entire childhood seems to be shadowed

---

VOCABULARY

retrospect: Looking back (*retro-* means to look back; *-spec-* means to look. ". . . one recalls . . ." is a clue.

compensatory: Making up for the lack of something (*com-* here means mutually; *-pen-* refers to weighing).

henchmen: Loyal supporters.

notorious: Known for unacceptable deeds; infamous (*noto-* means known). The prior sentence offers clues.

perverse: Going away from what is acceptable and considered good (*per-* means completely; *-ver-* means to turn).

chagrin: Embarrassment.

accentuated: Emphasized (*accent-* means to stress).

exploits: Here it means deeds of a hero. The next sentence is a clue.

CULTURAL NOTES

[3]*Division del Norte* is Spanish for "Division of the North."

by his presence. At our dinner table, almost every night, we would listen to endlessly repeated accounts of this battle, that stratagem,° or some great act of Robin Hood[4] kindness by *el centauro del norte.*[5] I remember how angry my parents were when they saw Wallace Beery[6] in *Viva Villa!*[7] "Garbage by stupid gringos," they called it. They were particularyly offended by the sweaty, unshaven sloppiness of Beery's portrayal. "Pancho Villa was clean and orderly, no matter how much he chased after women. This man's a dirty swine."

As if to deepen our sense of *Villismo,*° my parents also taught us "Adelita" and *"Se llevaron el cañon para Bachimba"* ("They took the cannons to Bachimba"), the two most famous songs of the Mexican revolution. Some twenty years later, (during my stint° at Harvard Law School), while strolling along the Charles River, I would find myself softly singing *"Se llevaron el cañon para Bachimba, para Bachimba, para Bachimba* over and over again. That's all I could remember of that poignant° rebel song. Though I had been born there, I had always regarded "Bachimba" as a fictitious, made-up, Lewis Carroll[8] kind of word. So that eight years ago, when I first returned to Mexico, I was literally stunned when I came to a crossroad south of Chihuahua and saw an old road marker: "Bachimba 18 km." Then it really exists—I shouted inwardly—Bachimba is a real town! Swinging onto the narrow, poorly paved road, I gunned the motor and sped toward the town I'd been singing about since infancy. It turned out to be a quiet, dusty village with a bleak worn-down plaza that was surrounded by nondescript buildings of uncertain vintage°.

VOCABULARY
stratagem: Deceptive strategy.
Villismo: Strong belief in Pancho Villa.
stint: A given time period.
poignant: Bringing about strong emotions (*poign-* means point).
vintage: Here it means age. It usually refers to wine.

CULTURAL NOTES
[4]Robin Hood was the famous twelfth-century robber in British folklore who stole from the rich to give to the poor.
[5]*El centauro del norte* is Spanish for "the centaur of the north" which refers to Pancho Villa. A *centaur* in Greek methodology was a creature who had the head and upper body of a man and the legs and lower body of a horse.
[6]Wallace Beery was an American actor in the film industry. He lived from 1885 to 1949.
[7]*Viva Villa!* is Spanish for "Long Live [Pancho] Villa!"
[8]Lewis Carroll was the pen name of British nineteenth-century writer and mathematician Charles Dodgson, who wrote *Alice's Adventures in Wonderland.*

Aside from the songs about Bachimba and Adelita and all the fold tales about Villa's guerrilla fighters, my early years were strongly influenced by our neighborhood celebrations of Mexico's two most important patriotic events: Mexican Independence Day on September 16 and the anniversary of the battle of Puebla on May 5. On those two dates Mexicans all over the world are likely to become extremely chauvinistic.° In Denver we would stage annual parades that included three or four floats skimpily decorated with crepe paper streamers, a small band, several adults in threadbare battle dress, and hundreds of kids marching in wild disorder. It was during one of these parades—I was ten years old then—that I was seized with acute appendicitis° and had to be rushed to a hospital. The doctor subsequently told my mother that I had made a long, impassioned speech about the early revolutionist Miguel Hidalgo while the anesthetic° was taking hold, and she explained with pardonable pride that it was the speech I was to make at Turner Hall that evening. Mine was one of the twenty-three *discursos*° scheduled on the postparade program, a copy of which my mother still retains. My only regret was missing the annual *discursos* of Don Miguel Gómez, my godfather, a deep-throated orator who would always climax his speech by falling to his knees and dramatically kissing the floor, almost weeping as he loudly proclaimed: *"Ay, Mexico! Beso tu tierra, tu mero corazon"* ("Ah, Mexico! I kiss your sacred soil, the very heart of you"). He gave the same oration for seventeen years, word for word and gesture for gesture, and it never failed to bring tears to his eyes. But not once did he return to Chihuahua, even for a brief visit.

My personal Mexican-ness eventually produced serious problems for me. Upon entering grade school I learned English

---

VOCABULARY

chauvinistic: Being so attached to a person, group, or an idea that one thinks there is no equal. The soldier, Nicholas Chauvin, of French folklore was said to be completely devoted to Napoleon.

appendicitis: An infected appendix. ". . . had to be rushed to a hospital. . ." is a clue.

anesthetic: Something that causes one to be insensitive to pain.

discursos: The Spanish word meaning speeches or orations.

CULTURAL NOTES

[9]Mexican Independence Day is celebrated on September 16 to commemorate the march on the capital in 1810. Actually, Mexico won its independence from Spain with the signing of the treaty of Córdoba in 1821.

[10]The battle of Puebla on May 5 marks a defeat of the French in 1862.

rapidly, and rather well, always ranking either first or second in my class; yet the hard core of me remained stubbornly Mexican. This chauvinism may have been a reaction to the constant racial prejudice we encountered on all sides. The neighborhood cops were always running us off the streets and calling us "dirty greasers," and most of our teachers frankly regarded us as totally inferior. I still remember the galling° disdain of my sixth-grade teacher, whose constant mimicking of our heavily accented speech drove me to a desperate study of *Webster's Dictionary* in the hope of acquiring a vocabulary larger than hers. Sadly enough, I succeeded only too well, and for the next few years I spoke the most ridiculous high-flown rhetoric° in the Denver public schools. One of my favorite words was "indubitably,°" and it must have driven everyone mad. I finally got rid of my accent by constantly reciting "Peter Piper picked a peck of pickled peppers" with little round pebbles in my mouth. Somewhere I had read about Desmosthenes.[11]

During this phase of my childhood the cultural tug of war known as "Americanization' almost pulled me apart. There were moments when I would identify completely with the gringo world (what could have been more American than my earnest high-voiced portrayal of George Washington, however ridiculous the cotton wig my mother had fashioned for me?); then quite suddenly I would feel so acutely Mexican that I would stammer over the simplest English phrase. I was so ready to take offense at the slightest slur against Mexicans that I would imagine prejudice where none existed. But on other occasions, in full confidence of my belonging, I would venture forth into social areas that I should have realized were clearly forbidden to little chicanos° from Curtis Park. The inevitable rebuffs° would leave me floundering° in self-pity; it was small comfort to know that other minority groups suffered even worse rebuffs than we did.

VOCABULARY
galling: Causing much discomfort.
rhetoric: Here it means speech that sounds good but has little substance.
indubitably (in du' bit ablē): Without doubt.
chicanos: Mexican-Americans.
rebuffs: Snubs.
floundering: Moving in a clumsy way; off-balance.

CULTURAL NOTES
[11]Demosthenes was a Greek orator and politician who lived in the fourth century B.C.

The only non-Mexican boy on our street was a Negro°
named Leroy Logan, who was probably my closest childhood
friend. Leroy was the best athlete, the best whistler, the best
liar, the best horseshoe player, the best marble shooter, the best
mumblety-pegger,° and the best shoplifter in our neighborhood.
He was also my "partner," and I thus entitled myself to a fifty-
fifty share of all his large triumphs and petty thefts. Because he
considered "Mexican" a derogatory word bordering on
obscenity, Leroy would pronounce it "Mesican" so as to soften
its harshness. But once in a while, when he'd get angry with me,
he would call me a "lousy Mesican greasy spik" with the most
extraordinarily effective hissing one can imagine. And I'm
embarrassed to admit that I would retaliate by calling him
"alligator bait."¹² As a matter of fact, just after I had returned
from the hospital, he came to visit me, and I thoughtlessly
greeted him with a flippant,° "Hi, alligator ba—" I never finished
the phrase because Leroy whacked me on the stomach with a
Ping-Pong paddle and rushed out of my house with great,
sobbing anger.

Weeks later, when we had re-established a rather cool
rapport,° I tried to make up for my stupid insult by helping him
steal cabbages from the vegetable trucks that rumbled through
our neighborhood on their way to the produce markets. They
would come down Larimer Street in the early dawn, and Leroy
and I would sneak up behind them at the 27th Street stop sign,
where they were forced to pause for cross traffic. Then Leroy,
with a hooked pole he had invented, would stab the top
cabbages and roll them off the truck. I would be waiting below
to catch them with an open gunny sack. Our system was
fabulously successful for a while, and we found a ready market
for the stolen goods; but one morning, as I started to unfurl my
sack, a fairly large cabbage conked me on the head. Screaming
with pain, I lunged at Leroy and tried to bite him. He, laughing

---

VOCABULARY

Negro: A Black or African-American. Not currently used.

mumblety-pegger: A player in the game mumblety-peg, in which a pocket knife is flipped to the
ground from various positions. The object of the game is to get the knife to stick in the gound
so it doesn't fall over.

flippant: Disrespectful, without thinking.

rapport (ra por): Showing mutual trust and respect.

CULTURAL NOTES

¹²In the southern United States, it has been reported that African-Americans were sometimes
abandoned in swamp areas where there were alligators.

all the while—it was obviously a funny scene—glided out of my reach, and finally ran into a nearby alley. We never engaged in commercial affairs thereafter.

Still and all, I remember him with great affection and a touch of sadness. I say sadness because eventually Leroy was to suffer the misery of being an outsider in an already outside ghetto. As he grew older, it was apparent that he longed to be a Mexican, that he felt terribly dark and alone. "Sometimes," he would tell me, "I feel like my damn skin's too tight, like I'm gonna bust out of it." One cold February night I found him in the coal shed behind Pacheco's store, desperately scraping his forearm with sandpaper, the hurt tears streaming down his face. "I got to get this off, man, I can't stand all this blackness." We stood there quietly staring at the floor for a long, anguished moment, both of us miserable beyond word or gesture. Finally he drew a deep breath, blew his nose loudly, and mumbled half audibly, "Man, you sure lucky to be a Mesican."

Not long after this incident Leroy moved out of Denver to live with relatives in Georgia. When I saw him off at the bus station, he grabbed my shoulder and whispered huskily, "You gonna miss me, man. You watch what I tellya." "Indubitably," I said. "Aw, man, cut that stuff. You the most fancy-pants Mesican I know." Those were his last words to me, and they caused a considerable dent in my ego. Not enough, however, to diminish my penchant° for fancy language. The dictionary continued to be my comic book well into high school.

Speaking of language, I am reminded of a most peculiar circumstance: almost every Mexican American lawyer that I've ever met speaks English with a noticeable Spanish accent, this despite the fact that they have all been born, reared, and educated exclusively in America. Of the forty-eight lawyers I have in mind, only three of us are free of any accent. Needless to say, our "cultural drag" has been weighty and persistent. And one must presume that our ethnic hyphens shall be with us for many years to come.

My own Mexican-ness, after years of decline at Harvard University, suddenly burst forth again when I returned to Chihuahua and stumbled on the town of Bachimba. I had long conversations with an uncle I'd never met before, my father's

---

VOCABULARY

penchant: A strong preference.

younger brother, Ramón. It was Tio° Ramón who chilled my spine with eyewitness stories about Pancho Villa's legendary *dorados*, one of whom was Martin López. "He was your second cousin. The bravest young buck in Villa's army. And he became a *dorado* when he was scarcely seventeen years old because he dared to defy Pancho Villa himself. As your papa may have told you, Villa had a bad habit of burying treasure up in the mountains and also burying the man he took with him to dig the hole for it. Well, one day he chose Martin López to go with him. Deep in the mountains they went, near Parral. And when they got to a suitably lonely place, Pancho Villa told him to dig a hole with pick and shovel. Then, when Martin had dug down to his waist, Villa leveled a gun at the boy. "Say your prayers, *muchacho*.° You shall stay here with the gold—forever." But Martin had come prepared. In his large right boot he had a gun, and when he rose from his bent position, he was pointing that gun at Villa. They stood there, both ready to fire, for several seconds, and finally Don Pancho started to laugh in that wonderful way of his. "*Bravo, bravo, muchacho!* You've got more guts than a man. Get out of that hole, boy. I need you for my *dorados.*"

Tio Ramón's eyes were wet with pride. "But what is more important, he died with great valor. Two years later, after he had terrorized the *federales* and Pershing's[13] gringo soldiers, he was finally wounded and captured here in Bachimba. It was a bad wound in his leg, finally turning to gangrene.° Then one Sunday morning they hauled Martin López and three other prisoners to the plaza. One by one they executed the three lesser prisoners against that wall. I was up on the church tower watching it all. Finally it was your uncle's turn. They dragged him off the buckboard wagon and handed him his crutches. Slowly, painfully, he hobbled to the wall and stood there. Very straight he stood. 'Do you have any last words?' asked the captain of the firing squad. With great pride Martin tossed his crutches aside and stood very tall on his one good leg. 'Give me, you yellow bastards, give me a gun—and I'll show you who is

---

VOCABULARY
tio: The Spanish word for uncle.
muchacho: The Spanish word for boy.
gangrene: The decay and death of the tissues of the body due to disease or injury. "It was a bad wound in his leg. . ." is a clue.

CULTURAL NOTES
[13]John Joseph Pershing was an American general who led the troops against Pancho Villa in 1916.

the man among . . .' Eight bullets crashed into his chest and face, and I never heard that final word. That was your second cousin. You would have been proud to know him."

As I listened to Tio Ramón's soft nostalgic° voice that evening, there in the sputtering light of the kerosene lamp on his back patio, I felt as intensely Mexican as I shall ever feel.

But not for long. Within six weeks I was destined to feel *less* Mexican than I had ever felt. The scene of my trauma was the Centro Mexicano de Escritores, where the finest young writers of Mexico met regularly to discuss works in progress and to engage in erudite° literary and philosophical discussions. Week after week I sat among them, dumbstruck by my inadequacy in Spanish and my total ignorance of their whole frame of reference. How could I have possibly imagined that I was Mexican? Those conversations were a dense tangle of local and private allusions,° and the few threads I could grasp only magnified my ignorance. The novelist Juan Rulfo was then reading the initial drafts of his *Pedro Páramo*, later to be acclaimed the best avant-garde° fiction in Mexican literature. Now that I have soaked myself in the *ambiance*° of Mexico, Rulfo's novel intrigues me beyond measure; but when he first read it at the Centro, he might just as well have been reading "Jabberwocky"[14] in Swahili[15] for all I understood of it. And because all of the other Mexican writers knew and greatly appreciated *Páramo*, I could only assume that I was really "too gringo" to comprehend it. For this reason, I, a person with no great talent for reticence,° never opened my mouth at the Centro. In fact, I was so shell-shocked by those sessions that I even found it difficult to converse with my housekeeper about such simple matters as dirty laundry or the loose doorknob in the bathroom.

VOCABULARY

nostalgic: Showing a pleasant sadness about the past.
erudite: Scholarly.
allusions: Meaningful references that are made indirectly.
avant-garde: Something that is ahead of its time.
ambiance: The atmosphere or environment.
reticence: The state of being quiet and reserved (*re-* means again; *-tic-* refers here to being silent). ". . . never opened my mouth. . ." is a clue.

CULTURAL NOTES

[14]Jabberwocky is a nonsense poem from *Through the Looking Glass* by Lewis Carroll.
[15]Swahili is an important language in eastern and central Africa and often is used in commerce between nations of the region.

Can any of us really go home again? I, for one, am convinced that I have no true home, that I must reconcile myself to a schizo-cultural limbo, with a mere hyphen to provide some slight cohesion between my split selves. This inevitable splitting is a plague and a pleasure. Some mornings as I glide down the Paseo de la Reforma, perhaps the most beautiful boulevard in the world, I am suddenly angered by the *machismo*, or aggressive maleness, of Mexican drivers who crowd and bully their screeching machines through dense traffic. What terrible insecurity, what awful dread of emasculation,° produces such assertive bully-boy conduct behind a steering wheel? Whatever the reasons, there is a part of me that can never accept this much-celebrated *machismo*. Nor can I accept the exaggerated nationalism one so frequently encounters in the press, on movie screens, over the radio, in daily conversations—that shrill barrage of slogans proclaiming that "there is only one Mexico."

Recently, when I expressed these views to an old friend, he smiled quite knowingly: "Let's face it, Hank, you're not really a Mexican—despite that long, comical name of yours. You're an American through and through." But that, of course, is a minority view and almost totally devoid° of realism. One could just as well say that Martin Luther King[16] was not a Negro, that he was merely an American. But the plain truth is that neither I nor the Martin Luther Kings of our land can escape the fact that we are Mexican and Negro with roots planted so deeply in the United States that we have grown those strong little hyphens that make us Mexican-American and Nego-American. This assertion may not please some idealists who would prefer to blind themselves to our obvious ethnic and racial differences, who are unwittingly patronizing° when they insist that we are all alike and indistinguishable. But the politicians, undoubtedly the most pragmatic creatures in America, are completely aware that ethnic groups *do* exist and that they seem to huddle together, bitch together, and sometimes vote together.

VOCABULARY

emasculation: Being made less masculine (*e-* means away from *-mascul-* refers to male).
   ". . . assertive bully-boy conduct behind a steering wheel. . ." is a clue.
devoid: Empty; completely lacking (*de-* here means completely; *-void-* means to empty).
patronizing: Acting superior to those considered lower in status (*pat-* means father).

CULTURAL NOTES

[16]Martin Luther King, Jr., was a famous twentieth-century civil rights leader in the United States.

When all is said and done, we hyphenated Americans are here to stay, bubbling happily or unhappily in the great non-melting pot. Much has been gained and will be gained from the multiethnic aspects of the United States, and there is no useful purpose in attempting to wish it away or to homogenize° it out of existence. In spite of the race riots in Watts[17] and ethnic unrest elsewhere, there would appear to be a kind of modus vivendi° developing on almost every level of American life.

And if there are those of us who may never feel completely at home, we can always make that brief visit to Bachimba.

QUESTIONS FOR REFLECTION/DISCUSSION

1. Why was the author resentful of those claiming to be Spanish Americans? Why do you think the people to whom he is referring call themselves Spanish Americans? Many people have a label for themselves that reflects a pride in the ethnic group or those cultures to which they feel they belong. Do you have such a label? If so, what is it? If you don't have a label but wanted to have one, what would it be? Discuss your feelings about having a label with a partner. Summarize your discussion in your journal.

2. The author describes the prejudice he faced at the hands of the police and teachers. Have you ever had similar experiences, or do you know someone who has? Why do you think such prejudice occurs? How can a person best deal with it? Discuss these questions with a partner. Share your conclusions with a small group.

3. Describe the relationship between the author and Leroy Logan. What was unusual about this relationship? Have you ever had a similar relationship with someone from another ethnic group?

4. What do you think the author means when he talks about "ethnic hyphens"? How important are they? Why do you think the author feels that it is not a good idea to ignore one's roots ? He feels that acknowledging one's roots "may not please some idealists who would prefer to blind themselves to our obvious ethnic and racial differences, who are unwittingly patronizing when they insist that we are all alike

VOCABULARY
homogenize: To make something uniform so all the parts are alike (*homo-* means the same).
modus vivendi: Latin for "a way of living."

CULTURAL NOTES
[17]Watts refers to the 1965 race riots in Watts, an African-American community in Los Angeles, California.

and indistinguishable" (p. 58). What does he mean? Do you agree or disagree with him? Might the answer be different for those who *look like* the persons in the dominant culture? Why or why not?

5. Think about these words: "Can any of us really go home again? I, for one am convinced that I have no true home, that I must reconcile myself to a schizo-cultural limbo, with a mere hyphen to provide some slight cohesion between my split selves. This inevitable splitting is a plague and a pleasure" (p. 58). What do you think the author means? Is the phrase "schizo-cultural limbo" overstating his dilemma a bit? In what ways might a culturally split self be both plague and pleasure? If you are an immigrant yourself, relate the author's experience to your own. Discuss these questions with a small group.

6. The author claims that much has been gained and will be gained from the multiethnic aspects of the United States. Think of all the areas in which the country in which you live has benefited from its multicultural heritage. Consider the areas of science, entertainment and the arts, literature, education, food, medicine, and so forth. What might happen if a society became too "homogenized"?

7. Do you see any humor in this selection? If so, what makes it humorous? Find an example or two. Do you like his humor? Why or why not?

EXPLORING OTHER SOURCES

1. Interview several persons who have come from another country. Write several questions to ask them. You will find a sample interview and "Guide to Interviewing" on the Internet at http://world-views.wadsworth.com. Following are a few sample questions.
   a. Where are you from?
   b. Why did you come to this country? How long have you been here?
   c. Did you have problems when you first came? What were they? What did you do to overcome your problems?
   d. What joys have you experienced since coming to this country?
   e. What advice would you give to others who are thinking of moving here?
   Share what you learn with a small group.

2. Find out as much as you can about the contributions made by various immigrant groups to the country in which you live. Consider contributions made by individuals within those groups to the fields of science, entertainment and the arts, literature, education, food, medicine, and so forth. Use your library, the Internet, and your community as resources. Share what you learn with a small group.

Synthesis Through Writing

1. In your journal, address one of the following questions:

   a. At one point in the story, Leroy says, "Sometimes I feel like my damn skin's too tight, like I'm gonna bust out of it" (p. 55). Have you ever felt that way yourself? What were the circumstances? How long did the feeling last? What helped you appreciate your own ethnicity?

   b. What experiences have you or someone you know had that were similar to one of those described by the author?

2. The author talks of the "great non-melting pot" (p. 59). What do you think he means? Write an essay about *assimilation*, as represented by the melting pot, versus *pluralism*, as represented by the great *non-melting pot*. Which one is healthier for individuals in a society as diverse as the one found in the United States? Discuss these questions. Before you begin, you may want to use a graphic organizer, such as the following, to clarify your thinking. If needed, refer to the writing strategies listed on page xix.

ASSIMILATION (characteristics)	PLURALISM (characteristics)

3. Write an essay about moving from one culture to another. Consider adjustments that need to be made to both a new language and a new culture. What sorts of behaviors might ease the process? To help you get started, divide a piece of paper into two columns (see the graphic organizer in item 2). In one column, list the adjustments to be made; in the other column, list the behaviors that might ease the problems involved with each adjustment. See the writing strategies on page xix.

4. Write an essay about the contributions made by various immigrant groups to the country in which you live. Consider contributions made by individuals within those groups to the fields of science, entertainment and the arts, literature, education, food, medicine, and so forth. Base your paper on what you learned from your research in the previous section, Exploring Other Resources. First, make a column on the far left on a piece of paper for the name of the field; then create two columns, one for the ethnic group and/or the individual and the other for a description of the contribution. Complete a graphic organizer like the one below and use it as a guide for writing your essay.

	NAME OF THE ETHNIC GROUP AND/OR INDIVIDUAL	DESCRIPTION OF CONTRIBUTION
Science		
Entertainment		
The Arts		
etc.		

MAKING CONNECTIONS: IDEAS FOR DISCUSSION AND/OR COMPOSITION

1. Think about all the selections you read in this unit. Which one do you think best expresses the idea of brotherhood? Justify your choice.

2. Think of the theme in relation to what is happening in the world today. In what ways might the world be a better place if people cared for each other more? Try to be as specific as possible.

3. The song that begins this unit, "He Ain't Heavy. . . He's My Brother" was first performed by the Hollies in the 1960s. The lyrics were written by Bob Russell and the music by Bobby Scott. How does the song relate to specific selections in this unit? Think of the word "brother" in the universal sense.

4. Use the Internet to find additional information about or written by the authors and/or topics in this unit that you find of particular interest.

Go to World Views Online at http://worldviews.wadsworth.com for suggestions and links to other sites.

READING FOR ENRICHMENT

The Dream Book: An Anthology of Writings by Italian-American Women

edited by Helen Barolini
Schocken Books, 1985

A collection of readings about Italian-American family life in the United States from the point of view of immigrant women.

Ceremony

by Leslie Marmon Silko
Viking, 1985

Leslie Marmon Silko, raised on the Laguna Pueblo reservation in New Mexico, weaves a tale of the Native American culture and the problems of Native Americans in the modern world. See the excerpt from this book beginning on page 27 in this unit.

Dogsong

by Gary Paulsen
Puffin Books, 1987

The exciting adventure of a courageous young Eskimo youth who leaves his village to find his own "song" and become a man.

Fifth Chinese Daughter

by Jade Snow Wong
Harper and Row, 1950

A high school girl from a Chinese-American family wins a scholarship to an American college and challenges parental authority and cultural tradition to follow her dream.

Home to Stay: Asian-American Women's Fiction

edited by Tina Koyama
Greenfield Review Press, 1991

A third-generation Japanese-American woman put together this collection of stories reflecting the emotional pressures, conflicts, and embarrassments of immigrant life in the United States.

I Remember Mama

by John van Druten
Harcourt Brace Jovanovich, 1944

This classic drama about a Norwegian immigrant family shows their struggle against poverty in order to survive in the United States.

Sarah, Plain and Tall

by Patricia MacLaclan
HarperCollins, 1985

A woman named Sarah brings unexpected happiness into the lives of a family after the untimely death of the mother.

"When you go to China," I told her, "you don't even need to open your mouth. They already know you are an outsider."

—Amy Tan
from "Double Face"

"Most of them in it are not our kind of people," she said, "but I can be gracious to anybody. . ."

—Flannery O'Conner
from "Everything that Rises Must Converge"

When they saw all that was sacred to them laid waste, the Navajos lost heart. They did not surrender; they simply ceased to fight. . . .

—Willa Cather
from Death Comes for the Archbishop

I've known rivers;
Ancient, dusky rivers
My soul has grown deep like rivers.

—Langston Hughes
from Selected Poems of Langston Hughes, 1974

Unit 2

WANTING TO UNDERSTAND AND TO BE UNDERSTOOD

Introduction

Our quest for understanding and for being understood comes from an intense desire to take pride in who we are and a yearning to reach our potential as human beings, both on personal and on societal levels. Encounters and the misgivings that can result from them often get in the way of our being understood by others. The most common encounters are those between one cultural group and another or one nation and another, between a parent and a child and between the sexes. These encounters often involve prejudice of one form or another, which can be overcome if we try.

An Overview

In this unit, you will read about a mother-daughter relationship in an excerpt entitled "Double Face" from Amy Tan's novel *The Joy Luck Club*. In this story, the mother represents Chinese traditional values, and the daughter represents modern values associated with life in the United States

67

as a second-generation Chinese American. In addition, you will explore prejudice through an encounter between a mother and her son in Flannery O'Connor's "Everything That Rises Must Converge." And you will see how it is possible for an encounter between nations to end in genocide in an excerpt from *Death Comes for the Archbishop* by Willa Cather. Included also is an excerpt from Chief Sealth's letter to the United States government that highlights one man's battle to try to preserve the environment for future generations. This is followed by a reading concerning encounters between the sexes entitled "Different Words, Different Worlds" from Deborah Tannen's best-selling book *You Just Don't Understand: Women and Men in Conversation*. In this last selection, you will find a linguist's attempt to explain the intense verbal encounters in which men and women often find themselves at odds with one another.

Thinking Critically About the Theme

The quotes beginning this unit come from some of the selections you will be reading. Think about the quotes in relation to the Unit 2 theme, Wanting to Understand and to Be Understood. Choose one or two to write about in your journal. Predict what might happen in the selection, based on the quote you chose and on the overview you just read.

Now look back at the poem by Langston Hughes. How does it relate to the theme? Write your response in your journal. Do you like the poem? Why or why not?

Double Face

Amy Tan

"Double Face" is taken from the novel *The Joy Luck Club* by Amy Tan. The excerpt presented here is about Lindo Jong and her daughter, Waverly. They form one of the four mother-daughter relationships described in this novel about women's lives in China before 1949 compared to their daughters' lives in modern-day America. Lindo Jong, who was promised in marriage at the age of two to the son of a prominent Chinese family and given to them when she was only 12, revealed a keen intelligence as she cleverly freed herself from their grasp. Under much stress, she eventually managed to come to the United States, where she later married and had children of her own. It is not until her daughter Waverly is about to marry for the second time that Lindo begins to understand the contrasts in their lives and the things that have driven them apart. It is with both humor and sadness that she confronts her daughter in "Double Face." While you are reading, think about your own relationship with a parent. Are there any ways in which your relationship might be similar to the one described here?

Amy Tan herself was born to immigrant parents soon after their arrival to the United States from China in 1949. In addition to *The Joy Luck Club* (her first book), she has written *The Kitchen God's Wife*, which focuses on a similar theme.

Before You Read

As mentioned above, the novel from which this selection comes shows a comparison between women's lives in China before 1949 and their daughters' lives today in the United States. In what ways do you think the two kinds of lives might differ? In what ways might they be similar? Talk about it with a small group or write about it in your journal.

My daughter wanted to go to China for her second honeymoon, but now she is afraid.

"What if I blend in so well they think I'm one of them?" Waverly asked me. "What if they don't let me come back to the United States?"

"When you go to China," I told her, "you don't even need to open your mouth. They already know you are an outsider."

"What are you talking about?" she asked. My daughter likes to speak back. She likes to question what I say.

"Aii-ya," I said, "Even if you put on their clothes, even if you take off your makeup and hide your fancy jewelry, they know.

They know just watching the way you walk, the way you carry your face. They know you do not belong."

My daughter did not look pleased when I told her this, that she didn't look Chinese. She had a sour American look on her face. Oh, maybe ten years ago, she would have clapped her hands—hurray!—as if this were good news. But now she wants to be Chinese, it is so fashionable. And I know it is too late. All those years I tried to teach her! She followed my Chinese ways only until she learned how to walk out the door by herself and go to school. So now the only Chinese words she can say are *sh-sh, houche, chr fan,* and *gwan deng shweijyau.* How can she talk to people in China with these words? Pee-pee, choo-choo train, eat, close light sleep. How can she think she can blend in? Only her skin and her hair are Chinese. Inside—she is all American-made.

It's my fault she is this way. I wanted my children to have the best combination: American circumstances° and Chinese character.° How could I know these two things do not mix?

I taught her how American circumstances work. If you are born poor here, it's no lasting shame. You are first in line for a scholarship. If the roof crashes on your head, no need to cry over this bad luck. You can sue anybody, make the landlord fix it. You do not have to sit like a Buddha under a tree letting pigeons drop their dirty business on your head. You can buy an umbrella. Or go inside a Catholic church. In America, nobody says you have to keep the circumstances somebody else gives you.

She learned these things, but I couldn't teach her about Chinese character. How to obey parents and listen to your mother's mind. How not to show your own thoughts, to put your feelings behind your face so you can take advantage of hidden opportunities. Why easy things are not worth pursuing. How to know your own worth and polish it, never flashing it around like a cheap ring. Why Chinese thinking is best.

No, this kind of thinking didn't stick to her. She was too busy chewing gum, blowing bubbles bigger than her cheeks. Only that kind of thinking stuck.

VOCABULARY

circumstances: The facts surrounding a situation; basic conditions beyond one's control (*circum-* means around; -*stance* means to stand).

character: Here it means the qualities or moral strength of a particular group or of persons within that group.

"Finish your coffee," I told her yesterday. "Don't throw your blessings away."

"Don't be so old-fashioned, Ma," she told me, finishing her coffee down the sink. "I'm my own person."

And I think, How can she be her own person? When did I give her up?

My daughter is getting married a second time. So she asked me to go to her beauty parlor, her famous Mr. Rory. I know her meaning. She is ashamed of my looks. What will her husband's parents and his important lawyer friends think of this backward old Chinese woman?

"Auntie An-mei can cut me," I say.

"Rory is famous," says my daughter, as if she had no ears. "He does fabulous work."

So I sit in Mr. Rory's chair. He pumps me up and down until I am the right height. Then my daughter criticizes me as if I were not there. "See how it's flat on one side," she accuses my head. "She needs a cut and a perm. And this purple tint in her hair, she's been doing it at home. She's never had anything professionally done."

She is looking at Mr. Rory in the mirror. He is looking at me in the mirror. I have seen this professional look before. Americans don't really look at one another when talking. They talk to their reflections. They look at others or themselves only when they think nobody is watching. So they never see how they really look. They see themselves smiling without their mouth open, or turned to the side where they cannot see their faults.

"How does she want it?" asked Mr. Rory. He thinks I do not understand English. He is floating his fingers through my hair. He is showing how his magic can make my hair thicker and longer.

"Ma, how do you want it?" Why does my daughter think she is translating English for me? Before I can even speak, she explains my thoughts: "She wants a soft wave. We probably shouldn't cut it too short. Otherwise it'll be too tight for the wedding. She doesn't want it to look kinky° or weird."

VOCABULARY
kinky: Here it means tightly curled.

And now she says to me in a loud voice, as if I had lost my hearing, "Isn't that right, Ma? Not too tight?"

I smile. I use my American face. That's the face Americans think is Chinese, the one they cannot understand. But inside I am becoming ashamed. I am ashamed she is ashamed. Because she is my daughter and I am proud of her, and I am her mother but she is not proud of me.

Mr. Rory pats my hair more. He looks at me. He looks at my daughter. Then he says something to my daughter that really displeases her: "It's uncanny° how much you two look alike!"

I smile, this time with my Chinese face. But my daughter's eyes and her smile become very narrow, the way a cat pulls itself small just before it bites. Now Mr. Rory goes away so we can think about this. I hear him snap his fingers. "Wash! Mrs. Jong is next!"

So my daughter and I are alone in this crowded beauty parlor. She is frowning at herself in the mirror. She sees me looking at her.

"The same cheeks," she says. She points to mine and then pokes her cheeks. She sucks them outside in to look like a starved person. She puts her face next to mine, side by side, and we look at each other in the mirror.

"You can see your character in your face," I say to my daughter without thinking. "You can see your future."

"What do you mean?" she says.

And now I have to fight back my feelings. These two faces, I think, so much the same! The same happiness, the same sadness, the same good fortune, the same faults.

I am seeing myself and my mother, back in China, when I was a young girl.

My mother—your grandmother—once told me my fortune, how my character could lead to good and bad circumstances. She was sitting at her table with the big mirror. I was standing behind her, my chin resting on her shoulder. The next day was the start of the new year.[1] I would be ten years by my Chinese

---

VOCABULARY

uncanny: Strange or amazing.

CULTURAL NOTES

[1] The Chinese lunar new year is a celebration whose exact date is determined by the appearance of a new moon.

age, so it was an important birthday for me. For this reason maybe she did not criticize me too much. She was looking at my face.

She touched my ear. "You are lucky," she said. "You have my ears, a big thick lobe, lots of meat at the bottom, full of blessings. Some people are born so poor. Their ears are so thin, so close to their head, they can never hear luck calling to them. You have the right ears, but you must listen to your opportunities."

She ran her thin finger down my nose. "You have my nose. The hole is not too big, so your money will not be running out. The nose is straight and smooth, a good sign. A girl with a crooked nose is bound for misfortune. She is always following the wrong things, the wrong people, the worst luck."

She tapped my chin and then hers. "Not too short, not too long. Our longevity° will be adequate, not cut off too soon, not so long we become a burden."

She pushed my hair away from my forehead. "We are the same," concluded my mother. "Perhaps your forehead is wider, so you will be even more clever. And your hair is thick, the hairline is low on your forehead. This means you will have some hardships in your early life. This happened to me. But look at my hairline now. High! Such a blessing for my old age. Later you will learn to worry and lose your hair, too."

She took my chin her hand. She turned my face toward her, eyes facing eyes. She moved my face to one side, then the other. "The eyes are honest, eager," she said. "They follow me and show respect. They do not look down in shame. They do not resist and turn the opposite way. You will be a good wife, mother, and daughter-in-law."

When my mother told me these things, I was still so young. And even though she said we looked the same, I wanted to look more the same. If her eye went up and looked surprised, I wanted my eye to do the same. If her mouth fell down and was unhappy, I too wanted to feel unhappy.

I was so much like my mother. This was before our circumstances separated us: a flood that caused my family to leave me behind, my first marriage to a family that did not want me, a war from all sides, and later, an ocean that took me to a

---

VOCABULARY

longevity: Length or duration of life. The words following offer clues.

Double Face

new country. She did not see how my face changed over the years. How my mouth began to droop. How I began to worry but still did not lose my hair. How my eyes began to follow the American way. She did not see that I twisted my nose bouncing forward on a crowded bus in San Francisco. Your father and I, we were on our way to church to give many thanks to God for all our blessings, but I had to subtract some for my nose.

It's hard to keep your Chinese face in America. At the beginning, before I even arrived, I had to hide my true self. I paid an American-raised Chinese girl in Peking to show me how.

"In America," she said, "you cannot say you want to live there forever. If you are Chinese, you must say you admire their schools, their ways of thinking. You must say you want to be a scholar and come back to teach Chinese people what you have learned."

"What should I say I want to learn?" I asked. "If they ask me questions, if I cannot answer . . ."

"Religion, you must say you want to study religion," said this smart girl. "Americans all have different ideas about religion, so there are no right and wrong answers. Say to them, I'm going for God's sake, and they will respect you."

For another sum of money, this girl gave me a form filled out with English words. I had to copy these words over and over again as if they were English words formed from my own head. Next to the word NAME, I wrote *Lindo Sun*. Next to the word BIRTHDATE, I wrote *May 11, 1918*, which this girl insisted was the same as three months after the Chinese lunar new year. Next to the word BIRTHPLACE, I put down *Taiyuan, China*. And next to the word OCCUPATION, I wrote *student of theology.*°

I gave the girl even more money for a list of addresses in San Francisco, people with big connections. And finally, this girl gave me, free of charge, instructions for changing my circumstances. "First," she said, "you must find a husband. An American citizen is best."

She saw my surprise and quickly added, "Chinese! Of course, he must be Chinese. 'Citizen' does not mean Caucasian.° But if he is not a citizen, you should immediately do number two. See

---

VOCABULARY
theology: Religion.
Caucasian: Belonging to the white race.

here, you should have a baby. Boy or girl, it doesn't matter in the United States. Neither will take care of you in your old age, isn't that true?" And we both laughed.

"Be careful, though," she said. "The authorities there will ask you if you have children now or if you are thinking of having some. You must say no. You should look sincere and say you are not married, you are religious, you know it is wrong to have a baby."

I must have looked puzzled, because she explained further: "Look here now, how can an unborn baby know what it is not supposed to do? And once it has arrived, it is an American citizen and can do anything it wants. It can ask its mother to stay. Isn't that true?"

But that is not the reason I was puzzled. I wondered why she said I should look sincere. How could I look any other way when telling the truth?

See how truthful my face still looks. Why didn't I give this look to you? Why do you always tell your friends that I arrived in the United States on a slow boat from China? This is not true. I was not that poor. I took a plane. I had saved the money my first husband's family gave me when they sent me away. And I had saved money from my twelve years' work as a telephone operator. But it is true I did not take the fastest plane. The plane took three weeks. It stopped everywhere: Hong Kong, Vietnam, the Philippines. Hawaii. So by the time I arrived, I did not look sincerely glad to be here.

Why do you always tell people that I met your father in the Cathay House, that I broke open a fortune cookie and it said I would marry a dark, handsome stranger, and that when I looked up, there he was, the waiter, your father. Why do you make this joke? This is not sincere. This was not true! Your father was not a waiter, I never ate in that restaurant. The Cathay House had a sign that said "Chinese Food," so only Americans went there before it was torn down. Now it is a McDonald's restaurant with a big Chinese sign that says *mai dong lou*—"wheat," "east," "building." All nonsense. Why are you attracted only to Chinese nonsense? You must understand my real circumstances, how I arrived, how I married, how I lost my Chinese face, why you are the way you are.

When I arrived, nobody asked me questions. The authorities looked at my papers and stamped me in. I decided to go first to a San Francisco address given to me by this girl in Peking. The bus put me down on a wide street with cable cars. This was California Street. I walked up this hill and then I saw a tall building. This was Old St. Mary's. Under the church sign, in handwritten Chinese characters,° someone had added: "A Chinese Ceremony to Save Ghosts from Spiritual Unrest 7 A.M. and 8:30 A.M." I memorized this information in case the authorities asked me where I worshipped my religion. And then I saw another sign across the street. It was painted on the outside of a short building: "Save Today for Tomorrow, at Bank of America." And I thought to myself, This is where American people worship. See, even then I was not so dumb! Today that church is the same size, but where that short bank used to be, now there is a tall building, fifty stories high, where you and your husband-to-be work and look down on everybody.

My daughter laughed when I said this. Her mother can make a good joke.

So I kept walking up this hill. I saw two pagodas,° one on each side of the street, as though they were the entrance to a great Buddha[2] temple. But when I looked carefully, I saw the pagoda was really just a building topped with stacks of tile roofs, no walls, nothing else under its head. I was surprised how they tried to make everything look like an old imperial° city or an emperor's tomb. But if you looked on either side of these pretend-pagodas, you could see the streets became narrow and crowded, dark, and dirty. I thought to myself, Why did they choose only the worst Chinese parts for the inside? Why didn't they build gardens and ponds instead? Oh, here and there was the look of a famous ancient cave or a Chinese opera. But inside it was always the same cheap stuff.

So by the time I found the address the girl in Peking gave me, I knew not to expect too much. The address was a large green building, so noisy, children running up and down the outside stairs and hallways. Inside number 402, I found an old woman who told me right away she had wasted her time waiting for me all week. She quickly wrote down some addresses and gave

---

VOCABULARY

characters: Here it means symbols or letters. "Handwritten" is a clue.
pagodas: Buildings with many levels shaped like towers.
imperial: Belonging to an empire (*imper-* refers to command). See the words following.

CULTURAL NOTES

[2]Buddha, a philosopher from India, founded the Buddhist religion.

them to me, keeping her hand out after I took the paper. So I gave her an American dollar and she looked at it and said, "*Syaujye*"—Miss—"we are in America now. Even a beggar can starve on this dollar." So I gave her another dollar and she said, "Aii, you think it is so easy getting this information?" So I gave her another and she closed her hand and her mouth.

With the addresses this old woman gave me, I found a cheap apartment on Washington Street. It was like all the other places, sitting on top of a little store. And through this three-dollar list, I found a terrible job paying me seventy-five cents an hour. Oh, I tried to get a job as a salesgirl, but you had to know English for that. I tried for another job as a Chinese hostess, but they also wanted me to rub my hands up and down foreign men, and I knew right away this was as bad as fourth-class prostitutes in China! So I rubbed that address out with black ink. And some of the other jobs required you to have a special relationship. They were jobs held by families from Canton and Toishan and the Four Districts, southern people who had come many years ago to make their fortune and were still holding on to them with the hands of their great-grandchildren.

So my mother was right about my hardships. This job in the cookie factory was one of the worst. Big black machines worked all day and night pouring little pancakes onto moving round griddles. The other women and I sat on high stools, and as the little pancakes went by, we had to grab them off the hot griddle just as they turned golden. We would put a strip of paper in the center, then fold the cookie in half and bend its arms back just as it turned hard. If you grabbed the pancake too soon, you would burn your fingers on the hot, wet dough. But if you grabbed too late, the cookie would harden before you could even complete the first bend. And then you had to throw these mistakes in a barrel, which counted against you because the owner could sell those only as scraps.

After the first day, I suffered ten red fingers. This was not a job for a stupid person. You had to learn fast or your fingers would turn into fried sausages. So the next day only my eyes burned, from never taking them off the pancakes. And the day after that, my arms ached from holding them out ready to catch the pancakes at just the right moment. But by the end of my first week, it became mindless work and I could relax enough to notice who else was working on each side of me. One was an older woman who never smiled and spoke to herself in

Cantonese[3] when she was angry. She talked like a crazy person. On my other side was a woman around my age. Her barrel contained very few mistakes. But I suspected she ate them. She was quite plump.

"Eh, *Syaujye*," she called to me over the loud noise of the machines. I was grateful to hear her voice, to discover we both spoke Mandarin,[4] although her dialect was coarse-sounding. "Did you ever think you would be so powerful you could determine someone else's fortune?" she asked.

I didn't understand what she meant. So she picked up one of the strips of paper and read it aloud, first in English: "Do not fight and air your dirty laundry in public. To the victor go the soils." Then she translated in Chinese: "You shouldn't fight and do your laundry at the same time. If you win, your clothes will get dirty."

I still did not know what she meant. So she picked up another one and read in English: "Money is the root of all evil. Look around you and dig deep." And then in Chinese: "Money is a bad influence. You become restless and rob graves."

"What is this nonsense?" I asked her, putting the strips of paper in my pocket, thinking I should study these classical American sayings.

"They are fortunes," she explained. "American people think Chinese people write these sayings."

"But we never say such things!" I said. "These things don't make sense. These are not fortunes, they are bad instructions."

"No, Miss," she said, laughing, "it is our bad fortune to be here making these and somebody else's bad fortune to pay to get them."

So that is how I met An-mei Hsu. Yes, yes, Auntie An-mei, now so old-fashioned. An-mei and I still laugh over those bad fortunes and how they later became quite useful in helping me catch a husband.

"Eh, Lindo," An-mei said to me one day at our workplace. "Come to my church this Sunday. My husband has a friend who is looking for a good Chinese wife. He is not a citizen, but I'm sure he knows how to make one." So that is how I first heard

---

CULTURAL NOTES

[3]Cantonese is the dialect of Chinese spoken by the people of Canton; it also refers to the people of that region.

[4]Mandarin is a dialect of Chinese spoken around the Peking area.

about Tin Jong, your father. It was not like my first marriage, where everything was arranged. I had a choice. I could choose to marry your father, or I could choose not to marry him and go back to China.

I knew something was not right when I saw him: He was Cantonese! How could An-mei think I could marry such a person? But she just said: "We are not in China anymore. You don't have to marry the village boy. Here everybody is now from the same village even if they come from different parts of China." See how changed Auntie An-mei is from those old days.

So we were shy at first, your father and I, neither of us able to speak to each other in our Chinese dialects. We went to English class together, speaking to each other in those new words and sometimes taking out a piece of paper to write a Chinese character to show what we meant. At least we had that, a piece of paper to hold us together. But it's hard to tell someone's marriage intentions when you can't say things aloud. All those little signs—the teasing, the bossy, scolding words— that's how you know if it is serious. But we could talk only in the manner of our English teacher. I see cat. I see rat. I see hat.

But I saw soon enough how much your father liked me. He would pretend he was in a Chinese play to show me what he meant. He ran back and forth, jumped up and down, pulling his fingers through his hair, so I knew—*mangjile!*—what a busy, exciting place this Pacific Telephone was, this place where he worked. You didn't know this about your father—that he could be such a good actor? You didn't know your father had so much hair?

Oh, I found out later his job was not the way he described it. It was not so good. Even today, now that I can speak Cantonese to your father, I always ask him why he doesn't find a better situation. But he acts as if we were in those old days, when he couldn't understand anything I said.

Sometimes I wonder why I wanted to catch a marriage with your father. I think An-mei put the thought in my mind. She said, "In the movies, boys and girls are always passing notes in class. That's how they fall into trouble. You need to start trouble to get this man to realize his intentions. Otherwise, you will be an old lady before it comes to his mind."

That evening An-mei and I went to work and searched through strips of fortune cookie papers, trying to find the right instructions to give to your father. An-mei read them aloud,

Double Face

putting aside ones that might work: "Diamonds are a girl's best friend. Don't ever settle for a pal." "If such thoughts are in your head, it's time to be wed." "Confucius say a woman is worth a thousand words. Tell your wife she's used up her total."

We laughed over those. But I knew the right one when I read it. It said: "A house is not home when a spouse is not at home." I did not laugh. I wrapped up this saying in a pancake, bending the cookie with all my heart.

After school the next afternoon, I put my hand in my purse and then made a look, as if a mouse had bitten my hand. "What's this?" I cried. Then I pulled out the cookie and handed it to your father. "Eh! So many cookies, just to see them makes me sick. You take this cookie."

I knew even then he had a nature that did not waste anything. He opened the cookie and he crunched it in his mouth, and then read the piece of paper.

"What does it say?" I asked. I tried to act as if it did not matter. And when he still did not speak, I said, "Translate, please."

We were walking in Portsmouth Square and already the fog had blown in and I was very cold in my thin coat. So I hoped your father would hurry and ask me to marry him. But instead, he kept his serious look and said, "I don't know this word 'spouse.' Tonight I will look in my dictionary. Then I can tell you the meaning tomorrow."

The next day he asked me in English, "Lindo, can you spouse me?" And I laughed at him and said he used that word incorrectly. So he came back and made a Confucius joke, that if the words were wrong, then his intentions must also be wrong. We scolded and joked with each other all day long like this, and that is how we decided to get married.

One month later we had a ceremony in the First Chinese Baptist Church, where we met. And nine months later your father and I had our proof of citizenship, a baby boy, your big brother Winston. I named him Winston because I liked the meaning of those two words "wins ton." I wanted to raise a son who would win many things, praise, money, a good life. Back then, I thought to myself, At last I have everything I wanted. I was so happy, I didn't see we were poor. I saw only what we had. How did I know Winston would die later in a car accident? So young! Only sixteen!

Two years after Winston was born, I had your other brother, Vincent. I named him Vincent, which sounds like "win cent," the sound of making money, because I was beginning to think we did not have enough. And then I bumped my nose riding on the bus. Soon after that you were born.

I don't know what caused me to change. Maybe it was my crooked nose that damaged my thinking. Maybe it was seeing you as a baby, how you looked so much like me, and this made me dissatisfied with my life. I wanted everything for you to be better. I wanted you to have the best circumstances, the best character. I didn't want you to regret anything. And that's why I named you Waverly. It was the name of the street we lived on. And I wanted you to think, This is where I belong. But I also knew if I named you after this street, soon you would grow up, leave this place, and take a piece of me with you.

Mr. Rory is brushing my hair. Everything is soft. Everything is black.

"You look great, Ma," says my daughter. "Everyone at the wedding will think you're my sister."

I look at my face in the beauty parlor mirror. I see my reflection. I cannot see my faults, but I know they are there. I gave my daughter these faults. The same eyes, the same cheeks, the same chin. Her character, it came from my circumstances. I look at my daughter and now it is the first time I have seen it.

"Ai-ya! What happened to your nose?"

She looks in the mirror. She sees nothing wrong. "What do you mean? Nothing happened," she says. "It's just the same nose."

"But how did you get it crooked?" I ask. One side of her nose is bending lower, dragging her cheek with it.

"What do you mean?" she asks. "It's your nose. You gave me this nose."

"How can that be? It's drooping. You must get plastic surgery and correct it."

But my daughter has no ears for my words. She puts her smiling face next to my worried one. "Don't be silly. Our nose isn't so bad," she says. "It makes us look devious." She looks pleased.

"What is this word, 'devious,'" I ask.

"It means we're looking one way, while following another.

We're for one side and also the other. We mean what we say, but our intentions are different."

"People can see this in our face?"

My daughter laughs. "Well, not everything that we're thinking. They just know we're two-faced."

"This is good?"

"This is good if you get what you want."

I think about our two faces. I think about my intentions. Which one is American? Which one is Chinese? Which one is better? If you show one, you must always sacrifice the other.

It is like what happened when I went back to China last year, after I had not been there for almost forty years. I had taken off my fancy jewelry. I did not wear loud colors. I spoke their language. I used their local money. But still, they knew. They knew my face was not one hundred percent Chinese. They still charged me high foreign prices.

So now I think, What did I lose? What did I get back in return? I will ask my daughter what she thinks.

Questions for Reflection/Discussion

1. Lindo tells her daughter, Waverly, that even if she were to go to China for her second honeymoon, she would be considered an "outsider." Why might this be true, according to Lindo? Why would this have pleased her daughter ten years ago? Why does it not please her daughter now? If you are an immigrant with children, do you think your children would be treated as "outsiders" were they to return to the country from which you came? Why or why not?

2. In what ways do you think Waverly is different from the young women her age in the China her mother knew? Consider behavior towards parents, self-expression, divorce, remarriage, for example.

3. What does Lindo mean when she says, "I wanted my children to have the best combination: American circumstances and Chinese character"? What is there about each that she considers to be positive? If you are an immigrant to the United States with children, do you want your children to have American circumstances but the character typical of people in the country from which you came? Explain.

4. Lindo mentions several superstitions about good luck/bad luck. What are a few of them? Do you have any such superstitions? Discuss these questions with a partner. Share your superstitions with another pair of classmates.

5. How do their reactions differ when they are both told that they look like their mothers? What does this tell you about the culture to which each was exposed?

6. Why does Lindo feel it is difficult to "keep your Chinese face in America" (p. 74)?

7. Why do you think it was all right for Lindo to marry a Cantonese person in the United States, but not in China? Do you know of similar ironies?

8. We discover that Lindo has a sense of humor. Find three or four instances of humor. What makes these instances seem humorous to you? Discuss them with a partner. Share your ideas with another pair of classmates.

 ## EXPLORING OTHER SOURCES

1. Make your own collection of superstitions. Ask friends, family members, and people in the community to share a few with you. Or you may want to look at library collections and select those that are most interesting to you. Make sure you note the source of each superstition.

2. Using library resources and/or the Internet, find out as much as you can about women's lives in China before 1949. Are their lives much different today? If so, in what ways? Key words might include "China," "Chinese women," "Chinese marriage customs," for example. To search the Internet, point your browser to World Views Online (http://worldviews.wadsworth.com). Ask your instructor or the librarian for assistance if you need it. Share your information with a small group.

3. Lindo and her new husband, even though they spoke different dialects of Chinese, were able to communicate by notes written in Chinese. How was this possible? Discover as much as you can about the Chinese written language. How does it differ from a written system such as one finds in English? If you are an immigrant or live in a non–English-speaking country, how does English differ from your own first language?

4. From a variety of sources, find out as much as possible about mother-daughter relationships in the United States today. In what ways are they similar to the relationship between Lindo and Waverly? In what ways are they generally different? Discuss these questions with a small group.

Synthesis Through Writing

1. In your journal, respond to one or both of the items below:
   a. Is there such a thing as an "American character"? If so, what is it? Is it easier or more difficult to define than a "Chinese character"? If so, why? How would you describe the "character" of the community in which you grew up?
   b. Are you an immigrant from another country? If so, explain the circumstances of your arrival to your new land. Were your experiences in any way similar to Lindo's? Did you see any humor in your situation?

2. Why do you think some people/cultures are more superstitious than others? Make a list of your reasons. Then develop a short essay giving examples to support your position. Refer to the writing strategies on page xix before you begin.

3. Lindo makes a joke about taking care of the elderly in society. How does caring for the elderly differ in China and the United States today?

   Divide a piece of paper into two columns. Label one column "China" and the other "United States." In each column, list what you know about taking care of the elderly in each country. You may want to find additional information from library resources or other resources available to you. Now examine what you have listed and note the differences between the treatment of the elderly in the two countries. Write an essay describing these differences. Use your graphic organizer to help you in this process.

4. Write an essay comparing women's lives in China before 1949 with their lives in China today. First, draw a Venn diagram like the following:

The Lives of Women Living in China

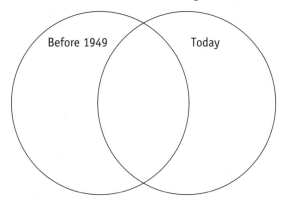

Before 1949   Today

Place the differences in the two circles. Place the similarities in the overlapping area. Use what you learned in the preceding activity, Exploring Other Sources, to fill in the circles. Use this diagram to help you develop your paper.

5. Write an essay comparing Lindo and Waverly's relationship with a typical mother-daughter relationship in the United States today. Create a Venn Diagram like the one in item 4 to help you. In addition, you may use the writing strategies on page xix.

Everything That Rises Must Converge
Flannery O'Connor

This story by Flannery O'Connor examines the nature of prejudice and how it affects attitudes towards others. What the reader will see here, at least on the surface, is an angry son condemning the prejudice he sees in his mother. This encounter between mother and son reveals not only the complexity of prejudice but also the many places where it can be found. It is probable that one would not have to look very far to find it.

Flannery O'Connor is best known for her short stories and novels about the southern region of the United States and its apparent inability to adjust easily to a changing world. "Everything That Rises Must Converge" is among her most popular short stories dealing with the prejudice that often accompanies the fear and anxiety that change can bring. Prejudice is a theme that is commonly found throughout her work. The stories "Good Country People" and "A Good Man Is Hard to Find" and the novels *Wise Blood* and *The Violent Bear It Away* are among her most cherished contributions to American literature.

Before You Read

Think about the meaning of the word "prejudice." How might you define it? How much prejudice do you think there is in the society in which you live? Is it a serious problem? Discuss it with a small group or write about it in your journal.

$\mathcal{H}$er doctor had told Julian's mother that she must lose twenty pounds on account of her blood pressure, so on Wednesday nights Julian had to take her downtown on the bus for a reducing class at the Y.[1] The reducing class was designed for working girls over fifty who weighed from 165 to 200 pounds. His mother was one of the slimmer ones, but she said ladies did not tell their age or weight. She would not ride the buses by herself at night since they had been integrated, and because the reducing class was one of her few pleasures, necessary for her health, and *free*, she said Julian could at least put himself out to take her, considering all she did for him. Julian did not like to consider all she did for him, but every Wednesday night he braced himself and took her.

She was almost ready to go, standing before the hall mirror, putting on her hat, while he, his hands behind him, appeared pinned to the door frame, waiting like Saint Sebastian[2] for the arrows to begin piercing him. The hat was new and had cost her seven dollars and a half. She kept saying, "Maybe I shouldn't have paid that for it. No, I shouldn't have. I'll take it off and return it tomorrow. I shouldn't have bought it."

Julian raised his eyes to heaven. "Yes, you should have bought it," he said. "Put it on and let's go." It was a hideous hat. A purple velvet flap came down on one side of it and stood up on the other; the rest of it was green and looked like a cushion with the stuffing out. He decided it was less comical than jaunty° and pathetic. Everything that gave her pleasure was small and depressed him.

She lifted the hat one more time and set it down slowly on top of her head. Two wings of gray hair protruded on either side of her florid° face, but her eyes, sky-blue, were as innocent and untouched by experience as they must have been when she was ten. Were it not that she was a widow who had struggled fiercely to feed and clothe and put him through school and who

---

VOCABULARY

jaunty: Appearing to be carefree and self-confident.
florid: Flushed with a reddish color (*flor-* means bloom).

CULTURAL NOTES

[1]The Y refers to the YWCA, which is the acronym for the Young Women's Christian Association. This group organizes sporting events and exercise programs for women in many cities across the United States.
[2]Saint Sebastian was a Roman martyr of the third century A.D. who was killed by arrows because he became a Christian.

was supporting him still, "until he got on his feet," she might have been a little girl that he had to take to town.

"It's all right, it's all right," he said. "Let's go." He opened the door himself and started down the walk to get her going. The sky was a dying violet and the houses stood out darkly against it, bulbous° liver-colored monstrosities of a uniform ugliness though no two were alike. Since this had been a fashionable neighborhood forty years ago, his mother persisted in thinking they did well to have an apartment in it. Each house had a narrow collar of dirt around it in which sat, usually, a grubby child. Julian walked with his hands in his pockets, his head down and thrust forward and his eyes glazed with the determination to make himself completely numb during the time he would be sacrificed to her pleasure.

The door closed and he turned to find the dumpy figure, surmounted° by the atrocious hat, coming toward him. "Well," she said, "you only live once and paying a little more for it, I at least won't meet myself coming and going."

"Some day I'll start making money," Julian said gloomily—he knew he never would—"and you can have one of those jokes whenever you take the fit." But first they would move. He visualized a place where the nearest neighbors would be three miles away on either side.

"I think you're doing fine," she said, drawing on her gloves. "You've only been out of school a year. Rome wasn't built in a day."

She was one of the few members of the Y reducing class who arrived in hat and gloves and who had a son who had been to college. "It takes time," she said, "and the world is in such a mess. This hat looked better on me than any of the others, though when she brought it out I said, 'Take that thing back. I wouldn't have it on my head,' and she said, 'Now wait till you see it on,' and when she put it on me, I said, 'We-ull,' and she said, 'If you ask me, that hat does something for you and you do something for the hat, and besides,' she said, 'with that hat, you won't meet yourself coming and going.'"

Julian thought he could have stood his lot better if she had been selfish, if she had been an old hag who drank and screamed at him. He walked along, saturated in depression, as if

---

VOCABULARY

bulbous: Like a bulb.
surmounted: Here it means topped (*sur*- means above; -*mounted*- means to get on top of).

in the midst of his martyrdom° he had lost his faith. Catching sight of his long, hopeless, irritated face, she stopped suddenly with a grief-stricken look, and pulled back on his arm. "Wait on me," she said. "I'm going back to the house and take this thing off and tomorrow I'm going to return it. I was out of my head. I can pay the gas bill with that seven-fifty."

He caught her arm in a vicious grip. "You are not going to take it back," he said. "I like it."

"Well," she said. "I don't think I ought . . . "

"Shut up and enjoy it," he muttered, more depressed than ever.

"With the world in the mess it's in," she said, "it's a wonder we can enjoy anything. I tell you, the bottom rail is on the top."

Julian sighed.

"Of course," she said, "if you know who you are, you can go anywhere." She said this every time he took her to the reducing class. "Most of them in it are not our kind of people," she said, "but I can be gracious to anybody. I know who I am."

"They don't give a damn for your graciousness," Julian said savagely. "Knowing who you are is good for one generation only. You haven't the foggiest idea where you stand now or who you are."

She stopped and allowed her eyes to flash at him. "I most certainly do know who I am," she said, "and if you don't know who you are, I'm ashamed of you."

"Oh hell," Julian said.

"Your great-grandfather was a former governor of this state," she said. "Your grandfather was a prosperous landowner. Your grandmother was a Godhigh."

"Will you look around you," he said tersely,° "and see where you are now?" and he swept his arm jerkily out to indicate the neighborhood, which the growing darkness at least made less dingy.°

"You remain what you are," she said. "Your great-grandfather had a plantation and two hundred slaves."

"There are no more slaves," he said irritably.

"They were better off when they were," she said. He groaned to see that she was off on that topic. She rolled onto it every few

---

VOCABULARY

martyrdom: The state of suffering for a cause beyond oneself.
tersely: concisely, using few words.
dingy (dĭn' jē): Drab or dull looking. ". . . growing darkness" is a clue.

days like a train on an open track. He knew every stop, every junction, every swamp along the way, and knew the exact point at which her conclusion would roll majestically into the station: "It's ridiculous. It's simply not realistic. They should rise, yes, but on their own side of the fence."

"Let's skip it," Julian said.

"The ones I feel sorry for," she said, "are the ones that are half white. They're tragic."

"Will you skip it?"

"Suppose we were half white. We would certainly have mixed feelings."

"I have mixed feelings now," he groaned.

"Well let's talk about something pleasant," she said. "I remember going to Grandpa's when I was a little girl. Then the house had double stairways that went up to what was really the second floor—all the cooking was done on the first. I used to like to stay down in the kitchen on account of the way the walls smelled. I would sit with my nose pressed against the plaster and take deep breaths. Actually the place belonged to the Godhighs but your grandfather Chestny paid the mortgage and saved it for them. They were in reduced circumstances," she said, "but reduced or not, they never forgot who they were."

"Doubtless that decayed mansion reminded them," Julian muttered. He never spoke of it without contempt or thought of it without longing. He had seen it once when he was a child before it had been sold. The double stairways had rotted and been torn down. Negroes[3] were living in it. But it remained in his mind as his mother had known it. It appeared in his dreams regularly. He would stand on the wide porch, listening to the rustle of oak leaves, then wander through the high-ceilinged hall into the parlor that opened onto it and gaze at the worn rugs and faded draperies. It occurred to him that it was he, not she, who could have appreciated it. He preferred its threadbare elegance to anything he could name and it was because of it that all the neighborhoods they had lived in had been a torment to him— whereas she had hardly known the difference. She called her insensitivity "being adjustable."

CULTURAL NOTES
[3]"Negroes" is an old-fashioned term meaning African-Americans.

"And I remember the old darky who was my nurse, Caroline. There was no better person in the world. I've always had a great respect for my colored friends," she said. "I'd do anything in the world for them and they'd . . . "

"Will you for God's sake get off that subject?" Julian said. When he got on a bus by himself, he made it a point to sit down beside a Negro, in reparation° as it were for his mother's sins.

"You're mighty touchy tonight," she said. "Do you feel all right?"

"Yes I feel all right," he said. "Now lay off."

She pursed her lips. "Well, you certainly are in a vile humor," she observed. "I just won't speak to you at all."

They had reached the bus stop. There was no bus in sight and Julian, his hands still jammed in his pockets and his head thrust forward, scowled down the empty street. The frustration of having to wait on the bus as well as ride on it began to creep up his neck like a hot hand. The presence of his mother was borne in upon him as she gave a pained sigh. He looked at her bleakly. She was holding herself very erect under the preposterous° hat, wearing it like a banner of her imaginary dignity. There was in him an evil urge to break her spirit. He suddenly unloosened his tie and pulled if off and put it in his pocket.

She stiffened. "Why must you look like *that* when you take me to town?" she said. "Why must you deliberately embarrass me?"

"If you'll never learn where you are," he said, "you can at least learn where I am."

"You look like a—thug," she said.

"Then I must be one," he murmured.

"I'll just go home," she said. "I will not bother you. If you can't do a little thing like that for me . . . "

Rolling his eyes upward, he put his tie back on. "Restored to my class," he muttered. He thrust his face toward her and hissed, "True culture is in the mind, the *mind,*" he said, and tapped his head, "the mind."

"It's in the heart," she said, "and in how you do things and how you do things is because of who you *are.*"

"Nobody in the damn bus cares who you are."

"I care who I am," she said icily.

VOCABULARY

reparation: The act of making amends or making up for something done that was wrong (*repar-* means repair). ". . . for his mother's sins" is a clue.
preposterous: Ridiculous or absurd.

The lighted bus appeared on top of the next hill and as it approached, they moved out into the street to meet it. He put his hand under her elbow and hoisted her up on the creaking step. She entered with a little smile, as if she were going into a drawing room where everyone had been waiting for her. While he put in the tokens, she sat down on one of the broad front seats for three which faced the aisle. A thin woman with protruding° teeth and long yellow hair was sitting on the end of it. His mother moved up beside her and left room for Julian beside herself. He sat down and looked at the floor across the aisle where a pair of thin feet in red and white canvas sandals were planted.

His mother immediately began a general conversation meant to attract anyone who felt like talking. "Can it get any hotter?" she said and removed from her purse a folding fan, black with a Japanese scene on it, which she began to flutter before her.

"I reckon it might could," the woman with the protruding teeth said, "but I know for a fact my apartment couldn't get no hotter."

"It must get the afternoon sun," his mother said. She sat forward and looked up and down the bus. It was half filled. Everybody was white. "I see we have the bus to ourselves," she said. Julian cringed.°

"For a change," said the woman across the aisle, the owner of the red and white canvas sandals. "I come on one the other day and they were thick as fleas—up front and all through."

"The world is in a mess everywhere," his mother said. "I don't know how we've let it get in this fix."

"What gets my goat is all those boys from good families stealing automobile tires," the woman with the protruding teeth said. "I told my boy, I said you may not be rich but you been raised right and if I ever catch you in any such mess, they can send you on to the reformatory. Be exactly where you belong."

"Training tells," his mother said. "Is your boy in high school?"

"Ninth grade," the woman said.

"My son just finished college last year. He wants to write but he's selling typewriters until he gets started," his mother said.

VOCABULARY
protruding: Sticking out (*pro-* means forth or forward; *trud-* means to thrust).
cringed (krĭnjd): Here it means showed distress in facial expression or moved back in disgust.

The woman leaned forward and peered at Julian. He threw her such a malevolent° look that she subsided against the seat. On the floor across the aisle there was an abandoned newspaper. He got up and got it and opened it out in front of him. His mother discreetly continued the conversation in a lower tone but the woman across the aisle said in a loud voice, "Well, that's nice. Selling typewriters is close to writing. He can go right from one to the other."

"I tell him," his mother said, "that Rome wasn't built in a day."

Behind the newspaper Julian was withdrawing into the inner compartment of his mind where he spent most of his time. This was a kind of mental bubble in which he established himself when he could not bear to be a part of what was going on around him. From it he could see out and judge but in it he was safe from any kind of penetration from without. It was the only place where he felt free of the general idiocy of his fellows. His mother had never entered it but from it he could see her with absolute clarity.

The old lady was clever enough and he thought that if she had started from any of the right premises,° more might have been expected of her. She lived according to the laws of her own fantasy world, outside of which he had never seen her set foot. The law of it was to sacrifice herself for him after she had first created the necessity to do so by making a mess of things. If he had permitted her sacrifices, it was only because her lack of foresight had made them necessary. All of her life had been a struggle to act like a Chestny without the Chestny goods, and to give him everything she thought a Chestny ought to have; but since, said she, it was fun to struggle, why complain? And when you had won, as she had won, what fun to look back on the hard times! He could not forgive her that she had enjoyed the struggle and that she thought *she* had won.

What she meant when she said she had won was that she had brought him up successfully and had sent him to college and that he had turned out so well—good looking (her teeth had gone unfilled so that his could be straightened), intelligent (he realized he was too intelligent to be a success), and with a future ahead of him (there was of course no future ahead of

---

VOCABULARY

malevolent (mə lev' lənt): Full of evil; malicious (*mal-* means bad; *-vol-* refers to wishing).
premises: Conclusions upon which an argument is based (*pre-* means before).

him). She excused his gloominess on the grounds that he was still growing up and his radical ideas on his lack of practical experience. She said he didn't yet know a thing about "life," that he hadn't even entered the real world—when already he was as disenchanted with it as a man of fifty.

The further irony° of all this was that in spite of her, he had turned out so well. In spite of going to only a third-rate college, he had, on his own initiative, come out with a first-rate education; in spite of growing up dominated by a small mind, he had ended up with a large one; in spite of all her foolish views, he was free of prejudice and unafraid to face fact. Most miraculous of all, instead of being blinded by love for her as she was for him, he had cut himself emotionally free of her and could see her with complete objectivity. He was not dominated by his mother.

The bus stopped with a sudden jerk and shook him from his meditation. A woman from the back lurched forward with little steps and barely escaped falling in his newspaper as she righted herself. She got off and a large Negro got on. Julian kept his paper lowered to watch. It gave him a certain satisfaction to see injustice in daily operation. It confirmed his view that with a few exceptions there was no one worth knowing within a radius of three hundred miles. The Negro was well dressed and carried a briefcase. He looked around and then sat down on the other end of the seat where the woman with the red and white canvas sandals was sitting. He immediately unfolded a newspaper and obscured himself behind it. Julian's mother's elbow at once prodded instantly into his ribs. "Now you see why I won't ride on these buses by myself," she whispered.

The woman with the red and white canvas sandals had risen at the same time the Negro sat down and had gone further back in the bus and taken the seat of the woman who had got off. His mother leaned forward and cast her an approving look.

Julian rose, crossed the aisle, and sat down in the place of the woman with the canvas sandals. From this position, he looked serenely across at his mother. Her face had turned an angry red. He started at her, making his eyes the eyes of a stranger. He felt his tension suddenly lift as if he had openly declared war on her.

VOCABULARY

irony: When things turn out the opposite of what one might expect. ". . . in spite of her, he had turned out so well" is a clue.

He would have liked to get in conversation with the Negro and to talk with him about art or politics or any subject that would be above the comprehension of those around them, but the man remained entrenched° behind his paper. He was either ignoring the change of seating or had never noticed it. There was no way for Julian to convey his sympathy.

His mother kept her eyes fixed reproachfully° on his face. The woman with the protruding teeth was looking at him avidly as if he were a type of monster new to her.

"Do you have a light?" he asked the Negro.

Without looking away from his paper, the man reached in his pocket and handed him a packet of matches.

"Thanks," Julian said. For a moment he held the matches foolishly. A NO SMOKING sign looked down upon him from over the door. This alone would not have deterred° him; he had no cigarettes. He had quit smoking some months before because he could not afford it. "Sorry," he muttered, and handed back the matches. The Negro lowered the paper and gave him an annoyed look. He took the matches and raised the paper again.

His mother continued to gaze at him but she did not take advantage of his momentary discomfort. Her eyes retained their battered look. Her face seemed to be unnaturally red, as if her blood pressure had risen. Julian allowed no glimmer of sympathy to show on his face. Having got the advantage, he wanted desperately to keep it and carry it through. He would have liked to teach her a lesson that would last her a while, but there seemed no way to continue the point. The Negro refused to come out from behind his paper.

Julian folded his arms and looked stolidly° before him, facing her but as if he did not see her, as if he had ceased to recognize her existence. He visualized a scene in which, the bus having reached their stop, he would remain in his seat and when she said, "Aren't you going to get off?" he would look at her as at a stranger who had rashly addressed him. The corner they off on was usually deserted, but it was well lighted and it would not hurt her to walk by herself the four blocks to the Y. He decided

---

VOCABULARY

entrenched: Defended or hidden, as though in a trench. ". . . behind his newspaper" is a clue.
reproachfully: Expressing blame.
deterred: Stopped or prevented (de- means away from; -ter- refers to being frightened).
stolidly: Not showing much emotion.

to wait until the time came and then decide whether or not he would let her get off by herself. He would have to be at the Y at ten to bring her back, but he could leave her wondering if he was going to show up. There was no reason for her to think she could always depend on him.

He retired again into the high-ceilinged room sparsely settled with large pieces of antique furniture. His soul expanded momentarily but then he became aware of his mother across from him and the vision shriveled. He studied her coldly. Her feet in little pumps dangled like a child's and did not quite reach the floor. She was training on him an exaggerated look of reproach. He felt completely detached from her. At that moment he could with pleasure have slapped her as he would have slapped a particularly obnoxious child in his charge.

He began to imagine various unlikely ways by which he could teach her a lesson. He might make friends with some distinguished Negro professor or lawyer and bring him home to spend the evening. He would be entirely justified but her blood pressure would rise to 300. He could not push her to the extent of making her have a stroke, and moreover, he had never been successful at making any Negro friends. He had tried to strike up an acquaintance on the bus with some of the better types, with ones that looked like professors or ministers or lawyers. One morning he had sat down next to a distinguished-looking dark brown man who had answered his questions with a sonorous° solemnity° but who had turned out to be an undertaker. Another day he had sat down beside a cigar-smoking Negro with a diamond ring on his finger, but after a few stilted° pleasantries, the Negro had rung the buzzer and risen, slipping two lottery tickets into Julian's hand as he climbed over him to leave.

He imagined his mother lying desperately ill and his being able to secure only a Negro doctor for her. He toyed with that idea for a few minutes and then dropped it for a momentary vision of himself participating as a sympathizer in a sit-in demonstration. This was possible but he did not linger with it. Instead, he approached the ultimate horror. He brought home a

---

VOCABULARY

sonorous: Producing a deep, rich sound (*sonor-* means sound).
solemnity (so lem' nə tē): The state of being very serious (solemn means serious).
stilted: Stiff and very formal.

beautiful suspiciously Negroid woman. Prepare yourself, he said. There is nothing you can do about it. This is the woman I've chosen. She's intelligent, dignified, even good and she's suffered and she hasn't thought it *fun*. Now persecute us, go ahead and persecute us. Drive her out of here, but remember, you're driving me too. His eyes were narrowed and through the indignation° he had generated, he saw his mother across the aisle, purple-faced, shrunken to the dwarf-like proportions of her moral nature, sitting like a mummy beneath the ridiculous banner of her hat.

He was tilted out of his fantasy again as the bus stopped. The door opened with a sucking hiss and out of the dark a huge, gaily dressed, sullen-looking° colored woman got on with a little boy. The child, who might have been four, had on a short plaid suit and a Tyrolean[4] hat with a blue feather in it. Julian hoped that he would sit down beside him and that the woman would push in beside his mother. He could think of no better arrangement.

As she waited for her tokens, the woman was surveying the seating possibilities—he hoped with the idea of sitting where she was least wanted. There was something familiar-looking about her but Julian could not place what it was. She was a giant of a woman. Her face was set not only to meet opposition but to seek it out. The downward tilt of her large lower lip was like a warning sign: DON'T TAMPER WITH ME. Her bulging figure was encased in a green crepe dress and her feet overflowed in red shoes. She had on a hideous hat. A purple velvet flap came down on one side of it and stood up on the other: the rest of it was green and looked like a cushion with the stuffing out. She carried a mammoth red pocketbook that bulged throughout as if it were stuffed with rocks.

To Julian's disappointment, the little boy climbed up on the empty seat beside his mother. His mother lumped all children, black and white, into the common category, "cute," and she thought little Negroes were on the whole cuter than little white children. She smiled at the little boy as he climbed on the seat.

VOCABULARY

indignation: Anger due to unjust treatment.
sullen-looking: Appearing to be full of resentment.

CULTURAL NOTES

[4]*Tyrolean* comes from the word *Tyrol*, which is a province of western Austria.

Meanwhile the woman was bearing down upon the empty seat beside Julian. To his annoyance, she squeezed herself into it. He saw his mother's face change as the woman settled herself next to him and he realized with satisfaction that this was more objectionable to her than it was to him. Her face seemed almost gray and there was a look of dull recognition in her eyes, as if suddenly she had sickened at some awful confrontation. Julian saw that it was because she and the woman had, in a sense, swapped sons. Though his mother would not realize the symbolic° significance of this, she would feel it. His amusement showed plainly on his face.

The woman next to him muttered something unintelligible° to herself. He was conscious of a kind of bristling next to him, a muted growling like that of an angry cat. He could not see anything but the red pocketbook upright on the bulging green thighs. He visualized the woman as she had stood waiting for her tokens—the ponderous° figure, rising from the red shoes upward over the solid hips, the mammoth bosom, the haughty° face, to the green and purple hat.

His eyes widened.

The vision of the two hats, identical, broke upon him with the radiance of a brilliant sunrise. His face was suddenly lit with joy. He could not believe that Fate had thrust upon his mother such a lesson. He gave a loud chuckle so that she would look at him and see that he saw. She turned her eyes on him slowly. The blue in them seemed to have turned a bruised purple. For a moment he had an uncomfortable sense of her innocence, but it lasted only a second before principle rescued him. Justice entitled him to laugh. His grin hardened until it said to her as plainly as if he were saying aloud: Your punishment exactly fits your pettiness. This should teach you a permanent lesson.

Her eyes shifted to the woman. She seemed unable to bear looking at him and to find the woman preferable. He became conscious again of the bristling presence at his side. The woman was rumbling like a volcano about to become active. His mother's mouth began to twitch slightly at one corner. With a

VOCABULARY
symbolic: A symbol is a word used to describe something concrete that represents an abstract idea.
unintelligible: Not understandable or comprehensible (*un-* means not; *-intelli-* refers to perceiving).
ponderous: Very large; massive (*ponde-* refers to weight). ". . . solid hips, the mammoth bosom . . ." is a clue.
haughty (hô' tē): Proud to the point of being arrogant and filled with self-importance.

Everything That Rises Must Converge

sinking heart, he saw incipient° signs of recovery on her face and realized that this was going to strike her suddenly as funny and was going to be no lesson at all. She kept her eyes on the woman and an amused smile came over her face as if the woman were a monkey that had stolen her hat. The little Negro was looking up at her with fascinated eyes. He had been trying to attract her attention for some time.

"Carver!" the woman said suddenly. "Come heah!"

When he saw that the spotlight was on him at last, Carver drew his feet up and turned himself toward Julian's mother and giggled.

"Carver!" the woman said. "You heah me? Come heah!"

Carver slid down from the seat but remained squatting with his back against the base of it, his head turned slyly around toward Julian's mother, who was smiling at him. The woman reached a hand across the aisle and snatched him to her. He righted himself and hung backwards on her knees, grinning at Julian's mother. "Isn't he cute?" Julian's mother said to the woman with the protruding teeth.

"I reckon he is," the woman said without conviction.

The Negress yanked him upright but he eased out of her grip and shot across the aisle and scrambled, giggling wildly, onto the seat beside his love.

"I think he likes me," Julian's mother said, and smiled at the woman. It was the smile she used when she was being particularly gracious to an inferior. Julian saw everything lost. The lesson had rolled off her like rain on a roof.

The woman stood up and yanked the little boy off the seat as if she were snatching him from contagion.° Julian could feel the rage in her at having no weapon like his mother's smile. She gave the child a sharp slap across his leg. He howled once and then thrust his head into her stomach and kicked his feet against her shins. "Be-have," she said. vehemently.°

The bus stopped and the Negro who had been reading the newspaper got off. The woman moved over and set the little boy down with a thump between herself and Julian. She held him firmly by the knee. In a moment he put his hands in front of his face and peered at Julian's mother through his fingers.

VOCABULARY

incipient: Beginning to become noticeable.
contagion: A disease that can be given to another person through contact; a contagious disease.
vehemently (vē'ə mənt lē): With strong emotion or conviction.

"I see yoooooooo!" she said and put her hand in front of her face and peeped at him.

The woman slapped his hand down. "Quit yo' foolishness," she said, "before I knock the living Jesus out of you!"

Julian was thankful that the next stop was theirs. He reached up and pulled the cord. The woman reached up and pulled it at the same time. Oh my God, he thought. He had the terrible intuition that when they got off the bus together, his mother would open her purse and give the little boy a nickel. The gesture would be as natural to her as breathing. The bus stopped and the woman got up and lunged to the front, dragging the child, who wished to stay on, after her. Julian and his mother got up and followed. As they neared the door, Julian tried to relieve her of her pocketbook.

"No," she murmured, "I want to give the little boy a nickel."

"No!" Julian hissed. "No!"

She smiled down at the child and opened her bag. The bus door opened and the woman picked him up by the arm and descended with him, hanging at her hip. Once in the street she set him down and shook him.

Julian's mother had to close her purse while she got down the bus step but as soon as her feet were on the ground, she opened it again and began to rummage inside. "I can't find but a penny," she whispered, "but it looks like a new one."

"Don't do it!" Julian said fiercely between his teeth. There was a streetlight on the corner and she hurried to get under it so that she could better see into her pocketbook. The woman was heading off rapidly down the street with the child still hanging backward on her hand.

"Oh little boy!" Julian's mother called and took a few quick steps and caught up with them just beyond the lamppost. "Here's a bright new penny for you," and she held out the coin, which shone bronze in the dim light.

The huge woman turned and for a moment stood, her shoulders lifted and her face frozen with frustrated rage, and stared at Julian's mother. Then all at once she seemed to explode like a piece of machinery that had been given one ounce of pressure too much. Julian saw the black fist swing out with the red pocketbook. He shut his eyes and cringed as he heard the woman shout, "He don't take nobody's pennies!" When he opened his eyes, the woman was disappearing down the street with the little boy staring wide-eyed over her shoulder. Julian's mother was sitting on the sidewalk.

"I told you not to do that," Julian said angrily. "I told you not to do that!"

He stood over her for a minute, gritting his teeth. Her legs were stretched out in front of her and her hat was on her lap. He squatted down and looked her in the face. It was totally expressionless. "You got exactly what you deserved," he said. "Now get up."

He picked up her pocketbook and put what had fallen out back in it. He picked the hat up off her lap. The penny caught his eye on the sidewalk and he picked that up and let it drop before her eyes into the purse. Then he stood up and leaned over and held his hands out to pull her up. She remained immobile. He sighed. Rising above them on either side were black apartment buildings, marked with irregular rectangles of light. At the end of the block a man came out of the door and walked off in the opposite direction. "All right," he said, "suppose somebody happens by and wants to know why you're sitting on the sidewalk?"

She took the hand and, breathing hard, pulled heavily up on it and then stood for a moment, swaying slightly as if the spots of light in the darkness were circling around her. Her eyes, shadowed and confused, finally settled on his face. He did not to try conceal his irritation. "I hope this teaches you a lesson," he said. She leaned forward and her eyes raked his face. She seemed trying to determine his identity. Then, as if she found nothing familiar about him, she started off with a headlong movement in the wrong direction.

"Aren't you going to the Y?" he asked.

"Home," she muttered.

"Well, are we walking?"

For answer she kept going. Julian followed along, his hands behind him. He saw no reason to let the lesson she had had go without backing it up with an explanation of its meaning. She might as well be made to understand what had happened to her. "Don't think that was just an uppity Negro woman," he said. "That was the whole colored race which will no longer take your condescending° pennies. That was your black double.

VOCABULARY

condescending: Looking down on someone one considers inferior (-de- means down; -scend- refers to climbing).

She can wear the same hat as you, and to be sure," he added gratuitously° (because he thought it was funny), "it looked better on her than it did on you. What all this means," he said, "is that the old world is gone. The old manners are obsolete and your graciousness is not worth a damn." He thought bitterly of the house that had been lost for him. "You aren't who you think you are," he said.

She continued to plow ahead, paying no attention to him. Her hair had come undone on one side. She dropped her pocketbook and took no notice. He stopped and picked it up and handed it to her but she did not take it.

"You needn't act as if the world had come to an end," he said, "because it hasn't. From now on you've got to live in a new world and face a few realities for a change. Buck up," he said, "it won't kill you."

She was breathing fast.

"Let's wait on the bus," he said.

"Home," she said thickly.

"I hate to see you behave like this," he said. "Just like a child. I should be able to expect more of you." He decided to stop where he was and make her stop and wait for a bus. "I'm not going any farther," he said, stopping. "We're going on the bus."

She continued to go on as she if she had not heard him. He took a few steps and caught her arm and stopped her. He looked into her face and caught his breath. He was looking into a face he had never seen before. "Tell Grandpa to come get me," she said.

He stared, stricken.

"Tell Caroline to come get me," she said.

Stunned, he let her go and she lurched forward again, walking as if one leg were shorter than the other. A tide of darkness seemed to be sweeping her from him. "Mother!" he cried. "Darling, sweetheart, wait!" Crumpling, she fell to the ground. He dashed forward and fell at her side, crying. "Mamma, Mamma!" He turned her over. Her face was fiercely distorted. One eye, large and staring, moved slightly to the left as if it had become unmoored.° The other remained fixed on him, raked his face again, found nothing and closed.

VOCABULARY
gratuitously: Freely, without expecting something in return (*grat-* means as a favor).
unmoored: Loosened from something that was holding it (its moorings).

"Wait here, wait here!" he cried and jumped up and began to run for help toward a cluster of lights he saw in the distance ahead of him. "Help, help!" he shouted, but his voice was thin, scarcely a thread of sound. The lights drifted farther away the faster he ran and his feet moved numbly as if they carried him nowhere. The tide of darkness seemed to sweep him back to her, postponing from moment to moment his entry into the world of guilt and sorrow.

QUESTIONS FOR REFLECTION/DISCUSSION

1. From whose point of view is this story told? How do you know?

2. To what extent do you think Julian is a success in life? How would his mother rate his success? What about Julian himself?

3. What does Julian long for most of all? Does he think he will ever achieve his vision? What seems to be his general attitude toward himself and others? Do you know any people who have attitudes similar to Julian's? How do you feel about them? Discuss these questions with a partner. Share your ideas with another pair of classmates.

4. Julian's mother repeats several times in the story, "With the world in the mess it's in . . . " What "mess" is she talking about?

5. Julian's mother is obviously prejudiced against African Americans. Find several details that show the extent of her prejudice. Make a list.

6. Why do you think Julian's mother calls black children "cute" and proclaims that she respects black friends such as her childhood nurse? In fact, she says that she would do anything in the world "for them" (p. 89). What do such proclamations tell you about prejudice in general?

7. What are some of the things Julian does or would like to do to prove that he is not prejudiced against African Americans? Do you see any irony in his need to prove his open-mindedness to his mother?

8. Is this story about prejudice only against African Americans? What other kinds of prejudice seem to be present here?

9. How is the fact that the two women have the same hats significant? Do you see any irony in this fact? Consider Julian's mother's reason for buying the hat in the first place.

10. In what way is it symbolic that the two women with the same hats appear to have swapped sons (p. 97)? Why does Julian seem to be delighted with this prospect?

11. Characters are often seen differently through the eyes of different people. Discuss how Julian's mother is viewed from the following perspectives:
    a. How she sees herself
    b. How Julian sees her
    c. How the African American lady with the identical hat sees her
    d. How the lady with the protruding teeth sees her

12. Julian and his mother hold very different attitudes about their poverty. Which one has made the better adjustment to their current economic and social status? How do you know?

13. Discuss the relationship between Julian and his mother. What basic problem or problems seem to keep them in constant conflict? Why does he emphasize that he is not dominated by her (p. 93)? Why does he seem obsessed with "teaching her a lesson"? How do you think they really feel about each other? Explain. Do you have a relationship of your own that is in constant conflict? Why do you think your relationship became conflictive? What can you do to change it? Write about it in your journal.

14. Discuss the following comparisons found in the story:
    a. "The sky was a dying violet" (p. 86)
    b. "Each house had a narrow collar of dirt around it" (p. 87)
    c. "The frustration of having to wait on the bus as well as ride on it began to creep up his neck like a hot hand" (p. 90)

    Did these comparisons increase your enjoyment of the story? If so, in what ways? Did you notice any other comparisons that you felt to be significant? Discuss these questions with your class and the instructor.

15. Relate the title "Everything That Rises Must Converge" to the story. What do you think it means? Do you think it fits? What title would you have given the story if you had been its author?

Exploring Other Sources

In the library and/or on the Internet, find out as much as you can about the following topics. Identify key words for research. Ask your instructor or the librarian for assistance if you need it. Go to Worldviews Online (http://worldviews.wadsworth.com) for further suggestions and/or links to specific sites.

  a. The issue of slavery in the United States—how it came about, its effects on the victims, its demise, its influence on African Americans living today
  b. The history of African Americans' struggle for freedom and the people that made a difference in that struggle
  c. The nature of prejudice—its causes, its effects, and any solutions to resulting problems

Share what you learn with a small group.

Synthesis Through Writing

1. In your journal, write about the different kinds of prejudice that you have encountered in your own world. What do you think are the basic causes of the kinds that are most evident to you?

2. Julian argued that *true culture* is in the mind, and his mother disagreed by saying it is in the heart (p. 90). What do they each mean? With whom do you agree most? Write a short essay about your views. First create a graphic organizer like the one below. Use the writing strategies on page xix to help you.

"TRUE CULTURE"	
JULIAN'S VIEW:	
HIS MOTHER'S VIEW:	
MY VIEW:	

3. How might the story differ if it were written from another perspective? Rewrite part of the story from the point of view of one of the other characters (e.g., Julian's mother or the African-American woman with the identical hat). Share your writing with a small group.

4. Write an essay on a related topic you researched in the library or on the Internet. See the previous activity in Exploring Other Sources. See additional writing strategies on page xix. Create your own graphic organizer to help you develop your paper.

Death Comes for the Archbishop [excerpt]
Willa Cather

In this selection, Father Latour, the main character in Willa Cather's novel *Death Comes for the Archbishop*, has spent much of his adult life building and expanding the Catholic church in New Mexico in the mid-1800s. Now that he is facing death himself, he recalls the terrible tragedy that occurred in one of the many encounters between the United States government and the Navajo Indian nation when the Navajo were expelled from their own territory.

Willa Cather's prose is as gripping today as it was in 1927 when it first became available to readers. Her other works include *O Pioneers!*, *My Àntonia*, and *One of Ours*, for which she received a Pulitzer Prize[1] in 1923.

Before You Read

Try to imagine what it might be like to be forced from your home and the only way of life you had ever known to a strange land without the resources to which you have been accustomed. How might such circumstances affect your children, spouse, parents, or guardians? What about your friends? Discuss it with a small group or write about it in your journal.

hrough his friendship with Eusabio he had become interested in the Navajos soon after he first came to his new diocese,° and he admired them; they stirred his imagination. Though this nomad° people were much slower to adopt white man's ways than the home-staying Indians who

---

VOCABULARY
diocese: The group of churches under the direction of one bishop.
nomad: Moving from place to place.

CULTURAL NOTES
[1]The Pulitzer Prize is an annual award given to people who excel in the fields of American literature, journalism, and music. It was established by Joseph Pulitzer, an American publisher and journalist who immigrated from Hungary.

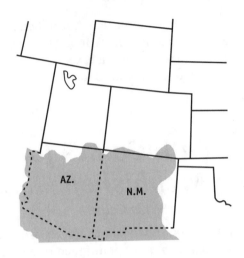

dwelt in pueblos,° and were much more indifferent to missionaries and the white man's religion. Father Latour felt a superior strength in them. There was purpose and conviction behind their inscrutable° reserve; something active and quick, something with an edge. The expulsion° of the Navajos from their country, which had been theirs no man knew how long, had seemed to him an injustice that cried to Heaven. Never could he forget that terrible winter when they were being hunted down and driven by thousands from their own reservation to the Bosque Redondo, three hundred miles away on the Pecos River. Hundreds of them, men, women, and children, perished from hunger and cold on the way; their sheep and horses died from exhaustion crossing the mountains. None ever went willingly; they were driven by starvation and the bayonet; captured in isolated bands, and brutally deported.

It was his own misguided friend, Kit Carson,[2] who finally subdued the last unconquered remnant° of that people; who followed them into the depths of the Canyon de Chelly, whither they had fled from their grazing plains and pine forests to make their last stand. They were shepherds, with no property but

---

VOCABULARY

pueblos: Small villages.
inscrutable: Mysterious; not easily understood.
expulsion: The state of being driven or forced out (ex- means out; -pul- refers to driving). ". . . of the Navajos from their country. . ." is a clue.
remnant: What was left or what remained (remn- refers to the remainder).

CULTURAL NOTES
[2]Kit Carson was a frontiersman and a hunter who became an Indian agent in 1853.

their live-stock, encumbered° by their women and children, poorly armed and with scanty ammunition. But this canyon had always before proved inpenetrable° to white troops. The Navajos believed it could not be taken. They believed that their old gods dwelt in the fastnesses° of that canyon; like their Shiprock, it was an inviolate° place, the very heart and centre° of their life.

Carson followed them down into the hidden world between those towering walls of red sandstone, spoiled their stores, destroyed their deep-sheltered corn-fields, cut down the terraced peach orchards so dear to them. When they saw all that was sacred to them laid waste,° the Navajos lost heart. They did not surrender; they simply ceased to fight, and were taken. Carson was a soldier under orders, and he did a soldier's brutal work. But the bravest of the Navajo chiefs he did not capture. Even after the crushing defeat of his people in the Canyon de Chelly, Manuelito[3] was still at large. It was then that Eusabio came to Santa Fe to ask Bishop Latour to meet Manuelito at Zuñi. As a priest, the Bishop knew that it was indiscreet° to consent to a meeting with this outlawed chief; but he was a man, too, and a lover of justice. The request came to him in such a way that he could not refuse it. He went with Eusabio.

Though the Government was offering a heavy reward for his person, living or dead, Manuelito rode off his own reservation° down into Zuñi in broad daylight, attended by some dozen followers, all on wretched, half-starved horses. He had been in hiding out in Eusabio's country on the Colorado Chiquito.

It was Manuelito's hope that the Bishop would go to Washington and plead his people's cause before they were utterly destroyed. They asked nothing of the Government, he

---

VOCABULARY

encumbered: Weighed down (-cumber- refers to hindrance).

impenetrable: Not capable of being entered or penetrated (im- means not). "The Navajos believed it [the canyon] could not be taken" is a clue.

fastnesses: Secret places.

inviolate: Not disturbed or violated (in- here means not).

centre: An alternate spelling for center.

laid waste: Destroyed.

indiscreet: Not wise or prudent (in- here means not). " . . . meeting with this outlawed chief" is a clue.

reservation: Pieces of land set aside by the United States goverment for Native Americans.

CULTURAL NOTES

[3]Manuelito, who was known for his courage and fairness, was a Navajo chief in the mid-1800s.

told Father Latour, but their religion, and their own land where they had lived from immemorial° times. Their country, he explained, was a part of their religion; the two were inseparable. The Canyon de Chelly the Padre knew; in that canyon his people had lived when they were a small weak tribe; it had nourished and protected them; it was their mother. Moreover, their gods dwelt there—in those inaccessible° white houses set in caverns up in the face of the cliffs, which were older than the white man's world, and which no living man had ever entered. Their gods were there, just as Padre's God was in his church.

And north of the Canyon de Chelly was the Shiprock, a slender crag rising to a dizzy height, all alone out on a flat desert. Seen at a distance of fifty miles or so, that crag presents the figure of a one-masted° fishing-boat under full sail, and the white man named it accordingly. But the Indian has another name; he believes that rock was once a ship of the air. Ages ago, Manuelito told the Bishop, that crag had moved through the air, bearing upon its summit the parents of the Navajo race from the place in the far north where all peoples were made,— and wherever it sank to earth was to be their land. It sank in a desert country, where it was hard for men to live. But they had found the Canyon de Chelly, where there was shelter and unfailing water. That canyon and the Shiprock were like kind parents to his people, places more sacred to them than churches, more sacred than any place is to the white man. How, then, could they go three hundred miles away and live in a strange land?

Moreover, the Bosque Redondo was down on the Pecos, far east of the Rio Grande. Manuelito drew a map in the sand, and explained to the Bishop how, from the very beginning, it had been enjoined° that his people must never cross the Rio Grande on the east, or the Rio San Juan on the north, or the Rio Colorado on the west; if they did, the tribe would perish. If a great priest, like Father Latour, were to go to Washington and explain these things, perhaps the Government would listen.

Father Latour tried to tell the Indian that in a Protestant country the one thing a Roman priest could not do was to

---

VOCABULARY
immemorial: Beyond what one can remember (*im-* here means not; *-memor-* refers to memory).
inaccessible: Not easily reached, obtained, or accessed (*in-* here means not).
one-masted: Having only one pole on a boat to support the sails.
enjoined: Officially commanded.

interfere in matters of Government. Manuelito listened respectfully, but the Bishop saw that he did not believe him. When he had finished, the Navajo rose and said:

"You are the friend of Christóbal,[4] who hunts my people and drives them over the mountains to the Bosque Redondo. Tell your friend that he will never take me alive. He can come and kill me when he pleases. Two years ago I could not count my flocks; now I have thirty sheep and a few starving horses. My children are eating roots, and I do not care for my life. But my mother and my gods are in the West, and I will never cross the Rio Grande."

He never did cross it. He lived in hiding until the return of his exiled people. For an unforeseen thing happened:

The Bosque Redondo proved an utterly unsuitable country for the Navajos. It could have been farmed by irrigation, but they were nomad shepherds, not farmers. There was no pasture for their flocks. There was no firewood; they dug mesquite roots and dried them for fuel. It was an alkaline° country, and hundreds of Indians died from bad water. At last the Government at Washington admitted its mistake—which governments seldom do. After five years of exile, the remnant of the Navajo people were permitted to go back to their sacred places.

In 1875 the Bishop took his French architect on a pack trip into Arizona to show him something of the country before he returned to France, and he had the pleasure of seeing the Navajo horsemen riding free over their great plains again. The two Frenchmen went as far as the Canyon de Chelly to behold the strange cliff ruins; once more crops were growing down at the bottom of the world between the towering sandstone walls; sheep were grazing under the magnificent cottonwoods and drinking at the streams of sweet water; it was like an Indian Garden of Eden.[5]

Now, when he was an old man and ill, scenes from those bygone times, dark and bright, flashed back to the Bishop: the terrible faces of the Navajos waiting at the place on the Rio Grande where they were being ferried° across into exile; the

---

VOCABULARY
alkaline: A mineral salt found in water.
ferried: Carried by a flat boat called a ferry, used to transport goods.

CULTURAL NOTES
[4]Christóbal is another name for Kit Carson, Kit being a shortened form of Christopher.
[5]A Garden of Eden is a paradise like the one in which Adam and Eve of the Bible once lived.

long streams of survivors going back to their own country, driving their scanty flocks, carrying their old men and their children. Memories, too, of that time he had spent with Eusabio on the Little Colorado, in the early spring, when the lambing season° was not yet over,—dark horsemen riding across the sands with orphan lambs in their arms—a young Navajo woman, giving a lamb her breast until a ewe° was found for it.

"Bernard," the old Bishop would murmur, "God has been very good to let me live to see a happy issue° to those old wrongs. I do not believe, as I once did, that the Indian will perish. I believe that God will preserve him."

QUESTIONS FOR REFLECTION/DISCUSSION

1. To what extent is it wise for nonwhites, such as the Native Americans, to adopt "white man's ways"? Does such assimilation usually make sense economically for persons who do not look white? What about socially? Might a better solution be pluralism, in which persons are able to function in the dominant culture but at the same time keep their own cultural identity? What might the advantages of pluralism be over assimilation, especially for groups who do not look like the persons in the dominant culture? Discuss these questions with a small group. Share the group's conclusions with your class.

2. What was Father Latour's attitude toward Kit Carson and his role in the encounter between the Government and the Navajos? How do you know?

3. With whom did Father Latour's loyalties lie more strongly—the Government or the Navajos? Provide evidence from the selection for your opinion.

4. For what reasons was it so difficult for the Navajos to leave their home, the Canyon de Chelly?

5. The United States Government eventually admitted that it had made a mistake in forcing the Navajos from their lands. What does this tell you about the government? How do you think it could have made such a terrible mistake in the first place? What can be learned from this unfortunate encounter?

VOCABULARY

lambing season: The time of year when many lambs are born.
ewe: A female adult sheep.
issue: Here it means outcome or result.

6. Father Latour believed that "God will preserve him [the Native American]." What did he mean? To what extent has the Native American been preserved?

ℰXPLORING 𝒪THER 𝒮OURCES

1. In the library and/or on the Internet, locate as much information as you can about the Navajo. Include the Navajo's history, resources, and problems in the modern world. Key words for research might include "Native Americans," "Navajo Indians," and Navajos," for example. If you need assistance, ask your instructor or the librarian for help. Share what you learn with a small group.

2. Research what happened to other Native American tribes during the period of great expansion in the 1800s. To what extent was their experience similar to that of the Navajo? Ask your instructor or the librarian for assistance if you need it. Discuss what you learn with a small group. If your research includes sources on the Internet, begin by pointing your browser to http://worldviews.wadsworth.com for suggestion and/or links to other sites.

𝒮YNTHESIS 𝒯HROUGH 𝒲RITING

1. In your journal, write about your own personal reaction to what happened to the Navajo as it is described in this selection.

2. Write an informative essay about the Navajo. Include the Navajo's history, resources, and problems in the modern world. Divide a piece of paper into three columns: "History," "Resources," and "Problems." Use the information you gathered in the previous activity in Exploring Other Sources, to fill in the columns. Use the graphic organizer to help you develop your essay. Refer to the writing strategies on page xix, if necessary.

3. Write an essay about another Native American group you may have researched in Exploring Other Sources. See the writing strategies on page xix. Create your own graphic organizer.

This Earth Is Sacred
Chief Sealth

The following is an excerpt from a letter written by Chief Sealth in 1855 to the United States government. At that time, the government was interested in purchasing land in the state of Washington from the Duwamish tribe led by Chief Sealth. The letter reveals a man far advanced for his time, one who was willing to encounter forces that seemed beyond his control.

Before You Read

Have you ever wanted to write a letter to your government about forces or events that seemed beyond your control? Perhaps you wanted to complain about something your government had done or was about to do. Did you actually write the letter? If so, what happened? Discuss it with a partner or write about it in your journal.

How can you buy or sell the sky—the warmth of the land? The idea is strange to us. We do not own the freshness of the air or the sparkle of the water. How can you buy them from us?

We will decide in our time. Every part of this earth is sacred to my people. Every shining pine needle, every sandy shore, every mist in the dark woods, every clearing and humming insect is holy in the memory and experience of my people . . .

If I decide to accept, I will make one condition. The white man must treat the beasts of this land as his brothers . . . What is man without the beasts? If all the beasts were gone, men would die from a great loneliness of spirit, for whatever happens to the beast also happens to man. All things are connected. Whatever befalls the earth befalls the sons of the earth . . .

If we sell you our land, love it as we've loved it. Care for it, as we've cared for it. Hold in your mind the memory of the land, as it is when you take it. And with all your strength, with all your might, and with all your heart—preserve it for your children.

QUESTIONS FOR REFLECTION/DISCUSSION

1. What kind of man do you think Chief Sealth was? Do you admire him? Why or why not?

2. What do you think Chief Sealth would think if he lived in the United States today? Would anything please him concerning the way in which its citizens have taken care of the environment? What might disappoint him? Explain.

*E*XPLORING *O*THER *S*OURCES

With a small group, research and discuss the environmental concern of your choice. Choose one concern from the list below to research in the library and/or on the Internet. What is the problem? How serious is it? What might be some solutions? If you need help, ask your instructor or the librarian for assistance. Or go to http://worldviews.wadsworth.com for suggestions and/or links to relevant sites.

a. Air pollution
b. Water pollution
c. Disappearing forests
d. Disappearing wild life
e. Another environmental concern of your choice

*S*YNTHESIS *T*HROUGH *W*RITING

1. In your journal, write about your greatest environmental concern in the world today. If you are a parent, how might the issues involved affect your children?

2. Write a letter to the editor of your local newspaper about an environmental problem you would like to see addressed by the community. Make sure you clearly state what you feel the problem to be. You may want to make some suggestions about possible solutions.

3. Write an essay about one of the environmental concerns you researched in the previous activity in Exploring Other Sources. First divide a piece of paper into three columns: "Problems," "Extent of Seriousness," and "Possible Solutions." Use this graphic representation to help you organize your essay.

PROBLEMS	EXTENT OF SERIOUSNESS	POSSIBLE SOLUTIONS

Different Words, Different Worlds [excerpt]

Deborah Tannen

Lack of understanding often creates a "gender gap." Encounters between men and women are as old as the human race. Today we know that such encounters sometimes end in disturbing animosity between the sexes that can be very mystifying. We may find ourselves asking, "Why did he react that way to her?" or "Why did she say what she did to him?" According to Deborah Tannen, a sociolinguist who has studied the conversations of men and women in the United States for a number of years, there are very real differences in the ways in which they tend to communicate with each other. By identifying and understanding the possible underlying motives of men and women generally and how these motives can effect differences in conversational style, perhaps we can begin putting the pieces of this puzzle together.

Deborah Tannen, who teaches linguistics at Georgetown University, wrote the book *You Just Don't Understand: Women and Men in Conversation* from which this excerpt comes. In addition, she has written a similar book entitled *That's Not What I Meant!*

Before You Read

Think of a time when you may have been involved in a conversation with a member of the opposite sex that left you perplexed and maybe even a bit hurt. Write about it in your journal.

SINGLE SLICES   by Peter Kohlsaat

$\mathcal{M}$any years ago I was married to a man who shouted at me, "I do not give you the right to raise your voice to me, because you are a woman and I am a man." This was frustrating, because I knew it was unfair. But I also knew just what was going on. I ascribed° his unfairness to his having grown up in a country where few people thought women and men might have equal rights.

Now I am married to a man who is a partner and friend. We come from similar backgrounds and share values and interests. It is a continual source of pleasure to talk to him. It is wonderful to have someone I can tell everything to, someone who understands. But he doesn't always see things as I do, doesn't always react to things as I expect him to. And I often don't understand why he says what he does.

At the time I began working on this book, we had jobs in different cities. People frequently expressed sympathy by making comments like "That must be rough," and "How do you stand it?" I was inclined to accept their sympathy and say things like "We fly a lot." Sometimes I would reinforce their concern: "The worst part is having to pack and unpack all the time." But my husband reacted differently, often with irritation. He might respond by de-emphasizing the inconvenience: As academics, we had four-day weekends together, as well as long vacations throughout the year and four months in the summer. We even benefited from the intervening° days of uninterrupted time for work. I once overheard him telling a dubious° man that we were lucky, since studies have shown that married couples who live together spend less than half an hour a week talking to each other; he was implying that our situation had advantages.

I didn't object to the way my husband responded—everything he said was true—but I was surprised by it. I didn't understand why he reacted as he did. He explained that he sensed condescension° in some expressions of concern, as if the questioner were implying,° "Yours is not a real marriage; your ill-chosen profession has resulted in an unfortunate

---

VOCABULARY
ascribed: Here it means blamed.
intervening: Coming between two things (*inter-* means between; *-ven-* refers to coming).
dubious (dōō' bē əs): Doubtful.
condescension: Acting superior or looking down on someone or something (*-de-* means down; *-scen-* refers to climbing). The next sentence is a clue.
implying: Suggesting.

arrangement. I pity you, and look down at you from the height of complacence,° since my wife and I have avoided your misfortune." It had not occurred to me that there might be an element of one-upmanship° in these expressions of concern, though I could recognize it when it was pointed out. Even after I saw the point, though, I was inclined to regard my husband's response as slightly odd, a personal quirk. He frequently seemed to see others as adversaries° when I didn't.

Having done the research that led to this book, I now see that my husband was simply engaging the world in a way that many men do: as an individual in a hierarchical° social order in which he was either one-up or one-down. In this world, conversations are negotiations° in which people try to achieve and maintain the upper hand if they can, and protect themselves from others' attempts to put them down and push them around. Life, then, is a contest, a struggle to preserve independence and avoid failure.

I, on the other hand, was approaching the world as many women do: as an individual in a network of connections. In this world, conversations are negotiations for closeness in which people try to seek and give confirmation° and support, and to reach consensus. They try to protect themselves from others' attempts to push them away. Life, then, is a community, a struggle to preserve intimacy° and avoid isolation. Though there are hierarchies in this world too, they are hierarchies more of friendship than of power and accomplishment.

Women are also concerned with achieving status and avoiding failure, but these are not the goals they are *focused* on all the time, and they tend to pursue them in the guise° of connection. And men are also concerned with achieving involvement and avoiding isolation, but they are not *focused* on these goals, and they tend to pursue them in the guise of opposition.

VOCABULARY

complacence: The state of being pleased with oneself (*complacen-* means to please).
one-upmanship: Trying to be better than another person or one rank higher.
adversaries: Enemies (*adversar-* refers to being an opponent).
hierarchical (hi'ərarkəkəl): Organized by using rank, the highest rank being at the top. "In which
    he was either one-up or one-down" is a clue.
negotiations: Discussions about something for the purpose of reaching an agreement.
confirmation: Verification, strengthening an idea (*con-* means with; *-firma-* means firm).
intimacy: Close, personal connections to others.
guise (gīz): The way something appears on the outside; pretense.

Discussing our differences from this point of view, my husband pointed out to me a distinction I had missed: He reacted the way I just described only if expressions of concern came from men in whom he sensed an awareness of hierarchy. And there were times when I too disliked people's expressing sympathy about our commuting° marriage. I recall being offended by one man who seemed to have a leering look in his eye when he asked, "How do you manage this long-distance romance?" Another time I was annoyed when a woman who knew me only by reputation approached us during the intermission° of a play, discovered our situation by asking my husband where he worked, and kept the conversation going by asking us all about it. In these cases, I didn't feel put down; I felt intruded upon. If my husband was offended by what he perceived as claims to superior status, I felt these sympathizers were claiming inappropriate intimacy.

Intimacy and Independence

Intimacy is key in a world of connection where individuals negotiate complex networks of friendship, minimize differences, try to reach consensus,° and avoid the appearance of superiority, which would highlight differences. In a world of status,° *independence* is key, because a primary means of establishing status is to tell others what to do, and taking orders is a marker of low status. Though all humans need both intimacy and independence, women tend to focus on the first and men on the second. It is as if their lifeblood ran in different directions.

These differences can give women and men differing views of the same situation, as they did in the case of a couple I will call Linda and Josh. When Josh's old high-school chum called him at work and announced he'd be in town on business the following month, Josh invited him to stay for the weekend. That evening he informed Linda that they were going to have a houseguest, and that he and his chum would go out together the first night to shoot the breeze like old times. Linda was upset. She was going to be away on business the week before, and the Friday

---

VOCABULARY

commuting: Traveling back and forth (-*mut*- refers to changing).
intermission: A break between the acts of a play (*inter*- means between).
consensus: Agreement (*consen*- means to agree).
status: Here it means social position or standing (*sta*- means to stand).

night when Josh would be out with his chum would be her first night home. But what upset her the most was that Josh had made these plans on his own and informed her of them, rather than discussing them with her before extending the invitation.

Linda would never make plans, for a weekend or an evening, without first checking with Josh. She can't understand why he doesn't show her the same courtesy and consideration that she shows him. But when she protests, Josh says, "I can't say to my friend, 'I have to ask my wife for permission'!"

To Josh, checking with his wife means seeking permission, which implies that he is not independent, not free to act on his own. It would make him feel like a child or an underling.° To Linda, checking with her husband has nothing to do with permission. She assumes that spouses discuss their plans with each other because their lives are intertwined,° so the actions of one have consequences for the other. Not only does Linda not mind telling someone, "I have to check with Josh"; quite the contrary—she likes it. It makes her feel good to know and show that she is involved with someone, that her life is bound up with someone else's.

Linda and Josh both felt more upset by this incident, and others like it, than seemed warranted,° because it cut to the core of their primary concerns. Linda was hurt because she sensed a failure of closeness in their relationship: He didn't care about her as much as she cared about him. And he was hurt because he felt she was trying to control him and limit his freedom.

A similar conflict exists between Louise and Howie, another couple, about spending money. Louise would never buy anything costing more than a hundred dollars without discussing it with Howie, but he goes out and buys whatever he wants and feels they can afford, like a table saw or a new power mower. Louise is disturbed, not because she disapproves of the purchases, but because she feels he is acting as if she were not in the picture.

Many women feel it is natural to consult with their partners at every turn, while many men automatically make more decisions without consulting their partners. This may reflect a broad

---

VOCABULARY
underling: Someone lower in status.
intertwined: Bound together.
warranted: Justified or logically fitting.

difference in conceptions° of decision making. Women expect decisions to be discussed first and made by consensus. They appreciate the discussion itself as evidence of involvement and communication. But many men feel oppressed° by lengthy discussions about what they see as minor decisions, and they feel hemmed in° if they can't just act without talking first. When women try to initiate a freewheeling discussion by asking, "What do you think?" men often think they are being asked to decide.

Communication is a continual balancing act, juggling the conflicting needs for intimacy and independence. To survive in the world, we have to act in concert with others, but to survive as ourselves, rather than simply as cogs° in a wheel, we have to act alone. In some ways, all people are the same. We all eat and sleep and drink and laugh and cough, and often we eat, and laugh at, the same things. But in some ways, each person is different, and individuals' differing wants and preferences may conflict with each other. Offered the same menu, people make different choices. And if there is cake for dessert, there is a chance one person may get a larger piece than another—and an even greater chance that one will *think* the other's piece is larger, whether it is or not. . . .

In Pursuit of Freedom

A woman was telling me why a long-term relationship had ended. She recounted a recurrent° and pivotal° conversation. She and the man she lived with had agreed that they would both be free, but they would not do anything to hurt each other. When the man began to sleep with other women, she protested, and he was incensed° at her protest. Their conversation went like this:

SHE: How can you do this when you know it's hurting me?
HE: How can you try to limit my freedom?
SHE: But it makes me feel awful.
HE: You are trying to manipulate me.

VOCABULARY
conceptions: Ideas or concepts.
oppressed: Pushed down (*op-* means against; *-pres-* means to press).
hemmed in: Confined.
cogs: Teeth on the rim of a wheel used to make another wheel go around.
recurrent: Happening again and again (*re-* means again; *-cur-* refers to running).
pivotal: Here it means an important conversation around which other conversations rotate or pivot.
incensed: Very upset, enraged (*incens-* means to set on fire).

Different Words, Different Worlds   **119**

On one level, this is simply an example of a clash of wills: What he wanted conflicted with what she wanted. But in a fundamental° way, it reflects the difference in focus I have been describing. In arguing for his point of view, the key issue for this man was his independence, his freedom of action. The key issue for the woman was their interdependence°—how what he did made her feel. He interpreted her insistence on their interdependence as "manipulation": She was using her feelings to control his behavior.

The point is not that women do not value freedom or that men do not value their connection to others. It is rather that the desire for freedom and independence becomes more of an issue for many men in relationships, whereas interdependence and connection become more of an issue for many women. The difference is one of focus and degree.

In a study of how women and men talk about their divorces, Catherine Kohler Riessman found that both men and women mentioned increased freedom as a benefit of divorce. But the word *freedom* meant different things to them. When women told her they had gained freedom by divorce, they meant that they had gained "independence and autonomy."° It was a relief for them not to have to worry about how their husbands would react to what they did, and not to have to be "responsive to a disgruntled° spouse." When men mentioned freedom as a benefit of divorce, they meant freedom from obligation—the relief of feeling "less confined," less "claustrophobic,"° and having "fewer responsibilities."

Riessman's findings illuminate° the differing burdens that are placed on women and men by their characteristic approaches to relationships. The burden from which divorce delivered the women was perceived as internally motivated: the continual preoccupation° with how their husbands would respond to them and how they should respond to their husbands. The burden from which it delivered the men was perceived as

---

VOCABULARY

fundamental: Very basic.
interdependence: Dependence or reliance on each other (*inter-* means between).
autonomy: Self-governing (*auto-* means self).
disgruntled: Cross and disagreeable.
claustrophobic: Extremely fearful of being enclosed in a small space (*claus-* refers to an enclosed space; *-phobic* means fearful).
illuminate: Shed light upon.
preoccupation: The state of having one's attention focused on something.

externally imposed: the obligations of the provider role and a feeling of confinement from having their behavior constrained° by others. Independence was not a gift of divorce for the men Riessman interviewed, because, as one man put it, "I always felt independent and I guess it's just more so now."

The Chronicle of Higher Education conducted a small survey, asking six university professors why they had chosen the teaching profession. Among the six were four men and two women. In answering the question, the two women referred to teaching. One said, "I've always wanted to teach." The other said, "I knew as an undergraduate that I wanted to join a faculty. . . . I realized that teaching was the thing I wanted to do." The four men's answers had much in common with each other and little in common with the women's. All four men referred to independence as their main motive. Here are excerpts from each of their responses:

I decided it was academe° over industry because I would have my choice of research. There's more independence.

I wanted to teach, and I like the freedom to set your own research goals.

I chose an academic job because the freedoms of academia outweighed the money disadvantages—and to pursue the research interest I'd like to, as opposed to having it dictated.

I have a problem that interests me. . . . I'd rather make $30,000 for the rest of my life and be allowed to do basic research than to make $100,000 and work in computer graphics.°

Though one man also mentioned teaching, neither of the women mentioned freedom to pursue their own research interests as a main consideration. I do not believe this means that women are not interested in research, but rather that independence, freedom from being told what to do, is not as significant a preoccupation for them.

In describing what appealed to them about teaching, these two women focused on the ability to influence students in a positive

---

VOCABULARY

constrained: Kept within close boundaries; confined (*con-* means together; *-strain-* means to draw tight).
academe: School or academic life.
graphics: Pictures or graphs formed with lines (*graph-* means to write).

way. Of course, influencing students reflects a kind of power over them, and teaching entails° an asymmetrical° relationship, with the teacher in the higher-status position. But in talking about their profession, the women focused on connection to students, whereas the men focused on their freedom from others' control.

Male-Female Conversation Is Cross-Cultural Communication

If women speak and hear a language of connection and intimacy, while men speak and hear a language of status and independence, then communication between men and women can be like cross-cultural communication, prey to a clash of conversational styles. Instead of different dialects, it has been said they speak different genderlects.°

The claim that men and women grow up in different worlds may at first seem patently° absurd. Brothers and sisters grow up in the same families, children to parents of both genders. Where, then, do women and men learn different ways of speaking and hearing?

It Begins at the Beginning

Even if they grow up in the same neighborhood, on the same block, or in the same house, girls and boys grow up in different worlds of words. Others talk to them differently and expect and accept different ways of talking from them. Most important, children learn how to talk, how to have conversations, not only from their parents but from their peers. After all, if their parents have a foreign or regional accent, children do not emulate° it; they learn to speak with the pronunciation of the region where they grow up. Anthropologists Daniel Maltz and Ruth Borker summarize research showing that boys and girls have very different ways of talking to their friends. Although they often play together, boys and girls spend most of their time playing in same-sex groups. And, although some of the activities they play at are similar, their favorite games are different, and their ways of using language in their games are separated by a world of difference.

VOCABULARY

entails: Involves out of necessity.
asymmetrical: Lack of balance and equality between two sides. (a- means without; sym- means like or same).
genderlect: A style of conversation based on one's sex.
patently: Obviously.
emulate: To copy something or try to be like someone else (emul- refers to imitating).

Boys tend to play outside, in large groups that are hierarchically structured. Their groups have a leader who tells others what to do and how to do it, and resists doing what other boys propose. It is by giving orders and making them stick that high status is negotiated. Another way boys achieve status is to take center stage by telling stories and jokes, and by sidetracking or challenging the stories and jokes of others. Boys' games have winners and losers and elaborate systems of rules that are frequently the subjects of arguments. Finally, boys are frequently heard to boast of their skill and argue about who is best at what.

Girls, on the other hand, play in small groups or in pairs; the center of a girl's social life is a best friend. Within the group, intimacy is key: Differentiation is measured by relative closeness. In their most frequent games, such as jump rope and hopscotch, everyone gets a turn. Many of their activities (such as playing house) do not have winners or losers. Though some girls are certainly more skilled than others, girls are expected not to boast about it, or show that they think they are better than the others. Girls don't give orders; they express their preferences as suggestions, and suggestions are likely to be accepted. Whereas boys say, "Gimme that!" and "Get outta here!" girls say, "Let's do this," and "How about doing that?" Anything else is put down as "bossy." They don't grab center stage—they don't want it—so they don't challenge each other directly. And much of the time, they simply sit together and talk. Girls are not accustomed to jockeying for status in an obvious way; they are more concerned that they be liked.

Gender differences in ways of talking have been described by researchers observing children as young as three. Amy Sheldon videotaped three- to four-year-old boys and girls playing in threesomes at a day-care center. She compared two groups of three—one of boys, one of girls—that got into fights about the same play item: a plastic pickle. Though both groups fought over the same thing, the dynamics° by which they negotiated their conflicts were different. In addition to illustrating some of the patterns I have just described, Sheldon's study also demonstrates the complexity of these dynamics.

VOCABULARY

dynamics: Changing actions brought about by interplay of forces (*dynam-* means powerful).

Different Words, Different Worlds   **123**

While playing in the kitchen area of the day-care center, a little girl named Sue wanted the pickle that Mary had, so she argued that Mary should give it up because Lisa, the third girl, wanted it. This led to a conflict about how to satisfy Lisa's (invented) need. Mary proposed a compromise,° but Sue protested:

MARY: I cut it in half. One for Lisa, one for me, one for me.
SUE: But, Lisa wants a *whole* pickle!

Mary comes up with another creative compromise, which Sue also rejects:

MARY: Well, it's a whole *half* pickle.
SUE: No, it isn't.
MARY: Yes, it is, a whole *half* pickle.
SUE: *I'll* give her a whole half. I'll give her a *whole whole*. I gave her a whole one.

At this point, Lisa withdraws from the alliance° with Sue, who satisfies herself by saying, "I'm pretending I gave you one."

On another occasion, Sheldon videotaped three boys playing in the same kitchen play area, and they too got into a fight about the plastic pickle. When Nick saw that Kevin had the pickle, he demanded it for himself:

NICK: [Screams] Kevin, but the, oh, I *have* to cut! I want to cut it! It's mine!

Like Sue, Nick involved the third child in his effort to get the pickle:

NICK: [Whining to Joe] Kevin is not letting me cut the pickle.
JOE: Oh, I know! I can pull it away from him and give it back to you. That's an idea!

The boys' conflict, which lasted two and a half times longer than the girls', then proceeded as a struggle between Nick and Joe on the one hand and Kevin on the other.

In comparing the boys' and girls' pickle fights, Sheldon points out that, for the most part, the girls mitigated° the conflict and

---

VOCABULARY

compromise: An agreement reached during which each side gives up one or more demands (*com-* means together).

alliance: Union or friendship (*alli-* refers to being a friend).

mitigated: Moderated, or made milder (*mit-* refers to mild). ". . . preserved harmony by compromise . . ." is a clue.

preserved harmony by compromise and evasion.° Conflict was more prolonged° among the boys, who used more insistence, appeals to rules, and threats of physical violence. However, to say these little girls and boys used *more* of one strategy or another is not to say that they didn't use the other strategies at all. For example, the boys did attempt compromise, and the girls did attempt physical force. The girls, like the boys, were struggling for control of their play. When Sue says by mistake, *"I'll give her a whole half,"* then quickly corrects herself to say, *"I'll give her a whole whole,"* she reveals that it is not really the size of the portion that is important to her, but who gets to serve it.

While reading Sheldon's study, I noticed that whereas both Nick and Sue tried to get what they wanted by involving a third child, the alignments° they created with the third child, and the dynamics they set in motion, were fundamentally different. Sue appealed to Mary to fulfill someone else's desire; rather than saying that *she* wanted the pickle, she claimed that Lisa wanted it. Nick asserted his own desire for the pickle, and when he couldn't get it on his own, he appealed to Joe to get it for him. Joe then tried to get the pickle by force. In both these scenarios, the children were enacting° complex lines of affiliation.°

Joe's strong-arm tactics° were undertaken not on his own behalf but, chivalrously°, on behalf of Nick. By making an appeal in a whining voice, Nick positioned himself as one-down in a hierarchical structure, framing himself as someone in need of protection. When Sue appealed to Mary to relinquish° her pickle, she wanted to take the one-up position of serving food. She was fighting not for the right to *have* the pickle, but for the right to *serve* it. (This reminded me of the women who said they'd become professors in order to teach.) But to accomplish her goal, Sue was depending on Mary's desire to fulfill others' needs.

This study suggests that boys and girls both want to get their way, but they tend to do so differently. Though social norms°

VOCABULARY

evasion: Avoidance.
prolonged: Drawn out; made to last longer.
alignments: Here it means groups formed by people who agree (*a-* means to; *-lign-* means line).
enacting: Performing.
affiliation: An association with or a connection to (*-filia-* refers to uniting with someone as though that person were a son).
tactics: Plans or strategies.
chivalrously: Like the knights or soldiers of the middle ages.
relinquish: Give up (*re-* here means behind; *-linqu-* refers to leaving).
norms: Behaviors that are considered to be normal in a given society.

Different Words, Different Worlds   **125**

encourage boys to be openly competitive and girls to be openly cooperative, different situations and activities can result in different ways of behaving. Marjorie Harness Goodwin compared boys and girls engaged in two task-oriented activities: The boys were making slingshots in preparation for a fight, and the girls were making rings. She found that the boys' group was hierarchical: The leader told the others what to do and how to do it. The girls' group was egalitarian:° Everyone made suggestions and tended to accept the suggestions of others. But observing the girls in a different activity—playing house— Goodwin found that they too adopted hierarchical structures: The girls who played mothers issued orders to the girls playing children, who in turn sought permission from their play-mothers. Moreover, a girl who was a play-mother was also a kind of manager of the game. This study shows that girls know how to issue orders and operate in a hierarchical structure, but they don't find that mode° of behavior appropriate when they engage in task activities with their peers. They do find it appropriate in parent-child relationships, which they enjoy practicing in the form of play.

These worlds of play shed light on the world views of women and men in relationships. The boys' play illuminates° why men would be on the lookout for signs they are being put down or told what to do. The chief commodity° that is bartered° in the boys' hierarchical world is status, and the way to achieve and maintain status is to give orders and get others to follow them. A boy in a low-status position finds himself being pushed around. So boys monitor° their relations for subtle° shifts in status by keeping track of who's giving orders and who's taking them.

These dynamics are not the ones that drive girls' play. The chief commodity that is bartered in the girls' community is intimacy. Girls monitor their friendships for subtle shifts in alliance, and they seek to be friends with popular girls. Popularity is a kind of status, but it is founded on connection. It also places

---

VOCABULARY

egalitarian: Believing that others are equal (*egal-* means equal). "Everyone made suggestions and tended to accept the suggestions of others" is a clue.
mode: Manner or way.
illuminates: Focuses light upon (*-lumin-* means light).
commodity: Something that can be bought or sold.
bartered: Traded, without using money.
monitor: Check.
subtle (Sŭt'l): Hardly noticeable.

popular girls in a bind. By doing field work in a junior high school, Donna Eder found that popular girls were paradoxically°—and inevitably°—disliked. Many girls want to befriend popular girls, but girls' friendships must necessarily be limited, since they entail° intimacy rather than large group activities. So a popular girl must reject the overtures° of most of the girls who seek her out—with the result that she is branded "stuck up."

The Key Is Understanding

If adults learn their ways of speaking as children growing up in separate social worlds of peers, then conversation between women and men is cross-cultural communication. Although each style is valid° on its own terms, misunderstandings arise because the styles are different. Taking a cross-cultural approach to male-female conversations makes it possible to explain why dissatisfactions are justified without accusing anyone of being wrong or crazy.

Learning about style differences won't make them go away, but it can banish mutual mystification° and blame. Being able to understand why our partners, friends, and even strangers behave the way they do is a comfort, even if we still don't see things the same way. It makes the world into more familiar territory. And having others understand why we talk and act as we do protects us from the pain of their puzzlement and criticism.

In discussing her novel *The Temple of My Familiar*, Alice Walker explained that a woman in the novel falls in love with a man because she sees in him "a giant ear." Walker went on to remark that although people may think they are falling in love because of sexual attraction or some other force, "really what we're looking for is someone to be able to hear us."

We all want, above all, to be heard—but not merely to be heard. We want to be understood—heard for what we think we are saying, for what we know we meant. With increased understanding of the ways women and men use language should come a decrease in frequency of the complaint "You just don't understand."

VOCABULARY
paradoxically: Puzzling because it appears as though the opposite should be true.
inevitably: Unavoidably.
entail: Involve out of necessity (*-tail* means limitation).
overtures: Actions to begin a relationship.
valid: Based on what is reasonable (*vali-* means to be strong).
mystification: The act of making something mysterious.

Different Words, Different Worlds   **127**

QUESTIONS FOR REFLECTION/DISCUSSION

1. To what extent do you think women operate in "a world of connection" in which *intimacy* is stressed and men operate in a "world of status" in which *independence* is stressed (p. 127)?

2. The author calls gender preferences in conversational style "cross-cultural." Do you agree with her? Explain.

3. Is it possible that the *same* distinctions between the sexes can be used to describe differences in communication between persons from different countries even if they are of the same sex? If so, can this behavior be reconciled with the author's views? Explain.

4. How do boys and girls behave differently in play according to the author? Do your experiences watching your own children or those of others at play bear out her conclusions?

5. Do you agree with the author that gender is the main predictive factor determining one's preference toward a certain conversational style?

6. To what extent do you feel using a certain conversational style is purposely manipulative and consciously applied? How much of it is subconscious?

7. Is the author convincing? Does she offer enough details and include examples to support her conclusions about gender differences? Are there ways she might improve this selection, in your opinion?

EXPLORING OTHER SOURCES

1. The author refers to a mini-survey conducted by the *Chronicle of Higher Education* in which six university professors (including both sexes) were asked why they had chosen the teaching profession. The researchers concluded that women tended to give reasons having to do more with connection, whereas men gave reasons associated more closely with status. With a partner, do a mini-survey using subjects from a profession other than teaching. Do your conclusions support the one done by the *Chronicle of Higher Education?* Do you think the profession from which you chose your subjects had any influence upon your results? Share your findings with a small group.

2. Conduct your own informal research of boys and girls at play. Listen to a few of their conversations. Does your own observation support the author's findings that boys and girls use very different conversational styles? Share your experiences with a small group.

3. The author mentions several studies upon which some of her conclusions are based; however, she does not cite the specific sources perhaps because her book is intended for the general public rather than for scholars. Try to locate one or two of her sources in a library or on the Internet to find out more information about the studies to which she refers. If you need assistance, ask your instructor or the librarian for help. Share what you learn with a small group.

SYNTHESIS THROUGH WRITING

1. In your journal, write a reflection based on your own experiences with misunderstandings between the sexes based on differences in conversational style. Did reading this selection give you greater insight into your own experiences? Explain.

2. Write an essay on cross-cultural misunderstandings between people of different countries due to differences in conversational styles. Use specific examples as much as possible. Refer to the writing strategies on page xix. Create your own graphic organizer.

3. Write an essay on gender as the main predictive factor determining one's preference toward a certain conversational style. Include the points at which you agree/disagree with the author of this selection. To help you in this task, divide a piece of paper into two columns. Label the first column "Points of agreement" and the second "Points of disagreement." Place the details in the appropriate columns and use them to organize your essay. For additional writing strategies, see page xix.

4. Write a summary of your own informal research done in conjunction with the previous activity in Exploring Other Sources. Include your basic plan for doing the research, describe the subjects, tell about your process, and discuss your conclusions. See the following graphic organizer.

THE OVERALL PLAN:
DESCRIPTION OF THE SUBJECTS:
DESCRIPTION OF THE PROCESS:
MY CONCLUSIONS:

MAKING CONNECTIONS: IDEAS FOR DISCUSSION AND/OR COMPOSITION

1. Think about how the various characters and/or authors to whom you were introduced in this unit dealt with the problems involved with wanting to understand and to be understood. Which people did you admire most? Why?

2. Look back at the quote by Langston Hughes that begins this unit on page 66. Show how it is applicable to several of the selections in this unit.

3. Compare your own struggle to understand and to be understood with that of one or more persons to whom you have been introduced in this unit. How was your own struggle different from theirs? How was it the same?

4. Use the Internet to find additional information about the authors and/or topics in this unit that you find of particular interest. First check out World Views Online at http://worldviews@ wadsworth.com for suggestions and/or links to other sites.

READING FOR ENRICHMENT

Giants in the Earth
by O.E. Rolvaag
Harper and Row, 1927

This now-classic novel tells a powerful story of the settling of the midwest by Norwegian American immigrants during the early part of the twentieth century.

How the Garcia Girls Lost Their Accents
by Julia Alvarez
Algonquin Books, 1991

The story of immigrants to the United States from the Dominican Republic and how they dealt with the issues of assimilation.

Home of the Brave
by Mary Motley Kalergis
Dutton, 1989

A collection of true stories told by immigrants to the United States. They tell of their experiences dealing with a new language and culture.

The Joy Luck Club
by Amy Tan
Ivy Books, 1989

This novel is about four mother-daughter relationships. It compares the lives of the mothers in China before 1949 to those of their daughters in modern-day America. "Double Face" on page 69 is an excerpt from this book. You might also enjoy *The Kitchen God's Wife* with a similar theme.

Lost in Translation
by Eva Hoffman
E.P. Dutton, 1989

Eva Hoffman describes her mixed emotions about emigrating from communist Poland in 1959 to settle in Canada.

Puerto Rican Writers at Home in the USA
edited by Judith Ortiz Cofer
Open Hand Publishing, 1991

A collection of writings, including poetry, about what daily life is like in America for Puerto Rican immigrants trying to make it their home.

Strangers from a Different Shore: A History of Asian Americans
by Ronald Takaki
Penguin, 1990

Ronald Takaki, the grandson of Japanese immigrants to Hawaii, writes about the Asian-American experience. See also *A Different Mirror: A History of Multicultural America* by the same author.

*To succeed, to be irreproachable,
to be American? She would be a
smart career girl in a tailored suit,
beautiful, and bold—an American
girl.*

—R. A. Sasaki
from "The Loom"

*We hear from so many students
that they have a white friend from
high school who couldn't get into
UCSB [University of California,
Santa Barbara], but a black kid got
in with no problem.*

—K. C. Cole
from "Brain's Use of Shortcuts
Can Be a Route to Bias"

*I became devoted to my
restlessness; to chasing down
poetry in the best of what I found;
to opening doors that allowed me
entrance into their universe, no
matter how small. If I found
nothing, I tried another door.*

—Gordon Parks
from "Voices in the Mirror"

Every One Sang

*Every one suddenly burst out singing:
And I was filled with such delight
As prisoned birds must find in freedom
Winging wildly across the white
Orchards and dark green fields; on; on;
   and out of sight.*

*Every one's voice was suddenly lifted,
And beauty came like the setting sun.
My heart was shaken with tears, and horror
Drifted away. . . . Oh, but every one
Was a bird; and the song was wordless; the
   singing will never be done.*

—Siegfried Sassoon
In Responding: Two, D. Rutledge & J. Walker, 1973

Unit 3

Breaking Through to Success

Introduction

There are many kinds of breakthroughs to success. Some are very dramatic breakthroughs, such as the one described in the poem that begins this unit. In the poem, those who have overcome serious obstacles feel very exalted and are sure that their time for success has come. Think of the people who have thrown off the shackles of dictatorships or those who, as whole groups, have overcome the devastating effects of racism and prejudice.

Then there are the more subtle breakthroughs that may not even have been noticed by anyone except the individuals who actually experienced them. These are the internal breakthroughs. Someone overcoming an unexplained fear or a deep-seated depression, for example. Or someone putting a traumatic event in perspective in order to move on in life without bitterness and hatred.

135

An Overview

The first selection, "The Loom" by R. A. Sasaki, shows how a Japanese American woman, who has suffered greatly from the effects of prejudice and internment during World War II, breaks through the psychological refuge she has hidden behind for so many years. Next is the poem "Strong Men" by Sterling A. Brown. Here we learn of the anguish of slavery through which persists a strong determination to overcome even the worse forms of degradation. Then we have the autobiographical experiences of Gordon Parks from his book *Voices in the Mirror*. We learn in this excerpt how a man can rise above poverty and racism and reach his goals in spite of great odds. Following is an excerpt from the *Los Angeles Times*, written by columnist and science writer K. C. Cole. The article explains how the mind is programmed to make snap judgments that can lead to prejudice and how programs such as affirmative action are needed to counteract this phenomenon. Last is the amazing story "Three Days to See" by Helen Keller, who was both blind and deaf. She imagines what she would do if she were given three days to see.

Thinking Critically About the Theme

The quotes beginning this unit come from the selections you will be reading. Think about the quotes in relation to the Unit 3 theme, Breaking Through to Success. Choose one or two to write about in your journal. Predict what might happen in the selection, based on the quote you chose and on the overview you just read.

Now look back at the poem by Siegfried Sassoon. Why do you think the word "everyone" has been made into two words in the poem? Is there a message in this use (misuse) of the language? How does the poem relate to the theme? Write your response in your journal. Do you like the poem? Why or why not?

The Loom

R. A. Sasaki

This story is among many told by the Japanese-American women and their families who had to overcome the prejudice aimed particularly at persons of non-European extraction in the United States. After the bombing of Pearl Harbor in 1941, Japanese Americans (the majority of whom were American-born) had to face, in addition to the prejudice, the extreme degradation of having their property taken away and of being placed in relocation centers designed to hold all Japanese Americans until the end of the war.

The mother in "The Loom" seems to be the character most overtly affected by what happened to her in her early years and later during the war. However, her daughters experience the effects of injustice too, if only indirectly. In addition to the story's focus on the long-term effects of injustice is the emphasis on mother-daughter relationships, not terribly unlike the relationship found in "Double Face" by Amy Tan (p. 69). Although the breakthrough to success is more subtle here than in the other selections in this unit, it is important nevertheless.

Before You Read

Try to imagine how such injustice might make you feel had you gone through World War II as a Japanese American. Discuss it with a small group or write about it in your journal.

And out of a pattern of lies, art weaves the truth.

—*D. H. Laurence*

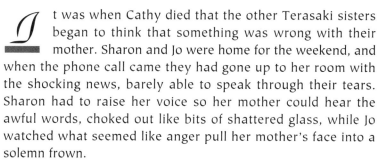

*I*t was when Cathy died that the other Terasaki sisters began to think that something was wrong with their mother. Sharon and Jo were home for the weekend, and when the phone call came they had gone up to her room with the shocking news, barely able to speak through their tears. Sharon had to raise her voice so her mother could hear the awful words, choked out like bits of shattered glass, while Jo watched what seemed like anger pull her mother's face into a solemn frown.

"You see?" their mother said. Her voice, harsh and trembling with a shocking vehemence,° startled the two sisters even in their grief. "Daddy told her not to go mountain climbing. He said it was too dangerous. She didn't listen."

VOCABULARY
vehemence (vē'əməns): Strong feeling.

Recalling her words later, Jo felt chilled.

They had always known about their mother's "ways"—the way she would snip off their straight black hair when they were children as soon as it grew past their ears, saying that hair too long would give people the wrong idea. Then later, when they were grown and defiant and wore their hair down to their waists, she would continue to campaign by lifting the long strands and snipping them with her fingers. There was also the way she would tear through the house in a frenzy° of cleaning just before they left on a family vacation, "in case there's a fire or someone breaks in and *yoso no hito*° have to come in." They never understood if it was the firemen, the police, or the burglar before whose eyes she would be mortally shamed if her house were not spotless. It was even in the way she cooked. She was governed not by inspiration or taste, but by what "they" did. The clothes she chose for them were what "they" were wearing these days. Who is this "they," her daughters always wanted to ask her. Her idiosyncrasies° were a source of mild frustration to which the girls were more or less resigned. "Oh, Mom," they would groan, or, to each other: "That's just Mom."

But this.

"It was as though she didn't feel anything at all," Jo recounted to her eldest sister, Linda, who had come home from Germany for the funeral. "It was as though all she could think about was that Cathy had broken the rules."

It wasn't until their father had come home that their mother cried, swept along in the wake of his massive grief. He had been away on a weekend fishing trip, and they had tried to get in touch with him, but failed. Jo had telephoned the highway patrol and park rangers at all his favorite fishing spots, saying, "No, don't tell him that his daughter has died. Would you just tell him to come home as soon as possible?" And it was Jo who was standing at the window watching when his truck turned the corner for home. The three women went down to the basement together. He and his fishing buddy had just emerged from the dusty, fish-odorous° truck, and he was rolling up the garage

---

VOCABULARY

frenzy: Crazed or overly excited state. " . . . she would tear through the house . . ." is a clue.
yoso no hito: A Japanese phrase meaning "other people."
idiosyncrasies: Behaviors that are unusual.
odorous: Giving off a distinct, not necessarily unpleasant odor (*od-* means to smell).

door when they reached him. He was caught between the bright spring sunlight and the dark coolness of the basement. His hand still on the garage door, he heard the news of his daughter's death. Their mother told him, with a hint of fear in her voice. He cried, as children cry who have awakened in the night to a nameless terror, a nameless grief; and for a suspended moment, as he stood alone sobbing his dead daughter's name, the three women deferred° to the sanctity° of his suffering. Then Sharon moved to encircle him in her arms, clinging flimsily to him against the tremendous isolation of grief.

It was only then that their mother had cried, but it seemed almost vicarious,° as if she had needed their father to process the raw stuff of life into personal emotion. Not once since the death had she talked about her own feelings. Not ever, her daughters now realized.

"It would probably do Mom good to get away for a while," Linda said. "I was thinking of taking her to Germany with me when I go back, just for a few weeks. She's never been anywhere. A change of scene might be just what she needs. Don't you think?"

"I suppose it's worth a try," said Jo.

So it was decided that when Linda flew back to join her husband, who was stationed in Heidelberg, their mother would go with her and stay a month. Except for a visit to Japan with her own mother when she was sixteen, it was their mother's first trip abroad. At first she was hesitant, but their father encouraged her; he would have gone too if he didn't have to stay and run the business.

It was hard to imagine their mother outside the context of their house. She had always been there when the children came back from school; in fact, the sisters had never had babysitters. Now, as they watched her at the airport, so small and sweet with her large purse clutched tightly in both hands and her new suitcase neatly packed and properly tagged beside her, they wondered just who this little person was, this person who was their mother.

VOCABULARY

deferred: Here it means submitted to another's feelings.

sanctity: Sacredness (*sanc*- refers to holiness).

vicarious: Experienced through someone else. " . . . she had needed their father to process the raw stuff of life into personal emotion" is a clue.

She had grown up in San Francisco, wearing the two faces of a second generation child born of immigrant parents. The two faces never met; there was no common thread running through both worlds. The duality was unplanned, untaught. Perhaps it had begun the first day of school when she couldn't understand the teacher and Eleanor Leland had called her a "Jap" and she cried. Before then there had never been a need to sort out her identity; she had met life headlong and with the confidence of a child.

Her world had been the old Victorian¹ flat in which her mother took in boarders—the long, narrow corridor, the spiral stairway, the quilts covered with bright Japanese cloth, and the smell of fish cooking in the kitchen. She had accepted without question the people who padded in and out of her world on stockinged feet; they all seemed to be friends of the family. She never wondered why most of them were men, and it never occurred to her child's mind to ask why they didn't have their own families. The men often couldn't pay, but they were always grateful. They lounged in doorways and had teasing affectionate words for her and her sister. Then they would disappear, for a month, for six months, a year. Time, to a child, was boundless and unmeasurable. Later crates of fruit would arrive and be stacked in the corridor.

"From Sato-san," her mother would say, or "*Kudoh-san kara.*" The young men sometimes came back to visit with new hats set jauntily° on their heads, if luck was good. But often luck was not good, and they came back to stay, again and again, each stay longer than the last; and each time they would tease less and drink more with her father in the back room. The slap of cards rose over the low mumble of their longing and despair. All this she accepted as her world.

The Victorian house which contained her world was on Pine Street, and so it was known as "Pine" to the young adventurers from her parents' native Wakayama prefecture° in Japan who made their way from the docks of Osaka to the lettuce fields and fruit orchards of California. "Stay at Pine," the word passed along the grapevine;° "Moriwaki-san will take care of you."

VOCABULARY

jauntily: In a carefree, self-confident manner.

prefecture: Office of official administrators.

passed along the grapevine: Told by one person who, in turn, told another, etc.

CULTURAL NOTES

¹Victorian means associated with the reign of Britain's Queen Victoria from 1837 to 1901. Victorian buildings were typically made of red brick and were ornate or highly decorated.

It was a short walk down the Buchanan Street hill from Pine to the flats where the Japanese community had taken root and was thriving like a tree whose seed had blown in from the Pacific and had held fast in this nook, this fold in the city's many gradations.° When she was a little older her world expanded beyond the Victorian called Pine. It expanded toward the heart of this community, toward the little shops from which her mother returned each day, string bag bulging with newspaper-wrapped parcels and a long white radish or two. She played hide-and-seek among the barrels of pickles and sacks of rice piled high in the garage which claimed to be the American Fish Market, while her mother exchanged news of the comings and goings of the community over the fish counter. "Ship coming in Friday? Do you think Yamashita-san's picture bride will come? She's in for a surprise!"

At the age of five she roller skated to the corner of her block, then on sudden impulse turned the corner and started down the Buchanan Street hill. Her elder sister, Keiko, who had expected her to turn around and come right back, threw down her jumprope and ran after her, screaming for her to stop. But she didn't stop. She made it all the way to the bottom, cheeks flushed red and black hair flying, before shooting off the curb and crumpling in the street. Her hands and knees were scraped raw, but she was laughing.

Before that first day of school there had been no need to look above Pine Street, where the city reached upwards to the Pacific Heights area and the splendid mansions of the rich, white people. The only Japanese who went to Pacific Heights were the ones employed to do housecleaning as day laborers. She had always known what was on the other side of Pine Street, and accepted early that it was not part of her world.

When it came time for her to go to school, she was not sent to the same school as the other Japanese American children because Pine was on the edge of Japantown and in a different school district. She was the only Japanese in her class. And from the instant Eleanor Leland pulled up the corners of her eyes at her, sneering "Jap!," a kind of radar system went to work in her. Afterward she always acted with caution in new surroundings,

---

VOCABULARY

gradations: Stages of development (*grad-* means step).

blending in like a chameleon° for survival. There were two things she would never do again: One was to forget the girl's name who had called her a Jap; the other was to cry.

She did her best to blend in. Though separated from the others by her features and her native tongue, she tried to be as inconspicuous as possible. If she didn't understand what the teacher said, she watched the other children and copied them. She listened carefully to the teacher and didn't do anything that might provoke° criticism. If she couldn't be outstanding she at least wanted to be invisible.

She succeeded. She muted° her colors and blended in. She was a quiet student and the other children got used to her; some were even nice to her. But she was still not really a part of their world because she was not really herself.

At the end of each school day she went home to the dark, narrow corridors of the old Victorian and the soothing, unconscious jumble of two tongues which was the two generations' compromise for the sake of communication. Theirs was a comfortable language, like a comfortable old sweater that had been well-washed and rendered shapeless by wear. She would never wear it outside of the house. It was a personal thing, like a hole in one's sock, which was perfectly all right at home but would be a horrible embarrassment if seen by *yoso no hito*.

In the outside world—the *hakujin* world—there was a watchdog at work which rigorously edited out Japanese words and mannerisms when she spoke. Her words became formal, carefully chosen and somewhat artificial. She never felt they conveyed° what she really felt, what she really was, because what she really was was unacceptable. In the realm of behavior, the watchdog was a tyrant. Respectability, as defined by popular novels and Hollywood heroines, must be upheld at all costs. How could she explain about the young men lounging in the doorways of her home and drinking in the back room with her father? How could she admit to the stories of the immigrant women who came to her mother desperate for protection from the beatings by

---

VOCABULARY
chameleon (kə-mēl' yən): A lizard that has the ability to change color in order to blend into the surrounding environment so as not to be noticed.
provoke: To cause or bring about.
muted: Toned down, muffled, of softened (*mu-* means silent). ". . . blended in" is a clue.
conveyed: Here it means communicated.

their frenzied° husbands? It was all so far from the drawing rooms of Jane Austen[2] and the virtue and gallantry° of Hollywood. The Japanese who passed through her house could drink, gamble, and philander,° but she would never acknowledge it. She could admit to no weakness, no peculiarity.° She would be irreproachable.° She would be American.

Poverty was irreproachably American in the Depression years. Her father's Oriental art goods business in Union Square had survived the 1906 earthquake only to be done in by the dishonesty of a *hakujin* partner who absconded° with the gross° receipts and the company car. The family survived on piecework and potatoes. Her mother organized a group of immigrant ladies to crochet° window shade rings. They got a penny apiece from the stores on Grant Avenue. Her father strung plastic birds onto multicolored rings. As they sat working in the back room day after day, they must have dreamed of better times. They had all gambled the known for the unknown when they left Japan to come to America. Apparently it took more than hard work. They could work themselves to death for pennies. Entrepreneurial° ventures were risky. They wanted to spare their sons and daughters this insecurity and hardship. Education was the key that would open the magical doors to a better future. Not that they hadn't been educated in Japan; indeed, some of them were better educated than the people whose houses they cleaned on California Street. But they felt the key was an American education, a college education. Immigrant sons and immigrant daughters would fulfill their dreams.

She and her peers acquiesced° in this dream. After all, wasn't it the same as their own? To succeed, to be irreproachable, to be American? She would be a smart career girl in a tailored suit, beautiful, and bold—an American girl.

VOCABULARY
frenzied: Filled with uncontrollable madness.
gallantry: Showy behavior.
philander: To go from love affair to love affair.
peculiarity: Oddity.
irreproachable: Beyond blame (*ir-* means not; reproach means to blame).
absconded: Left quicky (*ab-* means away).
gross: Here it means total amount.
crochet (krō-shā'): To make a hand-sewn item out of thread by looping it with a hooked needle.
entrepreneurial (äntrə-prə-nur' ē ŭl): Assuming the risk of starting one's own business.
acquiesced: Gave in passively without protest.

CULTURAL NOTES
[2]Jane Austen was a British novelist who lived from 1775 to 1817.

After the Depression her father opened a novelty store on Grant Avenue, and she was able to go to college. She set forth into the unknown with a generation of immigrant sons and daughters, all fortified° by their mutual vision of the American dream.

They did everything right. They lived at home to save expenses. Each morning they woke up at dawn to catch the bus to the ferry building. They studied on the ferry as it made the bay crossing, and studied on the train from the Berkeley marina to Shattuck, a few blocks from the majestic buildings of the University of California. They studied for hours in the isolation of the library on campus. They brought bag lunches from the dark kitchens of old Japantown flats and ate on the manicured° grass or at the Japanese Students' Club off campus. They went to football games and rooted for the home team. They wore bobby socks° and Cal sweaters. The women had pompadours° and the men parted their hair in the middle. They did everything correctly. But there was one thing they did not do: they did not break out of the solace° of their own society to establish contact with the outside world.

In a picture dated 1939, of the graduating members of the Nisei Students' Club, there are about sixty people in caps and gowns standing before California Hall. She is there, among the others, glowing triumphantly. No whisper of Pearl Harbor to cast a shadow on those bright faces. Yet all these young graduates would soon be clerking in Chinatown shops or pruning American gardens. Their degrees would get them nowhere, not because they hadn't done right, but because it was 1939 and they had Japanese faces. There was nowhere for them to go.

When the war came, her application for a teaching job had already been on file for two years. Since graduation she had been helping at her father's Grant Avenue store. Now she had to hand-letter signs for the store saying "Bargain Sale: Everything Must Go." Her father's back slumped in defeat as he watched the

---

VOCABULARY

fortified: Made stronger (fort- refers to being strong).
manicured: Shaped and clipped closely, as one might do to one's fingernails (man- means hand: (-cur- refers to care).
bobby socks: Thick socks rolled down at the top.
pompadours: Hairstyles featuring hair brushed up high from the forehead (popularized by the Marquise de Pompadour, mistress of Louis XV of France during the 1700s).
solace: Comfort.

business he had struggled to build melt away overnight. America was creating a masterpiece and did not want their color.

They packed away everything they could not carry. Tom the Greek, from whom they rented Pine, promised to keep their possessions in the basement, just in case they would be able to come back someday. The quilts of bright Japanese cloth, Imari dishes hand-carried by her mother from Japan, letters, photos, window-shade rings made in hard times, a copy of her junior college newspaper in which she had written a column, her Cal yearbook, faded pictures of bright Hollywood starlets—she put all her dreams in boxes for indefinite keeping. As instructed, they took along what was functional, only what would serve in the uncertain times to come—blankets, sweaters, pots, and pans. Then, tagged like baggage, they were escorted by the U.S. Army to their various pick-up points in the city. And when the buses took them away, it was as though they had never been.

They were taken to Tanforan Racetrack, south of the city, which was to be their new home. The stables were used as barracks, and horse stalls became "apartments" for families. As she viewed the dirt and manure left by the former occupants, she realized, "So this is what they think of me." Realization was followed by shame. She recalled how truly she had believed she was accepted, her foolish confidence, and her unfounded dreams. She and her nisei friends had been spinning a fantasy world that was unacknowledged by the larger fabric of society. She had been so carried away by the aura of Berkeley that she had forgotten the legacy° left her by Eleanor Leland. Now, the damp, dusty floor and stark cots reminded her sharply of her place. She was twenty-four. They lived in Tanforan for one year.

After a year they were moved to the Topaz Relocation Center in the wastelands of Utah. Topaz, Jewel of the Desert they called it sardonically.° Outside the barbed wire fence, the sagebrush traced aimless patterns on the shifting gray sands. Her sister Keiko could not endure it; she applied for an office job in Chicago and left the camp. Her brother enrolled at a Midwestern university. She stayed and looked after her parents.

After a time she began to have trouble with her hearing. At first, it was only certain frequencies she could not year, like

---

VOCABULARY
legacy: Something handed down; willed.
sardonically: Mockingly; scornfully.

some desert insects. Then it was even human voices, particularly when there was background noise. She couldn't be sure, but sometimes she wondered if it was a matter of choice, that if she only concentrated, she would be able to hear what someone was saying. But the blowing dust seemed to muffle everything anyway.

She left camp only once, and briefly, to marry the young man who had courted her wordlessly in the prewar days. He was a *kibei*—born in America and taken back to Japan at the age of eight. He had then returned to San Francisco to seek his fortune at the age of eighteen. He got off the boat with seven dollars in his pocket. He was one of those restless, lonely young men who would hang out at the Japantown poolhall, work at odd jobs by day, and go to school at night. He lived with a single-minded simplicity that seemed almost brash to someone who had grown up with so many unspoken rules. He wanted this sophisticated, college-educated American girl to be his wife, and she was completely won over. So she got leave from camp, and he from his unit, which was stationed at Fort Bragg, and they met in Chicago to cast a humble line into the uncertain future, a line they hoped would pull them out of this war into another, better life. Then they each returned to their respective barracks.

As defeat loomed inevitable° for Japan, more and more people were allowed to leave the camps. Some of them made straight for the Midwest or East Coast where feelings did not run so high against their presence, but her family could only think of going back home. The longing for San Francisco had become so strong that there was no question as to where they would go when they were released. They went straight back to Pine, and their hearts fell when they saw the filth and damage caused by three years of shifting tenancy.° But they set about restoring it nevertheless because it was the only thing left of their lives.

The three years that had passed seemed like wasted years. The experience had no connection to the rest of her life; it was like a pocket in time, or a loose string. It was as though she had fallen asleep and dreamed the experience. But there was certainly no time to think about that now; they were busy rebuilding their lives.

VOCABULARY
inevitable: Unavoidable.
tenancy: Period of temporary possession.

She was pregnant with her first child. Her husband pleated skirts at a factory that hired Japanese. Later he ventured into the wholesale flower business where the future might be brighter. His hours were irregular; he rose in the middle of the night to deliver fresh flowers to market. Her sister had an office job with the government. Her parents were too old to start over, though her father hired out to do day work. But it shamed him so much that he did not want anyone else to know, and he died shortly afterward.

She was busy with the babies who came quickly, one after another, all girls. She was absorbed in their nursing and bodily functions, in the sucking, smacking world of babies. How could she take time to pick up the pieces of her past selves, weave them together into a pattern, when there were diapers to be changed and washed, bowel movements to be recorded, and bottles sterilized. Her world was made up of Linda's solicitude° for her younger sister Cathy, Cathy's curiosity, and the placidity° of the third baby, Sharon. Then there was Jo, who demanded so much attention because of her frail health. The house was filled with babies. Her husband was restless, fiercely independent—he wanted to raise his family in a place of his own.

So they moved out to the Avenues, leaving the dark corridors and background music of mixed tongues for a sturdy little house in a predominantly *hakujin* neighborhood, where everyone had a yard enclosed by a fence.

When their mother died, Keiko also moved out of Pine and closed it up for good. The old Victorian was too big for one person to live in alone. But before all the old things stored away and forgotten in the basement were thrown out or given away, was there anything she wanted to keep? Just her college yearbook from Cal. That was all she could think of. She couldn't even remember what had been so important, to have been packed away in those boxes so carefully when the war had disrupted their lives. She couldn't take the time with four babies to sift through it all now. It would take days. No, just her yearbook. That was all.

Sealed off in her little house in the fog-shrouded° Avenues, the past seemed like a dream. Her parents, the old Victorian, the

---

VOCABULARY
solicitude: State of being concerned.
placidity: Outwardly calm (*plac-* refers to flat).
fog-shrouded: Covered with fog.

shuffling of slippered guests, and the low mumble of Japanese, all gone from her life. Her college friends were scattered all over the country, or married and sealed off in their own private worlds. But she felt no sense of loss. Their lives, after all, were getting better. There was no time to look back on those days before the war. The girls were growing. They needed new clothes for school. She must learn to sew. Somer & Kaufman was having a sale on school shoes. Could she make this hamburger stretch for two nights?

Linda was a bright and obedient child. She was very much the big sister. Jo, the youngest, was volatile,° alternating between loving and affectionate, and strong and stubborn. Sharon was a quiet child, buffered° from the world on both sides by sisters. She followed her sister, Cathy, demanding no special attention. Cathy was friendly and fearless, an unredeemable tomboy. When she slid down banisters and bicycled down the big hill next to their house in the Avenues, her mother's eyes would narrow as if in recognition, watching her.

As a mother, she was without fault. Her girls were always neatly dressed and on time. They had decent table manners, remembered to excuse themselves and say thank you. They learned to read quickly and loved books because she always read to them. She chose the books carefully and refused to read them any slang or bad grammar. Her children would be irreproachable.

She conscientiously attented PTA meetings, although this was a trial for her. She wasn't able to tell people about her hearing problem; somehow she was unable to admit to such a deficiency. So she did her best, sometimes pretending to hear when she didn't, nodding her head and smiling. She wanted things to go smoothly; she wanted to appear normal.

Linda, Cathy, and Jo excelled in school and were very popular. Linda held class offices and was invariably the teacher's pet. "A nice girl," her teachers said. Cathy was outgoing and athletic and showed great talent in art and design—"a beautiful girl," in her teachers' estimation. Jo was rebellious, read voraciously,° and wrote caustic° essays and satires.° Teachers sometimes disliked

---

VOCABULARY

volatile: Changeable.
buffered: Protected.
voraciously: Extremely; hungrily (vora- refers to devour).
caustic: Cutting and bitter.
satires: Pieces of literature written to make fun of something.

her, but they all thought she was "intelligent." Sharon was termed "shy." Although she liked the arts, Cathy was the artist of the family. And though Sharon read quite a bit, Jo was the one who liked to read. Sharon was not popular like Linda, and of all the Terasaki girls, she had to struggle the hardest, often unsuccessfully, to make the Honor Roll. But all in all, the girls vindicated° their mother, and it was a happy time, the happiest time of her life.

Then they were grown up and gone. They left one by one. The house emptied room by room until it seemed there was nothing but silence. She had to answer the phone herself now, if she heard it ring. She dreaded doing so because she could never be sure if she was hearing correctly. Sometimes she let the telephone ring, pretending not to be home. The one exception was when her sister called every night. Then she would exhange news on the phone for an hour.

When her daughters came home to visit she came alive. Linda was doing the right things. She had a nice Japanese American boyfriend; she was graduating from college; and she was going to get married.

Cathy was a bit of a free soul, and harder to undertand. She wore her hair long and straight, and seldom came home from Berkeley. When she did she seemed to find fault: Why didn't her mother get a hearing aid? Did she enjoy being left out of the hearing world? But Cathy had friends, interesting friends, *hakujin* friends, whom she sometimes brought home with her. She moved easily in all worlds, and her mother's heart swelled with pride to see it.

Sharon sometimes came home, sometimes stayed away. When she did come home she did not have much to say. She was not happy in school. She liked throwing pots° and weaving.

Then there was Jo, who would always bring a book home, or notebook, and whose "evil pen" would pause absently in midstroke when her mother hovered near, telling her little bits of information that were new since the last visit. Jo, whose thoughts roamed far away, would gradually focus on the little figure of her mother. She had led such a sheltered life.

And then Cathy had died, and her mother didn't even cry.

VOCABULARY

vindicated: Cleared from blame.
throwing pots: Placing clay on a potter's wheel to shape it into a pot as the wheel turns.

Linda sent pictures from Germany of their mother in front of Heidelberg Castle, and cruising down the Rhine. "She's just like a young girl," her letters proclaimed triumphantly. "She's excited about everything." But when their mother came home she talked about her trip for about a week. Then the old patterns prevailed, as if the house were a mold and her soul molded to it. In a month, Germany seemed like another loose thread in the fabric of her life. When Joe visited two months later, her mother was once again effaced,° a part of the house almost, in her faded blouse and shapeless skirt, joylessly adding too much seasoned salt to the dinner salad.

"If only," Jo wrote Linda facetiously,° "we could slip her out to some exotic place every other month."

In the fall Jo went to New York to study. "I have to get away," she wrote Linda. "The last time I went home I found myself discussing the machine washability of acrylics° with Mom. There has got to be more to life than that." In the spring she had her mother come for a visit. No trip to the top of the Empire State Building, no Staten Island ferry, with Jo. She whisked her mother straight from Kennedy Airport to her cramped flat in the Village, and no sooner had they finished dinner than Jo's boyfriend, Michael, arrived.

Her mother was gracious. "Where do you live, Michael?" she asked politely.

He and Jo exchanged looks. "Here," he said.

Despite her mother's anxiety about the safety of New York streets, the two of them walked furiously in the dusk and circled Washington Square several times, mother shocked and disappointed, daughter reassuring. At the end of an hour they returned to the flat for tea, and by the end of the evening the three of them had achieved an uneasy truce.

"I knew you wouldn't be happy about it," Jo said to her, "but I wanted you to know me. To know the truth. I hate pretending."

"Things were different when we were your age," her mother said. "What's Daddy going to say?"

VOCABULARY
effaced: Erased (ef- refers to remove).
facetiously: Playfully or jokingly.
acrylics: Pieces of cloth made of chemical substances.

She stayed for two weeks. Every morning Michael cooked breakfast, and the three of them ate together. Her attitude towards the situation softened from one of guarded assessment° to tentative° acceptance. Michael was very articulate,° Jo as level-headed as ever. Their apartment was clean and homey. She began to relax over morning coffee at the little round table by the window.

She remembered the trip she made to Chicago during the war to get married. She had traveled from Topaz to Chicago by train. It was her first trip alone. Her parents and camp friends had seen her off at Topaz, and her sister and future husband had met her at the station in Chicago. But as the train followed its track northeastward across the country, she had been alone in the world. Her senses had been heightened. She remembered vividly the quality of light coming through the train window, and how it had bathed the passing countryside in a golden wash. Other passengers had slept, but she sat riveted° at the window. Perhaps the scenery seemed so beautiful because of the bleakness and sensual° deprivation° of Topaz. She didn't know why she remembered it now.

Jo took her to the Metropolitan and to the Statue of Liberty. In a theater on Broadway they sat in the front row to see Deborah Kerr,[3] her all-time favorite, and afterwards she declared she had heard every word.

When she left she shook Michael's hand and hugged Jo, saying, "I'll talk to Daddy."

But by the time Jo came home to visit a year later, the house, or whatever it was, had done its work. Her mother was again lost to her, a sweet little creature unable to hear very well, relaying little bits of information.

"I give up," said Jo. "We seem to lose ground every time. We dig her out, then she crawls back in, only deeper."

Linda loyally and staunchly defended the fortress in which her mother seemed to have taken refuge.

VOCABULARY
assessment: Evaluation or analysis.
tentative: Here it means hesitant or doubtful.
articulate: Able to speak using clear and effective language.
riveted: Here it means as if fastened to something with a bolt (rivet).
sensual: Appealing to the senses (sight, hearing, etc.).
deprivation: The condition of being denied basic rights or necessities.

CULTURAL NOTES
[3]Deborah Kerr was a famous 20th century American actress in the movies and on the stage.

The Loom 151

Jo defiantly wanted to break through. "Like shock treatment," she said. "It's the only way to bring her out."

Sharon, the middle daughter, gave her mother a loom.

And so, late in life, she took up weaving. She attended a class and took detailed notes, then followed them step by step, bending to the loom with painstaking attention, threading the warp° tirelessly, endlessly winding, threading, tying. She made sampler° after sampler, using the subdued, muted colors she liked: Five inches of one weave, two inches of another, just as the teacher instructed.

For a year she wove samplers, geometric and repetitious, all in browns and neutral shades, the colors she preferred. She was fascinated by some of the more advanced techniques she began to learn. One could pick up threads from the warp selectively, so there could be a color on the warp that never appeared in the fabric if it were not picked up and woven into the fabric. This phenomenon meant she could show a flash of color, repeated flashes of the color, or never show it at all. The color would still be there, startling the eye when the piece was turned over. The backside would reveal long lengths of a color that simply hadn't been picked up from the warp and didn't appear at all in the right side of the fabric.

She took to her loom with new excitement, threading the warp with all the shades of her life: Gray, for the cold, foggy mornings when she had, piece by piece, warmed little clothes by the heater vent as Jo, four, stood shivering in her underwear; brown, the color of the five lunch bags she packed each morning with a sandwich, cut in half and wrapped in waxed paper, napkin, fruit, and potato chips; Dark brown, like the brownies they had baked "to make Daddy come home" from business trips—Sharon and Jo had believed he really could smell them, because he always came home.

Now when the daughters came home they always found something new she had woven. Linda dropped by almost every week to leave her own daughter, Terry, at "Bachan's house" before dashing off to work. When Linda's husband came to pick her up, Terry never wanted to leave "Bachi" and would cling to her, crying at the door.

VOCABULARY
warp: Part of the underlying apparatus of a loom.
sampler: Here it is a piece of cloth with designs woven into it.

She continued to weave: White, the color of five sets of sheets, which she had washed, hung out, and ironed each week—also the color of the bathroom sink and the lather of shampoo against four small black heads; blue, Cathy's favorite color.

Sharon came by from time to time, usually to do a favor or bring a treat. She would cook Mexican food or borrow a tool or help trim trees in the garden. She was frustrated with the public school system where she had been substitute teaching and was now working part time in a gallery.

Sometimes Sharon brought yarn for her mother to weave: Golden brown, the color of the Central Valley in summer. The family had driven through the valley on their way to the mountains almost every summer. They would arrive hot and sweating and hurry into the cool, emerald green waters of the Merced River. The children's floats flashed yellow on the dark green water. Yellow, too, were the beaten eggs fried flat, rolled, and eaten cold, with dark brown pickled vegetables and white rice balls. She always sat in the shade.

Jo was working abroad and usually came home to visit once a year. She and Michael had broken up. During the visits the house would fill with Jo and her friends. They would sit in the back room to talk. Jo visited her mother's weaving class and met her weaving friends.

"So this is the daughter," one of them said. "Your mother's been looking forward to your visit. She never misses class except when her daughters are home."

Soon it was time for Jo to leave again. "Mom's colors," she remarked to Sharon as she fingered the brown muffler her mother had woven for her.

"Put it on," said Sharon.

Jo did, and as she moved toward the light, hidden colors leaped from the brown fabric. It came alive in the sunlight.

"You know, there's actually red in here," she marveled, "and even bits of green. You'd never know it unless you looked real close."

"Most people don't," Sharon said.

The two sisters fell silent, sharing a rare moment together before their lives diverged° again. The muffler was warm about Jo's neck.

VOCABULARY
diverged: Went in different directions (*di-* here means apart; *-verge-* means to bend).

At the airport, Jo's mother stood next to Jo's father, leaning slightly toward him as an object of lighter mass naturally tends toward a more substantial one. She was crying.

When Jo was gone she returned to the house, and her loom. And amidst the comings and goings of the lives around her, she sat, a woman bent over a loom, weaving the diverse threads of life into one miraculous, mystical fabric with timeless care.

QUESTIONS FOR REFLECTION/DISCUSSION

1. Why do you think the sisters were startled at their mother's reaction to Cathy's death? How did their father's reaction differ from their mother's? Why do you think their mother reacted the way she did?

2. Describe their mother's ways. What seems to be her main concern?

3. Their mother had worn "the two faces of a second generation child born to immigrant parents" (p. 140). Describe these two faces. Is there any connection between having two faces and being able to "blend in like a chameleon for survival" (p. 142)? What are the negative aspects of having two faces? Is it sometimes good to be able to wear two faces? Why or why not?

4. Tell about the mother's childhood at home. What did her family do for other Japanese immigrants? Why do you think most of the immigrants were men? If you are an immigrant, describe the help you received from other immigrants when you first arrived in the country in which you now live. Do you feel they could have done more? Explain.

5. What did Japanese Americans think was the "key" to success in America? Did this turn out to be true for college graduates at the time of the story? Explain. To what extent do you think the "key" is considered the same today?

6. On page 144 are the words "No whisper of Pearl Harbor to cast a shadow on those bright faces" [of those graduating]. What do these words mean?

7. Think about the line "America was creating a masterpiece and did not want their color" (p. 145). Did this notion have anything to do with the "legacy left her by Eleanor Leland" (p. 145)? Explain. Do you see any signs of such a "masterpiece" being created today in the United States , Canada, or elsewhere in the world? If so, upon what evidence do you base your answer?

8. How might the actions of the mother as a deaf person be typical of other deaf people?

9. In what ways did the daughters "vindicate" their mother?

10. How does the mother react to Jo's living arrangements with her boyfriend? How would your parents react? How would you react as a parent?

11. The daughter Cathy "moved easily in all worlds" (p. 149). What does it mean to move easily in all worlds? To what extent should it be a goal of immigrants? Does this have any connection to having more than one face? Explain.

12. In what way is the house significant to the mother? How does her behavior change when she is in it?

13. How did the loom change the mother's life? Did it change her relationship with her daughters in any way?

14. During the war, the United States fought Germany in addition to Japan. However, German Americans did not experience the same injustices as Japanese Americans. How might you explain the difference in the treatment of the two groups? To what extent is such a difference in treatment typical of relationships between the dominant group and nondominant groups in a given society? Explain.

15. Explain the following comparisons:

Sharon had to raise her voice so her mother could hear the awful words about Cathy's death "choked out like bits of shattered glass" (p. 137).

. . . the Japanese community had taken root and was thriving like a tree whose seed had blown in from the Pacific and had held fast in this nook, this fold in the city's many gradations (p. 141).

Theirs was a comfortable language, like a comfortable old sweater that had been well-washed and rendered shapeless by wear (p. 142).

Outside the barbed wire fence, the sagebrush traced aimless patterns on the shifting gray sands (p. 145).

. . . they met in Chicago to cast a humble line into the uncertain future, a line they hoped would pull them out of this war into another, better life (p. 146).

16. Explain the irony in the lines below:

Not that they [the Japanese Americans] hadn't been educated in Japan; indeed, some of them were better educated than the people whose houses they cleaned on California Street (p. 143).

After a year they were moved to the Topaz Relocation Center in the wastelands of Utah. Topaz, Jewel of the Desert, they called it sardonically (p. 145).

Exploring Other Sources

1. Using library resources and/or the Internet, find out as much as you can about the Japanese-American experience during World War II. Key words in your research might include "Internment Camps," "World War II," or "United States internment." Your instructor or the librarian may be able to help you. Share what you learn with a small group. If your search includes the Internet, begin by pointing your browser to http://worldviews.wadsworth.com for links to information on the Japanese-American experience in America during World War II.

2. Locate accounts of real persons affected by the Japanese internment in the United States during World War II in the library or among people you know. How were their experiences similar to or different from those of the mother in "The Loom"?

3. Research in your library and/or on the Internet other groups of people in other places around the world who have experienced similar injustice. Ask your instructor or the librarian for assistance if you need it. Share your findings with a small group. To research on the Internet, use the web site referred to in item 1 above.

4. Have nations that you know of tried to create "masterpieces" in which people of a certain color or ethnic/cultural background were the victims of prejudice or even forced out? Research these attempts in your library. Look at the events that appeared to lead up to such treatment. What were the long-term effects? Which attempts had the most devastating results?

Synthesis Through Writing

1. Are you now moving easily in more than one world? If so, begin a diary in which you can record your experiences. Note that a diary is usually more personal than a journal. Write in your diary at least three times a week. Record your feelings, actions, and reactions. What are you learning from being in more than one world?

2. In "The Loom," the Japanese language is compared to a comfortable old sweater. If your first language is a language other than English, tell how you feel about it. Write a personal essay that expresses your feelings. Refer to the writing strategies on page xix.

3. Has an object such as the loom in this story made a change in your life or in the life of someone you know well? If so, write a personal essay telling how that object has brought about change in you or in the person into whose life it has come. See the writing strategies on page xix if necessary.

4. Write an opinion paper based on your research of attempts to create ethnic/cultural "masterpieces" around the world. What do you think brings about such attempts? How can such attempts be prevented altogether? First divide a piece of paper into three columns: "Attempts," "Causes," and "Prevention." See the following sample. Include in the columns what you learned in the previous activity in Exploring Other Sources. Use your graphic representation to help you organize your essay. If necessary, refer to additional writing strategies on page xix.

ATTEMPTS	CAUSES	PREVENTION

5. Write a paper comparing the Japanese-American experience with similar experiences of at least one other ethnic/cultural group in history. In what ways were their experiences similar? In what ways were they different? Divide a piece of paper into two columns. Label the first column "Similarities" and the second "Differences." Fill in the columns with the appropriate details. Use them to help you organize your essay. See the writing strategies on page xix if necessary.

SIMILARITIES	DIFFERENCES
1.	1.
2.	2.
3.	3.

The Loom

Strong Men
Sterling A. Brown

The African experience in the United States began when Africans were first brought to Virginia as slaves in 1619. At that time, the British were trading goods for slaves in Africa and bringing the slaves to the United States. Here the slaves were again traded for goods, which were then transported to Britain. In 1807 the British abolished slave trading and later abolished slavery itself in England and all its territories. Unfortunately, slavery by then had become an integral part of plantation life in the southern United States. One of the results of the Civil War between the northern states and the southern states was the freeing of the slaves in 1863. The United Nations in recent years has carried on efforts to abolish slavery worldwide. Still, millions of people around the world are slaves or live slave-like lives.

Author Sterling A. Brown was born and raised in Washington, D.C. In 1921, he was elected to Phi Beta Kappa[1] at Williams College. He graduated with an M.A. degree from Harvard in 1923. He has served for many years as a professor of English at Howard University. He has written *Southern Road*, which is a collection of his poems, and has published two volumes of literary criticism.

Before You Read

Think about what it might be like to live the life of a slave. Talk about it with a partner or write about it in your journal. Then read the following to learn what one African-American author thinks slavery may have been like for those who actually experienced it.

The strong men keep coming—Sandburg

> They dragged you from homeland,
> They chained you in coffles,°
> They huddled you spoon-fashion in filthy hatches,°
> They sold you to give a few gentlemen ease.
>
> They broke you in like oxen,
> They scourged you,
> They branded you,

VOCABULARY
coffles: Lines of people or animals chained together.
hatches: Openings in the deck of a boat.

CULTURAL NOTES
[1]Phi Beta Kappa is a scholarship honor society that began in 1776 at the College of William and Mary in Williamsburg, Virginia.

They made your women breeders,
They swelled your numbers with bastards . . .
They taught you the religion they disgraced.

You sang:
   Keep a-inchin'[2] along
   Lak a po'[3] inch worm . . .

You sang:
   Bye and bye
   I'm gonna lay down dis heaby[4] load . . .

You sang:
   Walk togedder, chillen,[5]
   Dontcha git[6] weary . . .
     The strong men keep a'comin'[7] on
     The strong men git stronger.

They point with pride to the roads you built for them,
They ride in comfort over the rails you laid for them.
They put hammers in your hand
And said—Drive so much before sundown.

You sang:
   Ain't no hammah[8]
   In dis lan',[9]
   Strikes lak mine, bebby,[10]
   Strikes lak mine.

They cooped° you in their kitchens,
They penned you in their factories,

VOCABULARY
cooped: Shut in.

CULTURAL NOTES
Seventeenth-century Black dialect:
[2]"a-inchin": " . . . inching . . ." (moving one inch at a time).
[3]"Lak a po'": "Like a poor . . ."
[4]"dis heaby": " . . . this heavy . . ."
[5]"togedder, chillen": " . . . together, children"
[6]"dontcha get": "Don't you get . . ."
[7]"a-comin'": " . . . coming . . ."
[8]"Ain't no hammah": "There isn't any hammer . . ."
[9]"dis lan'": " . . . this land . . ."
[10]"bebby": " . . . baby . . ."

They gave you the jobs that they were too good for,
They tried to guarantee happiness to themselves
By shunting° dirt and misery to you.

You sang:
    Me an' muh[11] baby gonna shine shine
    Me an' muh baby gonna shine.
        The strong men keep a-comin' on
        The strong men git stronger . . .

They bought off some of your leaders
You stumbled, as blind men will . . .
They coaxed you, unwontedly° soft-voiced . . .
You followed a way.
Then laughed as usual.

They heard the laugh and wondered;
Uncomfortable;
Unadmitting a deeper terror . . .
        The strong men keep a-comin' on
        Gittin' stronger . . .

What, from the slums
Where they have hemmed you,
What, from the tiny huts
They could not keep from you—
What reaches them
Making them ill at ease, fearful?
Today they shout prohibition° at you
"Thou° shalt° not this"
"Thou shalt not that"
"Reserved for whites only"
You laugh.

VOCABULARY
shunting: Shifting.
unwontedly: Not in the usual way.
prohibition: The act of forbidding or not allowing (*pro-* means in front; *-hibi-* refers to holding).
    "Thou shalt not this" and "Thou shalt not that" are clues.
thou: Previously used word meaning "you."
shalt: Previously used word meaning "shall."

CULTURAL NOTES
[11]"an' muh'": " . . . and my . . ."

160   UNIT 3—BREAKING THROUGH TO SUCCESS

One thing they cannot prohibit—
The strong men . . . coming on
The strong men gittin' stronger.
Strong men . . .
STRONGER . . .

QUESTIONS FOR REFLECTION/DISCUSSION

1. From what you learned in the poem, describe what life was like for African Americans under slavery in the southern United States. How close does your description come to what you thought about slavery before you read the poem? Discuss with a small group.

2. Does the poem indicate that there might be a better life at sometime in the future? How can you tell?

3. What feelings toward slavery are expressed in the poem?

EXPLORING OTHER SOURCES

Find information about the African-American experience in America today. In what areas have African Americans made recent gains? What problems do African Americans still face in this society? What is the hope for the future? Use library resources and/or the Internet. Key words for research might include "African-Americans" and "Blacks," for example. Ask your instructor or the librarian for assistance if you need it. Discuss what you learn with a small group. If your search includes sources on the internet begin by pointing your browser to http://worldviews.wadsworth.com for information about African Americans today.

SYNTHESIS THROUGH WRITING

1. In your journal, react to the feelings expressed in the poem. How did the poem make you feel?

2. Write an essay on the African-American experience in America today. Use the information you found in the Exploring Other Sources activity. Refer to the writing strategies on page xix. Create your own graphic organizer to help you develop your paper.

Voices in the Mirror *[excerpt]*

Gordon Parks

In spite of their experiences with poverty and racism, many individuals are able to overcome despair and rise above it to succeed. One such individual is Gordon Parks, an African American of many talents—photography, writing, composing music, and directing films, to name a few. He grew up in Kansas in a loving but poverty-stricken family who were all too familiar with the humiliation and anger associated with poverty and racism. When his mother died, he went to live with his sister in Minnesota, only to be thrown out into the cold by her less-than-sensitive husband. Because he was now homeless, he rode the streetcars by night to keep warm and took on odd jobs wherever he could find them during the day.

Fortunately, Gordon Parks' struggles made him even more determined to break through the barriers of poverty and racism. Instead of dwelling on his misery, he focused on his strengths and devoted himself completely to his work. His efforts paid off handsomely. Eventually he became a respected photographer for two popular magazines, *Vogue* and *Life*. Among his most well-known photographs are the portraits of actress Ingrid Bergman, Italian film director Roberto Rossellini, and England's famed World War II leader, Winston Churchill. He also captured on film leaders of various Black groups in the United States: Malcolm X, Eldridge Cleaver, Richard Wright, and many others. Later, turning to film directing in Hollywood, he was acclaimed for his direction of the movie *Shaft*. In addition, Gordon Parks became a productive writer. *The Learning Tree*, *A Choice of Weapons*, and *To Smile in Autumn* are among his most popular books.

Before You Read

Try to imagine what it might be like to find yourself homeless, without food and shelter. If you have children or are pregnant, how might this change the decisions that you make and the actions you might be forced to take? What might some of the related problems be? Discuss these questions with a small group or write about them in your journal.

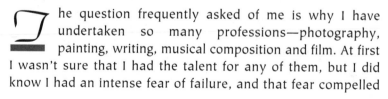

he question frequently asked of me is why I have undertaken so many professions—photography, painting, writing, musical composition and film. At first I wasn't sure that I had the talent for any of them, but I did know I had an intense fear of failure, and that fear compelled me to fight off anything that might abet° it—bigotry,° hatred, discrimination, poverty or hunger. I suffered those evils, but without allowing them to rob me of the freedom to expand. They came. I bottled them up inside me, closed them off and went on doing what I had to do. Why? I suppose it was good common horse sense. Perhaps it was then that those evils began churning into my subconscious, then to erupt much later through those violent dreams.

Nothing came easy. I was just born with a need to explore every tool shop of my mind, and with long searching and hard work. I became devoted to my restlessness; to chasing down poetry in the best of what I found; to opening doors that allowed me entrance into their universe, no matter how small. If I found nothing, I tried another door. Today my imagination refuses to be confined to boredom. It stays hungry and I feed it with things that surround me.

In my formative° years I was ill-prepared and I tried to make up for that by exploring every possibility. If one failed me I turned to another, but I was never just a dabbler.° I gave all of myself to every effort, and I still do. Calculation always figures strongly in my desire to doggedly° hold on to my creative pursuits. Sometimes I play the piano with my eyes firmly shut— considering the small possibility of blindness. Under such a handicap, I would learn to photograph an object or person by the feel of the light. If I lost my legs I could still write. And if I should lose both arms I am sure I would try painting with my toes.

Despite the fears that so often invade my sleep, I sometimes awake with a poem, or perhaps a musical theme, coursing° my mind. Memories too come streaming in from the past—good memories that I never want to forget, or bad memories, some of which I have learned to make peace with.

VOCABULARY

abet: Bring about or incite.
bigotry: Holding strong beliefs about religious, racial, or political issues and not respecting others rights to disagree and take other views.
formative: Experiencing change and development.
dabbler: One who dabbles, or tries one thing and then another, often without reason or serious intent (*dab* means the short stroke of a brush or a little bit).
doggedly: Stubbornly.
coursing: Here it means moving fast through something.

Here in the autumn of my life I still feel that there is a lot more to do, that there are other opportunities waiting to be grabbed. The signals are clear every morning when I get up; I know for sure that I will be working at something I like, and those are the kinds of mornings I've worked toward for so long.

I know too that there are a multitude of incalculable° forces lying in wait to do me in; to burn me up like firewood and scatter my ashes when nothing is left. But those forces still have trouble with me. Their language is despair, and I refuse to have any truck with° it. I've liked being a stranger to failure since I was a young man, and I still feel that way. I'm still occupied with survival; still very single-minded about keeping my life moving—but not for fame or fortune. I simply want to stay alive to learn more about the world we live in, a world that we, in spite of all its opportunities, are failing to live up to. I'm puzzled by all the illiteracy° that surrounds us in the midst of so many schools and teachers. I'm puzzled by all the crime, poverty, hunger and bigotry. Something is wrong, awfully wrong.

There have been times when I was even puzzled about the term success. Some dubious° characters have staked claims for it. To argue that Willie Sutton, the bank robber, was not successful is to lose the argument. In one haul—and there were many of them—he walked away with more money than Jessie James laid eyes on during his entire career of banditry.° Other gangsters like Al Capone, John Dillinger and "Pretty Boy" Floyd graduated *summa cum laude*[1] in their nefarious° fields. I could question the morality of their accomplishments if I liked, but all of them spelled success the same way John D. Rockefeller[2]

VOCABULARY

incalculable: Not able to guess or estimate (*in-* here means not).
truck with: Here it means to have dealings with.
illiteracy: The inability to read or write (*il-* means not).
dubious: Doubtful; questionable (*dub-* refers to moving in two directions).
banditry: The state of being a bandit.
nefarious: Evil (*ne-* means not; *-fari-* refers to divine law).

CULTURAL NOTES

[1]*Summa cum laude* is the highest award that can be given a university graduate.
[2]John Davison Rockefeller made a huge fortune for himself and his family by establishing the Standard Oil Company in the latter part of the 1800s. He was known not only for his ruthlessness in business dealings but also for his generosity during later years. He founded the Rockefeller Institute for Medical Research (which eventually became Rockefeller University), the Rockefeller Foundation, and the University of Chicago. His son, John Davison Rockefeller, Jr., founded the famous Rockefeller Center in New York City.

spelled it, and all of them gained national recognition. Yet, in the end, they proved as worthless to society as skeletons of dead fish. Only another crook would choose them as role models, and unfortunately a lot of them have, and it was my good fortune not to have been one of them.

Those parental sermons had prepared me to reach for a nobler kind of success, and during those frowning, adolescent days that threatened me, it took on a strange physical bearing, and a personality as well. I imagined it tall, skinny, sly and aloof—as mercurial° as quicksilver.° And I envisaged° it hovering secretively in dark corners and veiled in blue obscure shadows, always playing hide and seek with me.

I'm often asked if I thought of failure during those days. At that time there wasn't much to lose. I was starting in the pits, and up was the only direction available to me. What I needed most was motivation, and a need to escape my despair supplied plenty of that. There was no time for weeping, or for drumming up excuses to justify that despair. I had to do some fast growing or remain in the pits. It was a bad time, but I learned more with every setback. Luck, coupled with youth and determination, proved a worthy force against those detractors who kept the books on my strengths and weaknesses—those white teachers back in Kansas who had discouraged me, and later those Minnesota blacks who scoffed at my greenness. There were those other enemies too—cold, hunger and desolation.° Had my father seen me so distressed he would probably have given his usual advice. "Think, boy. Use that good common sense the Lord gave you." For him common sense was responsible for anything that turned out to be right—a fine crop of corn, the profitable sale of a horse, or perhaps the sale of a couple of hogs. To the contrary, all failures happened because "somebody didn't use their head."

I don't pretend to be an authority on common sense. I speak from only seventy-seven years of experience—which tells you

---

VOCABULARY

mercurial: Changeable; unpredictable (*mercur-* refers to the Roman god Mercury who served the other gods as a messenger).

quicksilver: The element mercury, which is silvery-white, is used in thermometers and other instruments to indicate the temperature.

envisaged: Saw future possibilities.

desolation: Here it means the state of being without hope; abandoned (*de-* here means completely; *-sol-* here refers to being alone).

next to nothing. As a term it has been undefined fully for centuries, and will probably remain so for centuries to come. I like to think of it as wisdom, and I've learned not to confuse wisdom with intelligence. There is a difference.

No doubt it was wisdom that taught me that my most dangerous enemy could be myself. One morning, with shaving razor in hand, I had stared into the mirror and asked myself some rather bothersome questions. With hard eyes I stared back at myself and reeled off some disturbing facts, along with some advice: "You're approaching manhood and you dislike yourself. That's why you're interrogating° me. [*Well, make up your mind to do something about it.*] You're so thin-skinned that the softest criticism rubs you raw. [*Accept criticism, man. It can't hurt, and it could be helpful.*] Envy of others' success hangs around your neck like a rope. [*That's stupid. Use their success to give you inspiration.*] You squander too much time on trivial things, always hurrying to nowhere, and in a rush to get there. [*Take your time, man. Think things out first, then go.*] You avoid questions about yourself that you find hard to answer. [*Figure things out. You just don't have the right answers. So admit to it.*] You talk rapid-fire just to be heard, and without having anything worthwhile to say. [*That's downright ego. Listen more. Keep your big mouth shut and keep your ears open. Your insecurity's showing.*] Well, enough for now. There's plenty left on the list for tomorrow. [*One last thing: Until you're sure of yourself, you won't be sure of anything. Think it over. See you tomorrow morning.*]"

I remember that session with the mirror so well because it forced me to take stock of myself. I was struggling for a positive image. But it was one thing to acknowledge my faults, and another thing to do something about them. I recall using four of my closest friends to learn from; to help me through the crisis. Adolph Thomas and Bud Kelly were likable, but both were gregarious° and suffered from diarrhea of the mouth. George Berry and Howard Barksdale were just as likable, but they were more reserved and usually spoke when they had something worthwhile to say. The four of them were near-perfect subjects for me to observe in helping to correct my own faults, and I used them well. But the mirror went right on watching, accusing, badgering like a nagging mother. Plainly it could see

---

VOCABULARY

interrogating: Asking a formal set of questions (*inter-* means between; *-rogat-* refers to asking).
gregarious: Very friendly and outgoing.

that I was weary of climbing into bed every night to cover myself with agony. It had helped me declare war with myself, and all the faults that were set to foul me up. The enemy—my faults—was confronted with the truth, and truth wielded the more powerful weapon.

Little by little I grew to feel better about myself, but having knocked one fault off, I had to remember that others were waiting to take over. They seemed to live in every shadow, knowing how hard it was to live without them. It was hard, while trying to beat the cold and scrounging for food, not to feel envy for my friends with secure homes, who wore nicely cut suits and talked about plans for college. I had finally bought my first new suit after I turned seventeen. I put two dollars down on it, and Ben Myers, the man who made it for me, got another dollar or so whenever he could catch me. Even then it took me a year to satisfy that debt. As for college, poverty purged° it from my thoughts.

That past comes galloping in sometimes like an enraged warrior, hawk-eyed, scowling, admonishing° itself for not having cut me down somewhere along the way. Angrily, it seems to point back at the smoke-filled pool hall, to the greasy eatery in St. Paul where I washed a million dirty dishes every weekend, to a rat-infested flophouse° on St. Peter Street where I mopped up the vomit of the bums, to that lowly brothel where I wearily thumped out the blues on a beatup piano for two years. It seemed as though I was serving out a sentence in hell. Remembering now, I sometimes shake my head and wonder how I survived it.

In St. Paul I met a wall of indifference—raised by blacks as well as whites. I never really expected much from the whites; to them I seemed to be invisible. But I hadn't bargained for the cold shoulders of blacks. Yet, their "private" clubs appeared as bigoted as those of the whites. Their members, intoxicated° with their upper lower class stations, altered my thoughts about the sense of caring blacks were supposed to have for one

---

VOCABULARY
purged: Cleansed.
admonishing: Here it means criticizing or scolding (*ad-* means to; *-monish-* here means to advise).
flophouse: A cheap hotel.
intoxicated: Here it means excited.

another. No hungry black boy would have gone unfed by other blacks in my hometown. There was always room for another plate at our supper table, regardless of how little food there was in the larder.° Up there in the North, blacks mistook the hunger in my eyes for daydreaming, and their houses seemed to be doorless. They made it clear to me that people, no matter what their color, could be unfeeling.

Surprisingly, some blacks who were thought to be living close to the devil showed me the most concern. The gamblers and hustlers always had a pat on the back for me, and they found odd jobs for me that brought in a few bucks. The tarnished world they were rooted in had not discolored their regard for a youngster like me. A foggy sense of paternalism° showed through their perverseness.° Ben Wilson, the gun-toting gambler and pimp° who had given me my finery° to play the piano, ordered me out of his place when he found me at the crap table.° "This joint can turn you into a bad egg overnight," he said as he showed me to the door. . . .

In 1929 hard luck backed off for a while when I got a job at the wealthy, prestigious,° white Minnesota Club as a bus boy in the day, and as a general lackey° at night. There I had the opportunity to observe what success was supposed to be, and to learn the rules I needed to know if I wanted to claim success. The rarefied° world inside the Minnesota Club was one of spacious rooms with high-beamed mahogany ceilings, of thick carpeting, of master and servant, of expensive clothes, wines and liquors, elegant table settings and epicurean° tastes. Influential men arrived there daily and I, dressed in a uniform of blue tails white tie and striped vest, served them brandy and coffee, and listened to their talk of stock markets, boating, traveling, golfing, financial deals and politics. I would take their coats, and the camel's hair

---

VOCABULARY

larder: A room or cupboard where food supplies, including meat, are kept (lard is pork fat).
paternalism: Fatherly behavior (*pater-* means father).
perverseness: Improper behavior. A *pervert* is one who participates in unacceptable behavior.
pimp: A person who sells prostitutes.
finery: Beautiful or showy clothes.
crap table: A table where people play craps, a game using dice.
prestigious: Having high status because of one's success, wealth, and/or fame.
lackey: A servant.
rarefied: Here it means reserved for a very select or special group.
epicurean: Devoted to fancy food and other such pleasures (*epicur-* refers to the Greek philosopher, Epicurus, who around 300 B.C. pursued a life without pain).

and the velvet-collared chesterfields° felt good to my calloused° hands. Their suits were well cut and well pressed, their oxfords° and grained brogues° discreetly polished. Their faces looked scrubbed, their hair neatly trimmed and they smelled of bay rum.° There was always the aroma of good food—great platters of roast pheasant, duck, guinea hen° banked with wild rice; huge buttered steaks served on planks of wood, garnished with steaming vegetables; spicy rum cakes, ices and creamy desserts. I was never hungry in those days; the leftovers amounted to a feast. There was a lot an unlettered° black boy could learn there, and what I learned I tucked deep inside, determined meanwhile to put each lesson into use whenever I could. I began to read more, borrowing newspapers, novels and books of poetry from the club library. And there a whole world opened up to me, one that would have been impossible to imagine on our small dirt farm back in Kansas.

Margaret Armstead, one of my grade school teachers in Kansas, had long before primed° my interest in reading literary works, those beyond comic strips and fairy tales. Twice a week she would have certain of her pupils make up stories spontaneously° and recite them before the rest of the class. "It's to improve your imagination," she would explain. The class itself had the privilege of selecting the storyteller they enjoyed most. My imagination must have been the wildest of the group, for it was me for whom they usually raised their hands to hear. Buster Jones, my antagonist,° declared that the reason for my always winning was because I was the biggest liar. If the novelists I began to read in the books I filched° from the club library were also liars, then they were obviously famous and rich liars—so I thought. Nevertheless, my mind was being

---

VOCABULARY

chesterfields: Overcoats with velvet collars and buttons that are usually hidden from view.
calloused: Hardened and rough to the touch.
oxfords: Low shoes with laces.
brogues: Low shoes with laces and patterns of ornate little holes punched in for decoration.
bay rum: A nice-smelling liquid made from the leaves of the West Indian bay tree mixed with alcohol and various oils.
guinea hen: A bird with blackish feathers and small white spots, similar to a pheasant.
unlettered: Uneducated.
primed: Started; caused to happen. Usually it refers to a water pump into which water must be first poured to get the operation started.
spontaneously: Unplanned; arising from the moment (*sponta-* means of free will).
antagonist: A person who is against another (*anta-* means against).
filched: To steal in a secretive way.

pushed into the foreign worlds of Thomas Mann, Sinclair Lewis and James Joyce.[3] Justice Pierce Butler, a member at the club, had, after several brandies, engaged me in conversation. Rather blithely° I told him about my interest in reading. A couple of days later he handed me an edition of Edith Wharton's[4] *The Age of Innocence.*

During 1929 fate smiled at me more than she had for a long time. I was still in school and working evenings at the club. Then Black Thursday[5] came—and with it panic and depression. I had no idea that my small world would be affected; surely a market crash concerned only the rich. But very quickly I, along with millions of others, was without a job. Desperately I searched for work, but I always failed to get any. On the seventh of November I went to school and cleaned out my locker. It was impossible to stay on. The blunt feel of winter returned with a snowstorm that same evening, and my hopes dwindled° once more.

I still had my room at Mrs. Brookins, and what little money I had saved soon ran out, but she didn't press for her rent. Then when everything seemed blackest I got a job playing at a northside Minneapolis brothel called Mattie's. Since I was full of melancholy° the music I fed them was filled with my mood and it seemed to soothe their souls. Friends began calling me "Blue," because of the blues I played for the prostitutes and their pimps, who were ripe for big tips. "Butterfly," bemoaning° the fate of a beautiful prostitute, became the big favorite, and I got one request for it after another. After a spat with Sally Alvis[6] I composed a song called "No Love," and that had silver dollars falling like tears. The job ended with a gruesome murder one Saturday night. The dead man, with a knife still lodged deep into his chest, fell a few feet from the piano. Along with the night

---

VOCABULARY
blithely: Casually, without serious thought.
dwindled: Became lessened gradually (*dwin-* means to waste away).
melancholy: Great sadness and depression (*mel-* here means black; *-chol-* refers to bile).
bemoaning: Mourning, or expressing sadness and regret (*be-* means about; *moan* means to express sadness).

CULTURAL NOTES
[3]Thomas Mann, Sinclair Lewis, and James Joyce are all very well-known writers.
[4]Edith Wharton was a famous American author who lived from 1862 to 1937.
[5]Black Thursday refers to the day in 1929 when the stock market lost much of its value and the Great Depression began.
[6]Sally Alvis was Gordon Parks' girlfriend at the time.

ladies, their customers and pimps, I fled that place and never went back. I can never forget the final moment in that room. The silence was startling.

Trouble was still coming in measured doses, and from all directions, rambling in out of order. If it didn't find me on Monday, it was bound to catch up with me on Tuesday. Had I been smart I might have saved myself some trouble by just sitting on a street corner and waiting for it to arrive. It took discipline to keep running away from it; and I ran hard if somewhat slow. Now the grass had turned to snow again, and I was still running.

QUESTIONS FOR REFLECTION/DISCUSSION

1. Do you think it was a good idea for the author to keep his fear of bigotry, hatred, discrimination, poverty, and hunger "bottled up" inside him? What can be the effects of bottling up such negative feelings? What effects can such feelings have on one's children, spouse, parents, or guardians? Is there a way he could have faced these feelings, dealt with them, and still have accomplished what he did in life?

2. What do you think the author means when he says, "I became devoted to my restlessness; to chasing down poetry in the best of what I found" (p. 163)? What do you think the "poetry" represents or symbolizes here? Is it a good idea to move on to something else if "poetry" is not found in what one is doing? If so, how long should one keep looking for the poetry in a certain endeavor before moving on to a new challenge? Explain.

3. The author feels that "Something is wrong, awfully wrong [with society]" (p. 164). Here he is referring to illiteracy in the midst of so many schools and teachers and to the presence of so much crime, poverty, hunger, and bigotry. Do you agree with the author that something is wrong? If so, *what* do you think is wrong? Can all of these problems be blamed on a single cause? Explain.

4. What does the author mean when he says, ". . . I've learned not to confuse wisdom with intelligence. There is a difference" (p. 166). Give an example or two to illustrate his meaning.

5. *Personification* is used often by the author to bring life to his descriptions. It sometimes involves comparisons in which objects or ideas are given human qualities. An example is "The past comes

galloping in sometimes like an enraged warrior, hawk-eyed, scowling, admonishing itself for not having cut me down somewhere along the way" (p. 167). Here, the past is compared to an enraged warrior. Find more examples of personification and other comparisons in the selection. Discuss them with your instructor and your class. To what extent do they increase your enjoyment of the reading?

6. Do you see any irony in the fact that the author was shunned by economically advantaged African Americans in Minneapolis? Why do you think this experience was particularly painful for him to bear?

EXPLORING OTHER SOURCES

In the library and/or on the Internet, find out as much as you can about the life of Gordon Parks. Ask your instructor or the librarian for assistance if you need it. Share what you learn with a small group. If you search the Internet, first go to World Views Online (http://worldviews. wadsworth.com) to find links to information about Gordon Parks.

SYNTHESIS THROUGH WRITING

1. In your journal, respond to one of the following questions:
   a. Were you to look in the mirror as did the author (see p. 166), what questions might you ask yourself? Then, give the answers to your own questions.
   b. Summarize what you feel to be Gordon Parks's philosophy about life based on what you learned from this selection. With what parts of his philosophy do you agree? Disagree?

2. Select one of the questions the author asks himself in the mirror. Reword it as a topic and write an essay about it. If you chose 1a to write about in your journal, you may want to use one of your own questions there to prime your topic. Refer to the writing strategies on page xix. Create your own graphic organizer to help you develop your paper.

Brain's Use of Shortcuts Can Be a Route to Bias [excerpt]

K. C. Cole

Affirmative action programs, which began in the 1960s, gave many members of nondominant groups in the United States the breakthrough they needed to succeed. Colleges and universities made special efforts to have diverse student bodies. Employers recruited both men and women from various ethnic and cultural backgrounds. Unfortunately, in the mid-1990s affirmative action became a political football as its fairness became questioned, predominantly by those who felt society had gone too far in trying to correct the evils of the past. Preference should be based "on merit alone" rather than on a person's membership in a nondominant group was the argument. While it is true that in an ideal society, preference probably would be based on merit alone, our society is generally not considered ideal in this respect. Jobs, promotions, higher salaries, educational advantages, and so forth are still being bestowed upon the members of the dominant group in greater numbers than upon members of nondominant groups, including females of all races and backgrounds.

The article you are about to read was taken from the *Los Angeles Times* for which K. C. Cole is a science writer and columnist.

Before You Read

Have you or has someone you know benefited from affirmative action or some program similar to it? If so, in what ways were there benefits? Discuss the question with a small group or write about it in your journal.

*A*ffirmative action stirs up powerful emotions in both supporters and opponents. But while both sides battle for the hearts of voters, psychologists say the real issues have more to do with the mechanisms of the mind.

Human brains are finely tuned, decision-making machines designed to make quick judgments on a wide variety of confusing events. How far away is that car in the distance? Is that form in the shadows a garbage can or a man with a gun? Is that round red thing a cherry or a marble?

In general, the brain uses past experience to jump to the "most likely" conclusion. Yet these same assumptions can lead people grossly° astray.

"This acceptance by the brain of the most probable answer," writes British perceptual° psychologist Richard Gregory, makes it "difficult, perhaps somewhat impossible, to see very unusual objects."

When "unusual objects" are women and minorities, it may be impossible to see them as qualified for a variety of jobs, psychologists say.

"Even if you have absolutely no prejudice, you are influenced by your expectations," said Diane Halpern, professor of psychology at Cal State San Bernardino. "A small woman of color doesn't look like a corporate executive. If you look at heads of corporations, they are tall, slender, white males. They are not fat. They are not in a wheelchair. They are not too old. Anything that doesn't conform to the expectation is a misfit."

"Similarity is a strong predictor of attraction," said David Kravitz, psychologist at Florida International University. "So there is a natural human tendency to prefer and hire people like you."

A growing number of behavioral studies point to patterns of perception that infuence how people view everything from the moon to minority job candidates. These patterns, experts say, confirm that perception is an active process in which people color the world with their expectations. They do not so much believe what they see as see what they believe.

VOCABULARY

grossly: Here it means totally.
perceptual: Having to do with the way the mind takes things in or perceives them (-cept- refers to seizing something).

The ideal of a society free of prejudice may not be possible, experts say, simply because of the makeup of the human mind. Stereotypes° are not only inevitable, but essential for survival. If people couldn't make lightning-fast decisions on limited information, they would not be able to discriminate between friend or foe, shadow or object, far or near. To a very real extent, people have to judge every book by its cover. And once a judgment is made, virtually° no amount of contrary evidence can turn it around.

People aren't normally aware of the amount of guesswork that goes on in the brain because these perceptual tricks hit upon the right answer the vast majority of the time. Not only do perceptual processes work to ensure survival, they allow people to make music, play baseball, create art. In fact, one of the great puzzles of cognitive° science is how a mind capable of dreaming up the music of Mozart and the equations of quantum mechanics° can make so many egregious° mistakes.

Social psychologists are finding that the occasional errors that the mind makes reveal the hidden rules it uses to make decisions. For example, the brain uses apparent size to judge distance: People don't mistake a car in the distance for a toy because the brain knows through past experience that distant objects appear smaller; therefore the brain compensates,° automatically making it larger.

But when the information is ambiguous,° the brain often leaps to the wrong conclusion. For example, the moon appears to be much larger when it floats just above the horizon than when it shines overhead. The moon doesn't change size, but the brain's estimation of its distance does—in turn automatically changing its apparent size.

VOCABULARY

stereotypes: Judgments formed on the basis of limited knowledge. "If people couldn't make lightning-fast decisions on limited information . . ." is a clue.

virtually: Nearly; almost but not quite.

cognitive: Having to do with how we think (*cogni-* means to learn). ". . . how a mind capable of dreaming up . . ." is a clue.

quantum mechanics: A mathematical theory of how atoms and molecules are structured and how they behave.

egregious: Very, very bad.

compensates: Makes up for (*-pensa-* means to weigh).

ambiguous: Not clear (*ambi-* means around). ". . . the brain often leaps to the wrong conclusion" is a clue.

Brain's Use of Shortcuts Can Be a Route to Bias   **175**

By studying how the mind can fool us, psychologists explore the nature of cognitive weak points. They have found that to a large extent, people see what they expect to see, and reject any information that would challenge their already established point of view. "It's the one thing that everyone agrees on," said psychologist Rachel Hare-Mustin, formerly of Harvard. "Unconscious prevailing° ideologies° are like sand at the picnic. They get into everything."

Errors about everyday objects tend to provide immediate feedback, which makes people unlikely to repeat them. Even a slight mistake in estimating the size of a step can lead to a serious fall.

But errors about other people can more easily slip by unnoticed. "If you're wrong about that car coming at you, it's going to run you down," said psychologist Jennifer Crocker of the State University of New York at Buffalo. "But if you're wrong about whether someone is stupid, you don't hire that person and you never find out how brilliant they are."

The subversive° nature of unconscious thought is revealed by this riddle:

A father and son are enroute to a baseball game when their car stalls on the railroad tracks. The father can't restart the car. An oncoming train hits the car. The father dies. An ambulance rushes the boy to a nearby hospital. In the emergency room, the surgeon takes one look and says: "I can't operate on this child; he's my son."

As cognition researcher Douglas Hofstadter pointed out, even intelligent, broad-minded people go out of their way to invent bizarre scenarios—sometimes involving extraterrestrials°—to solve the riddle. What prevents most people from seeing that the surgeon is the boy's mother is the reliance of the brain on the "default assumption"° that a surgeon is a man.

"A default assumption," Hofstadter explained, "is what holds true in what you might say is the 'simplest' or 'most likely'

VOCABULARY
prevailing: Having the most influence (*pre-* means before; *-vail-* means to be strong).
ideologies: Sets of ideas strongly believed by certain groups or individuals.
subversive: Intended to destroy, ruin, or overthrow (*sub-* means under; *-ver-* means to turn).
extraterrestrials: Beings from outer space.
default assumption: An assumption that is made because no other possibilities are considered
    (*-fault-* here means lack or failure).

case. But the critical thing is that they are made automatically, not as a result of consideration and elimination."

Default assumptions are one of the strategies the brain uses to judge the most likely interpretation of an ambiguous situation. In effect, the brain calculates what psychologists call a "base rate"— the normal frequency of a certain event in a normal population.

Base rates have enormous survival value. A mail carrier who assumes that most pit bulls are dangerous is more likely to escape injury than a more open-minded colleague.

Other peculiarities of social perception have been uncovered in a wide variety of controlled experiments, mostly with college students. For example, subjects judge attractive colleagues as smarter, kinder and happier than their unattractive (but otherwise similar) counterparts.

They judge people perceived to be powerful as taller than less powerful people, even when they are actually the same height. They judge people living in poverty as less intelligent than people in affluent° neighborhoods.

In one experiment, college students watched a short film of a girl taking a math test and getting a numerical grade. When the girl was portrayed in a suburban neighborhood, viewers remembered her score as higher than when she was shown in a ghetto—even though both the girl and the score were the same in both cases.

The brain also grabs for the most readily available image at hand. This automatic response—which psychologists refer to by the tongue-tangling term "availability-mediated° influence"— can be easily manipulated.°

In one frequently cited° series of experiments, three groups of people were introduced to one of two bogus prison guards— one sweet natured and humane, the other sadistic° and brutish. All three groups were later asked to make inferences about "prison guards in general."

The first group was told that whatever guard they met was typical of all prison guards. The second group was told nothing.

VOCABULARY
affluent: Wealthy.
mediated: Brought about an agreement (*media-* here means middle).
manipulated: To control by skill in a shrewd way.
cited: Referred to.
sadistic: Taking pleasure in being cruel. ". . . and brutish" is a clue.

The third group was told that the guard they met was not at all typical; in fact, they were specifically warned that any inferences they made from this one case was likely to be wrong.

Nonetheless, all three groups described "prison guards in general" as either kind or brutish, depending on which guard they met.

The experiment, described in the classic book, "Human Inference" by Lee Ross of Stanford and Richard Nisbett of the University of Michigan, presents what the authors describe as "a humbling picture of human . . . frailty.°" When presented with a single vivid "available" example, the mind tends to bury all other evidence under the carpet of the unconscious.

This reliance on one vivid example sheds light on one of the most painful contradictions of the affirmative action debate. Many white males, studies show, are angry because they are convinced that less qualified women and minorities are taking their jobs. . . .

"So much of the public discourse on this is debate by anecdote,"° said William Bielby, chairman of the sociology department at UC Santa Barbara.[1] "We hear from so many students that they have a white friend from high school who couldn't get into UCSB, but a black kid got in with no problem. And we know how many black kids are on campus. If all those anecdotes were true, then 15% of our students, rather than 3%, would be black."

In the same way, Bielby said, it's easier to hang onto stereotypes in settings where only one or two women, for example, are in management positions. When only one woman occupies the executive suite, she becomes a target for all expectations about women in general. "But when the proportion of women is 40% or 50%," Bielby said, "[their colleagues] can see the extent to which the women differ among themselves and the men differ among themselves."

Psychologist Faye Crosby of Smith College conducted an experiment with a group of Yale undergraduate men that vividly

---

VOCABULARY
frailty: Weakness.
anecdote: The telling of real or imagined experience. The example given in the same paragraph is a clue.

CULTURAL NOTES
[1] UC Santa Barbara refers to the University of California in Santa Barbara.

The Lessons of Illusions

Psychologists use illusions to catch the brain in the act of jumping to conclusions. Most of the time, these perceptual shortcuts work quite well, so we don't notice them. But in unusual situations— such as considering women and minority applicants for jobs traditionally held by white males—the same tricks can lead to egregious mistakes. Many psychologists believe that the unconscious mechanisms people employ to make judgments about other people are very similar to those behind visual illusions.

TRUE MOON

■ **THE ILLUSION:** The moon appears larger when it's low on the horizon than when it's high overhead, even though the moon doesn't change size.

■ **HOW IT WORKS:** When the moon sits low in the sky, the horizon serves as a reference point, making the moon seem unnaturally bigger. (If you view the moon upside down and the horizon becomes the sky—thereby changing the apparent distance—the illusion disappears.)

■ **WHAT IT SHOWS:** That the brain can jump to the wrong conclusions when information is ambiguous. Also, that knowing something is an illusion does not make the illusion go away.

Note: The moon on the right has been made smaller to simulate the illusion.

SHAPE AND FORM

■ **THE ILLUSION:** A white triangle appears to float in front of three black circles, even though no triangle exists.

■ **HOW IT WORKS:** The brain constructs the triangle as the most likely solution to the figure of three pie-shaped wedges. People who don't immediately see it usually find it after someone points it out to them.

■ **WHAT IT SHOWS:** That people can see something that doesn't exist, especially if they go looking for it. Also, that it's much easier to see something familiar.

PARIS, PARIS

PARIS
IN THE
THE SPRING

■ **THE ILLUSION:** A sign appears to read "Paris in the spring," but it actually has an extra "the."

■ **HOW IT WORKS:** Since people do not expect to see a double "the," most do not perceive it.

■ **WHAT IT SHOWS:** That expectation influences what people see.

Source: The Exploratorium, San Francisco Researched by K.C. COLE / Los Angeles Times

Los Angeles Times

VOCABULARY

illusions: False perceptions of reality. ". . . jumping to conclusions. . ." is a clue.
simulate: Imitate (*simul-* means similar).

Brain's Use of Shortcuts Can Be a Route to Bias   **179** showed how inequality becomes imperceptible° on a case-by-case basis. Patterns of discrimination° that are easy to see in a broad context become invisible when seen in individual instances.

Crosby and her colleagues created bogus job descriptions of various men and women at a hypothetical° company. The students were instructed to look for unfairness in the salaries. Unknown to them, the women's salaries were rigged to be 80% of the salaries of comparable men.

When the students compared one man with one woman at a time, they did not see any unfairness. But when they saw all the salaries of all the men and all the women at the same time, they could easily spot the pattern.

Crosby stresses that this inability to see unfairness on a case-by-case basis has nothing to do with sexism or bad attitudes. It has to do with how the mind works. "We're not saying people are stupid. It's just [a normal cognitive process] like optical° illusions."

However one's perceptions are planted, they soon become almost impossible to root out.

In a process psychologists call "belief perseverance,"° people do almost anything to cling to cherished notions. "If we were constantly changing the way we view the world, things would be too confusing," Crocker said. So people tend to discount evidence that contradicts their "schema," or theory about the world. "If you believe lawyers are slimy and you meet some who aren't, you don't revise your schema; you say, oh, that's an exception."

People also routinely change their memories, Halpern said, to fit their beliefs. If you think that successful people have to be aggressive, and you work with a successful person who is not aggressive "you remember that person as more aggressive," Halpern said. "What we remember depends very much on our biases and beliefs."

VOCABULARY

imperceptible: Not able to be perceived (*im-* means not; *-cept-* refers to seizing something). "Patterns . . . become invisible when seen in individual instances" is a clue.
discrimination: Here it means an action based on prejudice (*discrim-* means to divide).
hypothetical: Existing in the mind.
optical: Referring to sight (*optic-* means visible).
perseverance: Holding on to something; steadfast (*-sever-* means serious). ". . . people do almost anything to cling to cherished notions" is a clue.

These self-fulfilling prophecies,° known to psychologists as "behavioral confirmation biases," were dramatically illustrated by a series of experiments in which similar black and white job applicants were questioned by a white intervewer while researchers watched behind a one-way mirror. When the job applicants were black, interviewers sat farther back in their chairs, avoided eye contact, stumbled over their speech and posed fewer questions.

The next part of the test was designed to look at the behavior of the job applicants. This time, the researchers became the interviewers. For consistency; all the applicants were white. With half of the applicants, the researchers intentionally mimicked° the behaviors that the interviewers in the first part of the experiment used on blacks (sitting back, stumbling over words and so on); with the other half, they behaved as the interviewers had with whites—that is, they sat forward in the chairs, maintained eye contact, spoke clearly and asked more questions.

Other researchers watching from behind one-way mirrors evaluated how the applicants seemed to perform during the interview. The result was that the white applicants, when treated as the black applicants had been, were rated less confident, less articulate and less qualified for the job.

What makes these behaviors hard to correct is that they're completely unconscious; the brain jumps to conclusions in less than 100 milliseconds, "the time it takes to recognize your mother," Hofstadter noted.

In study after study, "the most important finding is that [biases] operate unconsciously, even in people who don't want them to," said Anthony G. Greenwald, psychologist at the University of Washington. One of the greatest misconceptions that people have, he said, "is that wanting to be fair is enough to enable you to be fair—not recognizing the unconscious forces that infuence your judgments."

In the end, he says, the best approach to affirmative action may have nothing to do with putting people's hearts in the right place. Instead, it should come from understanding what goes on in the brain.

VOCABULARY

prophecies: Beliefs about the future (*pro-* means before; *-phec-* refers to speaking).
mimicked: Copied or imitated. A *mimic* is an imitator.

"If you understand that your car tends to drive to the left because your wheels are out of line, you correct it," he said. Affirmative action, says Greenwald, is a way to compensate not only for past discrimination, but also for future discrimination "by persons who have no intent to discriminate."

QUESTIONS FOR REFLECTION/DISCUSSION

1. In what ways might women and minorities be perceived as "unusual objects"? Explain.

2. The article quotes Diane Halpern, a professor of psychology, as saying, "Even if you have absolutely no prejudice, you are influenced by your expectations" (p. 174). Is it possible for a human being to have "absolutely no prejudice"? Explain. How does the author react to the possibility of a "society free of prejudice" (p. 175)? Does he think it is possible? Why or why not? Is it desirable? Why or why not?

3. Psychologist David Kravitz said, "Similarity is a strong predictor of attraction, so there is a natural human tendency to prefer and hire people like you" (p. 174). How true do you think his words are? Can you think of examples? Share your reactions and/or examples with a small group.

4. What does the author mean by the words, ". . . people color the world with their expectations. They do not so much believe what they see as see what they believe" (p. 174). Do you agree with this assessment? If so, list some examples of this. Compare your list with that of a partner.

5. Psychologist Anthony Greenwald feels that it is not enough to want to be fair; people also need to understand what happens within the brain in order to make a real contribution to the debate about affirmative action. Do you agree with him? If so, why do you think this is true? What do you think could happen if most people understood how the brain works when it comes to discrimination? Do you think it would be a better world for members of nondominant groups? Explain.

6. Look carefully at the article from a critical standpoint. Is it well organized? Are the conclusions adequately supported by facts, examples, and other details? Do the ideas flow smoothly? Are they presented clearly? In your opinion, what could the author do to improve the article?

EXPLORING OTHER SOURCES

1. Because this article was written for a daily newspaper readership, the author does not give citations for the studies or quotes mentioned in the article. See if you can find, in the library or on the Internet, one or more of the sources to which the author referred. Your instructor or the librarian may be able to help you. Share the source(s) with your class. Discuss what other information you learned from the source(s) that may shed light on discrimination in society in the United States or in societies in general.

2. Find out as much as you can about affirmative action or a similar concept with which you are familiar, including its history, goals, applications, misapplications, and results. Use library resources and/or the Internet. Ask your instructor or the librarian for assistance if you need it. Share what you learn with a small group. You and your class may want to formally or informally debate affirmative action or a similar concept and/or related issues. If your search includes the Internet, go first to http://worldviews.wadsworth.com for links to information on affirmative action.

SYNTHESIS THROUGH WRITING

1. In your journal, express your own opinion(s) about affirmative action or a similar concept with which you are familiar and/or related issues.

2. Write an essay on affirmative action or on a similar concept. Include what you feel to be important from what you learned in the previous activities in Exploring Other Sources. Make sure you express and support your opinion. Create your own graphic organizer. For additional writing strategies, see page xix.

3. Write an essay on a related topic you learned about in your reading in Exploring Other Sources. Refer to the writing strategies on page xix. Create your own graphic organizer to help you develop your paper.

Three Days to See
Helen Keller

Helen Keller was one of the more remarkable authors and lecturers of the early to mid-1900s in America. From before the age of two, she could neither see nor hear.

Helen Keller's breakthrough to success came when her beloved teacher Anne Sullivan Macy helped her "to see and hear." By tapping her fingers gently into the palm of Helen's hand, she began to communicate letters of the alphabet. First, Helen had to realize that the taps into her palm had meaning in that they symbolized letters that could be formed into words. Her first awareness of this came through the association of the taps with common, everyday things. From then on she knew she could have a language and could communicate with those around her. She no longer had to remain in the lonely world of isolation.

Subsequently, Helen Keller received an education and went on to graduate from Radcliffe College with honors. She wrote books and magazine articles with the use of a Braille typewriter and spoke around the world on behalf of the blind until her death in 1968. Helen Keller's life was an example to us all. She taught us that whether we are disabled in some way or not, we can all lead productive lives and can make a contribution to society, provided we are given assistance and the right tools and the confidence to take advantage of them.

Before You Read

Close your eyes and try to imagine what it might be like to be both blind and deaf. How might your having such a disability affect you? How might your disability affect your children, spouse, parents, or guardians? Imagine the difficulties. Talk about them with a partner or write about it in your journal.

All of us have read thrilling stories in which the hero had only a limited and specified time to live. Sometimes it was as long as a year; sometimes as short as twenty-four hours. But always we were interested in discovering just how the doomed man chose to spend his last days or his last hours. I speak, of course, of free men who have a choice, not condemned criminals whose sphere of activities is strictly delimited.°

VOCABULARY
delimited: Given clear boundaries or limits.

Such stories set us thinking, wondering what we should do under similar circumstances. What events, what experiences, what associations should we crowd into those last hours as mortal° beings? What happiness should we find in reviewing the past, what regrets?

Sometimes I have thought it would be an excellent rule to live each day as if we should die tomorrow. Such an attitude would emphasize sharply the values of life. We should live each day with a gentleness, a vigor, and a keenness of appreciation which are often lost when time stretches before us in the constant panorama° of more days and months and years to come. There are those, of course, who would adopt the epicurean° motto of "Eat, drink, and be merry," but most people would be chastened° by the certainty of impending° death.

In stories, the doomed hero is usually saved at the last minute by some stroke of fortune, but almost always his sense of values is changed. He becomes more appreciative of the meaning of life and its permanent spiritual values. It has often been noted that those who live, or have lived, in the shadow of death bring a mellow sweetness to everything they do.

Most of us, however, take life for granted. We know that one day we must die, but usually we picture that day as far in the future. When we are in buoyant° health, death is all but unimaginable. We seldom think of it. The days stretch out in an endless vista. So we go about our petty tasks, hardly aware of our listless attitude toward life.

The same lethargy,° I am afraid, characterizes the use of all our faculties and senses. Only the deaf appreciate hearing, only the blind realize the manifold° blessings that lie in sight. Particularly does this observation apply to those who have lost sight and hearing in adult life. But those who have never suffered impairment° of sight or hearing seldom make the fullest use of these blessed faculties. Their eyes and ears take in all sights and sounds hazily, without concentration, and with

---

VOCABULARY

mortal: Not living forever.
panorama: A wide view.
epicurean: Devoted to pleasure.
chastened: (chăs' nd): Disciplined.
impending: Ready to happen (-pend- refers to hanging). ". . . by the certainty . . ." is a clue.
buoyant: Here it means having the ability to recover quickly.
lethargy: Drowsiness; laziness.
manifold: Many kinds of.
impairment: Something that takes away or lowers the quality of (-pair- here it means worse).

little appreciation. It is the same old story of not being grateful for what we have until we lose it, of not being conscious of health until we are ill.

I have often thought it would be a blessing if each human being were stricken° blind and deaf for a few days at some time during his early adult life. Darkness would make him more appreciative of sight; silence would teach him the joys of sound.

Now and then I have tested my seeing friends to discover what they see. Recently I was visited by a very good friend who had just returned from a long walk in the woods, and I asked her what she had observed. "Nothing in particular," she replied. I might have been incredulous° had I not been accustomed to such responses, for long ago I became convinced that the seeing see little.

How was it possible, I asked myself, to walk for an hour through the woods, and see nothing worthy of note? I who cannot see find hundreds of things to interest me through mere touch. I feel the delicate symmetry° of a leaf. I pass my hand lovingly about the smooth skin of a silver birch, or the rough shaggy bark of a pine. In spring I touch the branches of trees hopefully in search of a bud, the first sign of awakening Nature after her winter's sleep. I feel the delightful, velvety texture of a flower, and discover its remarkable convolutions,° and something of the miracle of Nature is revealed to me. Occasionally, if I am very fortunate, I place my hand gently on a small tree and feel the happy quiver of a bird in full song. I am delighted to have the cool waters of a brook rush through my open fingers. To me a lush carpet of pine needles or spongy grass is more welcome than the most luxurious Persian rug.[1] To me the pageant° of seasons is a thrilling and unending drama, the action of which streams through my finger tips.

At times my heart cries out with longing to see all these things. If I can get so much pleasure from mere touch, how much more beauty must be revealed by sight. Yet, those who have eyes apparently see little. The panorama of color and

---

VOCABULARY

stricken: Struck by something overwhelming.
incredulous: Not believing; skeptical (*in-* means not; *-cred-* means believe).
symmetry: Identical on each side, if divided in half (*sym-* means same; *-metr-* means measure).
convolutions: Here it means folds.
pageant: A public presentation full of drama.

CULTURAL NOTES

[1] A Persian rug is a very ornate rug made in Iran (formerly called Persia).

action which fills the world is taken for granted. It is human, perhaps, to appreciate little that which we have and to long for that which we have not, but it is a great pity that in the world of light the gift of sight is used only as a mere convenience rather than as a means of adding fullness to life.

If I were the president of a university I should establish a compulsory° course in "How to Use Your Eyes." The professor would try to show his pupils how they could add joy to their lives by really seeing what passes unnoticed before them. He would try to awake their dormant° and sluggish faculties.°

Perhaps I can best illustrate by imagining what I should most like to see if I were given the use of my eyes, say, for just three days. And while I am imagining, suppose you, too, set your mind to work on the problem of how you would use your eyes if you had only three more days to see. If with the oncoming darkness of the third night you knew that the sun would never rise for you again, how would you spend those three precious intervening days? What would you most want to let your gaze rest upon?

I, naturally, should want most to see the things which have become dear to me through my years of darkness. You, too, would want to let your eyes rest long on the things that have become dear to you so that you could take the memory of them with you into the night that loomed before you.

If, by some miracle, I were granted three seeing days, to be followed by a relapse° into darkness, I should divide the period into three parts.

The First Day

On the first day, I should want to see the people whose kindness and gentleness and companionship have made my life worth living. First I should like to gaze long upon the face of my dear teacher, Mrs. Anne Sullivan Macy, who came to me when I was a child and opened the outer world to me. I should want not merely to see the outline of her face, so that I could cherish it in my memory, but to study that face and find in it the living evidence of the sympathetic tenderness and patience with which she accomplished the difficult task of my education. I should like

---

VOCABULARY
compulsory: Required.
dormant: Sleeping; not active.
faculties: Here it means abilities.
relapse: Falling back into (*re-* here means back; *-lapse-* means to slide).

to see in her eyes that strength of character which has enabled her to stand firm in the face of difficulties, and that compassion for all humanity which she has revealed to me so often.

I do not know what it is to see into the heart of a friend through that "window of the soul," the eye. I can only "see" through my finger tips the outline of a face, I can detect laughter, sorrow, and many other obvious emotions. I know my friends from the feel of their faces. But I cannot really picture their personalities by touch. I know their personalities, of course, through other means, through the thoughts they express to me, through whatever of their actions are revealed to me. But I am denied that deeper understanding of them which I am sure would come through sight of them, through watching their reactions to various expressed thoughts and circumstances, through noting the immediate and fleeting reactions of their eyes and countenance.°

Friends who are near to me I know well, because through the months and years they reveal themselves to me in all their phases; but of casual friends I have only an incomplete impression, an impression gained from a handclasp, from spoken words which I take from their lips with my finger tips, or which they tap into the palm of my hand.

How much easier, how much more satisfying it is for you who can see to grasp quickly the essential qualities of another person by watching the subtleties° of expression, the quiver of a muscle, the flutter of a hand. But does it ever occur to you to use your sight to see into the inner nature of a friend or acquaintance? Do not most of you seeing people grasp casually the outward features of a face and let it go at that?

For instance, can you describe accurately the faces of five good friends? Some of you can, but many cannot. As an experiment, I have questioned husbands of long standing about the color of their wives' eyes, and often they express embarrassed confusion and admit that they do not know. And, incidentally, it is a chronic° complaint of wives that their husbands do not notice new dresses, new hats, and changes in household arrangements.

VOCABULARY
countenance: Facial expression.
subtleties: Very small changes.
chronic: Recurring over a long time (*chron-* means time).

The eyes of seeing persons soon become accustomed to the routine of their surroundings, and they actually see only the startling and spectacular. But even in viewing the most spectacular sights the eyes are lazy. Court records reveal every day how inaccurately "eyewitnesses" see. A given event will be "seen" in several different ways by as many witnesses. Some see more than others, but few see everything that is within the range of their vision.

Oh, the things that I should see if I had the power of sight for just three days!

The first day would be a busy one. I should call to me all my dear friends and look long into their faces, imprinting upon my mind the outward evidences of the beauty that is within them. I should let my eyes rest, too, on the face of a baby, so that I could catch a vision of the eager, innocent beauty which precedes° the individual's consciousness of the conflicts which life develops.

And I should like to look into the loyal, trusting eyes of my dogs—the grave, canny little Scottie, Darkie, and the stalwart,° understanding great Dane, Helga, whose warm, tender, and playful friendships are so comforting to me.

On that busy first day I should also view the small simple things of my home. I want to see the warm colors in the rugs under my feet, the pictures on the walls, the intimate trifles° that transform a house into home. My eyes would rest respectfully on the books in raised type which I have read, but they would be more eagerly interested in the printed books which seeing people can read, for during the long night of my life the books I have read and those which have been read to me have built themselves into a great shining lighthouse, revealing to me the deepest channels of human life and the human spirit.

In the afternoon of that first seeing day, I should take a long walk in the woods and intoxicate° my eyes on the beauties of the world of Nature, trying desperately to absorb in a few hours the vast splendor which is constantly unfolding itself to those who can see. On the way home from my woodland jaunt° my

---

VOCABULARY

precedes: Goes before (*pre-* means before; *-cede-* means going).
stalwart: Here it means sturdy and strong.
trifles: Little things.
intoxicate: Here it means to excite or stimulate.
jaunt: A short walk for pleasure.

path would lie near a farm so that I might see the patient horses plowing in the field (perhaps I should see only a tractor!) and the serene content of men living close to the soil. And I should pray for the glory of a colorful sunset.

When dusk had fallen, I should experience the double delight of being able to see by artificial light, which the genius of man has created to extend the power of his sight when Nature decrees° darkness.

In the night of that first day of sight, I should not be able to sleep, so full would be my mind of the memories of the day.

The Second Day

The next day—the second day of sight—I should arise with the dawn and see the thrilling miracle by which night is transformed into day. I should behold with awe the magnificent panorama of light with which the sun awakens the sleeping earth.

This day I should devote to a hasty glimpse of the world, past and present. I should want to see the pageant on of man's progress, the kaleidoscope° of the ages. How can so much be compressed into one day? Through the museums, of course. Often I have visited the New York Museum of Natural History to touch with my hands many of the objects there exhibited, but I have longed to see with my eyes the condensed history of the earth and its inhabitants displayed there—animals and the races of men pictured in their native environment; gigantic carcasses of dinosaurs and mastodons° which roamed the earth long before man appeared, with his tiny stature° and powerful brain, to conquer the animal kingdom; realistic presentations of the processes of evolution in animals, in man, and in the implements which man has used to fashion for himself a secure home on this planet; and a thousand and one other aspects of natural history.

I wonder how many readers of this article have viewed this panorama of the face of living things as pictured in that inspiring museum. Many, of course, have not had the opportunity, but I am sure that many who *have* had the opportunity have not made use of it. There, indeed, is a place to

---

VOCABULARY

decrees: Orders officially.
kaleidoscope: Here it means frequently changing colors.
mastodons: Large animals that no longer exist on earth. They resembled elephants.
stature: Height (*sta*- means to stand).

use your eyes. You who see can spend many fruitful days there, but I, with my imaginary three days of sight, could only take a hasty glimpse, and pass on.

My next stop would be the Metropolitan Museum of Art, for just as the Museum of Natural History reveals the material aspects of the world, so does the Metropolitan show the myriad° facets° of the human spirit. Throughout the history of humanity the urge to artistic expression has been almost as powerful as the urge for food, shelter, and procreation°. And here, in the vast chambers of the Metropolitan Museum, is unfolded before me the spirit of Egypt, Greece, and Rome, as expressed in their art. I know well through my hands the sculptured gods and goddesses of the ancient Nile-land. I have felt copies of Parthenon friezes,[2] and I have sensed the rhythmic beauty of charging Athenian warriors.[3] Apollos[4] and Venuses[5] and the Wingèd Victory of Samothrace[6] are friends of my finger tips. The gnarled, bearded features of Homer[7] are dear to me, for he, too, knew blindness.

My hands have lingered upon the living marble of Roman sculpture as well as that of later generations. I have passed my hands over a plaster cast of Michelangelo's[8] inspiring and heroic Moses;[9] I have sensed the power of Rodin;[10] I have been awed by the devoted spirit of Gothic[11] wood carving. These arts which can be touched have meaning for me, but even they were meant to be seen rather than felt, and I can only guess at the beauty which remains hidden from me. I can admire the simple lines of a Greek vase, but its figured decorations are lost to me.

VOCABULARY
myriad: A very large indefinite number.
facets: Sides or aspects.
procreation: Giving birth to offspring.

CULTURAL NOTES
[2]Parthenon friezes are ornamental, richly sculptured bands of marble that decorate the walls of the temple in Athens, Greece.
[3]Athenian warriors were fighting men from Athens, Greece.
[4]Apollo was the Greek god of the sun.
[5]Venus was the Roman goddess of love.
[6]The Wingèd Victory of Samothrace is a statue of the Greek goddess of victory.
[7]Homer was a poet of ancient Greece. He wrote the *Iliad* and the *Odyssey*.
[8]Michelangelo was a famous Italian 16th Century sculptor, painter, poet, and architect.
[9]Moses, the lawgiver described in the Christian Bible, led the Israelites out of Egypt in the 13th Century, B.C.
[10]Rodin (1840–1917) was a French sculptor.
[11]Gothic is a style of architecture popular in the 12th to 15th Century in western Europe. It is characterized by vaulted ceilings and pointed arches.

So on this, my second day of sight, I should try to probe into the soul of man through his art. The things I knew through touch I should now see. More splendid still, the whole magnificent world of painting would be opened to me, from the Italian Primitives, with their serene religious devotion, to the Moderns, with their feverish visions. I should look deep into the canvases of Raphael, Leonardo da Vinci, Titian, Rembrandt. I should want to feast my eyes upon the warm colors of Veronese, study the mysteries of El Greco, catch a new vision of Nature from Corot.[12] Oh, there is so much rich meaning and beauty in the art of the ages for you who have eyes to see!

Upon my short visit to this temple of art I should not be able to review a fraction of that great world of art which is open to you. I should be able to get only a superficial impression. Artists tell me that for a deep and true appreciation of art one must educate the eye. One must learn through experience to weigh the merits of line, of composition, of form and color. If I had eyes, how happily would I embark upon so fascinating a study! Yet I am told that, to many of you who have eyes to see, the world of art is a dark night, unexplored and unilluminated.°

It would be with extreme reluctance that I should leave the Metropolitan Museum, which contains the key to beauty—a beauty so neglected. Seeing persons, however, do not need a Metropolitan to find this key to beauty. The same key lies waiting in smaller museums, and in books on the shelves of even small libraries. But naturally, in my limited time of imaginary sight, I should choose the place where the key unlocks the greatest treasures in the shortest time.

The evening of my second day of sight I should spend at a theater or at the movies. Even now I often attend theatrical performances of all sorts, but the action of the play must be spelled into my hand by a companion. But how I should like to see with my own eyes the fascinating figure of Hamlet,[13] or the gusty Falstaff[14] amid colorful Elizabethan trappings![15] How I

VOCABULARY

unilluminated: Not lit up or highlighted (*un-* means not; *-luminat-* means light). ". . . a dark night, unexplored . . ." is a clue.

CULTURAL NOTES

[12]Raphael, Leonardo da Vinci, Titian, Rembrandt, Veronese, El Greco, and Corot are all famous artists.
[13]Hamlet is the main character in Shakespeare's tragedy with that name.
[14]Falstaff is one of Shakespeare's comic characters. See especially *Henry IV*.
[15]Elizabethan trappings are things typical of the times in Shakespeare's England when Elizabeth I was the queen.

should like to follow each movement of the graceful Hamlet, each strut° of the hearty Falstaff! And since I could see only one play, I should be confronted by a many-horned dilemma, for there are scores of plays I should want to see. You who have eyes can see any you like. How many of you, I wonder, when you gaze at a play, a movie, or any spectacle, realize and give thanks for the miracle of sight which enables you to enjoy its color, grace, and movement?

I cannot enjoy the beauty of rhythmic movement except in a sphere restricted to the touch of my hands. I can vision only dimly the grace of a Pavlova,[16] although I know something of the delight of rhythm, for often I can sense the beat of music as it vibrates through the floor. I can well imagine that cadenced° motion must be one of the most pleasing sights in the world. I have been able to gather something of this by tracing with my fingers the lines in sculptured marble; if this static grace can be so lovely, how much more acute must be the thrill of seeing grace in motion.

One of my dearest memories is of the time when Joseph Jefferson[17] allowed me to touch his face and hands as he went through some of the gestures and speeches of his beloved Rip Van Winkle.[18] I was able to catch thus a meager° glimpse of the world of drama, and I shall never forget the delight of that moment. But, oh, how much I must miss, and how much pleasure you seeing ones can derive from watching and hearing the interplay of speech and movement, in the unfolding of a dramatic performance! If I could see only one play, I should know how to picture in my mind the action of a hundred plays which I have read or had transferred to me through the medium of the manual° alphabet.

So, through the evening of my second imaginary day of sight, the great figures of dramatic literature would crowd sleep from my eyes.

VOCABULARY
strut: A stiff walk that shows self-importance.
cadenced: Having rhythm or a beat. ". . . often I can sense the beat of music as it vibrates through the floor" is a clue.
meager: Very small.
manual: Using the hand (*man-* refers to hand).

CULTURAL NOTES
[16]Pavlova refers to Anna Pavlova, a famous Russian dancer who lived from 1885 to 1931.
[17]Joseph Jefferson was an American actor who lived from 1829 to 1905.
[18]Rip van Winkle is the main character in a story by American writer Washington Irving. The character fell asleep for many years and woke up to discover a changed world.

The Third Day

The following morning, I should again greet the dawn, anxious to discover new delights, for I am sure that, for those who have eyes which really see, the dawn of each day must be a perpetually° new revelation° of beauty.

This, according to the terms of my imagined miracle, is to be my third and last day of light. I shall have no time to waste in regrets or longings; there is too much to see. The first day I devoted to my friends, animate° and inanimate. The second revealed to me the history of man and Nature. Today I shall spend in the workaday world of the present, amid the haunts of men going about the business of life. And where can one find so many activities and conditions of men as in New York? So the city becomes my destination.

I start from my home in the quiet little suburb of Forest Hills, Long Island. Here, surrounded by green lawns, trees, and flowers, are neat little houses, happy with the voices and movements of wives and children, havens° of peaceful rest for men who toil° in the city. I drive across the lacy structure of steel which spans the East River, and I get a new and startling vision of the power and ingenuity° of the mind of man. Busy boats chug and scurry about the river—racy speedboats, stolid,° snorting tugs. If I had long days of sight ahead, I should spend many of them watching the delightful activity upon the river.

I look ahead, and before me rise the fantastic towers of New York, a city that seems to have stepped from the pages of a fairy story. What an awe-inspiring sight, these glittering spires, these vast banks of stone and steel—structures such as the gods might build for themselves! This animated picture is a part of the lives of millions of people every day. How many, I wonder, give it so much as a second glance? Very few, I fear. Their eyes are blind to this magnificent sight because it is so familiar to them.

VOCABULARY

perpetually: Always, or continually.
revelation: Something revealed or made known.
animate: Here it means alive; filled with life or enthusiasm.
havens: Places where one can be safe for a while.
toil: Work.
ingenuity: Cleverness.
stolid: Not being affected by anything.

I hurry to the top of one of those gigantic structures, the Empire State Building, for there, a short time ago, I "saw" the city below through the eyes of my secretary. I am anxious to compare my fancy with reality. I am sure I should not be disappointed in the panorama spread out before me, for to me it would be a vision of another world.

Now I begin my rounds of the city. First, I stand at a busy corner, merely looking at people, trying by sight of them to understand something of their lives. I see smiles, and I am happy. I see serious determination, and I am proud. I see suffering, and I am compassionate.

I stroll down Fifth Avenue. I throw my eyes out of focus so that I see no particular object but only a seething° kaleidoscope of color. I am certain that the colors of women's dresses moving in a throng° must be a gorgeous spectacle of which I should never tire. But perhaps if I had sight I should be like most other women—too interested in styles and the cut of individual dresses to give much attention to the splendor° of color in the mass. And I am convinced, too, that I should become an inveterate° window shopper, for it must be a delight to the eye to view the myriad articles of beauty on display.

From Fifth Avenue I make a tour of the city—to Park Avenue, to the slums, to factories, to parks where children play. I take a stay-at-home trip abroad by visiting the foreign quarters. Always my eyes are open wide to all the sights of both happiness and misery so that I may probe deep and add to my understanding of how people work and live. My heart is full of the images of people and things. My eye passes lightly over no single trifle; it strives to touch and hold closely each thing its gaze rests upon. Some sights are pleasant, filling the heart with happiness; but some are miserably pathetic. To these latter I do not shut my eyes, for they, too, are part of life. To close the eye on them is to close the heart and mind.

My third day of sight is drawing to an end. Perhaps there are many serious pursuits to which I should devote the few remaining hours, but I am afraid that on the evening of that last

---

VOCABULARY
seething: To churn as though being boiled.
throng: A crowd.
splendor: A grand display.
inveterate: Never stopping; constant; habitual.

Three Days to See   195

day I should again run away to the theater, to a hilariously funny play, so that I might appreciate the overtones of comedy in the human spirit.

At midnight my temporary respite° from blindness would cease, and permanent night would close in on me again. Naturally in those three short days I should not have seen all I wanted to see. Only when darkness had again descended upon me should I realize how much I had left unseen. But my mind would be so crowded with glorious memories that I should have little time for regrets. Thereafter the touch of every object would bring a glowing memory of how that object looked.

Perhaps this short outline of how I should spend three days of sight does not agree with the program you would set for yourself if you knew that you were about to be stricken blind. I am, however, sure that if you actually faced that fate, your eyes would open to things you had never seen before, storing up memories for the long night ahead. You would use your eyes as never before. Everything you saw would become dear to you. Your eyes would touch and embrace every object that came within your range of vision. Then, at last, you would really see, and a new world of beauty would open itself before you.

I who am blind can give one hint to those who see—one admonition° to those who would make full use of the gift of sight: Use your eyes as if tomorrow you would be stricken blind. And the same method can be applied to the other senses. Hear the music of voices, the song of a bird, the mighty strains of an orchestra, as if you would be stricken deaf tomorrow. Touch each object you want to touch as if tomorrow your tactile° sense would fail. Smell the perfume of flowers, taste with relish° each morsel,° as if tomorrow you could never smell and taste again. Make the most of every sense; glory in all the facets of pleasure and beauty which the world reveals to you through the several means of contact which Nature provides. But of all the senses, I am sure that sight must be the most delightful.

VOCABULARY
respite: Relief or rest.
admonition: Warning.
tactile: Relating to the sense of touch (*tact-* means touch).
relish: Full appreciation.
morsel: Small piece.

QUESTIONS FOR REFLECTION/DISCUSSION

1. Helen Keller feels that most of us take life for granted and don't appreciate each moment as we should. To what extent do you think this is true? Discuss this question with a partner. Summarize your discussion in your journal.

2. How do you think a language system in which taps were made into the palm of a hand would work? What might the problems be with such a system? Can you think of a better system her teacher might have used? Discuss this question with your class and the instructor.

3. React to the quote, "It is human, perhaps, to appreciate little that which we have and to long for that which we have not, but it is a great pity that in the world of light the gift of sight is used only as a mere convenience rather than as a means of adding fullness to life." With a partner, list some examples of a lack of appreciation for what we have and a longing for what we do not have. Talk about how we can use sight to add fullness to our lives.

4. If you were the president of your local university or college and could add any course you wanted to the curriculum, what would it be? How might such a course be beneficial? Discuss these questions with a small group. Share your ideas with the class.

5. If you could have spent one of Helen Keller's three days with her, which day of sight would you have chosen? What was there about that day that you especially liked?

EXPLORING OTHER SOURCES

1. Choose a few of the pieces of art that she mentions and find out as much as you can about them in your library and/or on the Internet. Learn about their artists. Why do you think she would like these pieces of art? See if you can find pictures of them. Ask your instructor or the librarian for help, if you need it. Share the information you have found and the pictures (if you can bring them to class) with a small group. If your search includes sources on the Internet, go to World Views Online (http://worldviews.wadsworth.com) for links to the information you seek.

2. Find information about being blind in the modern world. What medical advances have been developed to help the blind? Are there recent inventions or new laws you know of that have made the lives of the blind a little bit easier? What organizations can the blind turn to

for help when they need it? What kinds of help can the blind expect to receive? Use library resources and/or the Internet. Your instructor or the librarian may be able to assist you in your search. If you are using the Internet, go to http://worldviews.wadsworth.com for links to information about the blind.

Synthesis Through Writing

1. In your journal, write about what you learned from Helen Keller's life that might help you make your own life fuller.

2. Imagine that you are blind and have only three days to see. What things would you want to see? Describe each day in your own personal essay. Use Helen Keller's essay as a guide. Refer to the writing strategies on page xix.

3. Write an essay on one of the topics you researched in the previous activity in Exploring Other Sources. See the writing strategies on page xix if necessary. Create your own graphic organizer to help you develop your paper.

MAKING CONNECTIONS: IDEAS FOR DISCUSSION AND/OR COMPOSITION

1. Several of the selections in this unit have had to do with overcoming the effects of prejudice. Using prejudice as a topic, draw examples from several of the selections to support your point of view.

2. Think again about the poem on page 134. How does it relate to several of the selections in the unit?

3. Interview one or two people you know who have experienced breakthroughs to success of one kind or another. Compare their experiences with some of the people to whom you were introduced in this unit. In addition, you may want to take a look at the sample interview and the "Guide to Interviewing" on the Internet at http://worldviews.wadsworth.com.

4. Use the Internet to find additional information about the authors and/or topics in this unit that you find of particular interest. First check out World Views Online. Go to the site mentioned in item 3 for the information you seek.

READING FOR ENRICHMENT

Isamu Noguchi: The Life of a Sculptor
by Toby Tobias
Crowell, 1974

The success story of a Japanese youth who comes to America and overcomes many obstacles to achieve fame as an artist.

Making Waves: An Anthology of Writings By and About Asian-American Women
edited by Asian Women United of California
Beacon, 1989

The stories of immigrant women from various countries in Asia. They tell about their families and their struggles as they try to make their lives better in the United States. "The Loom" on page 137 comes from this collection.

Martin Luther King, Jr., and the March Toward Freedom
by Rita Hakim
Millbrook Press, 1991

The courage and inner strength of this man enabled him to advocate nonviolence and, at the same time, to rise above his circumstances and become a great African-American leader who led the fight against segregation.

Pathblazers: Eight People Who Made a Difference
by M. K. Fullen
Open Hand Publishing, 1992

The true stories of eight famous African Americans who worked hard to defeat racism and to achieve greatness.

The Pride of Puerto Rico—The Life of Roberto Clemente
by Paul Robert Walker
Harcourt Brace Jovanovich, 1988

Roberto Clemente had to fight against both oppression and poverty to become the first Latin American to gain election to the Baseball Hall of Fame.

Philadelphia
by Christopher Davis
Screenplay by Ron Nyswaner
Bantam Books, 1993

Andrew Beckett, a gay lawyer, tries to save his reputation and his life while battling AIDS and the law firm that has just fired him.

We were Black Americans in West Africa, where for the first time in our lives, the color of our skin was accepted as correct and normal.

—Maya Angelou
from "All God's Children Need
Traveling Shoes"

"The place has a reputation—a bad one." "Cannibals?" suggested Rainsford. "Hardly. Even cannibals wouldn't live in such a God-forsaken place."

—Richard Connell
from "A Most Dangerous Game"

"I tell you it wasn't fair. You didn't give him time enough to choose. Everybody saw that."

—Shirley Jackson
from "The Lottery"

*"How would you have us, as we are?
Or sinking 'neath the load we bear,
Our eyes fixed forward on a star,
Or gazing empty at despair?"*

—Weldon Johnson
from "To America," 1933

Unit 4

ILLUSION VERSUS REALITY

Introduction

Most of us as children tended to believe what our eyes and ears told us. We seldom looked below the surface of what we saw or heard. Most of us were too young to question tradition or the actions we witnessed. Often it was not until we grew older that we began to realize that not all things were as they appeared. At that time we may have become disillusioned or disappointed about what was revealed to us. Perhaps a person we thought we knew well did something to show us another, darker side. Or maybe it was an action by a group we once admired that left us wondering about our earlier impressions. Both had appealing veneers, but under the surface something else was lurking.

An Overview

In this unit, you will discover much about the civilization beneath the veneer. The first selection, a classic entitled "The Lottery" by Shirley Jackson, introduces us to a community involved in a traditional act that they can't seem to shake off or change in any major way. Next, we are introduced to General Zaroff of "The Most Dangerous Game" by Richard Connell. We will soon see that he plays a game like no other, to the horror of his unsuspecting guests. Then comes an excerpt from Maya Angelou's *All God's Children Need Traveling Shoes,* in which strangers care enough about Maya Angelou to tell her a truth she doesn't want to hear. Next is Robert Tallman's drama "The Man Who Liked Dickens," written for television and based on the famous story of the same name written by Evelyn Waugh. In this story we explore the character of a man who has created a rather ideal world for himself deep in the Amazon jungle—but at whose expense? And last is an excerpt from Frederick Douglass's "An American Slave," which awakens us to several of the common practices of slavery in the United States before the Civil War, fought between the northern states and the southern states in the 1860s.

Thinking Critically About the Theme

The quotes beginning this unit come from the selections you will be reading. Think about the quotes in relation to the Unit 4 theme, Illusion Versus Reality. Choose one or two to write about in your journal. Predict what might happen in the selection, based on the quote you chose and on the overview you just read.

Now look back at the words from the poem by Weldon Johnson. How do they relate to the theme? Write your response in your journal. Do you like the words? Why or why not?

The Lottery

Shirley Jackson

When we read, it is important for us to pay very close attention to the details and, in a sense, to read between the lines. Perhaps there was a time when the story we were reading led to something much different from what we anticipated. Later, when we looked back at the story, we realized that we should have been more aware of the details and maybe the tone or mood that was being established. But reading carefully doesn't always lead us to the right conclusion. The author may have purposely misled us for effect.

Shirley Jackson, in her short story "The Lottery," presents an experience you will probably never forget, so vivid is it. It first appeared in 1948 in *The New Yorker* magazine. Even today, people are still fascinated by its artistic qualities as well as by its haunting message.

Before You Read

Think about a time when you may have been misled by an event or by people in your own life. Or think about a time when you were misled by something you read. Write about the experience in your journal.

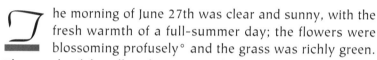

he morning of June 27th was clear and sunny, with the fresh warmth of a full-summer day; the flowers were blossoming profusely° and the grass was richly green. The people of the village began to gather in the square, between the post office and the bank, around ten o'clock; in some towns there were so many people that the lottery took two days and had to be started on June 26th, but in this village, where there were only about three hundred people, the whole lottery took less than two hours, so it could begin at ten o'clock in the morning and still be through in time to allow the villagers to get home for noon dinner.

The children assembled° first, of course. School was recently over for the summer, and the feeling of liberty sat uneasily on most of them; they tended to gather together quietly for a while before they broke into boisterous° play, and their talk was still of the classroom and the teacher, of books and reprimands.°

VOCABULARY

profusely: Abundantly; freely giving or producing much (*pro-* here means forth; *-fuse-* refers to pouring out).
assembled: Came together. The next sentence in the text is a clue.
boisterous: Very loud and noisy; without restraint.
reprimands: Strong expressions of disapproval.

Bobby Martin had already stuffed his pockets full of stones, and the other boys soon followed his example, selecting the smoothest and roundest stones; Bobby and Harry Jones and Dickie Delacroix—the villagers pronounced this name "Dellacroy"—eventually made a great pile of stones in one corner of the square and guarded it against the raids of the other boys. The girls stood aside, talking among themselves, looking over their shoulders at the boys, and the very small children rolled in the dust or clung to the hands of their older brothers or sisters.

Soon the men began to gather, surveying their own children, speaking of planting and rain, tractors and taxes. They stood together, away from the pile of stones in the corner, and their jokes were quiet and they smiled rather than laughed. The women, wearing faded house dresses and sweaters, came shortly after their menfolk. They greeted one another and exchanged bits of gossip as they went to join their husbands. Soon the women, standing by their husbands, began to call to their children, and the children came reluctantly, having to be called four or five times. Bobby Martin ducked under his mother's grasping hand and ran, laughing, back to the pile of stones. His father spoke up sharply, and Bobby came quickly and took his place between his father and his oldest brother.

The lottery was conducted—as were the square dances, the teenage club, the Halloween program—by Mr. Summers, who had time and energy to devote to civic activities. He was a round-faced, jovial° man and he ran the coal business, and people were sorry for him, because he had no children and his wife was a scold.° When he arrived in the square, carrying the black wooden box, there was a murmur of conversation among the villagers, and he waved and called, "Little late today, folks." The postmaster, Mr. Graves, followed him, carrying a three-legged stool, and the stool was put in the center of the square and Mr. Summers set the black box down on it. The villagers kept their distance, leaving a space between themselves and the stool, and when Mr. Summers said, "Some of you fellows want to give me a hand?" there was a hesitation before two men,

---

VOCABULARY
jovial: Very cheeful in manner (jov- means to shine).
scold: A person who scolds or reprimands others.

Mr. Martin and his oldest son, Baxter, came forward to hold the box steady on the stool while Mr. Summers stirred up the papers inside it.

The original paraphernalia° for the lottery had been lost long ago, and the black box now resting on the stool had been put into use even before Old Man Warner, the oldest man in town, was born. Mr. Summers spoke frequently to the villagers about making a new box, but no one liked to upset even as much tradition as was represented by the black box. There was a story that the present box had been made with some pieces of the box that had preceded it, the one that had been constructed when the first people settled down to make a village here. Every year, after the lottery, Mr. Summers began talking again about a new box, but every year the subject was allowed to fade off without anything's being done. The black box grew shabbier each year; by now it was no longer completely black but splintered badly along one side to show the original wood color, and in some places faded or stained.

Mr. Martin and his oldest son, Baxter, held the black box securely on the stool until Mr. Summers had stirred the papers thoroughly with his hand. Because so much of the ritual had been forgotten or discarded, Mr. Summers had been successful in having slips of paper substituted for the chips of wood that had been used for generations. Chips of wood, Mr. Summers had argued, had been all very well when the village was tiny, but now that the population was more than three hundred and likely to keep on growing, it was necessary to use something that would fit more easily into the black box. The night before the lottery, Mr. Summers and Mr. Graves made up the slips of paper and put them in the box, and it was then taken to the safe of Mr. Summers' coal company and locked up until Mr. Summers was ready to take it to the square next morning. The rest of the year, the box was put away, sometimes one place, sometimes another; it had spent one year in Mr. Graves's barn and another year underfoot in the post office, and sometimes it was set on a shelf in the Martin grocery and left there.

There was a great deal of fussing to be done before Mr. Summers declared the lottery open. There were the lists to make

---

VOCABULARY
paraphernalia: The items used.

up—of heads of families, heads of households in each family, members of each household in each family. There was the proper swearing-in of Mr. Summers by the postmaster, as the official of the lottery; at one time, some people remembered, there had been a recital of some sort, performed by the official of the lottery, a perfunctory,° tuneless chant that had been rattled off duly° each year; some people believed that the official of the lottery used to stand just so when he said or sang it, others believed that he was supposed to walk among the people, but years and years ago this part of the ritual had been allowed to lapse. There had been, also, a ritual salute, which the official of the lottery had had to use in addressing each person who came up to draw from the box, but this also had changed with time, until now it was felt necessary only for the official to speak to each person approaching. Mr. Summers was very good at all this; in his clean white shirt and blue jeans, with one hand resting carelessly on the black box, he seemed very proper and important as he talked interminably° to Mr. Graves and the Martins.

Just as Mr. Summers finally left off talking and turned to the assembled villagers, Mrs. Hutchinson came hurriedly along the path to the square, her sweater thrown over her shoulders, and slid into place in the back of the crowd. "Clean forgot what day it was," she said to Mrs. Delacroix, who stood next to her, and they both laughed softly. "Thought my old man was out back stacking wood," Mrs. Hutchinson went on, "and then I looked out the window and the kids was gone, and then I remembered it was the twenty-seventh and came a-running." She dried her hands on her apron, and Mrs. Delacroix said, "You're in time, though. They're still talking away up there."

Mrs. Hutchinson craned° her neck to see through the crowd and found her husband and children standing near the front. She tapped Mrs. Delacroix on the arm as a farewell and began to make her way through the crowd. The people separated good-humoredly to let her through; two or three people said, in

---

VOCABULARY

perfunctory: Here it means usual or routine (-*func*- means performing). ". . . chant that had been rattled off duly each year" is a clue.

duly: In the proper way.

interminably: In a neverending way; constantly.

craned: Stretched [the neck] to see better. ". . . to see through the crowd . . ." is a clue.

voices just loud enough to be heard across the crowd, "Here comes your Missus, Hutchinson," and "Bill, she made it after all." Mrs. Hutchinson reached her husband, and Mr. Summers, who had been waiting, said cheerfully, "Thought we were going to have to get on without you, Tessie." Mrs. Hutchinson said, grinning, "Wouldn't have me leave m'dishes in the sink, now, would you, Joe?" and soft laughter ran through the crowd as the people stirred back into position after Mrs. Hutchinson's arrival.

"Well, now," Mr. Summers said soberly, "guess we better get started, get this over with, so's we can go back to work. Anybody ain't here?"

"Dunbar," several people said. "Dunbar, Dunbar."

Mr. Summers consulted his list. "Clyde Dunbar," he said. "That's right. He's broke his leg, hasn't he? Who's drawing for him?"

"Me, I guess," a woman said, and Mr. Summers turned to look at her. "Wife draws for her husband," Mr. Summers said. "Don't you have a grown boy to do it for you, Janey?" Although Mr. Summers and everyone else in the village knew the answer perfectly well, it was the business of the official of the lottery to ask such questions formally. Mr. Summers waited with an expression of polite interest while Mrs. Dunbar answered.

"Horace's not but sixteen yet," Mrs. Dunbar said regretfully. "Guess I gotta fill in for the old man this year."

"Right," Mr. Summers said. He made a note on the list he was holding. Then he asked, "Watson boy drawing this year?"

A tall boy in the crowd raised his hand. "Here," he said. "I'm drawing for m'mother and me." He blinked his eyes nervously and ducked his head as several voices in the crowd said things like "Good fellow, Jack," and "Glad to see your mother's got a man to do it."

"Well," Mr. Summers said, "guess that's everyone. Old Man Warner make it?"

"Here," a voice said, and Mr. Summers nodded.

A sudden hush fell on the crowd as Mr. Summers cleared his throat and looked at the list. "All ready?" he called. "Now, I'll read the names—heads of families first—and the men come up and take a paper out of the box. Keep the paper folded in your hand without looking at it until everyone has had a turn. Everything clear?"

The people had done it so many times that they only half listened to the directions; most of them were quiet, wetting their lips, not looking around. Then Mr. Summers raised one hand high and said, "Adams." A man disengaged himself from the crowd and came forward. "Hi, Steve," Mr. Summers said, and Mr. Adams said, "Hi, Joe." They grinned at one another humorlessly and nervously. Then Mr. Adams reached into the black box and took out a folded paper. He held it firmly by one corner as he turned and went hastily back to his place in the crowd, where he stood a little apart from his family, not looking down at his hand.

"Allen," Mr. Summers said. "Anderson. . . . Bentham."

"Seems like there's no time at all between lotteries any more," Mrs. Delacroix said to Mrs. Graves in the back row. "Seems like we got through with the last one only last week."

"Time sure goes fast," Mrs. Graves said.

"Clark. . . . Delacroix."

"There goes my old man," Mrs. Delacroix said. She held her breath while her husband went forward.

"Dunbar," Mr. Summers said, and Mrs. Dunbar went steadily to the box while one of the women said, "Go on, Janey," and another said, "There she goes."

"We're next," Mrs. Graves said. She watched while Mr. Graves came around from the side of the box, greeted Mr. Summers gravely, and selected a slip of paper from the box. By now, all through the crowd there were men holding the small folded papers in their large hands, turning them over and over nervously. Mrs. Dunbar and her two sons stood together, Mrs. Dunbar holding the slip of paper.

"Harburt. . . . Hutchinson."

"Get up there, Bill," Mrs. Hutchinson said, and the people near her laughed.

"Jones."

"They do say," Mr. Adams said to Old Man Warner, who stood next to him, "that over in the north village they're talking of giving up the lottery."

Old Man Warner snorted. "Pack of crazy fools," he said. "Listening to the young folks, nothing's good enough for *them*. Next thing you know, they'll be wanting to go back to living in caves, nobody work any more, live *that* way for a while. Used to be a saying about 'Lottery in June, corn be heavy soon.' First thing you know, we'd all be eating stewed chickweed and

acorns. There's *always* been a lottery," he added petulantly.°
"Bad enough to see young Joe Summers up there joking with
everybody."

"Some places have already quit lotteries," Mrs. Adams said.

"Nothing but trouble in *that*," Old Man Warner said stoutly.°
"Pack of young fools."

"Martin." And Bobby Martin watched his father go forward.
"Overdyke. . . . Percy."

"I wish they'd hurry," Mrs. Dunbar said to her older son. "I
wish they'd hurry."

"They're almost through," her son said.

"You get ready to run tell Dad," Mrs. Dunbar said.

Mr. Summers called his own name and then stepped forward
precisely and selected a slip from the box. Then he called,
"Warner."

"Seventy-seventh year I been in the lottery," Old Man Warner
said as he went through the crowd. "Seventy-seventh time."

"Watson." The tall boy came awkwardly through the crowd.
Someone said, "Don't be nervous, Jack," and Mr. Summers said,
"Take your time, son."

"Zanani."

After that, there was a long pause, a breathless pause, until
Mr. Summers, holding his slip of paper in the air, said, "All
right, fellows." For a minute, no one moved, and then all the
slips of paper were opened. Suddenly, all the women began to
speak at once, saying, "Who is it?," "Who's got it?," "Is it the
Dunbars?," "Is it the Watsons?" Then the voices began to say,
"It's Hutchinson. It's Bill," "Bill Hutchinson's got it."

"Go tell your father," Mrs. Dunbar said to her older son.

People began to look around to see the Hutchinsons. Bill
Hutchinson was standing quiet, staring down at the paper in his
hand. Suddenly, Tessie Hutchinson shouted to Mr. Summers,
"You didn't give him time enough to take any paper he wanted.
I saw you. It wasn't fair."

"Be a good sport, Tessie," Mrs. Delacroix called, and Mrs.
Graves said, "All of us took the same chance."

"Shut up, Tessie," Bill Hutchinson said.

VOCABULARY

petulantly: In a very irritated manner.
stoutly: Here it means firmly.

"Well, everyone," Mr. Summers said, "that was done pretty fast, and now we've got to be hurrying a little more to get done in time." He consulted his next list. "Bill," he said, "you draw for the Hutchinson family. You got any other households in the Hutchinsons?"

"There's Don and Eva," Mrs. Hutchinson yelled. "Make *them* take their chance!"

"Daughters draw with their husbands' families, Tessie," Mr. Summers said gently. "You know that as well as anyone else."

"It wasn't *fair*," Tessie said.

"I guess not, Joe," Bill Hutchinson said regretfully. "My daughter draws with her husband's family, that's only fair. And I've got no other family except the kids."

"Then, as far as drawing for families is concerned, it's you," Mr. Summers said in explanation, "and as far as drawing for households is concerned, that's you, too. Right?"

"Right," Bill Hutchinson said.

"How many kids, Bill?" Mr. Summers asked formally.

"Three," Bill Hutchinson said. "There's Bill, Jr., and Nancy, and little Dave. And Tessie and me."

"All right, then," Mr. Summers said. "Harry, you got their tickets back?"

Mr. Graves nodded and held up the slips of paper. "Put them in the box, then," Mr. Summers directed. "Take Bill's and put it in."

"I think we ought to start over," Mrs. Hutchinson said, as quietly as she could. "I tell you it wasn't *fair*. You didn't give him time enough to choose. *Every*body saw that."

Mr. Graves had selected the five slips and put them in the box, and he dropped all the papers but those onto the ground, where the breeze caught them and lifted them off.

"Listen, everybody," Mrs. Hutchinson was saying to the people around her.

"Ready, Bill?" Mr. Summers asked, and Bill Hutchinson, with one quick glance around at his wife and children, nodded.

"Remember," Mr. Summers said, "take the slips and keep them folded until each person has taken one. Harry, you help little Dave." Mr. Graves took the hand of the little boy, who came willingly with him up to the box. "Take a paper out of the box, Davy," Mr. Summers said. Davy put his hand into the box and laughed. "Take just *one* paper," Mr. Summers said. "Harry, you hold it for him." Mr. Graves took the child's hand and removed the folded paper from the tight fist and held it while little Dave stood next to him and looked up at him wonderingly.

"Nancy next," Mr. Summers said. Nancy was twelve, and her school friends breathed heavily as she went forward, switching her skirt, and took a slip daintily from the box. "Bill, Jr.," Mr. Summers said, and Billy, his face red and his feet over-large, nearly knocked the box over as he got a paper out. "Tessie," Mr. Summers said. She hesitated for a minute, looking around defiantly, and then set her lips and went up to the box. She snatched a paper and held it behind her.

"Bill," Mr. Summers said, and Bill Hutchinson reached into the box and felt around, bringing his hand out at last with the slip of paper in it.

The crowd was quiet. A girl whispered, "I hope it's not Nancy," and the sound of the whisper reached the edges of the crowd.

"It's not the way it used to be," Old Man Warner said clearly. "People ain't the way they used to be."

"All right," Mr. Summers said. "Open the papers. Harry, you open little Dave's."

Mr. Graves opened the slip of paper and there was a general sigh through the crowd as he held it up and everyone could see that it was blank. Nancy and Bill, Jr., opened theirs at the same time, and both beamed and laughed, turning around to the crowd and holding their slips of paper above their heads.

"Tessie," Mr. Summers said. There was a pause, and then Mr. Summers looked at Bill Hutchinson, and Bill unfolded his paper and showed it. It was blank.

"It's Tessie," Mr. Summers said, and his voice was hushed. "Show us her paper, Bill."

Bill Hutchinson went over to his wife and forced the slip of paper out of her hand. It had a black spot on it, the black spot Mr. Summers had made the night before with the heavy pencil in the coal-company office. Bill Hutchinson held it up, and there was a stir in the crowd.

"All right, folks," Mr. Summers said. "Let's finish quickly."

Although the villagers had forgotten the ritual and lost the original black box, they still remembered to use stones. The pile of stones the boys had made earlier was ready; there were stones on the ground with the blowing scraps of paper that had come out of the box. Mrs. Delacroix selected a stone so large she had to pick it up with both hands and turned to Mrs. Dunbar. "Come on," she said. "Hurry up."

Mrs. Dunbar had small stones in both hands, and she said, gasping for breath, "I can't run at all. You'll have to go ahead and I'll catch up with you."

The children had stones already, and someone gave little Davy Hutchinson a few pebbles.

Tessie Hutchinson was in the center of a cleared space by now, and she held her hands out desperately as the villagers moved in on her. "It isn't fair," she said. A stone hit her on the side of the head.

Old Man Warner was saying, "Come on, come on, everyone." Steve Adams was in the front of the crowd of villagers, with Mrs. Graves beside him.

"It isn't fair, it isn't right," Mrs. Hutchinson screamed, and then they were upon her.

QUESTIONS FOR REFLECTION/DISCUSSION

1. What was the history of the lottery? Did anyone question it over time? Explain.

2. What kind of mood is established in the story? When did you first realize that something awful was going to happen?

3. Shirley Jackson at one time referred to the lottery as "a ritual of blood sacrifice." What do you think she meant? What other type of events in the history of humankind other than blood sacrifice, might the story represent? Think about a time when one person or group was singled out for public ridicule or persecution. To what extent was chance a factor? Are some more immune than others to this kind of treatment? Do you see this story as perhaps being symbolic of some events in our own world? If so, what kind of events? Is there anything we can do to stop such events from occurring? Discuss these questions with a small group. Share your group's conclusions with the class.

4. The intention of the author is clearly to shock the reader at the end. What techniques does she use to accomplish this successfully?

5. Often you can look back in the story and find very subtle *foreshadowing* or clues that allow us to believe the ending, no matter how shocking. Go back and find the bits of foreshadowing that make the ending credible. With a partner, make a list.

6. Do you find irony in this story? If so, explain what it is that you find ironical and why.

7. Why do events such as the lottery occur in society? If they do indeed represent "blood sacrifices," is there anything we can do to stop such events from happening? Discuss these questions with a small group. Share your group's conclusions with the class.

Exploring Other Sources

Further explore one or more of the events in history discussed in item 3 in the previous section. What happened? Why did the event(s) occur? What were the results? What might have been done to prevent the event(s) from happening? Use library resources and/or the Internet. Ask your instructor or the librarian for assistance if you need it. Share what you learn with a small group.

Synthesis Through Writing

1. In your journal, react to the lottery. How did the story make you feel? Do you personally know of a time when one person or group was singled out for public ridicule, persecution, or death? To what extent may chance have been a factor?

2. Write an essay about an event you researched in the previous section, Exploring Other Sources. Refer to the writing strategies on page xix. Create your own graphic organizer to help you develop your paper.

The Most Dangerous Game
Richard Connell

Physical confrontations in history have involved humans against each other, humans against animals, and animals against animals. Of the three types of confrontations, the first one, humans against humans, is perhaps the most disturbing, and at the same time the most complex.

Richard Connell presents us with a chilling adventure story with surprising results. As you read, think about whether or not it is really just an adventure story or if its meaning goes far beyond the surface to reveal a darker side of the human character.

Before You Read

Think of a physical confrontation that you may have witnessed between two people or between one group and another. What was the situation? Was the confrontation spontaneous or planned? What was the result of it? How did the confrontation make you feel inside? Share your experience with a small group or write about it in your journal.

Part I

"Off there to the right—somewhere—is a large island," said Whitney. "It's rather a mystery—"

"What island is it?" Rainsford asked.

"The old charts call it 'Ship-Trap Island,'" Whitney replied: "A suggestive name, isn't it? Sailors have a curious dread of the place. I don't know why. Some superstition—"

"Can't see it," remarked Rainsford, trying to peer through the dank,° tropical night that was palpable° as it pressed its thick, warm blackness in upon the yacht.°

"You've got good eyes," said Whitney, with a laugh, "and I've seen you pick off° a moose moving in the brown fall bush at four hundred yards, but even you can't see four miles or so through a moonless Caribbean night."

"Not four yards," admitted Rainsford. "Ugh! It's like moist black velvet."

"It will be light enough where we're going," promised Whitney. "We should make it in a few days. I hope the jaguar guns have come. We'll have good hunting up the Amazon. Great sport, hunting."

"The best sport in the world," agreed Rainsford.

"For the hunter," amended Whitney. "Not for the jaguar."

"Don't talk rot, Whitney," said Rainsford. "You're a big-game hunter, not a philosopher. Who cares how a jaguar feels?"

"Perhaps the jaguar does," observed Whitney.

"Bah! They've no understanding."

"Even so, I rather think they understand one thing—fear. The fear of pain and the fear of death."

VOCABULARY

dank: Very damp. ". . .as it [the night] pressed its thick, warm blackness in upon the yacht" is a clue.

palpable: Capable of being felt (*pal-* means to touch).

yacht (yăt): An expensive boat used for pleasure or racing.

pick off: Here it means shoot.

"Nonsense," laughed Rainsford. "This hot weather is making you soft, Whitney. Be a realist. The world is made up of two classes—the hunters and the hunted. Luckily, you and I are hunters. Do you think we've passed that island yet?"

"I can't tell in the dark. I hope so."

"Why?" asked Rainsford.

"The place has a reputation—a bad one."

"Cannibals?" suggested Rainsford.

"Hardly. Even cannibals wouldn't live in such a God-forsaken place. But it's got into sailor lore, somehow. Didn't you notice that the crew's nerves seemed a bit jumpy today?"

"They were a bit strange, now that you mention it. Even Captain Nielsen—"

"Yes, even that tough-minded old Swede,° who'd go up to the devil himself and ask him for a light. Those fishy blue eyes held a look I never saw there before. All I could get out of him was: 'This place has an evil name among seafaring men, sir.' Then he said to me, very gravely: 'Don't you feel anything?'—as if the air about us was actually poisonous. Now, you mustn't laugh when I tell you this—I did feel something like a sudden chill."

"There was no breeze. The sea was as flat as a plateglass window. We were drawing near the island then. What I felt was a—a mental chill; a sort of sudden dread."

"Pure imagination," said Rainsford. "One superstitious sailor can taint° the whole ship's company with his fear."

"Maybe. But sometimes I think sailors have an extra sense that tells them when they are in danger. Sometimes I think evil is a tangible° thing—with wave lengths, just as sound and light have. An evil place can, so to speak, broadcast vibrations of evil. Anyhow, I'm glad we're getting out of this zone. Well, I think I'll turn in now, Rainsford.

"I'm not sleepy," said Rainsford. "I'm going to smoke another pipe up on the afterdeck."

"Good night, then, Rainsford. See you at breakfast."

"Right. Good night, Whitney."

VOCABULARY

Swede: A person from Sweden.

taint: Contaminate or make bad.

tangible (tan jĭbl): Capable of being felt; palpable (-tang- means to touch).

The Most Dangerous Game   **217**

There was no sound in the night as Rainsford sat there but the muffled throb of the engine that drove the yacht swiftly through the darkness, and the swish and ripple of the wash of the propeller.

Rainsford, reclining in a steamer chair, indolently° puffed on his favorite briar.° The sensuous drowsiness of the night was on him. "It's so dark," he thought, "that I could sleep without closing my eyes; the night would be my eyelids—"

An abrupt sound startled him. Off to the right he heard it, and his ears, expert in such matters, could not be mistaken. Again he heard the sound, and again. Somewhere, off in the blackness, someone had fired a gun three times.

Rainsford sprang up and moved quickly to the rail, mystified. He strained his eyes in the direction from which the reports had come, but it was like trying to see through a blanket. He leaped upon the rail and balanced himself there, to get greater elevation; his pipe, striking a rope, was knocked from his mouth. He lunged for it; a short, hoarse cry came from his lips as he realized he had reached too far and had lost his balance. The cry was pinched off short as the blood-warm waters of the Caribbean Sea closed over his head.

He struggled up to the surface and tried to cry out, but the wash from the speeding yacht slapped him in the face and the salt water in his open mouth made him gag and strangle. Desperately he struck out with strong strokes after the receding° lights of the yacht, but he stopped before he had swum fifty feet. A certain cool-headedness had come to him; it was not the first time he had been in a tight place. There was a chance that his cries could be heard by someone aboard the yacht, but that chance was slender, and grew more slender as the yacht raced on. He wrestled himself out of his clothes, and shouted with all his power. The lights of the yacht became faint and ever-vanishing fireflies; then they were blotted out entirely by the night.

Rainsford remembered the shots. They had come from the right, and doggedly° he swam in that direction, swimming with slow, deliberate strokes, conserving his strength. For a

---

VOCABULARY

indolently: Lazily. ". . . reclining in a steamer chair" and ". . . drowsiness of the night was on him" are clues.
briar: A pipe made from a woody stem or root of a shrub.
receding: Becoming more distant (*re-* here means back; *-ced-* means to go).
doggedly: Stubornly; willfully.

seemingly endless time he fought the sea. He began to count his strokes; he could do possibly a hundred more and then—

Rainsford heard a sound. It came out of the darkness, a high screaming sound, the sound of an animal in an extremity of anguish and terror.

He did not recognize the animal that made the sound—he did not try to; with fresh vitality he swam toward the sound. He heard it again; then it was cut short by another noise, crisp, staccato.°

"Pistol shot," muttered Rainsford, swimming on.

Ten minutes of determined effort brought another sound to his ears—the most welcome he had ever heard—the muttering and growling of the sea breaking on a rocky shore. He was almost on the rocks before he saw them; on a night less calm he would have been shattered against them. With his remaining strength he dragged himself from the swirling waters. Jagged crags° appeared to jut into the opaqueness;° he forced himself upward, hand over hand. Gasping, his hands raw, he reached a flat place at the top. Dense jungle came down to the very edge of the cliffs. What perils that tangle of trees and underbrush might hold for him did not concern Rainsford just them. All he knew was that he was safe from his enemy, the sea, and that utter weariness was on him. He flung himself down at the jungle edge and tumbled headlong into the deepest sleep of his life.

When he opened his eyes he knew from the position of the sun that it was late in the afternoon. Sleep had given him new vigor; a sharp hunger was picking at him. He looked about him, almost cheerfully.

"Where there are pistol shots, there are men. Where there are men, there is food," he thought. But what kind of men, he wondered, in so forbidding a place? An unbroken front of snarled and jagged jungle fringed° the shore.

He saw no sign of a trail through the closely knit web of weeds and trees; it was easier to go along the shore, and Rainsford floundered° along by the water. Not far from where he had landed, he stopped.

VOCABULARY

staccato: Abrupt, disconnected [sounds]. The word "crisp" is a clue.
crags: Large, pointed rock formations.
opaqueness: Something through which light cannot pass.
fringed: Was on the edge of.
floundered: Moved in an awkward, clumsy manner.

Some wounded thing, by the evidence a large animal, had thrashed about in the underbrush; the jungle weeds were crushed down and the moss was lacerated;° one patch of weeds was stained crimson. A small, glittering object not far away caught Rainsford's eye and he picked it up. It was an empty cartridge.°

"A twenty-two," he remarked. "That's odd. It must have been a fairly large animal too. The hunter had his nerve with him to tackle it with such a light gun. It's clear that the brute put up a good fight. I suppose the first three shots I heard were when the hunter flushed° his quarry° and wounded it. The last shot was when he trailed it here and finished it."

He examined the ground closely and found what he had hoped to find—the print of hunting boots. They pointed along the cliff in the direction he had been going. Eagerly he hurried along, now slipping on a rotten log or a loose stone, but making headway; night was beginning to settle down on the island.

Bleak darkness was blacking out the sea and jungle when Rainsford sighted the lights. He came upon them as he turned a crook in the coast line, and his first thought was that he had come upon a village, for there were many lights. But as he forged° along he saw to his great astonishment that all the lights were in one enormous building—a lofty structure with pointed towers plunging upward into the gloom. His eyes made out the shadowy outlines of a palatial° château;° it was set on a high bluff, and on three sides of it cliffs dived down to where the sea licked greedy lips in the shadows.

"Mirage,"° thought Rainsford. But it was no mirage, he found, when he opened the tall spiked iron gate. The stone steps were real enough; the massive door with a leering gargoyle° for a knocker was real enough; yet about it all hung an air of unreality.

He lifted the knocker, and it creaked up stiffly, as if it had never before been used. He let it fall, and it startled him with its

---

VOCABULARY

lacerated: Here it means torn (*lacer-* means torn or mangled).
cartridge: The part of a bullet that holds the gun powder.
flushed: Frightened to make it come out from cover.
quarry: Prey; the thing hunted.
forged: Here it means went forward slowly but steadily.
palatial: Like a palace (*palat-* means palace).
château: A large castle-like house in the country.
mirage: A thing that appears that is not really there (*mir-* means to look).
gargoyle: An ugly carved figure of a person or animal whose open mouth carries away rain water from a roof or wall.

booming loudness. He thought he heard steps within; the door remained closed. Again Rainsford lifted the heavy knocker, and let it fall. The door opened then, opened as suddenly as if it were on a spring, and Rainsford stood blinking in the river of glaring gold light that poured out. The first thing Rainsford's eyes discerned° was the largest man Rainsford had ever seen— a gigantic creature, solidly made and black-bearded to the waist. In his hand the man held a long barreled revolver, and he was pointing it straight at Rainsford's heart.

Out of the snarl of beard two small eyes regarded Rainsford.

"Don't be alarmed," said Rainsford, with a smile which he hoped was disarming. "I'm no robber. I fell off a yacht. My name is Sanger Rainsford of New York City."

The menacing° look in the eyes did not change. The revolver pointed as rigidly as if the giant were a statue. He gave no sign that he understood Rainsford's words, or that he had even heard them. He was dressed in uniform, a black uniform trimmed with gray astrakhan.°

"I'm Sanger Rainsford of New York," Rainsford began again. "I fell off a yacht. I am hungry."

The man's only answer was to raise with his thumb the hammer of his revolver. Then Rainsford saw the man's free hand go to his forehead in a military salute, and he saw him click his heels together and stand at attention. Another man was coming down the broad marble steps, an erect, slender man in evening clothes. He advanced and held out his hand.

In a cultivated° voice marked by a slight accent that gave it added precision and deliberateness, he said: "It is a very great pleasure and honor to welcome Mr. Sanger Rainsford, the celebrated hunter, to my home." Automatically, Rainsford shook the man's hand.

"I've read your book about hunting snow leopards in Tibet[1], you see," explained the man. "I am General Zaroff."

Rainsford's first impression was that the man was singularly° handsome; his second was that there was an original, almost

---

VOCABULARY

discerned: Saw as separate and distinct (*dis-* means apart; *-cern-* means to separate).
menacing: Threatening.
astrakhan: Curly fur like the wool on a lamb.
cultivated: Refined to reveal a good education.
singularly: Uncommonly.

CULTURAL NOTES

[1]Tibet is a region in southern China.

bizarre quality about the man's face. He was a tall man past middle age, for his hair was a vivid white; but his thick eyebrows and pointed military mustache were as black as the night from which Rainsford had come. His eyes, too, were black and very bright. He had high cheekbones, a sharp cut nose, a spare, dark face, the face of a man used to giving orders, the face of an aristocrat.° Turning to the giant in uniform, the general made a sign. The giant put away his pistol, saluted, withdrew.

"Ivan is an incredibly strong fellow," remarked the general, "but he has the misfortune to be deaf and dumb. A simple fellow, but, I'm afraid, like all his race, a bit of a savage."

"Is he Russian?"

"He is a Cossack,"[2] said the general, and his smile showed red lips and pointed teeth. "So am I."

"Come," he said, "we shouldn't be chatting here. We can talk later. Now you want clothes, food, rest. You shall have them. This is a most restful spot."

Ivan had reappeared, and the general spoke to him with lips that moved but gave forth no sound.

"Follow Ivan, if you please, Mr. Rainsford," said the general. "I was about to have my dinner when you came. I'll wait for you. You'll find that my clothes will fit you, I think."

It was to a huge, beam-ceilinged bedroom with a canopied° bed big enough for six men that Rainsford followed the silent giant. Ivan laid out an evening suit, and Rainsford, as he put it on, noticed that it came from a London tailor who ordinarily cut and sewed for none below the rank of duke.

The dining room to which Ivan conducted him was in many ways remarkable. There was a medieval° magnificence about it; it suggested a baronial° hall of feudal° times with its oaken panels, its high ceiling, its vast refectory° table where twoscore° men could sit down to eat. About the hall were the

---

VOCABULARY

aristocrat: A member of the upper class (*arist-* means best).
canopied: Having an overhanging cover.
medieval: Associated with the Middle Ages in Europe from A.D. 476 to 1453.
baronial: Having to do with a lord or a noble (a baron).
feudal: Relating to feudalism, an economic system of ninth- through fifteenth-century Europe whereby land is granted in exchange for service.
refectory: A room where food is served at mealtime.
twoscore: Forty (twenty in each score).

CULTURAL NOTES

[2]A Cossack is a person from southern Russia.

mounted heads of many animals—lions, tigers, elephants, moose, bears; larger or more perfect specimens Rainsford had never seen. At the great table the general was sitting alone.

"You'll have a cocktail, Mr. Rainsford," he suggested. The cocktail was surpassingly good; and, Rainsford noted, the table appointments were of the finest—the linen, the crystal, the silver, the china.

They were eating *borsch,* the rich, red soup with whipped cream so dear to Russian palates.° Half apologetically General Zaroff said: "We do our best to preserve the amenities° of civilization here. Please forgive any lapses. We are well off the beaten track, you know. Do you think the champagne has suffered from its long ocean trip?"

"Not in the least," declared Rainsford. He was finding the general a most thoughtful and affable° host, a true cosmopolite.° But there was one trait of the general's that made Rainsford uncomfortable. Whenever he looked up he found the general studying him, appraising him narrowly.

"Perhaps," said General Zaroff, "you were surprised that I recognized your name. You see, I read all books on hunting published in English, French, and Russian. I have but one passion in my life, Mr. Rainsford, and it is the hunt."

"You have some wonderful heads here," said Rainsford as he ate a particularly well-cooked filet mignon.° "That Cape buffalo³ is the largest I ever saw."

"Oh, that fellow. Yes, he was a monster."

"Did he charge you?"

"Hurled me against a tree," said the general. "Fractured my skull. But I got the brute."

"I've always thought," said Rainsford, "that the Cape buffalo is the most dangerous of all big game."

For a moment the general did not reply; he was smiling his curious red-lipped smile. Then he said slowly: "No. You are wrong, sir. The Cape buffalo is not the most dangerous big

---

VOCABULARY

palates: Here it means senses of taste.
amenities: Social courtesies; pleasantries (*ameni-* means pleasant).
affable: Easy to approach or speak to.
cosmopolite: One who feels comfortable with people of all cultures, etc.; a citizen of the world
    (*cosmo-* means world; -*polit-* means citizen).
filet mignon: An expensive cut of beef.

CULTURAL NOTES
³Cape buffalo are buffalo from the Cape of Good Hope Province on the southwestern tip of Africa.

game." He sipped his wine. "Here in my preserve on this island," he said in the same slow tone, "I hunt more dangerous game."

Rainsford expressed his surprise. "Is there big game on this island?"

The general nodded. "The biggest."

"Really?"

"Oh, it isn't here naturally, of course. I have to stock the island."

"What have you imported, General?" Rainsford asked. "Tigers?"

The general smiled. "No," he said. "Hunting tigers ceased to interest me some years ago. I exhausted their possibilities, you see. No thrill left in tigers, no real danger. I live for danger, Mr. Rainsford."

The general took from his pocket a gold cigarette case and offered his guest a long black cigarette with a silver tip; it was perfumed and gave off a smell like incense.°

"We will have some capital hunting, you and I," said the general. "I shall be most glad to have your society."

"But what game—" began Rainsford.

"I'll tell you," said the general. "You will be amused, I know. I think I may say, in all modesty, that I have done a rare thing. I have invented a new sensation. May I pour another glass of port, Mr. Rainsford?"

"Thank you, General."

The general filled both glasses, and said: "God makes some men poets. Some He makes kings, some beggars. Me He made a hunter. My hand was made for the trigger, my father said. He was a very rich man with a quarter of a million acres in the Crimea,[4] and he was an ardent° sportsman. When I was only five years old he gave me a little gun, specially made in Moscow for me, to shoot sparrows with. When I shot some of his prize turkeys with it, he did not punish me; he complimented me on my marksmanship. I killed my first bear in the Caucacus[5] when

---

VOCABULARY

incense: A material made of a gum or wood that gives off a very pleasant sweet odor when burned.

ardent: Having much enthusiasm (*ard*- refers to burning).

CULTURAL NOTES

[4] The Crimea is a region bordered by the Black Sea on the southwest and the Sea of Azov on the northeast.

[5] The Caucasus is a region between the Black and Caspian seas.

I was ten. My whole life has been one prolonged hunt. I went into the army—it was expected of noblemen's sons—and for a time commanded a division of Cossack cavalry, but my real interest was always the hunt. I have hunted every kind of game in every land. It would be impossible for me to tell you how many animals I have killed."

The general puffed at his cigarette.

"After the debacle° in Russia I left the country, for it was imprudent° for an officer of the Czar to stay there. Many noble Russians lost everything. I, luckily, had invested heavily in American securities, so I shall never have to open a tearoom in Monte Carlo[6] or drive a taxi in Paris. Naturally, I continued to hunt—grizzlies in your Rockies, crocodiles in the Ganges,[7] rhinoceroses in East Africa. It was in Africa that the Cape buffalo hit me and laid me up for six months. As soon as I recovered I started for the Amazon[8] to hunt jaguars, for I had heard they were unusually cunning. They weren't." The Cossack sighed. "They were no match at all for a hunter with his wits about him, and a high-powered rifle. I was bitterly disappointed. I was lying in my tent with a splitting headache one night when a terrible thought pushed its way into my mind. Hunting was beginning to bore me! And hunting, remember, had been my life. I have heard that in America businessmen often go to pieces when they give up the business that has been their life."

"Yes, that's so," said Rainsford.

The general smiled. "I had no wish to go to pieces," he said. "I must do something. Now, mine is an analytical mind, Mr. Rainsford. Doubtless that is why I enjoy the problems of the chase."

"No doubt, General Zaroff."

"So," continued the general, "I asked myself why the hunt no longer fascinated me. You are much younger than I am, Mr. Rainsford, and have not hunted as much, but you perhaps can guess the answer."

VOCABULARY
debacle: A sudden collapse.
imprudent: Unwise or rash (*im-* means not; *prudent* means wise).

CULTURAL NOTES
[6]Monte Carlo is a resort town in Monaco where a gambling casino is located.
[7]The Ganges is a river in northern India and Bangladesh. It is considered sacred to the Hindus.
[8]The Amazon is a river in South America.

The Most Dangerous Game   **225**

"What was it?"

"Simply this: hunting had ceased to be what you call 'a sporting proposition.'° It had become too easy. I always got my quarry. Always. There is no greater bore than perfection."

The general lit a fresh cigarette.

"No animal had a chance with me any more. That is no boast; it is a mathematical certainty. The animal had nothing but his legs and his instinct. Instinct is no match for reason. When I thought of this it was a tragic moment for me, I can tell you."

Rainsford leaned across the table, absorbed in what his host was saying.

"It came to me as an inspiration what I must do," the general went on.

"And that was?"

The general smiled the quiet smile of one who has faced an obstacle and surmounted° it with success. "I had to invent a new animal to hunt," he said.

"A new animal? You're joking."

"Not at all," said the general. "I never joke about hunting. I needed a new animal. I found one. So I bought this island, built this house, and here I do my hunting. The island is perfect for my purposes—there are jungles with a maze of trails in them, hills, swamps—"

"But the animal, General Zaroff?"

"Oh," said the general, "it supplies me with the most exciting hunting in the world. No other hunting compares with it for an instant. Every day I hunt, and I never grow bored now, for I have a quarry with which I can match my wits."

Rainsford's bewilderment showed in his face.

"I wanted the ideal animal to hunt," explained the general. "So I said: 'What are the attributes of an ideal quarry?' And the answer was, of course: 'It must have courage, cunning, and, above all, it must be able to reason.'"

"But no animal can reason," objected Rainsford.

"My dear fellow," said the general, "there is one that can."

"But you can't mean—" gasped Rainsford.

"And why not?"

VOCABULARY

proposition: A plan put forward for consideration (*pro-* means forward; *-posit-* means to place).
surmounted: Overcame (*sur-* means above). The words "obstacle" and "success" are clues.

"I can't believe you are serious, General Zaroff. This is a grisly joke."

"Why should I not be serious? I am speaking of hunting."

"Hunting? Good God, General Zaroff, what you speak of is murder."

The general laughed with entire good nature. He regarded Rainsford quizzically.° "I refuse to believe that so modern and civilized a young man as you harbors romantic ideas about the value of human life. Surely your experiences in the war—"

"Did not make me condone° cold-blooded murder," finished Rainsford stiffly.

Laughter shook the general. "How extraordinarily droll° you are!" he said. "One does not expect nowadays to find a young man of the educated class, even in America, with such a naïve and, if I may say so, mid-Victorian[9] point of view. It's like finding a snuffbox in a limousine. Ah, well, doubtless you had Puritan[10] ancestors. So many Americans appear to have had. I'll wager you'll forget your notions when you go hunting with me. You've a genuine thrill in store for you, Mr. Rainsford."

"Thank you, I'm a hunter, not a murderer."

"Dear me," said the general, quite unruffled,° "again that unpleasant word. But I think I can show you that your scruples° are quite unfounded."

"Yes?"

"Life is for the strong, to be lived by the strong, and, if needs be, taken by the strong. The weak of the world were put here to give the strong pleasure. I am strong. Why should I not use my gift? If I wish to hunt, why should I not? I hunt the scum of the earth—sailors from tramp ships—lascars,° blacks, Chinese,

---

VOCABULARY

quizzically: Here it means in a teasing way. "The general laughed with entire good nature" is a clue.

condone: Overlook; to treat as trivial and unimportant (-don- means to give away).

droll: Laughable.

unruffled: Undisturbed.

scruples: Hesitation due to principles of personal conduct that keep one from doing wrong.

lascars: Sailors from the East Indies.

CULTURAL NOTES

[9]Mid-Victorian refers to the time period during which Queen Victoria ruled England in the nineteenth century. This period was characterized by severe moral codes and extreme conservatism.

[10]A Puritan was one who belonged to a group of English Protestants holding very strict religious beliefs in the sixteenth and seventeenth centuries.

whites, mongrels—a thoroughbred horse or hound is worth more than a score of them."

"But they are men," said Rainsford hotly.

"Precisely," said the general. "That is why I use them. It gives me pleasure. They can reason, after a fashion. So they are dangerous."

"But where do you get them?"

The general's eyelid fluttered down in a wink. "This island is called Ship-Trap," he answered. "Sometimes an angry god of the high seas sends them to me. Sometimes, when Providence[11] is not so kind, I help Providence a bit. Come to the window with me."

Rainsford went to the window and looked out toward the sea.

"Watch! Out there!" exclaimed the general, pointing into the night. Rainsford's eyes saw only blackness, and then, as the general pressed a button, far out to sea Rainsford saw the flash of lights.

The general chuckled. "They indicate a channel," he said, "where there's none: giant rocks with razor edges crouch like a sea monster with wide open jaws. They can crush a ship as easily as I crush this nut." He dropped a walnut on the hardwood floor and brought his heel grinding down on it. "Oh, yes," he said, casually, as if in answer to a question, "I have electricity. We try to be civilized here."

"Civilized? And you shoot down men?"

A trace of anger was in the general's black eyes, but it was there for but a second, and he said, in his most pleasant manner: "Dear me, what a righteous° young man you are! I assure you I do not do the thing you suggest. That would be barbarous.° I treat these visitors with every consideration. They get plenty of good food and exercise. They get into splendid physical condition. You shall see for yourself tomorrow."

"What do you mean?"

"We'll visit my training school," smiled the general, "It's in the cellar. I have about a dozen pupils down there now. They're from the Spanish bark,° *San Lucar*, that had the bad luck to go

---

VOCABULARY

righteous: Morally right.
barbarous: Cruel.
bark: A large ship with sails or masts.

CULTURAL NOTES

[11]Providence is another word for God.

on the rocks out there. A very inferior lot, I regret to say. Poor specimens° and more accustomed to the deck than to the jungle."

He raised his hand, and Ivan, who served as waiter, brought thick Turkish coffee. Rainsford, with an effort, held his tongue in check.

"It's a game, you see," pursued the general blandly.° "I suggest to one of them that we go hunting. I give him a supply of food and an excellent hunting knife. I give him three hours' start. I am to follow, armed only with a pistol of the smallest caliber° and range. If my quarry eludes° me for three whole days, he wins the game. If I find him," the general smiled, "he loses."

"Suppose he refuses to be hunted?"

"Oh," said the general, "I give him his option, of course. He need not play that game if he doesn't wish to. If he does not wish to hunt I turn him over to Ivan. Ivan once had the honor of serving as official knouter° to the Great White Czar,[12] and he has his own ideas of sport. Invariably, Mr. Rainsford, invariably they choose the hunt."

"And if they win?"

The smile on the general's face widened. "To date I have not lost," he said.

Then he added hastily: "I don't wish you to think me a braggart, Mr. Rainsford. Many of them afford only the most elementary sort of problem. Occasionally I strike a tartar.° One almost did win. I eventually had to use the dogs."

"The dogs?"

"This way, please. I'll show you."

The general steered Rainsford to a window. The lights from the window sent a flickering illumination that made grotesque patterns on the courtyard below, and Rainsford could see moving about there a dozen or so huge black shapes; as they turned toward him, their eyes glittered greenly.

VOCABULARY
specimens: Samples used to represent the whole.
blandly: Mildly; without irritation.
caliber: The diameter (inside size) of a gun.
eludes: Avoids through cunning (e- means away; -lude- means to play).
knouter: A person who whips or flogs criminals as punishment for their crimes.
tartar: An unexpectedly fierce or clever opponent.

CULTURAL NOTES
[12]The Great White Czar was one of the leaders of Russia in the nineteenth century.

The Most Dangerous Game

"A rather good lot, I think," observed the general. "They are let out at seven every night. If anyone should try to get into my house—or out of it—something extremely regrettable would occur to him." He hummed a snatch° of song from the Folies Bergere.[13]

"And now," said the general, "I want to show you my new collection of heads. Will you come with me to the library?"

"I hope," said Rainsford, "that you will excuse me tonight, General Zaroff. I'm really not feeling at all well."

"Ah, indeed?" the general inquired solicitously.° "Well, I suppose that's only natural, after your long swim. You need a good, restful night's sleep. Tomorrow you'll feel like a new man, I'll wager.° Then we'll hunt, eh? I've one rather promising prospect—"

Rainsford was hurrying from the room.

"Sorry you can't go with me tonight," called the general. "I expect rather fair sport—a big, strong black. He looks resourceful—Well, good night, Mr. Rainsford; I hope you have a good night's rest."

The bed was good and the pajamas of the softest silk, and he was tired in every fiber of his being, but nevertheless Rainsford could not quiet his brain with the opiate° of sleep. He lay, eyes wide open. Once he thought he heard stealthy steps in the corridor outside his room. He sought to throw open the door; it would not open. He went to the window and looked out. His room was high up in one of the towers. The lights of the château were out now, and it was dark and silent, but there was a fragment of sallow° moon, and by its wan° light he could see, dimly, the courtyard; there, weaving, in and out in the pattern of shadow, were black, noiseless forms; the hounds heard him at the window and looked up, expectantly, with their green eyes. Rainsford went back to the bed and lay down. By many methods he tried to put himself to sleep. He had achieved a doze when,

---

VOCABULARY

snatch: Here it means a brief bit of.

solicitously: Showing much concern (*sol-* refers to whole; *-cit-* means to put into action).

wager: Bet.

opiate: Something that relaxes or brings about restfulness. Opium is a drug that produces sedation or sleepiness.

sallow: Yellowish; pale.

wan: Pale.

CULTURAL NOTES

[13]The Folies Bergere is a famous musical review in Paris, France.

just as morning began to come, he heard, far off in the jungle, the faint report of a pistol.

General Zaroff did not appear until luncheon. He was dressed faultlessly in the tweeds of a country squire.° He was solicitous about the state of Rainsford's health.

"As for me," sighed the general, "I do not feel so well. I am worried, Mr. Rainsford. Last night I detected traces of my old complaint."

To Rainsford's questioning glance the general said: "Ennui.[14] Boredom."

Then, taking a second helping of crêpe suzette,[15] the general explained: "The hunting was not good last night. The fellow lost his head. He made a straight trail that offered no problems at all. That's the trouble with these sailors; they have dull brains to begin with, and they do not know how to get about in the woods. They do excessively stupid and obvious things. It's most annoying. Will you have another glass of Chablis,[16] Mr. Rainsford?"

"General," said Rainsford firmly, "I wish to leave this island at once."

The general raised his thickets of eyebrows; he seemed hurt. "But, my dear fellow," the general protested, "you've only just come. You've had no hunting—"

"I wish to go today," said Rainsford. He saw the dead black eyes of the general on him, studying him. General Zaroff's face suddenly brightened.

He filled Rainsford's glass with venerable° Chablis from a dusty bottle.

"Tonight," said the general, "we will hunt—you and I."

Rainsford shook his head. "No, General," he said. "I will not hunt."

The general shrugged his shoulders and nibbled delicately at a hothouse° grape. "As you wish, my friend," he said. "The choice rests entirely with you. But may I not venture to suggest that you will find my idea of sport more diverting than Ivan's?"

VOCABULARY
squire: Here it mean a gentleman.
venerable: Deserving of respect because of age.
hothouse: A heated greenhouse where plants are grown.

CULTURAL NOTES
[14]*Ennui* (ŏn wē') is the French word for boredom.
[15]A crêpe suzette is a thin French pancake served with a hot sauce made with orange juice and brandy.
[16]Chablis is a wine.

The Most Dangerous Game   **231**

He nodded toward the corner where the giant stood, scowling, his thick arms crossed on his hogshead° of chest.

"You don't mean—" cried Rainsford.

"My dear fellow," said the general, "have I not told you I always mean what I say about hunting? This is really an inspiration. I drink to a foeman° worthy of my steel—at last."

The general raised his glass, but Rainsford sat staring at him.

"You'll find this game worth playing," the general said enthusiastically. "Your brain against mine. Your woodcraft against mine. Your strength and stamina against mine. Outdoor chess. And the stake is not without value, eh?"

"And if I win—" began Rainsford huskily.

"I'll cheerfully admit myself defeated if I do not find you by midnight of the third day," said General Zaroff. "My sloop° will place you on the mainland near a town."

The general read what Rainsford was thinking.

"Oh, you can trust me," said the Cossack. "I will give you my word as a gentleman and a sportsman. Of course, you, in turn, must agree to say nothing of your visit here."

"I'll agree to nothing of the kind," said Rainsford.

"Oh," said the general, "in that case—but why discuss that now? Three days hence° we can discuss it over a bottle of Veuve Cliquot,[17] unless—"

The general sipped his wine.

Then a businesslike air animated him. "Ivan," he said to Rainsford, "will supply you with hunting clothes, food, a knife. I suggest you wear moccasins; they leave a poorer trail. I should suggest, too, that you avoid the big swamp in the southeast corner of the island. We call it Death Swamp. There's quicksand there. One foolish fellow tried it. The deplorable part of it was that Lazarus followed him. You can imagine my feelings, Mr. Rainsford. I loved Lazarus; he was the finest hound in my pack. Well, I must beg you to excuse me now. I always take a siesta after lunch. You'll hardly have time for a nap, I fear. You'll want to start, no doubt. I shall not follow till dusk. Hunting at night is

---

VOCABULARY

hogshead: A large barrel used for storing liquids.
foeman: Enemy.
sloop: A type of sailboat.
hence: From now.

CULTURAL NOTES

[17]Veuve Cliquot is a wine.

so much more exciting than by day, don't you think? Au revoir,[18] Mr. Rainsford, au revoir."

General Zaroff, with a deep, courtly bow, strolled from the room.

From another door came Ivan. Under one arm he carried khaki° hunting clothes, a haversack° of food, a leather sheath containing a long bladed hunting knife; his right hand rested on a cocked revolver thrust in the crimson sash around his waist . . . .

Part II

Rainsford had fought his way through the bush for two hours.

"I must keep my nerve. I must keep my nerve," he said through tight teeth.

He had not been entirely clear headed when the château gates snapped shut behind him. His whole idea at first was to put distance between himself and General Zaroff, and, to this end, he had plunged along, spurred on by the sharp rowels° of something very like panic. Now he had got a grip on himself, had stopped, and was taking stock of himself and the situation.

He saw that straight flight was futile; inevitably it would bring him face to face with the sea. He was in a picture with a frame of water, and his operations, clearly, must take place within that frame.

"I'll give him a trail to follow," muttered Rainsford, and he struck off from the rude path he had been following into the trackless wilderness. He executed a series of intricate loops; he doubled on his trail again and again, recalling all the lore of the fox hunt, and all the dodges of the fox. Night found him leg-weary, with hands and face lashed by the branches, on a thickly wooded ridge. He knew it would be insane to blunder on through the dark, even if he had the strength. His need for rest was imperative and he thought: "I have played the fox, now I must play the cat of the fable." A big tree with a thick trunk and outspread branches was near by, and, taking care to leave not

---

VOCABULARY
khaki: A light yellowish brown.
haversack: A bag with one strap worn over the shoulder.
rowels: Wheels with sharp teeth.

CULTURAL NOTES
[18]Au revoir means good-bye in French.

The Most Dangerous Game   **233**

the slightest mark, he climbed up into the crotch, and stretching out on one of the broad limbs, after a fashion, rested. Rest brought him new confidence and almost a feeling of security. Even so zealous° a hunter as General Zaroff could not trace him there, he told himself; only the devil himself could follow that complicated trail through the jungle after dark. But, perhaps, the general was a devil—

An apprehensive° night crawled slowly by like a wounded snake, and sleep did not visit Rainsford, although the silence of a dead world was on the jungle. Toward morning when a dingy gray was varnishing the sky, the cry of some startled bird focused Rainsford's attention in that direction. Something was coming through the bush, coming slowly, carefully, coming by the same winding way Rainsford had come. He flattened himself down on the limb, and through a screen of leaves almost as thick as tapestry, he watched. The thing that was approaching was a man.

It was General Zaroff. He made his way along with his eyes fixed in utmost concentration on the ground before him. He paused almost beneath the tree, dropped to his knees, and studied the ground before him. Rainsford's impulse was to hurl himself down like a panther, but he saw that the general's right hand held something small and metallic—an automatic pistol.

The hunter shook his head several times as if he were puzzled. Then he straightened up and took from his case one of his black cigarettes; its pungent° incenselike smoke floated up to Rainsford's nostrils.

Rainsford held his breath. The general's eyes had left the ground and were traveling inch by inch up the tree. Rainsford froze there, every muscle tensed for a spring. But the sharp eyes of the hunter stopped before they reached the limb where Rainsford lay; a smile spread over his brown face. Very deliberately he blew a smoke ring into the air; then he turned his back on the tree and walked carelessly away, back along the trail he had come. The swirls of the underbrush against his hunting boots grew fainter and fainter.

VOCABULARY

zealous: Filled with enthusiasm or zeal.

apprehensive: Anxious about what might happen.

pungent (pŭn jent): Sharp and biting to the sense of smell or taste (*pung-* means to prick or sting).

The pent-up air burst hotly from Rainsford's lungs. His first thought made him feel sick and numb. The general could follow a trail through the woods at night; he could follow an extremely difficult trail; he must have uncanny powers; only by the merest chance had the Cossack failed to see his quarry.

Rainsford's second thought was even more terrible. It sent a shudder of cold horror through his whole being. Why had the general smiled? Why had he turned back?

Rainsford did not want to believe what his reason told him was true, but the truth was as evident as the sun that had by now pushed through the morning mists. The general was playing with him. The general was saving him for another day's sport! The Cossack was the cat; he was the mouse. Then it was that Rainsford knew the full meaning of terror.

"I will not lose my nerve. I will not."

He slid down from the tree, and struck off again into the woods. His face was set and he forced the machinery of his mind to function. Three hundred yards from his hiding place he stopped where a huge dead tree leaned precariously° on a smaller living one. Throwing off his sack of food, Rainsford took his knife from its sheath and began to work with all his energy.

The job was finished at last, and he threw himself down behind a fallen log a hundred feet away. He did not have to wait long. The cat was coming again to play with the mouse.

Following the trail with the sureness of a bloodhound came General Zaroff. Nothing escaped those searching black eyes, no crushed blade of grass, no bent twig, no mark, no matter how faint, in the moss. So intent was the Cossack on his stalking that he was upon the thing Rainsford had made before he saw it. His foot touched the protruding bough that was the trigger. Even as he touched it, the general sensed his danger and leaped back with the agility of an ape. But he was not quite quick enough; the dead tree, delicately adjusted to rest on the cut living one, crashed down and struck the general a glancing blow on the shoulder as it fell; but for his alertness, he must have been smashed beneath it. He staggered, but he did not fall; nor did he drop his revolver. He stood there rubbing his injured shoulder, and Rainsford, with fear again gripping his heart, heard the general's mocking laugh ring through the jungle.

VOCABULARY
precariously: Dangerously.

The Most Dangerous Game　　　　**235**

"Rainsford," called the general, "if you are within sound of my voice, as I suppose you are, let me congratulate you. Not many men know how to make a Malay[19] man-catcher. Luckily, for me, I too have hunted in Malacca.[20] You are proving interesting, Mr. Rainsford. I am going now to have my wound dressed; it's only a slight one. But I shall be back. I shall be back."

When the general, nursing his bruised shoulder, had gone, Rainsford took up his flight again. It was flight now, a desperate, hopeless flight, that carried him on for some hours. Dusk came, then darkness, and still he pressed on. The ground grew softer under his moccasins; the vegetation grew ranker, denser; insects bit him savagely. Then, as he stepped forward, his foot sank into the ooze. He tried to wrench it back, but the muck sucked viciously at his foot as if it were a giant leech. With a violent effort, he tore his foot loose. He knew where he was now. Death Swamp and its quicksand.

His hands were tight closed as if his nerve were something tangible that someone in the darkness was trying to tear from his grip. The softness of the earth had given him an idea. He stepped back from the quicksand a dozen feet or so and, like some huge prehistoric beaver, he began to dig.

Rainsford had dug himself in, in France, when a second's delay meant death. That had been a placid° pastime compared to his digging now. The pit grew deeper; when it was above his shoulders, he climbed out and from some hard saplings cut stakes and sharpened them to a fine point. These stakes he planted in the bottom of the pit with the points sticking up. With flying fingers he wove a rough carpet of weeds and branches, and with it he covered the mouth of the pit. Then, wet with sweat and aching with tiredness, he crouched behind the stump of a lightning-charred tree.

He knew his pursuer was coming; he heard the padding sound of feet on the soft earth, and the night breeze brought him the perfume of the general's cigarette. It seemed to Rainsford that the general was coming with unusual swiftness; he was not feeling his way along foot by foot. Rainsford,

---

VOCABULARY

placid: Calm (*placi-* means gentle or pleasing).

CULTURAL NOTES

[19]Malay refers to things associated with Malaya, or Malaysia, a country of southeast Asia.
[20]Malacca is a state in Malaysia.

crouching there, could not see the general, nor could he see the pit. He lived a year in a minute. Then he felt an impulse to cry aloud with joy, for he heard the sharp crackle of the breaking branches as the cover of the pit gave way; he heard the sharp scream of pain as the pointed stakes found their mark. He leaped up from his place of concealment. Then he cowered back. Three feet from the pit a man was standing, with an electric torch in his hand.

"You've done well, Rainsford," the voice of the general called. "Your Burmese[21] tiger pit has claimed one of my best dogs. Again you score. I think, Mr. Rainsford, I'll see what you can do against my whole pack. I'm going home for a rest now. Thank you for a most amusing evening."

At daybreak Rainsford, lying near the swamp, was awakened by a sound that made him know that he had new things to learn about fear. It was a distant sound, faint and wavering, but he knew it. It was the baying of a pack of hounds.

Rainsford knew he could do one of two things. He could stay where he was and wait. That was suicide. He could flee. That was postponing the inevitable. For a moment he stood there, thinking. An idea that held a wild chance came to him, and, tightening his belt, he headed away from the swamp. The baying of the hounds drew nearer, then still nearer, ever nearer. On a ridge Rainsford climbed a tree. Down a watercourse, not a quarter of a mile away, he could see the bush moving. Straining his eyes, he saw the lean figure of General Zaroff; just ahead of him Rainsford made out another figure whose wide shoulders surged through the tall jungle weeds; it was the giant Ivan, and he seemed pulled forward by some unseen force; Rainsford knew that Ivan must be holding the pack in leash.

They would be on him any minute now. His mind worked fanatically He thought of a native trick he had learned in Uganda.[22] He slid down the tree. He caught hold of a springy young sapling° and to it he fastened his hunting knife, with the blade pointing down the trail; with a bit of wild grapevine he

---

VOCABULARY
sapling: A young tree.

CULTURAL NOTES
[21]Burmese refers to things associated with Myanmar (Burma), a republic in southeast Asia bordering India.
[22]Uganda is a country in east-central Africa.

The Most Dangerous Game　　　**237**

tied back the sapling. Then he ran for his life. The hounds raised their voices as they hit the fresh scent. Rainsford knew now how an animal at bay feels.

He had to stop to get his breath. The baying of the hounds stopped abruptly, and Rainsford's heart stopped too. They must have reached the knife.

He shinned° excitedly up a tree and looked back. His pursuers had stopped. But the hope that was in Rainsford's brain when he climbed died, for he saw in the shallow valley that General Zaroff was still on his feet. But Ivan was not. The knife, driven by the recoil of the springing tree, had not wholly failed.

Rainsford had hardly tumbled to the ground when the pack resumed the chase.

"Nerve, nerve, nerve!" he panted, as he dashed along. A blue gap showed between the trees dead ahead. Ever nearer drew the hounds. Rainsford forced himself on toward that gap. He reached it. It was the shore of the sea. Across a cove he could see the gloomy gray stone of the château. Twenty feet below him the sea rumbled and hissed. Rainsford hesitated. He heard the sounds. Then he leaped far out into the sea . . .

When the general and his pack reached the place by the sea, the Cossack stopped. For some minutes he stood regarding the blue-green expanse of water. He shrugged his shoulders. Then he sat down, took a drink of brandy from a silver flask, lit a perfumed cigarette, and hummed a bit from *Madame Butterfly*.[23]

General Zaroff had an exceedingly good dinner in his great paneled dining hall that evening. With it he had a bottle of Pol Roger and a half bottle of Chambertin.[24] Two slight annoyances kept him from perfect enjoyment. One was the thought that it would be difficult to replace Ivan; the other was that his quarry had escaped him; of course, the American hadn't played the game—so thought the general as he tasted his after-dinner liqueur. In his library he read, to soothe himself, from the works of Marcus Aurelius.[25] At ten he went up to his bedroom. He was deliciously tired, he said to himself, as he locked himself in. There was a little moonlight, so, before turning on his light, he

---

VOCABULARY

shinned: To climb using both hands and legs alternately.

CULTURAL NOTES

[23]*Madame Butterfly* is the name of an opera.

[24]Pol Roger and Chambertin are both wines.

[25]Marcus Aurelius was a Roman emperor from A.D. 121 to 180.

went to the window and looked down at the courtyard. To the great hounds he called: "Better luck another time!" Then he switched on the light.

A man, who had been hiding in the curtains of the bed, was standing there.

"Rainsford!" screamed the general. "How in God's name did you get here?"

"Swam," said Rainsford. "I found it quicker than walking through the jungle."

The general sucked in his breath and smiled. "I congratulate you," he said. "You have won the game."

Rainsford did not smile. "I am still a beast at bay," he said, in a low, hoarse voice. "Get ready General Zaroff."

The general made one of his deepest bows. "I see," he said. "Splendid! One of us is to furnish a repast° for the hounds. The other will sleep in this very excellent bed. On guard, Rainsford." . . .

He had never slept in a better bed, Rainsford decided.

$\mathcal{Q}$UESTIONS FOR $\mathcal{R}$EFLECTION/$\mathcal{D}$ISCUSSION

1. How would you describe the mood that the author tries to build in this story right from the beginning? Is the author successful in this attempt? Why or why not? List details that the author uses to establish the mood.

2. What details tell you that Rainsford is an ardent hunter and that he is a very experienced outdoorsman?

3. Do you see any irony in Rainsford's statement to Whitney, "The world is made up of two classes—the hunters and the hunted. Luckily, you and I are hunters" (page 217)? Explain.

4. What foreshadowing does the author use to lead you to the fact that men (not animals) are being hunted here on this island? When did you first realize that this was the case? What foreshadowing prepares you for Rainsford's being hunted? When does he first begin to realize what General Zaroff might have planned for him? When does he know for sure?

5. Do you see any irony in General Zaroff's manner, appearance, and style of living, once you find out what he does for sport? Explain.

VOCABULARY
repast: A meal.

The Most Dangerous Game   **239**

6. How might General Zaroff describe himself? How might Rainsford describe the General by the end of the story? How might Rainsford describe himself? How might General Zaroff describe Rainsford before the hunt? After the hunt?

7. Why is hunting Rainsford particularly exciting for the General?

8. Who wins? Why? What happens to the loser?

9. What do you think the author is saying about humankind with this story? To what extent do you agree with him? Discuss these questions with a small group. Share your conclusions with your class.

10. What is your opinion of hunting as a sport in general? With whom do you most agree in the discussion about attitudes toward the hunted, Rainsford or Whitney? See page 224. How different are your own ideas from those of either of these men? Discuss these questions with a small group. Share your opinions with the class.

 ## EXPLORING OTHER SOURCES

Research hunting as a sport in the country in which you live. What can be its effect on animals and the environment in general? To what extent is hunting dangerous to those who participate in it? Some say it is a way for fathers to spend time with their sons. Others say it is a way to keep animal populations under control in some areas. What would your response be to these people? Use library resources and/or the Internet. Ask your instructor or the librarian for assistance if you need it. Share what you learn and your conclusions with a small group. To search the Internet, go to http://worldviews.wadsworth.com for links to information about hunting as a sport.

SYNTHESIS THROUGH WRITING

1. In your journal, discuss your reaction to General Zaroff's actions and his character. In your opinion, does he have any good qualities?

2. Write your own story using the theme "Illusions Versus Reality." Establish the mood you want and use foreshadowing to prepare your reader for what happens (however, don't give the ending away). Refer to the writing strategies on page xix, if necessary.

3. Write an essay about what you researched in the Exploring Other Sources activity. Create your own graphic organizer. See page xix for additional writing strategies.

All God's Children Need Traveling Shoes [excerpt]

Maya Angelou

In this autobiographical sketch, Maya Angelou focuses on the African-American experience and recounts her reaction to her son's unexpected scrape with death. It all happened in Ghana, where her son was about to attend the University in Accra, the nation's largest city. She is surprised and even somewhat fearful of the intensity of her ensuing feelings, which cause her to behave in uncharacteristic ways. Two strangers then enter her life, care about her as a human being, and are not afraid to tell her the truth about what she has allowed herself to become.

All God's Children Need Traveling Shoes is only one of five autobiographical volumes written by Maya Angelou. Perhaps the most well known of these is *I Know Why the Caged Bird Sings*. In addition to her autobiographies, her poetry is also about the African-American experience.

Before You Read

Perhaps you too, at some time or other, met a person who has helped you see the reality others probably noticed but would not or could not tell you. Write about it in your journal.

*T*he breezes of the West African night were intimate and shy, licking the hair, sweeping through cotton dresses with unseemly intimacy, then disappearing into the utter° blackness. Daylight was equally insistent, but much more bold and thoughtless. It dazzled, muddling the sight. It forced through my closed eyelids, bringing me up and out of a borrowed bed and into brand new streets.

After living nearly two years in Cairo, I had brought my son Guy to enter the University of Ghana in Accra.¹ I planned staying for two weeks with a friend of a colleague, settling Guy into his dormitory, then continuing to Liberia² to a job with the Department of Information.

VOCABULARY
utter: Complete.

CULTURAL NOTES
¹Accra is the capitol of Ghana, a country in western Africa.
²Liberia is an African country west of Ghana.

Guy was seventeen and quick. I was thirty-three and determined. We were Black Americans in West Africa, where for the first time in our lives the color of our skin was accepted as correct and normal.

Guy had finished high school in Egypt, his Arabic[3] was good and his health excellent. He assured me that he would quickly learn a Ghanaian language, and he certainly could look after himself. I had worked successfully as a journalist in Cairo, and failed sadly at a marriage which I ended with false public dignity and copious° secret tears. But with all crying in the past, I was on my way to another adventure. The future was plump with promise.

For two days Guy and I laughed. We looked at the Ghanaian streets and laughed. We listened to the melodious° languages and laughed. We looked at each other and laughed out loud.

On the third day, Guy, on a pleasure outing, was injured in an automobile accident. One arm and one leg were fractured and his neck was broken.

July and August of 1962 stretched out like fat men yawning after a sumptuous° dinner. They had every right to gloat,° for they had eaten me up. Gobbled me down. Consumed my spirit, not in a wild rush, but slowly, with the obscene patience of certain victors. I became a shadow walking in the white hot streets, and a dark spectre° in the hospital.

There was no solace° in knowing that the doctors and nurses hovering around Guy were African, nor in the company of the Black American expatriates° who, hearing of our misfortune, came to share some of the slow hours. Racial loyalties and cultural attachments had become meaningless.

VOCABULARY

copious: In large supply.
melodious: Filled with pleasing sounds (*mel-* here means music).
sumptuous: Very lavish; extravagant.
gloat: Show an excessive amount of self-satisfied pleasure.
spectre (the British spelling for "specter"): An image or vision (*spect-* means to see).
solace: Comfort.
expatriates: Here it means those who have given up their citizenship and live in another country
    (*ex-* means out; *-patri-* refers to one's native land or land of one's father).

CULTURAL NOTES

[3]Arabic is the language of the Arabs and is spoken in northern Africa as well as many other
    countries in the region.

Trying utterly, I could not match Guy's stoicism.° He lay calm, week after week, in a prison of plaster from which only his face and one leg and arm were visible. His assurances that he would heal and be better than new drove me into a faithless silence. Had I been less timid, I would have cursed God. Had I come from a different background, I would have gone further and denied His very existence. Having neither the courage nor the historical precedent,° I raged inside myself like a blinded bull in a metal stall.

Admittedly, Guy lived with the knowledge that an unexpected and very hard sneeze could force the fractured vertebrae against his spinal cord, and he would be paralyzed or die immediately, but he had only an infatuation with life. He hadn't lived long enough to fall in love with this brutally delicious experience. He could lightly waft° away to another place, if there really was another place, where his youthful innocence would assure him a crown, wings, a harp, ambrosia,° free milk and an absence of nostalgic° yearning. (I was raised on the spirituals which ached to "See my old mother in glory" or "Meet with my dear children in heaven," but even the most fanciful lyricists° never dared to suggest that those cavorting° souls gave one thought to those of us left to moil° in the world.) My wretchedness reminded me that, on the other hand, I would be rudderless.°

I had lived with family until my son was born in my sixteenth year. When he was two months old and perched on my left hip, we left my mother's house and together, save for one year when I was touring, we had been each other's home and center for seventeen years. He could die if he wanted to and go off to wherever dead folks go, but I, I would be left without a home.

VOCABULARY

stoicism: Not showing pleasure or pain; being passive. "He lay calm, week after week, in a prison of plaster . . ." is a clue.
precedent: A previous act or decision that becomes the custom or tradition (*pre-* means before; *-ced-* means to go).
waft: Float.
ambrosia: Food of the gods.
nostalgic: Longing for things or persons from the past.
lyricists: Musicians who write the words to songs.
cavorting: Prancing around playfully.
moil: To work like a slave.
rudderless: Without something to steer or guide; without direction.

All God's Children Need Traveling Shoes   **243**

The man who caused the accident stood swaying at the foot of the bed. Drunk again, or, two months later, still drunk. He, the host of the motor trip and the owner of the car, had passed out on the back seat leaving Guy behind the steering wheel trying to start the stalled engine. A truck had careened° off a steep hill and plowed into Richard's car, and he had walked away unhurt.

Now he dangled loosely in the room, looking shyly at me. "Hello, Sister Maya." The slurred words made me hate him more. My whole body yearned for his scrawny neck. I turned my face from the scoundrel and looked at my son. The once white plaster that encased his body and curved around his face was yellowing and had begun to crumble.

I spoke softly, as people do to the very old, the very young and the sick. "Darling, how are you today?"

"Mother, Richard spoke to you." His already deep voice growled with disapproval.

"Hello, Richard," I mumbled, hoping he couldn't hear me.

My greeting penetrated the alcoholic fog, and the man lumbered into an apologetic monologue° that tested my control. "I'm sorry, Sister Maya. So sorry. If only it could be me, there on that bed . . . Oh, if only it could be me . . ."

I agreed with him.

At last he had done with his regrets, and saying good-bye to Guy, took my hand. Although his touch was repulsive, Guy was watching me, so I placed a silly grin on my face and said, "Good-bye, Richard." After he left I began quickly to unload the basket of food I had brought. (The teenage appetite is not thwarted° by bruises or even broken bones.)

Guy's voice stopped me.

"Mother, come so I can see you."

The cast prevented him from turning, so visitors had to stand directly in his vision. I put the basket down and went to stand at the foot of the bed.

His face clouded with anger.

"Mother, I know I'm your only child, but you must remember, this is my life, not yours." The thorn from the bush one has

---

VOCABULARY

careened: Sped forward without control.
monologue: A long speech given by one person (*mono-* means one; *-logue-* refers to talking).
thwarted: Prevented or blocked.

planted, nourished and pruned, pricks most deeply and draws more blood. I waited in agony as he continued, eyes scornful and lips curled, "If I can see Richard and understand that he has been more hurt than I, what about you? Didn't you mean all those sermons about tolerance? All that stuff about understanding? About before you criticize a man, you should walk a mile in his shoes?"

Of course I meant it in theory, in conversation about the underprivileged, misunderstood and oppressed miscreants,° but not about a brute who had endangered my son's life.

I lied and said, "Yes, I meant it." Guy smiled and said, "I know you did, Mother. You're just upset now." His face framed by the cast was beautiful with forgiveness. "Don't worry anymore. I'm going to get out of here soon, then you can go on to Liberia."

I made bitterness into a wad and swallowed it.

I puckered and grinned and said, "You're right, darling. I won't be upset anymore."

As always, we found something to laugh about. He fumbled, eating with his unbroken left hand and when he did have the food firmly in his grasp, he pretended not to know how to find his mouth. Crumbs littered his gown. "I'll figure it out, Mom. I promise you I won't starve to death." We played word games, and the visiting hours went by quickly.

Too soon I was back on the bright street with an empty basket in my hands and my head swimming in the lonely air.

I did know some people who would receive me, but reluctantly, because I had nothing to offer company save a long face and a self-pitying heart, and I had no intention of changing either. Black Americans of my generation didn't look kindly on public mournings except during or immediately after funerals. We were expected by others and by ourselves to lighten the burden by smiling, to deflect° possible new assaults by laughter. Hadn't it worked for us for centuries? Hadn't it?

On our first night in Ghana, our host (who was only a friend of a friend) invited Black American and South American expatriates to meet us. Julian Mayfield and his beautiful wife, Ana Livia, who was a medical doctor, were known to me from

---

VOCABULARY

miscreants: Villains or criminals (*mis-* here means bad; *-creant-* refers to believing).
deflect: To turn aside (*de-* means away; *-flect-* means to bend).

New York and the rest were not. But there is a kinship among wanderers, as operative° as the bond between bishops or the tie between thieves: We knew each other instantly and exchanged anecdotes, contacts and even addresses within the first hour.

Alice Windom, a wit from St. Louis, and Vicki Garvin, a gentle woman from New York City, were among the Americans laughing and entertaining in the small living room. In the two years which had passed since Guy had been in the company of so many Black Americans, he had grown from a precocious° adolescent into an adept° young man. He bristled with pleasure, discovering that he could hold his own in the bantering° company.

Each emigré° praised Ghana and questioned my plans to settle in Liberia. There was no need to tell them that I hungered for security and would have accepted nearly any promised permanence in Africa. They knew, but kept up the teasing. One asked, "You remember that Ray Charles[4] song where he says, 'When you leave New York, you ain't going nowhere'?"

I remembered.

"Well, when you leave Ghana, going to Liberia, you ain't going to Africa, in fact you ain't going nowhere."

Although I knew Liberians who were as African as Congo drums, I honored the traditional procedure and allowed the raillery° to continue.

Alice advised, "Honey, you'd better stay here, get a job and settle down. It can't get better than Ghana and it could be a lot worse." Everyone laughed and agreed.

The fast talk and jokes were packages from home and I was delighted to show the group that I still knew how to act in Black company. I laughed as hard as the teasers and enjoyed the camaraderie.°

VOCABULARY

operative: Influential (*oper-* refers to working).

precocious: Developing or maturing early (*pre-* means before; *-coci-* refers to cooking). "he had grown . . . into an adept young man" is a clue.

adept: Having highly developed skills.

bantering: Playfully teasing.

emigré: An emigrant who has fled his or her country during bad times.

raillery: Playful teasing or ridicule (*rail* here means to scold harshly). The next sentence is a clue.

camaraderie: Good relationships with friends (*camar-* refers to comrade).

CULTURAL NOTES

[4]Ray Charles is a current African-American song writer, pianist, and rhythm and blues singer who has been blind since the age of seven. His full name is Ray Charles Robinson.

But Guy's accident erased all traces of their names, their faces and conviviality.° I felt as if I had met no one, knew no one, and had lived my entire life as the bereft° mother of a seriously injured child.

Tragedy, no matter how sad, becomes boring to those not caught in its addictive caress. I watched my host, so sympathetic at the outset, become increasingly less interested in me and my distress. After a few weeks in his house, his discomfort even penetrated my self-centeredness. When Julian and Ana Livia Mayfield allowed me to store my books and clothes at their house, I gave my host only perfunctory° thanks and moved into a tiny room at the local YWCA.[5] I focused my attention on myself, with occasional concentrations on Guy. If I thought about it I was relieved that no one anticipated my company, yet, I took the idea of rejection as one more ornament on my string of worry beads.

One sunny morning Julian stood waiting for me in the YWCA lobby. His good looks drew attention and giggles from the young women who sat on the vinyl chairs pretending to read.

"I'm taking you to meet someone. Someone you should know." He looked at me without smiling. He was tall, Black, tough and brusque.°

"You need to have someone, a woman, talk to you. Let's go." I withdrew from his proprietary° air, but lack of energy prevented me from telling him that he wasn't my brother, he wasn't even a close friend. For want of resistance, I followed him to his car.

"Somebody needs to tell you that you have to give up this self-pity. You're letting yourself go. Look at your clothes. Look at your hair. Hell, it's Guy whose neck was broken. Not yours."

Anger jumped up in my mouth, but I held back the scorching words and turned to look at him. He was watching the road but

---

VOCABULARY

conviviality: Fun among friends (*con-* means together; *-viv-* means live).
bereft: Deprived or left without.
perfunctory: Routine; without caring.
brusque: Abrupt or overly blunt.
proprietary: Showing ownership (*proprie-* refers to property).

CULTURAL NOTES

[5]The YWCA is an acronym for the Young Women's Christian Association, which provides low-cost shelter and programmed activities for women in many cities around the world.

the side of his face visible to me was tense, his eyes were unblinking, and he had pushed his full lips out in a pout.

"Everybody understands . . . as much as anyone can understand another's pain . . . but you've . . . you've forgotten to be polite. Hell, girl, everybody feels sorry for you, but nobody owes you a damn thing. You know that. Don't forget your background. Your mother didn't raise you in a dog house."

Blacks concede that hurrawing,° jibing,° jiving,° signifying, disrepecting, cursing, even outright insults might be acceptable under particular conditions, but aspersions° cast against one's family call for immediate attack.

I said, "How do you know my business so well? Was that my daddy visiting your mother all those times he left our home?"

I expected an explosion from Julian. Yet his response shocked me. Laughter burst out of him, loud and raucous.° The car wobbled and slowed while he held tenuously° to the steering wheel. I caught his laughter, and it made me pull his jacket, and slap my own knee. Miraculously we stayed on the road. We were still laughing when he pulled into a driveway and let the engine die.

"Girl, you're going to be all right. You haven't forgotten the essentials. You know about defending yourself. All you have to do now is remember . . . sometimes you have to defend yourself from yourself."

When we got out of the car Julian hugged me and we walked together toward The National Theatre of Ghana, a round, white building set in an embrace of green-black trees.

Efua Sutherland could have posed for the original bust of Nefertiti.[6] She was long, lean, Black and lovely, and spoke so

---

VOCABULARY

hurrawing (often spelled "hurrahing"): Applauding and cheering.
jibing: Teasing.
jiving: Using glib or informal talk.
aspersions: Slanderous remarks. ". . . against one's family" is a clue.
raucous: Harsh; not pleasant to the ear.
tenuously: Weakly (tenu- refers to thin).

CULTURAL NOTES

[6]Nefertiti was the Queen of Egypt during the mid-1300s B.C. The bust of Nefertiti, which is made of limestone, is in the Berlin Museum.

softly I had to lean forward to catch her words. She wore an impervious° air as obvious as a strong perfume, and an austere° white floor-length gown.

She sat motionless as Julian recounted my dreadful tale and ended saying that my only child was, even as we spoke, in the Military Hospital. When Julian stopped talking and looked at her pointedly, I was pleased that Efua's serene face did not crumble into pity. She was silent and Julian continued, "Maya is a writer. We knew each other at home. She worked for Martin Luther King. She's pretty much alone here, so I have to be a brother to her, but she needs to talk to a woman, and pretty soon she'll need a job." Efua said nothing, but finally turned to me and I had the feeling that all of myself was being absorbed. The moment was long.

"Maya," she stood and walked to me. "Sister Maya, we will see about a job, but now you have need of a Sister friend." I had not cried since the accident. I had helped to lift Guy's inert° body onto the X-ray table at the first hospital, had assisted in carrying his stretcher to an ambulance for transfer to another hospital. I had slept, awakened, walked and lived in a thick atmosphere, which only allowed breathing and routine motor behavior.

Efua put her hand on my cheek and repeated, "Sister, you have need of a Sister friend because you need to weep, and you need someone to watch you while you weep." Her gestures and voice were mesmerizing.° I began to cry. She stroked my face for a minute then returned to her chair. She began speaking to Julian about other matters. I continued crying and was embarrassed when I couldn't stop the tears. When I was a child, my grandmother would observe me weeping and say, "Be careful, Sister. The more you cry, the less you'll pee, and peeing is more important." But the faucet, once opened, had to drain itself. I had no power over its flow.

Efua sent Julian away with assurances that she would return me to the hospital. I looked at her, but she had settled into herself sweetly, and I was freed to cry out all the bitterness and self-pity of the past days.

VOCABULARY

impervious: Incapable of being entered or penetrated (*im-* here means not; *pervious* means open to penetration).

austere: Here it means simple and without decoration.

inert: Not able to move. "I had helped to lift . . ." is a clue.

mesmerizing: Hypnotizing.

All God's Children Need Traveling Shoes

When I had finished, she stood again, offering me a handkerchief. "Now, Sister, you must eat. Eat and drink. Replenish yourself." She called her chauffeur, and we were taken to her home.

She was a poet, playwright, teacher, and the head of Ghana's National Theatre. We talked in the car of Shakespeare, Langston Hughes,[7] Alexander Pope,[8] and Sheridan.[9] We agreed that art was the flower of life and despite the years of ill-treatment Black artists were among its most glorious blossoms.

She knew the president and called him familiarly "Kwame."

She said, "Kwame has said that Ghana must use its own legends to heal itself. I have written the old tales in new ways to teach the children that their history is rich and noble."

Her house, white as chalk and stark, had rounded walls which enclosed a green lawn. Her three children came laughing to greet me, and her servant brought me food. Efua spoke in Fanti[10] to the maid, and a mixture of Fanti and English to the children.

"This is your Auntie Maya. She shall be coming frequently. Her son is ill, but you shall meet him, for he will soon be released from the hospital."

Esi Rieter, the oldest, a girl of ten, Ralph, seven, and the five-year-old, Amowi, immediately wanted to know how old my son was, what was his illness, did I have other children, what did I do. Efua sent them away assuring them that time would answer all questions.

I ate as I had cried, generously. After the meal, Efua walked me to the car.

"Sister, you are not alone. I, myself, will be at the hospital tomorrow. Your son is now my son. He has two mothers in this place." She put her hand on my face again. "Sister, exercise patience. Try."

When the driver stopped at the hospital, I felt cool and refreshed as if I had just gone swimming in Bethesda's pool,[11] and many of my cares had been washed away in its healing water.

CULTURAL NOTES

[7]Langston Hughes was a twentieth century African-American poet.
[8]Alexander Pope was a late eighteenth-century English poet.
[9]Richard Sheridan was a late eighteenth-century English dramatist.
[10]Fanti is a dialect in Ghana that has both spoken and written forms.
[11]Bethesda's pool is in Jerusalem and is reported to have the power to heal.

QUESTIONS FOR REFLECTION/DISCUSSION

1. Were you surprised to hear the author say, "We were Black Americans in West Africa, where for the first time in our lives the color of our skin was accepted as correct and normal" (p. 242)? What has to happen in a society such as the one in the United States before skin of all colors will be accepted as correct and normal?

2. Guy assured his mother that he would quickly learn a Ghanaian language? Do you think it is possible to *quickly* learn another language? If so, how? What strategies do you think successful language learners use when learning another language?

3. When Guy is seriously injured and near death in the hospital, why do you think his mother concludes that "Racial loyalties and cultural attachments became meaningless"? Would most of us come to the same conclusion in similar situations? Explain.

4. Why do you think the author raged inside herself "like a blinded bull in a metal stall"? What did she wish she had the courage to do? Think about and/or discuss with a partner a time when you felt a similar kind of anger.

5. When the author says that her son ". . . hadn't lived long enough to fall in love with this brutally delicious experience" (p. 243), to what experience is she referring? See the preceding paragraph. Do your personal beliefs or religion include such an experience? Discuss these questions with a partner. Summarize your discussion in your journal.

6. How is it possible for one person to be the "home" of another? (p. 243). Are there any dangers in having this kind of relationship with another person? Explain.

7. How does the way the mother reacts to Richard differ from the way her son reacts to him? What do their reactions tell you about both mother and son?

8. What is meant by the words "the thorn from the bush one has planted, nourished, and pruned pricks more deeply and draws more blood" (pp. 244–245)? How do the words apply to the author and her son?

9. What effect did Guy's accident have on his mother's social relationships? Is it natural for a parent to behave as she did considering the circumstances? Explain.

10. How were Julian and later Efua able to have such a dramatic influence on the author's state of mind? What do you think she learned from them?

All God's Children Need Traveling Shoes   **251**

11. The author seems to make extensive use of *personification* in this biographical sketch. For example, on page 242 she claims that the "future was plump with promise." Find other examples of personification in this selection. Share them with your class. Did such use of personification increase your enjoyment of the story? If so, in what way?

 ℰXPLORING ᴏTHER ᔑOURCES

1. In this autobiographical sketch, the author favors Ghana over Liberia as a place to live and work. In the library and/or on the Internet, find out as much as you can about the two countries as they existed before 1985. Pay particular attention to their governments and political systems. Was there justification for choosing one over the other as a place to live and work? What about today? Which one would you choose to live and work in? Your instructor or the librarian may be able to suggest sources to you. Share what you learn with a small group.

2. In the library, gather information about Ghana's culture, its languages, educational system, customs and traditions. Ask your instructor or the librarian for assistance, if you need it. Share the information with your class.

ᔑYNTHESIS ᔑHROUGH ᴡRITING

1. In your journal, address the following questions:
   a. What does the concept "brotherhood" mean to you?
   b. What do you learn about it from this selection?

2. Write your own autobiographical sketch. Choose an experience in your life during which you learned an important lesson. You may use Maya Angelou's autobiographical sketch as an example. See writing strategies on page xix.

3. The author claims that there is a kinship between wanderers "as operative as the bond between bishops or the tie between thieves . . ." (p. 246). Have you ever felt a similar kinship with others whom you had only known about an hour or so? Write about your experience in a personal essay. Refer to the writing strategies on page xix.

4. Use the words ". . . the thorn from the bush one has planted, nourished, and pruned pricks more deeply and draws more blood" (p. 244-245) as the subject of an essay. Think of examples supporting the conclusion expressed in this quote. Make a list of them before you begin your essay.

5. Develop an essay around the idea expressed by Maya Angelou in the words "Racial loyalties and cultural attachments became meaningless" (p. 242). Can you think of other situations in which this might be likely to happen? What does this tell us about human nature? Jot down any situations you can think of. Then choose one or two to develop more fully in your paper. The writing strategies on page xix may be helpful.

6. Write an essay about Ghana's culture, its languages, educational system, customs, and traditions. Use the information you found in the Exploring Other Sources section to develop your essay. First divide a piece of paper into five columns labeled "Culture," Languages," "Educational System," "Customs" and "Traditions." Then place the appropriate details in each column. Use this graphic representation to help you organize your essay. See page xix for additional writing strategies.

7. Write an essay comparing Ghana and Liberia as they existed before 1985. The information you collected in Exploring Other Sources can be used to develop your essay. You may want to limit your paper about the two countries to their governments and political systems. Divide a piece of paper into two columns. Label the first column "Ghana" and the second "Liberia." Place the appropriate details in each column. Use your paper to help you develop your essay.

The Man Who Liked Dickens

Evelyn Waugh
adapted for Television by Robert Tallman

This television play shows very clearly that a person may not be what he or she appears to be. We are introduced in this story to an authoritative man who ruthlessly controls the environment he has created for himself at the expense of others.

Authors Evelyn Waugh and Robert Tallman both wrote in the mid-1900s. Evelyn (pronounced Eve' lin) Waugh was a British social satirist who took great pleasure in making fun of upper-class society, which he knew very well from firsthand experience. Perhaps his satire best known in the United States was *The Loved One* (1948), which made fun of Hollywood mortuary customs. His moralistic *Brideshead Revisited* (1945), about the spiritual reawakening of a Catholic family, was also widely read both in England and abroad, particularly in literary circles.

Robert Tallman, who adapted this story for television, began his literary career as a reporter for the *New York Herald Tribune* and eventually became a script writer for radio and television. He also wrote a few early Hollywood films.

And now a word about Charles Dickens, whose name is in the title of this play. Dickens was a famous nineteenth-century British novelist. Although it is not necessary that you know much about Dickens's novels, the following information may interest you.

Dickens grew up in poverty in nineteenth-century England and experienced many of the brutalities of British society. His novels are admired particularly for their vivid descriptions of people, not only from the lower classes but from all stations in life. His novels include *Martin Chuzzlewit, Bleak House, Oliver Twist* (about street children who pick pockets to make a living), *Little Dorrit, Hard Times, A Tale of Two Cities* (in which a man goes to the guillotine), *Nicholas Nickleby, David Copperfield, Barnaby Rudge, Great Expectations, The Old Curiosity Shop, Dombey and Son,* and several others. His classic story, "A Christmas Carol," presents the character Ebenezer Scrooge, a very stingy and bitter businessman. His name has become a household word; a person who demonstrates characteristics similar to those of Ebenezer Scrooge is likely to be called a "scrooge."

Before You Read

Think of someone from your past who, like the man who liked Dickens, was very authoritarian in his or her dealings with you and/or with others you know. Write about that person in your journal. How did you and/or other people react to that person?

Act I

 CENE. *A clearing in the Amazonian jungle. We see a settlement of thatched° huts dominated by a bungalow° of the same native materials but having several rooms and a*

VOCABULARY
thatched: Roofed with straw or other similar materials.
bungalow: A house of only one level.

verandah.° This *is* MR. MCMASTER'S *house. On three sides the settlement is bounded by dense vegetation: on the fourth, by the river and one boat landing. The constant clamor° of jungle birds and monkeys is heard.*

MR. MCMASTER, *seated on the steps of his verandah, has just finished cleaning his shotgun and is reassembling° it. At the sound of the crackling of dry sticks underfoot,* MR. MCMASTER *lowers the gun and turns in the direction from which the sound seems to come. It becomes louder and the hoarse gasping breath of a man is heard. Then the branches of two palmettos° part and* JOHN HENTY *stumbles into the clearing and falls at full length.* MR. MCMASTER *goes forward to help him to his feet, supports him.*

MCMASTER. Steady there . . . my poor man, you're ill. Very ill.

HENTY. *(gasping, half sobbing, clinging to* MCMASTER*).* Tired. Can't go on any further. Too tired.

MCMASTER *(turning toward the house and pointing).* My house is just over there. Think you can make it?

HENTY. Don't know . . .

MCMASTER. It is a very short way. When we get there, I will give you something to make you better.

HENTY *(as they cross the verandah).* You speak English.

MCMASTER. As Mrs. Gamp might say, I speaks enough.

HENTY. Mrs. Gamp? Your wife?

MCMASTER. Oh, dear no. I live quite alone. *(They are on the verandah.* MCMASTER *helps* HENTY *toward a hammock. Mrs. Gamp, by the way, is a character in Dickens' novel* Martin Chuzzlewit.*)* How long have you been lost in the jungle?

HENTY. Don't know . . . days . . . several days . . . expedition° down the river . . . boat capsized° . . . all the others drowned.

MCMASTER. I see. You had better be quiet now. There will be much time for talking when you are better.

HENTY. You're . . . *(swallows)* kind.

VOCABULARY
verandah: An open area at the side of a house. It has a floor and a roof.
clamor: Continuous, loud, confused noise. ". . . of jungle birds and monkeys" is a clue.
reassembling: Putting back together; assembling again (re- means again).
palmettos: Small palm trees with fan-shaped leaves.
expedition: Organized travel done by a group of people going somewhere for a definite purpose.
capsized: Turned upside down.

The Man Who Liked Dickens

MCMASTER. My name is McMaster. You may have heard my name in Manáos?[1]

HENTY. No. My name is Henty.

MCMASTER (*nods*). Mr. Henty. Now if you will rest here for a moment, I will fetch something for you.

[HENTY *manages a faint smile of gratitude.* MCMASTER *enters the house, takes down an earthen crock and from a row of apothecary*° *bottles in the same shelf shakes out dried leaves and bits of bark, crumbles them into the crock.*]

MCMASTER (*calling*). Traddles![2] (*An Indian,* TRADDLES, *appears in the doorway.*) Is the water hot?

TRADDLES. Yes, master.

MCMASTER. Bring it here. Hurry. (MCMASTER *rubs his hands and looks up at an attic platform at the end of the room. Several straw-wrapped bundles are seen at the top of the ladder. Then he turns briskly toward the doorway through which* TRADDLES *has disappeared.*) Step lively there! Hurry up, I say! (*The Indian trots in with an ordinary old-fashioned teakettle.*)

TRADDLES. Water not boil yet, master. Fire burn too slow.

MCMASTER (*taking teakettle and lifting lid, it steams*). Hot enough. (*Pours the water on top of the herbs and bark and stirs with a stick. To* TRADDLES) Mr. Henty—the gentleman out there—is to be my guest. He will stay here in the house with me, as Mr. Barnabas did. Do you understand? (TRADDLES *nods.*) Fetch down that calabash.° I believe this stuff is ready. (TRADDLES *hands him a calabash hanging on a wall peg.* MR. MCMASTER *dips out some of the brew, tastes it, and spits it out.*) Ah. Exactly right. Put those things away. (*Going out to* HENTY) Mr. Henty . . . (HENTY *opens his eyes.*) I want you to drink this, Mr. Henty. (*He puts one arm under* HENTY'S *shoulders and lifts him up, holds the calabash under* HENTY'S *nose.* HENTY *winces.*)

HENTY. What is it?

MCMASTER. Medicine. In the forest, there is medicine for everything. There is medicine to make you well and to make you ill. Plants to cure you and give you fever; to kill you and send you mad.° My mother was an Indian, she taught me many of them.

VOCABULARY

apothecary: A druggist or pharmacist.

calabash: A cup made out of a gourd (often a calabash gourd) with a long handle; also called a dipper.

mad: Here it means crazy.

CULTURAL NOTES

[1]Manáos is a city in Brazil.
[2]Traddles is a character in *David Copperfield*, a novel by Charles Dickens.

(Walks to the edge of verandah and looks toward edge of clearing where two graves are marked with heavy crosses.) They say there is a medicine that can bring dead people to life, but I have not seen it done. *(Back to* HENTY *with a smile)* Perhaps I will live to see that, too. *(Arranges the pillow under* HENTY'S *head.)* Go to sleep, Mr. Henty.

[HENTY *closes his eyes, smiling gratefully.* MCMASTER *bends down over him.]*

MCMASTER. Can you read, Mr. Henty? *(Whispering)* You can read, of course?

HENTY *(drowsily).* Of course.

[MCMASTER *straightens up. He smiles contentedly. Fade out.]*

Fade in. Shortly before sunrise. TRADDLES *is blowing out a little lamp which burns on the verandah. He looks down, to see* HENTY *lying in the hammock staring up at him through insect netting.* HENTY *parts the net, looks about, slips his legs out, and gets to his feet a little unsteadily. He runs his hand over his stubble of beard and the Indian makes shaving motions on his own face and points.*

Following the direction, HENTY *walks to a mirror that hangs over a washstand. He eyes his stubble, sees shaving things laid out, picks up shaving mug and starts to lather. There is a thud off stage as* MCMASTER *throws down one of the straw bundles from the attic platform.* HENTY *peers around the door.*

HENTY. Need some help there?

MCMASTER. No, thank you, I can manage. *(He throws another bundle down, comes down the ladder, unwraps the bundles while* HENTY *shaves. They contain books.)* I hope that razor is satisfactory.

HENTY. Splendid.

MCMASTER. It belonged to poor Barnabas.

HENTY. Barnabas?

MCMASTER. He wandered into my village as you did—lost in the jungle and in the grip of a fever. He was a native, well-educated in Georgetown.[3] *(Putting books lovingly on shelf)* I buried him only a week before you arrived.

HENTY *(with razor poised).* Poor chap.° *(Resumes shaving.)* How long have you lived here?

VOCABULARY
chap: Here it is a British word meaning a man.

CULTURAL NOTES
[3]Georgetown refers to Georgetown University in the Washington, D.C., area.

The Man Who Liked Dickens   **257**

MCMASTER. All my life. (*Proudly*) My *father* was English. He came to British Guiana⁴ as a missionary and took a Shirianá⁵ woman as his wife. The Shirianá are ugly, but very devoted. Most of the men and women living in this savannah° are my children. This is why they obey me . . . (*picking up the shotgun*) . . . and because I have the gun. My father was a man of education, Mr. Henty. I suppose you, too, can read.

HENTY. Yes, of course.

MCMASTER. It is not everyone who is so fortunate. I cannot.

HENTY (*an apologetic laugh, looking at the books*). You're joking, Mr. McMaster. I mean, all the books—

MCMASTER. Oh, I have a great many books—a great many, Mr. Henty. (*To* THADDLES) Put those shaving things away. Lock up the razor. (*As* TRADDLES *gathers up things and* HENTY *looks curious*) Metal tools are a rarity among these Indians, you know. Have to keep the cutlery° under lock and key.

HENTY. How long was I sick? I've lost all track of time.

MCMASTER. Time is our most plentiful commodity° here in the jungle. It is two weeks since you arrived. You were very ill, Mr. Henty. Very. Come, I want to show you something.

[MCMASTER *leads him down the stairs of the verandah.* HENTY *is dizzy and has to lean on post for a moment.*]

HENTY. Sorry.

MCMASTER. You are still far from completely recovered, Mr. Henty.

HENTY. It's all right now. What is it you wanted to show me?

MCMASTER. Out here. (*Leads him to a carpenter's bench and takes a cross from vise.*) I started the day you came . . . to commemorate° your arrival. It is very hard mahogany,° like the others.

HENTY (*looking toward grave area; two crosses are visible*). Is that—?

VOCABULARY

savannah: An open, level grassland in the tropics.
cutlery: Knives, and other tools used for cutting. "Metal tools are a rarity . . ." is a clue.
commodity: Anything used to bring in a profit.
commemorate: To mark the memory of an event (*-memor-* refers to being mindful).
mahogany: A hard reddish-brown wood.

CULTURAL NOTES

⁴British Guiana is the part of an area known as Guiana in northeast South America.
⁵Shirianá is one of the Indian tribes in the Orinoco River valley of South America.

MCMASTER. Yes, that is where I buried poor Barnabas. The other is a man who died of snake bite many years ago. I never knew his name . . . he did not read as well as Barnabas.

HENTY. Then you must have intended this for—you must have expected me to die.

MCMASTER. I sincerely hoped not. Do you believe in God, Mr. Henty?

HENTY. *(embarrassed).* Why . . .

MCMASTER. Dickens did.

HENTY. Dickens?

MCMASTER. Yes. Charles Dickens. It is apparent in all his books. *(They start into the house.)* I just unpacked them again today. I had to put them away to preserve them after Barnabas died. I was not expecting another visitor quite so soon. (HENTY *gives him an uneasy look.)* Here they all are. It has been hard to keep out the worms and ants. *(Picks up two tattered volumes.)* These two were practically destroyed. But there is an oil the Indians make that is useful.

[HENTY *runs a finger along the row of titles:* Bleak House, Nicholas Nickleby, Oliver Twist, Martin Chuzzlewit, Pickwick Papers, David Copperfield, Barnaby Rudge, Little Dorrit, Great Expectations, Old Curiosity Shop, Christmas Books, Hard Times, Dombey and Son.]

HENTY. You're very fond of Dickens, I see.

MCMASTER. More than fond, Mr. Henty. Far more. You see, they are the only books I have ever heard. My father used to read them and then later poor Barnabas. He was very kind to me. Every afternoon until he died, he read to me. Do you enjoy reading aloud?

HENTY. Well, I think—yes.

MCMASTER. I have heard all these books many times now and I never get tired. So many characters . . . so many changes of scene . . . so many words. Each time I think I find more to enjoy and admire.

HENTY. Would you like me to read to you a bit now?

MCMASTER *(with heartfelt gratitude).* I had hardly dared to hope. Oh, *yes!*

HENTY *(taking down* A Tale of Two Cities *and leafing through).* Well, which one shall we begin with?

MCMASTER. It does not matter. I find them all equally delightful.

HENTY. *A Tale of Two Cities*—

The Man Who Liked Dickens   **259**

MCMASTER. Splendid! That is the one in which Sydney Carton goes to the guillotine.

HENTY. French Revolution, yes.

MCMASTER. A distressing story, but it has a lofty and noble ending, I recall. I believe there is just time for a chapter before teatime.

HENTY. Very well . . . (HENTY *sits down and opens the book.* MCMASTER *crouches on a low stool hugging his knees like a child.* HENTY *reads.*) "Book the first. 'Recalled to Life' . . . It was the best of times, it was the worst of times; it was the age of wisdom, it was the age of foolishness; it was the season of light, it was the season of darkness; it was the spring of hope, it was the winter of despair . . ."

[*Camera moves in on* MCMASTER'S *absorbed, rapt° face.*]

Slow dissolve° to: The boat landing. Part of a large native canoe in drydock. Indians are repairing it. All activity ceases as HENTY *approaches.*

HENTY. Good morning. (*Indians do not reply.*) Uh—me guest— Mr. McMaster. (*They echo* "MCMASTER" *like an incantation°* HENTY *is encouraged.*) You speak some English, don't you? (*No response*) Mr. McMaster says most of you are his children. ("MCMASTER" *routine again*) Look—I'll be leaving here soon and I'll be wanting a boat and a guide to take me up the river. (*No response*) Boat . . . (*Slaps hull of canoe.*) Canoe . . . (*Rowing motion*) You— take—me—river. (*Takes wallet from pocket.*) Look—money. Me pay much money guide. (HENTY *shows money, extends banknote. One man takes it, passes it around to the others. They jabber, hand it back to him.*) How—surely one of you speaks a little English. (*They jabber some more and run off the scene.*)

MCMASTER (*voice over*). Ah, here you are, Mr. Henty.

[HENTY *turns.* MCMASTER *comes on.*]

HENTY. I've been trying to get acquainted with some of your villagers. Without much success, I'm afraid.

MCMASTER. They're a shy lot,° the Shirianá. What is it you want of them, Mr. Henty?

HENTY. I was trying to find out about getting a boat and a guide to take me upriver.

VOCABULARY

rapt: Deeply engrossed or involved mentally. (-*rap*- means to seize).
dissolve: Fade into (or out of) view.
incantation: A chant given during a ceremony.
lot: Here it means bunch or group.

MCMASTER. Oh, Mr. Henty, you cannot reach the main channel of the river by boat until the *rainy* season.

HENTY. How far off is that?

MCMASTER. A month or so. *(He looks up at the sun.)* Two o'clock, Mr. Henty. *(He takes* HENTY *by the arm and they walk.)* I'm most anxious to get on with Dr. Manette's manuscript. What unendurable sufferings he experienced. You read beautifully, with a far better accent than Barnabas had. It is almost as though my father were here again.

[*They walk out of the picture. The Indians look after them, shrug, return to work on the boat. Dissolve to: Book. Close up of page in* A Tale of Two Cities. *Very slow pan° up to close-up of* HENTY'S *face.*]

HENTY *(voice over).* ". . . after having been long in danger at the hands of the villagers, I have been seized with great violence and indignity and brought a great journey on foot. And now, held here against my will, I suffer beyond hope. For the love of heaven, of justice, of generosity, I supplicate° you to succor° and release me from this prison of horror, where I find every hour nearer to destruction." (HENTY *looks up for a moment, thoughtfully, then sighs and returns to the book. Move in on volume—* A Tale of Two Cities—*dissolve to copy of* Oliver Twist, *chapter five.* HENTY'S *voice, reading—)* "He was alone in a strange place; and the boy had no friends to care for him. And he wished as he crept into his narrow bed, that it were his coffin."

[*Cut to* MCMASTER *listening as* HENTY *reads.*]

MCMASTER. Poor lad, poor little Oliver Twist. *(He weeps.)*

HENTY. Perhaps we'd better skip over this part.

MCMASTER *(weeping).* No, no. Every word. I must hear every word.

[HENTY *sighs and picks up the book again. There is the rumble of thunder.*]

HENTY. Thunder! It's going to rain!

MCMASTER. I believe you are right, Mr. Henty. We should be grateful for a roof over our heads, should we not?

VOCABULARY
pan: A movement of the camera as it films over a wide area.
supplicate: Beg in a humble way as if to pray.
succor: Help.

[*Torrent of rain starts to fall. Lightning flashes.* HENTY *drops the book and rushes to the window.*]

HENTY. It's started! The rainy season!

MCMASTER. Is that such a cause for rejoicing?

HENTY. I can get back home again! Back to civilization!

MCMASTER. I'm afraid that will not be possible—not for a while, Mr. Henty. Not until the rain stops, most certainly.

HENTY. But you said the rainy season was the only time . . .

MCMASTER. That is quite true, but the native canoes are not sturdy enough for upriver travel.

HENTY. But they can build a stronger boat!

MCMASTER. Yes. They are expert boat builders.

HENTY. Well, then?

MCMASTER. But they, unfortunately, are superstitious. It is absolutely taboo° to build a boat during the rainy season.

HENTY. I don't believe it.

MCMASTER. It is a fact that you can easily find out for yourself.

HENTY. You might have told me.

MCMASTER. Did I not mention it? I forgot.

HENTY. I must know when I can get a boat! I can't stand it! I've been thinking of nothing but getting away!

MCMASTER. Poor Barnabas was like that. He thought of it all the time. But he died here . . .

[*The full horrible realization comes to* HENTY. *He turns away from* MCMASTER'S *stare and clutches the window sill. A series of lightning flashes show the crosses, now three in number, casting long, eerie shadows across the rain-swept earth. Music swells to big climax. Fade out.*]

ACT II

SCENE. *Jungle village. The sun is breaking through. The leaves are dripping a little. It is the end of the rainy season.* THOMPSON, *a prospector° with a heavy pack on his back and a pickaxe at his belt, approaches the bungalow.*

VOCABULARY

taboo: Forbidden.

prospector: One who explores an area for gold, oil, or some other natural substance (*pro-* means forward; *-spect-* means to look). ". . . a pickaxe at his belt" is a clue.

THOMPSON. Hallo! Anyone at home? (HENTY *appears at the door. Haggard and untidy, he tries to speak, but cannot.*) Well, didn't know the old man had company.

[HENTY *looks up and down agitatedly,° leaps forward, grasps* THOMPSON'S *arm.*]

THOMPSON. What's the trouble, friend. Touch of the fever?

HENTY (*pulling* THOMPSON *away from the doorway.*) Listen to me— I don't know who you are, but you found your way here and you don't seem to be lost—you have a boat?

THOMPSON. I beached it ten miles upriver. Heading north on foot. Stopped here for supplies.

HENTY. Take me with you!

THOMPSON. Prospecting for gold?

HENTY. No. Back to the boat. Back upriver. I'll pay you. I'll pay you well.

THOMPSON. Couldn't take you nohow. Got a one-man canoe, just room for my own supplies.

HENTY. You've got to help. I'm being held prisoner here.

THOMPSON. Huh? What would he be holding you prisoner for?

HENTY. To read to him.

THOMPSON. What!

HENTY. He's buried two men out here—one supposedly died of snakes, the other he held prisoner here for more than 15 years.

THOMPSON. Barnabas. You mean Barnabas Washington?

HENTY. Yes. He died just before I arrived.

THOMPSON. Sorry to hear that. But you're wrong about Barnabas. He was devoted to McMaster.

HENTY. He was afraid to say anything. Wait. I'll prove it to you. He wrote down . . . (*Crosses to bookshelf, takes torn piece of notepaper from the leaves of book and hands it to* THOMPSON.) Here. Read this.

THOMPSON (*reads*). "June second, 1939. I James McMaster of Brazil do swear to Barnabas Washington of Georgetown that if he finish this book, in fact Martin Chuh-chuz—"

HENTY. Chuzzlewit. Martin Chuzzlewit.

THOMPSON. Who's he?

HENTY. It's the title of a book by Dickens.

VOCABULARY
agitatedly: In an excited way. ". . . leaps forward, grasps Thompson's arm" is a clue.

THOMPSON. "—if he finish this book, I will let him go away back home as soon as finished. Mr. McMaster made this mark, signed Barnabas Washington." Well, I'll be—Who are you, anyway?

HENTY. John Henty.

THOMPSON. Henty. I heard that name in Manáos. Your wife's looking for you. But they're pretty sure you're dead.

HENTY. Well, I pretty nearly am! There's my *grave*—right out there.

[THOMPSON *looks out at the crosses.*]

THOMPSON. I don't get it.

HENTY. The cross on the right. You'll see it has my name on it.

THOMPSON. McMaster can't write.

HENTY. I made the inscription. He said it was to commemorate my arrival.

THOMPSON. I *see.* Well! A rescue expedition here costs a lot of money. I doubt if they'd do it on the word of a crazy old prospector like me.

HENTY (*takes watch from pocket*). Take this watch with you. My wife will identify it.

THOMPSON. Okay. (*Reaches for it.*)

HENTY. Wait, I'd better write a note.

THOMPSON (*looking out door*). Better hurry. Here comes McMaster now.

HENTY (*rummaging° desperately*). Paper . . . paper . . .

THOMPSON. I'll talk to him outside. Slip it in my pocket later on.

HENTY. Don't leave without it. Promise?

THOMPSON. I promise. (THOMPSON *goes out and meets* MCMASTER *on the steps.* HENTY *moves desperately around the room looking for pencil and paper.*)

HENTY (*breathing hard, talking under breath.*) No paper, no pencil. He thought of everything. Paper . . . (*Suddenly*) the books . . .! (*Takes down* A Tale of Two Cities, *turns pages feverishly, comes to one. Reads*) "After having been long in danger . . ." It's got to work! It's got to work. . . . (*He tears out page. Folds it. Puts it in back of watch.* MCMASTER *comes in.*)

MCMASTER (*over shoulder*). Go on over to the smokehouse, Mr. Thompson. I'll send a man over with the keys.

VOCABULARY
rummaging: Looking through the contents of something in earnest.

THOMPSON (*offstage*). Okay, pop.

[MCMASTER *goes into the back room.* HENTY *runs after* THOMPSON.]

HENTY. Put it in your pocket.

THOMPSON. Where's the note?

HENTY. In the back of the watch. I couldn't find pencil and paper, but there's a page of a book. My wife—I hope she'll understand.

[MCMASTER *comes out after the two men part. There is no indication that he has seen anything.*]

MCMASTER. Ah, Mr. Henty—I was just about to have a look at my cocoa plantation.° Care to go along?

HENTY (*a little anxious to please*). No, thank you, Mr. McMaster.

MCMASTER. Excellent . . . excellent. I won't be long. (MCMASTER *checks the cartridge magazine*° *in his gun and goes out.*)

[TRADDLES *enters, puts down an empty plate.*]

HENTY (*looking at it*). What's this supposed to be?

TRADDLES. Master say you eat.

HENTY. What are you talking about? There's nothing . . .

TRADDLES. Master say you eat—this. (*There is an offstage shot.*)

HENTY. What was that?

TRADDLES. Master out hunting.

HENTY. He said he was going to the cocoa plantation.

TRADDLES. Master is a great hunter.

HENTY (*bored*). Yes, yes. I'm sure. Well, take this and put some food on it. (*He lifts up the empty plate.*)

[MCMASTER *enters, sits at table. The shotgun is pointed at Henty.*]

MCMASTER. Did you have an interesting day, Mr. Henty?

HENTY. Why do you ask?

MCMASTER. I did. Most interesting. (*He peers outside.*) Goodness. It must be well past our usual hour. May I trouble you for the time, Mr. Henty?

HENTY (*pretending to fish in pockets for watch*). That's strange. I don't seem to have it on me.

MCMASTER (*rising and dangling* HENTY'S *watch before him*). Is this it, Mr. Henty?

VOCABULARY

plantation: Here it means an area of ground where a crop is planted.
cartridge magazine: A compartment in a gun that holds the bullets.

The Man Who Liked Dickens

HENTY. Where did you get that?

MCMASTER (*peers outside*). A prospector stopped here this afternoon for supplies. He met with an accident a short distance from here. Apparently he was light-fingered as well as careless, for this was found on his person.

HENTY. You murdered him!

MCMASTER. Murder a man for stealing a watch? I do not believe there is an instance for that, even in Dickens.

HENTY. (*breaking*). Let me go—!

MCMASTER. I have told you repeatedly you are free to go. You are under no restraint.

HENTY. You know that I can't get to Manáos without help.

MCMASTER. In that case, you must humor an old man. Read me another chapter. (TRADDLES *enters with plate heaped high with food—roast duck, etc.*) Ah! Roast duck with wild rice—delicious. I am sorry there is not another portion, Mr. Henty. But perhaps this will be a lesson for you. I felt in your reading of *Oliver Twist* that you were not sufficiently sympathetic with the plight of that unfortunate lad. Let us hope you do better by *David Copperfield*. (*He begins to eat.* HENTY *watches him, broken. He reaches automatically for the book, opens it.*)

Dissolve to: Exterior. Day. TRADDLES *runs into clearing.* MCMASTER *comes out of the bungalow to greet him.*

TRADDLES. Master, big party, many boats, come this way.

MCMASTER. Where did they land?

TRADDLES. North of PyeWye village, one-two day journey.

MCMASTER. Send an escort of our men to meet them and bring them here.

TRADDLES. They look for white man, lost in jungle. Henty.

MCMASTER. Exactly.

TRADDLES. There is a woman with them.

MCMASTER. A woman? English?

TRADDLES. They say she is wife of man who reads for master, Henty.

MCMASTER. That is good. See that they are brought here, dear boy. I want the whole village to welcome them. There will be piwari° and dancing—a feast day. (MCMASTER *goes up to the verandah where* HENTY *lies sleeping in the hammock.*) Mr. Henty, wake up.

VOCABULARY

piwari: An intoxicating drink made from a type of bread.

HENTY. No. No, please, I feel too ill to read today.

MCMASTER. Today is a holiday, Mr. Henty.

HENTY. Holiday?

MCMASTER. One of the native feast days. We are invited to the chief's enclosure to drink *piwari.*

HENTY *(ironical).* You don't say.

MCMASTER. *Piwari* is a ceremonial drink of the Shiriana. The effects are quite pleasant. I believe it will cheer you up.

HENTY. If I thought it would cheer me up, I'd drink arsenic.°

MCMASTER. Then you accept the chief's invitation?

HENTY *(sits up, yawning).* By all means, Mr. McMaster. Tell him I'll be there.

Dissolve to compound° at night. Torches. Indian dance in progress. Indians drinking out of skin flagons.° Suddenly TRADDLES *taps* MCMASTER'S *shoulder and points off. Cut° to* MRS. HENTY *and two pith°-helmeted white men,* WILLIAMS *and* SMYTHE, *approaching the scene.* MCMASTER *comes to greet them.*

MCMASTER. My dear lady, my dear, dear lady. I regret that my welcome must be tempered with bad news.

MRS. HENTY. Bad news?

MCMASTER. You are Mrs. Henty, are you not?

MRS. HENTY. Yes. You have news of my husband?

MCMASTER. He found his way here six months ago—ill and delirious.° He spoke a few words and lapsed into a coma. The next morning he was dead.

MRS. HENTY *(dry sob).* Poor John. Where—? Where is—?

MCMASTER. Just over there. He shares a plot with two others whose journey ended here.

[He leads them to the graves. Camera pans slowly to: Lean-to° enclosure near the dancers. HENTY *and fat* CHIEF. CHIEF *drinks and hands calabash to* HENTY.]

HENTY. Wonderful. Wonderful party. Wonderful drinks. What you say this was called?

CHIEF *(mumbling native word).* Piwari.

VOCABULARY

arsenic: A poison.

compound: A group of buildings (in this case huts) together.

flagons: Containers with a handle and spout for holding wine and other drinks.

cut: Move to another scene quickly.

pith: The soft center in a stem of a plant.

delirious: In a state of great mental confusion.

lean-to: A shelter formed by resting a structure up against some other structure.

HENTY. *Piwari. (Giggles.)* Remind me to buy a case—take back to England. *(Lifts calabash.)* God save the Queen! *(Drinks, then suddenly looks toward groups at grave.)* There's my wife! Brenda! *(He rises and takes a few steps forward, reels, drops calabash. Collapses.* CHIEF *helps* HENTY *to a straw mat where he passes out. Cut to grave.)*

BRENDA. But I tell you it sounded exactly like John's voice, calling my name. Didn't you hear anything?

WILLIAMS. Nothing but the infernal° howling of those savages.

MCMASTER. Won't you come into the house? It will be quieter there.

MRS. HENTY. Thank you. You're very kind.

[They go ahead of MCMASTER, *enter bungalow.)*

MCMASTER *opens a cupboard and takes out* HENTY'S *watch).* I saved this out of your husband's effects. I thought—you might want a memento° of him.

MRS. HENTY. His watch . . . thank you. Mr. McMaster, you are very kind. . . .

MCMASTER. You may well be proud of him, Mrs. Henty. He died trying to find help for his friends. His epitaph° might well have said, like Sydney Carton: "It is a far, far better thing I do than I have ever done. It is a far better rest that I go to than I have ever known."

*[*MRS. HENTY *breaks down. Sobs on* WILLIAMS' *shoulder. She drops the watch. It falls open.* SMYTHE *picks it up.]*

SMYTHE *(unfolding the book page that was in the back of the watch).* This is peculiar . . .

MRS. HENTY *(stops weeping).* The watch—

SMYTHE. I picked it up. But look— *(Extends the page.)* This was in it.

MRS. HENTY. A page from out of a book.

MCMASTER *(outraged).* My book. He defaced° my book! *(Tries to grab page.)*

SMYTHE *(holds it away).* Wait a moment. *(Reads bits.)* "After having been long in danger . . . at the hands of the villagers . . . seized with great violence . . . held here against my will . . . for the love of heaven, of justice, of generosity, I supplicate you to succor and release me from this prison of horror. . . ."

VOCABULARY

infernal: As one might find in an everlasting hell.

mememto: A reminder.

epitaph: The words on a tombstone in memory of the person buried there (*epi-* means over; *-taph* means tomb).

defaced: To spoil the appearance of (*de-* here means ruin).

MRS. HENTY. Did you say my husband tore this from one of your books?

MCMASTER. By accident, I'm sure. While he was reading to me, I daresay.

MRS. HENTY. Reading to you? But you said he spoke only a few words and lapsed into a coma.

MCMASTER. I—I have had a most fatiguing day. I—I am not myself. The noise of the festival. So many visitors. We are so retired here as a rule. I must ask you to be tolerant of an old man's failing memory. *(Goes to door and shouts.)* Quiet! Stop that infernal howling and go to bed. *(Noise stops instantly.)* My guides will see you back to your camp.

WILLIAMS. You seem to be in a great hurry to be rid of us.

HENTY'S VOICE *(off—very faintly).* Brenda . . . Brenda . . .

MRS. HENTY. There it is again . . . his voice. *(Frantic)* I know it was his voice. I know. He's alive and that thing in the watch was meant as a message—

*[*MCMASTER *is frozen to the spot, his eyes darting from one to the other.]*

WILLIAMS. There's one simple way to make sure.

MRS. HENTY. What?

WILLIAMS. Dig up that grave.

MCMASTER. No!

[They turn. He raises the rifle.]

MRS. HENTY. What do you want of my husband? Why are you keeping him?

WILLIAMS. Three graves? Two occupied and one in readiness. Just what is your game, Mr. McMaster?

*[*HENTY *staggers into doorway.]*

HENTY. I'll tell you . . .

*[*MCMASTER *wheels around, is seized.]*

MRS. HENTY. John!

HENTY. Here's his game . . . and *(wildly)* here's the finish of it. *(Grabs a book.)* Bleak House! *(Throws it on the cooking fire in the hearth).* Little Dorrit! *(Throws.)* Hard Times! *(Takes armload. Throws all at once.)*

MCMASTER. My books. No! No! Don't! All my beautiful friends . . . .

[Drops on his knees before the fire, grasping at singed° pages of his books . . . as the curtain falls.]

VOCABULARY

singed (sĭnjed): Burned at the edges.

QUESTIONS FOR REFLECTION/DISCUSSION

1. It is interesting to discover someone's character through the eyes of different persons. Think about McMaster, for example. What words might he use to describe himself? What words might Henty use to describe him? How would you describe McMaster?

2. When did you realize that McMaster was not the man he appeared to be? When did Henty come to this same realization?

3. How does McMaster feel about the natives who work for him? Give examples to support your conclusion. How common is it for a man like McMaster to dominate the native people in an area? Think of other examples of this kind of oppression. Share them with a small group. Why do you think some people are able to be so successful in dominating others?

4. We have looked at irony before (see especially p. 14). Do you find irony in this play? If so, explain what it is that you find ironical and why.

5. Good authors very carefully prepare their readers with subtle hints about what is going to happen in a story. You learned earlier that this preparation is called *foreshadowing*. If authors did not use foreshadowing, readers would probably not believe the events when they occur. For example, we learn early on that McMaster is not able to read. This fact, along with many others, foreshadows later occurrences during which Henty is forced to read Dickens to McMaster. It causes us to accept these occurrences. Below are three events or possible eventualities that we accept when they are brought to our attention because they have been properly foreshadowed. With a partner, talk about the foreshadowing that leads to each one. Write down your ideas to share with your class and the instructor later.
   a. Henty is forced to read Dickens to McMaster.
   b. Henty may never be able to leave alive.
   c. Someone will come looking for Henty.

EXPLORING OTHER SOURCES

1. In a newspaper or a magazine, find one or two articles about real-life situations in which one or more people were able to successfully dominate others. What were the circumstances? How were they able to gain control? What were the results? Share what you learn with a small group.

2. Choose a novel by Charles Dickens to read. You can use the list on page 254 as a starting point. If you want something shorter in length, try "A Christmas Carol." From time to time, share what you are learning about his characters and the plot with others in your class. Do any of the characters turn out to be much different from the way they first appear?

3. See if you can locate the original story by Evelyn Waugh from his book *A Handful of Dust,* published by Little, Brown and Company in 1934. When you read it, you will notice that it has a very different ending. Read the ending aloud to a small group and ask them which ending they like best.

SYNTHESIS THROUGH WRITING

1. In your journal, discuss your reaction to McMaster's actions and his character. In your opinion, does he have any good qualities?

2. Rewrite one or more scenes from the play, shortening them for acting out or reading aloud. Using a small group of classmates to play the various roles, you may want to present a scene to your class.

3. Write an essay about the domination of one or more people over others, which you may have researched in the previous section, Exploring Other Sources. See the writing strategies on page xix if necessary. Create your own graphic organizer to help you develop your paper.

4. Write a critical essay on one of the novels of Charles Dickens that you read in Exploring Other Sources. Include these things:
   a. The plot or main events of the story
   b. An analysis of one or more main characters from more than one point of view, if possible
   c. The strengths and/or weaknesses of the novel from your point of view
   Refer to the writing strategies on page xix.

An American Slave [excerpt]

Frederick Douglass

Slavery is perhaps the most cruel act a society can inflict upon fellow human beings. It deprives them of their personhood and gives them little hope for a better tomorrow. Even after slaves become free, the degradation follows them throughout life and even affects future generations. The cost to society is enormous in terms of lost human potential.

Frederick Douglass, the author of this selection, was one who never lost hope, in spite of the fact that he himself was a slave from the day he was born in the early nineteenth century until 1838, when he escaped from bondage. At that time, he used his oratorical skills to round up black soldiers for the 54th and 55th Massachusetts Regiments to fight in the Civil War. After the war, he fought for the rights of African-Americans, for whom freedom finally had become a reality. He produced three biographies: *Narrative of the Life of Frederick Douglass, An American Slave; My Bondage and My Freedom;* and *Life and Times of Frederick Douglass.* At one time, he served as Minister of the United States to Haiti.

What you are about to read comes from his first book, *Narrative of the Life of Frederick Douglass, An American Slave,* published in 1845 by the Anti-Slavery Office in Boston. He wrote this book while his memories were still very vivid and fresh in his mind. Some of what is included here may be shocking to those readers unfamiliar with this shameful period in America's history. In addition, readers may find the language use and the writing style a bit odd, considering that the piece was written in an earlier century.

Before You Read

How do you think slaveowners might have justified their holding of slaves? What might your response have been to them? Write about it in your journal.

Part I

I was born in Tuckahoe, near Hillsborough, and about twelve miles from Easton, in Talbot county, Maryland. I have no accurate knowledge of my age, never having seen any authentic record containing it. By far the larger part of the slaves know as little of their ages as horses know of theirs, and it is the wish of most masters within my knowledge to keep their slaves thus ignorant. I do not remember to have ever met a slave who could tell of his birthday. They seldom come nearer to it than planting-time, harvest-time, cherry-time, spring-time, or fall-time. A want of information concerning my own was a source of unhappiness to me even during childhood. The white children could tell their ages. I could not tell why I ought to be deprived of the same privilege. I was not allowed to take any inquiries of my master concerning it. He deemed° all such inquiries on the part of a slave improper and impertinent,° and evidence of a restless spirit. The nearest estimate I can give makes me now between twenty-seven and twenty-eight years of age. I come to this, from hearing my master say, some time during 1835, I was about seventeen years old.

My mother was named Harriet Bailey. She was the daughter of Isaac and Betsey Bailey, both colored, and quite dark. My mother was of a darker complexion than either my grandmother or grandfather.

My father was a white man. He was admitted to be such by all I ever heard speak of my parentage. The opinion was also whispered that my master was my father; but of the correctness of this opinion, I know nothing; the means of knowing was withheld from me. My mother and I were separated when I was but an infant—before I knew her as my mother. It is a common custom, in the part of Maryland from which I ran away, to part children from their mothers at a very early age. Frequently, before the child has reached its twelfth month, the mother is taken from it, and hired out on some farm a considerable distance off, and the child is placed under the care of an old woman, too old for field labor. For what this separation is done, I do not know, unless it be to hinder the development of the child's affection toward its mother, and to blunt and destroy the natural affection of the mother for the child. This is the inevitable result.

I never saw my mother, to know her as such, more than four or five times in my life; and each of these times was very short in duration, and at night. She was hired by a Mr. Stewart, who lived about twelve miles from my home. She made her journeys to see me in the night, travelling the whole distance on foot, after the performance of her day's work. She was a field hand, and a whipping is the penalty of not being in the field at sunrise, unless a slave has special permission from his or her master to the contrary—a permission which they seldom get, and one that gives to him that gives it the proud name of being a kind master. I do not recollect of ever seeing my mother by the light of day.

VOCABULARY
deemed: Considered.
impertinent: Rude. The word "improper" is a clue.

She was with me in the night. She would lie down with me, and get me to sleep, but long before I waked she was gone. Very little communication ever took place between us. Death soon ended what little we could have while she lived, and with it her hardships and suffering. She died when I was about seven years old, on one of my master's farms near Lee's Mill. I was not allowed to be present during her illness, at her death, or burial. She was gone long before I knew any thing about it. Never having enjoyed, to any considerable extent, her soothing presence, her tender and watchful care, I received the tidings of her death with much the same emotions I should have probably felt at the death of a stranger.

Called thus suddenly away, she left me without the slightest intimation° of who my father was. The whisper that my master was my father, may or may not be true; and, true, or false, it is of but little consequence to my purpose whilst° the fact remains, in all its glaring odiousness,° that slaveholders have ordained,° and by law established, that the children of slave women shall in all cases follow the condition of their mothers; and this is done too obviously to administer to their own lusts, and make a gratification of their wicked desires profitable as well as pleasurable; for by this cunning arrangement, the slaveholder, in cases not a few, sustains to his slaves the double relation of master and father.

I know of such cases; and it is worthy of remark that such slaves invariably suffer greater hardships, and have more to contend with, than others. They are, in the first place, a constant offence to their mistress. She is ever disposed° to find fault with them; they can seldom do any thing to please her; she is never better pleased than when she sees them under the lash, especially when she suspects her husband of showing to his mulatto° children favors which he withholds from his black slaves. The master is frequently compelled to sell this class of his slaves, out of deference° to the feelings of his white wife; and, cruel as the deed may strike any one to be, for a man to

---

VOCABULARY

intimation: A hint.
whilst: An old-fashioned way to say "while."
odiousness: Offensiveness (*odi-* refers to hate).
ordained: Ordered by one's authority.
disposed: Willing.
mulatto: A person having one white parent and one black parent.
deference: Acting in a way that shows respect for the opinion or feelings of another person.

sell his own children to human flesh-mongers, it is often the dictate of humanity for him to do so; for, unless he does this, he must not only whip them himself, but must stand by and see one white son tie up his brother, of but few shades darker complexion than himself, and ply° the gory lash to his naked back; and if he lisp one word of disapproval, it is set down to his parental partiality, and only makes a bad matter worse, both for himself and the slave whom he would protect and defend.

Every year brings with it multitudes of this class of slaves. It was doubtless in consequence of a knowledge of this fact, that one great statesman of the south predicted the downfall of slavery by the inevitable laws of population. Whether this prophecy is ever fulfilled or not, it is nevertheless plain that a very different-looking class of people are springing up at the south, and are now held in slavery, from those originally brought to this country from Africa; and if their increase will do no other good, it will do away the force of the argument, that God cursed Ham,[1] and therefore American slavery is right. If the lineal° descendants of Ham are alone to be scripturally° enslaved, it is certain that slavery at the south must soon become unscriptural; for thousands are ushered° into the world, annually, who, like myself, owe their existence to white fathers, and those fathers most frequently their own masters.

I have had two masters. My first master's name was Anthony. I do not remember his first name. He was generally called Captain Anthony—a title which, I presume, he acquired by sailing a craft on the Chesapeake Bay.[2] He was not considered a rich slaveholder. He owned two or three farms and about thirty slaves. His farms and slaves were under the care of an overseer. The overseer's name was Plummer. Mr. Plummer was a miserable drunkard, a profane° swearer, and a savage monster. He always went armed with a cowskin and a heavy

---

VOCABULARY
ply: To use.
lineal: In a straight or direct line.
scripturally: According to the Bible.
ushered: Brought into.
profane: Very disrespectful of things that are sacred to others.

CULTURAL NOTES
[1]Ham was the son of Noah, who was chosen by God, according to the Bible, to build the ark (boat) that saved many humans and animals during the great Flood of ancient times. Some consider him to be an ancestor of the Egyptians.
[2]Chesapeake Bay is a waterway extending 200 miles inland from the Atlantic Ocean. It is located in the states of Virginia and Maryland.

cudgel.° I have known him to cut and slash the women's heads so horribly, that even master would be enraged at his cruelty, and would threaten to whip him if he did not mind himself. Master, however, was not a humane slaveholder. It required extraordinary barbarity on the part of an overseer to affect him. He was a cruel man, hardened by a long life of slaveholding. He would at times seem to take great pleasure in whipping a slave. I have often been awakened at the dawn of day by the most heart-rending shrieks of an own aunt of mine, whom he used to tie up to a joist,° and whip upon her naked back till she was literally covered with blood. No words, no tears, no prayers, from his gory victim, seemed to move his iron heart from its bloody purpose. The louder she screamed, the harder he whipped; and where the blood ran fastest, there he whipped longest. He would whip her to make her scream, and whip her to make her hush; and not until overcome by fatigue, would he cease to swing the blood-clotted cowskin. I remember the first time I ever witnessed this horrible exhibition. I was quite a child, but I well remember it. I never shall forget it whilst I remember any thing. It was the first of a long series of such outrages, of which I was doomed to be a witness and a participant. It struck me with awful force. It was the blood-stained gate, the entrance to the hell of slavery, through which I was about to pass. It was a most terrible spectacle. I wish I could commit to paper the feelings with which I beheld it.

This occurrence took place very soon after I went to live with my old master, and under the following circumstances. Aunt Hester went out one night,—where or for what I do not know,—and happened to be absent when my master desired her presence. He had ordered her not to go out evenings, and warned her that she must never let him catch her in company with a young man, who was paying attention to her belonging to Colonel Lloyd. The young man's name was Ned Roberts, generally called Lloyd's Ned. Why master was so careful of her, may be safely left to conjecture.° She was a woman of noble form, and of graceful proportions, having very few equals, and fewer superiors, in personal appearance, among the colored or white women of our neighborhood.

VOCABULARY

cudgel: A heavy, short club.
joist: A beam of wood used to support a floor or ceiling.
conjecture: Guesses.

Aunt Hester had not only disobeyed his orders in going out, but had been found in company with Lloyd's Ned; which circumstance, I found, from what he said while whipping her, was the chief offence. Had he been a man of pure morals himself, he might have been thought interested in protecting the innocence of my aunt; but those who knew him will not suspect him of any such virtue. Before he commenced° whipping Aunt Hester, he took her into the kitchen, and stripped her from neck to waist, leaving her neck, shoulders, and back, entirely naked. He then said to her,

". . . I'll learn you how to disobey my orders!" and after rolling up his sleeves, he commenced to lay on the heavy cowskin, and soon the warm, red blood (amid° heart-rending shrieks from her, and horrid oaths from him) came dripping to the floor. I was so terrified and horror-stricken at the sight, that I hid myself in a closet, and dared not venture out till long after the bloody transaction was over. I expected it would be my turn next. It was all new to me. I have never seen any thing like it before. I had always lived with my grandmother on the outskirts of the plantation,° where she was put to raise the children of the younger women. I had therefore been, until now, out of the way of the bloody scenes that often occurred on the plantation.

Part II

My new mistress proved to be all she appeared when I first met her at the door,—a woman of the kindest heart and finest feelings. She had never had a slave under her control previously to myself, and prior to her marriage she had been dependent upon her own industry for a living. She was by trade a weaver; and by constant application to her business, she had been in a good degree preserved from the blighting° and dehumanizing effects of slavery. I was utterly astonished at her goodness. I scarcely knew how to behave towards her. She was entirely unlike any other white woman I had ever seen. I could not approach her as I was accustomed to approach other white

---

VOCABULARY

commenced: Began.
amid: In the middle of.
plantation: Here it means an estate with lands for growing certain crops like tobacco, cotton, etc., that are harvested by the workers living on the estate.
blighting: Destructive.

ladies. My early instruction was all out of place. The crouching servility,° usually so acceptable a quality in a slave, did not answer when manifested° toward her. Her favor was not gained by it; she seemed to be disturbed by it. She did not deem it impudent° or unmannerly for a slave to look her in the face. The meanest slave was put fully at ease in her presence, and none left without feeling better for having seen her. Her face was made of heavenly smiles, and her voice of tranquil music.

But, alas!° this kind heart had but a short time to remain such. The fatal poison of irresponsible power was already in her hands, and soon commenced its infernal° work. That cheerful eye, under the influence of slavery, soon became red with rage; that voice, made all of sweet accord, changed to one of harsh and horrid discord; and that angelic face gave place to that of a demon.

Very soon after I went to live with Mr. and Mrs. Auld, she very kindly commenced to teach me the A, B, C. After I had learned this, she assisted me in learning to spell words of three or four letters. Just at this point of my progress, Mr. Auld found out what was going on, and at once forbade Mrs. Auld to instruct me further, telling her, among other things, that it was unlawful, as well as unsafe, to teach a slave to read. To use his own words, further, he said, "If you give a nigger an inch, he will take an ell.° A nigger should know nothing but to obey his master—to do as he is told to do. Learning would *spoil* the best nigger in the world. Now," said he, "if you teach that nigger (speaking of myself) how to read, there would be no keeping him. It would forever unfit him to be a slave. He would at once become unmanageable, and of no value to his master. As to himself, it could do him no good, but a great deal of harm. It would make him discontented and unhappy." These words sank deep into my heart, stirred up sentiments within that lay slumbering, and called into existence an entirely new train of thought. It was a new and special revelation, explaining dark and mysterious things, with which my youthful understanding had struggled, but struggled in vain. I now understood what had

---

VOCABULARY

servility: State of being in the service of others (*servi-* means slave).

manifested: Made obvious or revealed (*man-* means hand; *-fest-* here means gripped).

impudent: Rude (*im-* means not; *-pude-* refers to being ashamed). The word "unmannerly" is a clue.

alas: An old-fashioned way to express fear or sorrow.

infernal: Associated with or related to hell.

ell: A British measurement equal to 45 inches.

been to me a most perplexing difficulty—to wit,° the white man's power to enslave the black man. It was a grand achievement, and I prized it highly. From that moment, I understood the pathway from slavery to freedom. It was just what I wanted, and I got it at a time when I the least expected it. Whilst I was saddened by the thought of losing the aid of my kind mistress, I was gladdened by the invaluable instruction which, by the merest° accident, I had gained from my master. Though conscious of the difficulty of learning without a teacher, I set out with high hope, and a fixed purpose, at whatever cost of trouble, to learn how to read. The very decided manner with which he spoke, and strove to impress his wife with the evil consequences of giving me instruction, served to convince me that he was deeply sensible of the truths he was uttering. It gave me the best assurance that I might rely with the utmost confidence on the results which, he said, would flow from teaching me to read. What he most dreaded, that I most desired. What he most loved, that I most hated. That which to him was a great evil, to be carefully shunned, was to me a great good, to be diligently sought; and the argument which he so warmly urged, against my learning to read, only served to inspire me with a desire and determination to learn. In learning to read, I owe almost as much to the bitter opposition of my master, as to the kindly aid of my mistress. I acknowledge the benefit of both.

I had resided but a short time in Baltimore before I observed a marked difference, in the treatment of slaves, from that which I had witnessed in the country. A city slave is almost a freeman, compared with a slave on the plantation. He is much better fed and clothed, and enjoys privileges altogether unknown to the slave on the plantation. There is a vestige° of decency, a sense of shame, that does much to curb and check those outbreaks of atrocious cruelty so commonly enacted upon the plantation. He is a desperate slaveholder, who will shock the humanity of his non-slaveholding neighbors with the cries of his lacerated° slave. Few are willing to incur° the odium° attaching to the

---

VOCABULARY
to wit: Namely; that is to say.
merest: Slightest.
vestige: A trace.
lacerated: Here it means cut or wounded.
incur: Bring upon oneself.
odium: The state of being hateful (*odi-* refers to hate). ". . . attaching to the reputation of being a cruel master" is a clue.

reputation of being a cruel master; and above all things, they would not be known as not giving a slave enough to eat. Every city slaveholder is anxious to have it known of him, that he feeds his slaves well; and it is due to them to say, that most of them do give their slaves enough to eat. There are, however, some painful exceptions to this rule. Directly opposite to us, on Philpot Street, lived Mr. Thomas Hamilton. He owned two slaves. Their names were Henrietta and Mary. Henrietta was about twenty-two years of age, Mary was about fourteen; and of all the mangled and emaciated° creatures I ever looked upon, these two were the most so. His heart must be harder than stone, that could look upon these unmoved. The head, neck, and shoulders of Mary were literally cut to pieces. I have frequently felt her head, and found it nearly covered with festering sores, caused by the lash of her cruel mistress. I do not know that her master ever whipped her, but I have been an eye-witness to the cruelty of Mrs. Hamilton. I used to be in Mr. Hamilton's house nearly every day. Mrs. Hamilton used to sit in a large chair in the middle of the room, with a heavy cowskin always by her side, and scarce an hour passed during the day but was marked by the blood of one of these slaves. The girls seldom passed her without her saying, "Move faster, you *black gip!*" at the same time giving them a blow with the cowskin over the head or shoulders, often drawing the blood. She would then say, "Take that you *black gip!*"—continuing, "If you don't move faster, I'll move you!" Added to the cruel lashings to which these slaves were subjected, they were kept nearly half-starved. They seldom knew what it was to eat a full meal. I have seen Mary contending with the pigs for the offal° thrown into the street. So much was Mary kicked and cut to pieces, that she was oftener called *"pecked"* than by her name.

Part III

I lived in Master Hugh's family about seven years. During this time, I succeeded in learning to read and write. In accomplishing this, I was compelled to resort to various stratagems.° I had no regular teacher. My mistress, who had kindly commenced to

---

VOCABULARY

emaciated: Made thin by starvation or disease (*e-* here means completely; *-macia-* refers to making thin).
offal: The parts of a butchered animal that are thrown away.
stratagems: Deceptions.

instruct me, had, in compliance° with the advice and direction of her husband, not only ceased to instruct, but had set her face against my being instructed by any one else. It is due, however, to my mistress to say of her, that she did not adopt this course of treatment immediately. She at first lacked the depravity° indispensable to shutting me up in mental darkness. It was at least necessary for her to have some training in the exercise of irresponsible power, to make her equal to the task of treating me as though I were a brute.

My mistress was, as I have said, a kind and tender-hearted woman; and in the simplicity of her soul she commenced, when I first went to live with her, to treat me as she supposed one human being ought to treat another. In entering upon the duties of a slaveholder, she did not seem to perceive that I sustained° to her the relation of a mere chattel,° and that for her to treat me as a human being was not only wrong, but dangerously so. Slavery proved as injurious to her as it did to me. When I went there, she was a pious,° warm, and tenderhearted woman. There was no sorrow or suffering for which she had not a tear. She had bread for the hungry, clothes for the naked, and comfort for every mourner that came within her reach. Slavery soon proved its ability to divest° her of these heavenly qualities. Under its influence, the tender heart became stone, and the lamblike disposition gave way to one of tiger-like fierceness. The first step in her downward course was in her ceasing to instruct me. She now commenced to practise her husband's precepts.° She finally became even more violent in her opposition than her husband himself. She was not satisfied with simply doing as well as he had commanded; she seemed anxious to do better. Nothing seemed to make her more angry than to see me with a newspaper. She seemed to think that here lay the danger. I have had her rush at me with a face made all up of fury, and snatch from me a newspaper, in a manner that

---

VOCABULARY

compliance: Giving in to a wish, demand, or requirement. (". . . with the advice and direction of her husband) . . ." is a clue.

depravity: Moral corruption (*de-* here means completely; *-prav-* means distorted).

sustained: Kept in existence over time (*sus-* means up from under; *-tain-* means to hold).

chattel: Property or a slave.

pious: Having a deep respect for religion.

divest: To strip or take away.

precepts: Principles or rules.

An American Slave   281

fully revealed her apprehension. She was an apt° woman; and a little experience soon demonstrated, to her satisfaction, that education and slavery were incompatible with each other.

From this time I was most narrowly watched. If I was in a separate room any considerable length of time, I was sure to be suspected of having a book, and was at once called to give an account of myself. All this, however, was too late. The first step had been taken. Mistress, in teaching me the alphabet, had given me the *inch*, and no precaution could prevent me from taking the *ell*.

The plan which I adopted, and the one by which I was most successful, was that of making friends of all the little white boys whom I met in the street. As many of these as I could, I converted into teachers. With their kindly aid, obtained at different times and in different places, I finally succeeded in learning to read. When I was sent on errands, I always took my book with me, and by going one part of my errand quickly, I found time to get a lesson before my return. I used also to carry bread with me, enough of which was always in the house, and to which I was always welcome; for I was much better off in this regard than many of the poor white children in our neighborhood. This bread I used to bestow° upon the hungry little urchins,° who, in return, would give me that more valuable bread of knowledge. I am strongly tempted to give the names of two or three of those little boys, as a testimonial° of the gratitude and affection I bear them; but prudence° forbids;—not that it would injure me, but it might embarrass them; for it is almost an unpardonable offence to teach slaves to read in this Christian country. It is enough to say of the dear little fellows, that they lived on Philpot Street, very near Durgin and Bailey's shipyard. I used to talk this matter of slavery over with them. I would sometimes say to them, I wished I could be as free as they would be when they got to be men. "You will be free as soon as you are twenty-one, *but I am a slave for life!* Have not I as good a right to be free as you have?" These words used to

---

VOCABULARY

apt: Here it means capable.
bestow: To give as an award or honor.
urchins: Small uncared-for children.
testimonial: A formal declaration that something is true (*test*- means witness).
prudence: Wisdom.

trouble them; they would express for me the liveliest sympathy, and console me with the hope that something would occur by which I might be free.

I was now about twelve years old, and the thought of being *a slave for life* began to bear heavily upon my heart. Just about this time, I got hold of a book entitled "The Columbian Orator." Every opportunity I got, I used to read this book. Among much of other interesting matter, I found in it a dialogue between a master and his slave. The slave was represented as having run away from his master three times. The dialogue represented the conversation which took place between them, when the slave was retaken the third time. In this dialogue, the whole argument in behalf of slavery was brought forward by the master, all of which was disposed of by the slave. The slave was made to say some very smart as well as impressive things in reply to his master—things which had the desired though unexpected effect; for the conversation resulted in the voluntary emancipation° of the slave on the part of the master.

In the same book, I met with one of Sheridan's[3] mighty speeches on and in behalf of Catholic emancipation. These were choice documents to me. I read them over and over again with unabated° interest. They gave tongue to interesting thoughts of my own soul, which had frequently flashed through my mind, and died away for want of utterance. The moral which I gained from the dialogue was the power of truth over the conscience of even a slaveholder. What I got from Sheridan was a bold denunciation° of slavery, and a powerful vindication° of human rights. The reading of these documents enabled me to utter my thoughts, and to meet the arguments brought forward to sustain slavery; but while they relieved me of one difficulty, they brought on another even more painful than the one of which I was relieved. The more I read, the more I was led to abhor° and detest my enslavers. I could regard them in no other light than a

---

VOCABULARY
emancipation: The act of giving freedom from slavery.
unabated: Not reduced or lessened (*un-* means not).
denunciation: The act of denouncing or being strongly against.
vindication: The act of proving the worth of.
abhor: Hate. The word "detest" is a clue.

CULTURAL NOTES
[3]Philip Henry Sheridan, who lived from 1831 to 1888, was a commander of the Union cavalry during the Civil War.

band of successful robbers, who had left their homes, and gone to Africa, and stolen us from our homes, and in a strange land reduced us to slavery. I loathed them as being the meanest as well as the most wicked of men. As I read and contemplated° the subject, behold! that very discontentment which Master Hugh had predicted would follow my learning to read had already come to torment and sting my soul to unutterable anguish. As I writhed° under it, I would at times feel that learning to read had been a curse rather than a blessing. It had given me a view of my wretched° condition, without the remedy. It opened my eyes to the horrible pit, but to no ladder upon which to get out. In moments of agony, I envied my fellow-slaves for their stupidity. I have often wished myself a beast. I preferred the condition of the meanest reptile to my own. Any thing, no matter what, to get rid of thinking! It was this everlasting thinking of my condition that tormented me. There was no getting rid of it. It was pressed upon me by every object within sight or hearing, animate or inanimate. The silver trump of freedom had roused my soul to eternal wakefulness. Freedom now appeared, to disappear no more forever. It was heard in every sound, and seen in every thing. It was ever present to torment me with a sense of my wretched condition. I saw nothing without seeing it, I heard nothing without hearing it, and felt nothing without feeling it. It looked from every star, it smiled in every calm, breathed in every wind, and moved in every storm.

I often found myself regretting my own existence, and wishing myself dead; and but for the hope of being free, I have no doubt but that I should have killed myself, or done something for which I should have been killed. While in this state of mind, I was eager to hear any one speak of slavery. I was a ready listener. Every little while, I could hear something about the abolitionists.° It was some time before I found what the word meant. It was always used in such connections as to make it an interesting word to me. If a slave ran away and succeeded in getting clear, or if a slave killed his master, set fire to a barn, or did any thing very wrong in the mind of a slaveholder, it was spoken of as the fruit of *abolition*. Hearing the word in this

---

VOCABULARY
contemplated: Thought about.
writhed: Twisted the body.
wretched: Miserable.
abolitionists: Those who wanted to get rid of or abolish slavery.

connection very often, I set about learning what it meant. The dictionary afforded me little or no help. I found it was "the act of abolishing"; but then I did not know what was to be abolished. Here I was perplexed.° I did not dare to ask any one about its meaning, for I was satisfied that it was something they wanted me to know very little about. After a patient waiting, I got one of our city papers, containing an account of the number of petitions from the north, praying for the abolition of slavery in the District of Columbia, and of the slave trade between the States. From this time I understood the words *abolition* and *abolitionist*, and always drew near when that word was spoken, expecting to hear something of importance to myself and fellow-slaves. The light broke in upon me by degrees. I went one day down on the wharf of Mr. Waters; and seeing two Irishmen unloading a scow° of stone, I went, unasked, and helped them. When we had finished, one of them came to me and asked, "Are ye° a slave for life?" I told him that I was. The good Irishman seemed to be deeply affected by the statement. He said to the other that it was a pity so fine a little fellow as myself should be a slave for life. He said it was a shame to hold me. They both advised me to run away to the north; that I should find friends there, and that I should be free. I pretended not to be interested in what they said, and treated them as if I did not understand them; for I feared they might be treacherous.° White men have been known to encourage slaves to escape, and then, to get the reward, catch them and return them to their masters. I was afraid that these seemingly good men might use me so; but I nevertheless remembered their advice, and from that time I resolved° to run away. I looked forward to a time at which it would be safe for me to escape. I was too young to think of doing so immediately; besides, I wished to learn how to write, as I might have occasion to write my own pass. I consoled myself with the hope that I should one day find a good chance. Meanwhile I would learn to write.

The idea as to how I might learn to write was suggested to me by being in Durgin and Bailey's ship-yard, and frequently seeing

---

VOCABULARY

perplexed: Confused.
scow: A large boat with a flat bottom.
ye: A word meaning "you." It is no longer used.
treacherous: Full of deception or hidden dangers.
resolved: Firmly decided.

the ship carpenters, after hewing,° and getting a piece of timber ready for use, write on the timber the name of that part of the ship for which it was intended. When a piece of timber was intended for the larboard° side, it would be marked thus—"L." When a piece was for the starboard° side, it would be marked thus—"S." A piece for the larboard side forward, would be marked thus—"L. F." When a piece was for starboard side forward, it would be marked thus—"S. F." For larboard aft,° it would be marked thus—"L. A." For starboard aft, it would be marked thus—"S. A." I soon learned the names of these letters, and for what they were intended when placed upon a piece of timber in the ship-yard. I immediately commenced copying them, and in a short time was able to make the four letters named. After that, when I met with any boy who I knew could write, I would tell him I could write as well as he. The next word would be, "I don't believe you. Let me see you try it." I would then make the letters which I had been so fortunate as to learn, and ask him to beat that. In this way I got a good many lessons in writing, which it is quite possible I should never have gotten in any other way. During this time, my copy-book was the board fence, brick wall, and pavement; my pen and ink was a lump of chalk. With these, I learned mainly how to write. I then commenced and continued copying the Italics in Webster's Spelling Book, until I could make them all without looking on the book. By this time, my little Master Thomas had gone to school, and learned how to write, and had written over a number of copy-books. These had been brought home, and shown to some of our near neighbors, and then laid aside. My mistress used to go to class meeting at the Wilk Street meetinghouse every Monday afternoon, and leave me to take care of the house. When left thus, I used to spend this time writing in the spaces left in Master Thomas's copy-book, copying what he had written. I continued to do this until I could write a hand very similar to that of Master Thomas. Thus, after a long, tedious effort for years, I finally succeeded in learning how to write.

VOCABULARY

hewing: Shaping with a cutting tool such as a knife.

larboard: The side of the ship next to the port or dock for loading. In this context it may refer to the left-hand side of the ship.

starboard: The right-hand side of the ship if one is in it and facing forward.

aft: Near or close to the stern or the rear of the ship.

QUESTIONS FOR REFLECTION/DISCUSSION

1. What do the following lines from the selection tell you about slavery as it was practiced in the United States and the society that allowed it?

   a. "I do not remember to have ever met a slave who could tell of his birthday" (p. 272).

   b. I never saw my mother, to know her as such, more than four or five times in my life. . . ." (p. 273).

   c. ". . . she [his mother] left me without the slightest intimation of who my father was" (p. 274).

   d. "He is a desperate slaveholder, who will shock the humanity of his non-slaveholding neighbors with the cries of his lacerated slave" (p. 279-280).

   e. "Every city slaveholder is anxious to have it known of him, that he feeds his slaves well" (p. 280).

   f. ". . . for her [referring to Mrs. Auld] to treat me as a human being was not only wrong, but dangerously so. Slavery proved as injurious to her as it did to me" (p. 281).

   g. ". . . education and slavery were incompatible with each other" (p. 282).

   h. ". . . it is almost an unpardonable offense to teach slaves to read in this Christian country" (p. 282).

   i. "They [two Irishmen] both advised me to run away to the north; that I should find friends there, and that I should be free. I pretended not to be interested in what they said, and treated them as if I did not understand them . . ." (p. 285).

2. About Mr. Auld forbidding Mrs. Auld to teach a slave to read, the author said, "From that moment, I understood the pathway from slavery to freedom" (p. 279). What did he mean? Why was this such a critical point in his life?

3. Describe what you have learned about the character of Mrs. Auld. How and why do you think she changed? See especially the line "She now commenced to practice her husband's precepts" (p. 281). Are such changes common among humans? Why or why not? Can you think of any examples from your own experience?.

4. Which slaveholder was an exception to the statement "Every city slaveholder is anxious to have it known of him, that he feeds his slaves well" (item 1e above)? What do you think this reveals about him?

5. The author proclaimed, ". . . teaching me the alphabet, had given me the *inch*, and no precaution could prevent me from taking the *ell*" (p. 282). What did he mean? What actions would he be taking to "take the ell"?

6. Why did the author read specific selections from the book entitled *The Columbian Orator* over and over again in spite of the fact that they caused him great anguish? What kept him from ending his life altogether?

7. Why did it eventually become so important for the author to learn how to write? If you have children of your own or plan to have children, what skills will be important for them to have in today's world?

Exploring Other Sources

Find out as much as you can about the history of slavery in the United States. Where did the slaves come from? From whom were they bought? How did they get to the United States? What happened to them after they arrived? What kinds of lives did they lead? When and how did they become free? Use library resources and/or the Internet. If you need help, ask your instructor or the librarian for assistance. Share what you learn with a small group. To search the Internet, point your browser to http://worldviews.wadsworth.com for information about slavery in the United States.

Synthesis Through Writing

1. In your journal, react to the author's experiences as a slave. How did some of the things he told about make you feel? How would you have reacted to the some of the treatment slaves received at the hands of their masters?

2. Write an essay about what you learned about slavery in the United States in the previous activity, Exploring Other Sources. Create your own graphic organizer. See the writing strategies on page xix for additional strategies.

3. Write an essay about slavery in another country. Include how it compared with slavery in the United States. Create your own graphic organizer. Refer to other writing strategies on page xix if necessary.

MAKING CONNECTIONS: IDEAS FOR DISCUSSION AND/OR COMPOSITION

1. Think about all the selections you read in this unit and what each had to say about reality versus illusion. Which two were the most horrifying to you? Which were the least? Tell why.

2. Assume that all the major and minor characters you read about in this unit were alive today. What advice would you give to a few of them about changing their lives for the better?

3. Compare any two characters in this unit and their attitudes toward themselves and society. Tell how the two characters are similar and how they are different.

4. Use the Internet to find additional information about the authors and/or topics in this unit that you find of particular interest. Go to World Views Online at http://worldviews.wadsworth.com for suggestions and links to other sites.

READING FOR ENRICHMENT

False Love and Other Romantic Illusions
by Dr. Stan J. Katz and Aimee E. Liu
Ticknow and Fields, 1977
An insightful discussion of romantic illusions with all their deceptions versus the reality of love that goes beyond candlelight dinners to the very routine way we often live our lives.

I Know Why the Caged Bird Sings
by Maya Angelou
Random House, 1969
One of several books written by Maya Angelou based on the struggles and joys of her own life as an African American and as a woman.

Laughing Boy

by Oliver La Farge
Signet, 1957

A classic novel about a young Navajo couple who have high hopes for a long, fulfilling life. However, they soon become very disillusioned by the corruption of the world around them.

Narrative of the Life of Frederick Douglass, An American Slave

by Frederick Douglass
Signet, 1968

In this classic autobiography, Frederick Douglass reveals the reality of slavery and the treachery of the slaveowners who do their best to keep up appearances. The excerpt on p. 280 is from this book.

The Pearl

by John Steinbeck
Viking Penguin, 1973

The story of the fisherman, Kino, who finds the "pearl of the world," only to discover that it does not bring him the happiness he expects.

*So our struggle is to continue
working to be accepted in that
larger space of American
institutions and to participate fully.*

—Bill Moyers
from "An Interview with Arturo
Madrid"

*Change, of course, is intrinsic.
There is no way to prevent it and
no profit in fretting about it.*

—Margaret Cousins
from "One More Adventure"

*. . . the longing for a final house
is great in all men . . .*

—William Saroyan
from "Anybody Home?"

The Peace of Wild Things

*When despair for the world grows in me
and I wake in the night at the least sound
in fear of what my life and my children's lives may be,
I go and lie down where the wood drake
rests in his beauty on the water, and the great heron feeds.
I come into the peace of wild things
who do not tax their lives with forethought
of grief. I come into the presence of still water.
And I feel above me the day-blind stars
waiting with their light. For a time
I rest in the grace of the world, and am free.*

—Wendell Berry

Looking Ahead

Introduction

Hope is what helps us get through troubled times—hope for freedom, for an end to fighting, for the ways and means to solve our most pressing problems as members of cultural groups and as citizens of nations and of the world. We cannot live without hope. This last unit, Looking Ahead, includes dreams that give us hope and help us understand that if we seek a better tomorrow and are willing to work hard to achieve it, we will improve our chances to reach that goal.

An Overview

This unit begins with an excerpt from William Saroyan's "Anybody Home?" This essay examines the meaning of home and the various ways of looking at it. Next is an autobiographical sketch from the collection *The Courage to Grow Old*. It is entitled "One More Adventure" by Margaret Cousins. In it, she tells about what it is like to grow old. She refers to old age as just another adventure, different from the others in many ways, but, nevertheless, filled with its own challenges and joys. Then comes "An Interview with Arturo Madrid" by Bill Moyers, the popular television figure. Through his relevant, thoughtful questions, Mr. Moyers leads educator Arturo Madrid to reveal his innermost dreams for his people—people who often find themselves struggling in a society in which many of them feel alienated. The speeches in "Shalom, Salaam, Peace—Views of Three Leaders" turn our attention to a part of the world that has a long history of war and suffering—the Middle East. Three leaders, William Jefferson Clinton, Yitzhak Rabin, and Yasser Arafat, give the world renewed hope that, with perseverance and a strong desire to achieve harmony, peace can come even to one of the most troubled regions on earth. The last selection in this unit is James Baldwin's "The Creative Process." In this essay, he reminds us that artists, whether they are appreciated during their lifetimes or not, often provide insight into a society by giving perspective to the people and events that shape its history.

Thinking Critically About the Theme

The quotes beginning this unit come from the selections you will be reading. Think about the quotes in relation to the Unit 5 theme, Looking Ahead. Choose one or two to write about in your journal. Predict what might be a few of the attitudes and opinions expressed in the selection, based on the quote you chose and on the overview you just read.

Now look back at the poem by Wendell Berry. How does it relate to the theme? Write your response in your journal. Do you like the poem? Why or why not?

Anybody Home? *[excerpt]*

William Saroyan

Looking ahead often means deciding where we want to live or put our roots down, so to speak. Sometimes it is difficult to know where that place called "home" really is or to define it in a meaningful way. Is it the place where we came from? Is it the place where we now find ourselves or will find ourselves in the future? Or is home something that is in our minds?

William Saroyan examines the meaning of home in the selection that follows, and in the process, he gives us some very unusual ways of looking at it—both global and personal. William Saroyan was an American author who did much of his writing in the middle of the twentieth century. Among his works are several plays, novels, and short stories. His most well-known titles include *The Time of Your Life* (a play), *The Human Comedy* (a novel), and *The Daring Young Man on the Flying Trapeze* (a collection of short stories).

Before You Read

How might you define "home"? Discuss the definition with several students in your class. Write about it in your journal.

 don't know what home means to me, but then I don't know what anybody means by home. Home is the world, to begin with. A man reaches home when he's born. Home is also a man's nation, his native city, his neighborhood, and finally his house, his room, his table and chair and bed. That's geographical,° but there are other aspects to the matter. Home is a man's family, which first of all is the human family. A man finds himself one among many. Home is also his nationality—American, Mexican, English, French, Italian or something else. Home is also a man's own father and mother or the memory of them, and his own son and daughter . . . .

A man is himself his home, I suppose, and that's the reason it's not a simple thing to talk about. A home should mean everything, increasingly so all the time. The only real address I have ever had was my shoes, and I think that's the reason I have always had to stop at shoe stores to look at the shoes in

---

VOCABULARY

geographical: Having to do with the earth, its features, and locations (*geo-* means earth; *-graphi-* refers to writing or pictures).

the window. To become too devoted to a house, I think, is a profound° mistake, or the beginning of commonplace failure. And yet the longing for a final house is great in all men, it seems. I know I began to long for my own home before I was nine years old, and my own son, at ten, has a whole lore° of his own home—what a place, what a life, what fun, what ideas, what freedom, what intelligence, what wonders when he gets there. Will he make it? . . . Perhaps not, but in the meantime he's got his feet in his shoes, the sidewalk under his shoes, the world all around and that's where he is and where he lives, and in the end his only home. . . .

QUESTIONS FOR REFLECTION/DISCUSSION

1. Why do you think the author says, "To become too devoted to a house, I think, is a profound mistake, or the beginning of commonplace failure"? What does he mean? Do you agree with him? What can happen to a person who becomes too devoted to a house?

2. List the descriptions of home you like best in this selection. Share your list with a partner. Tell your partner why you made the choices you did.

3. Note that in the last line, the author comes to his conclusion about what home is "in the end." Can you explain what he means? Is his conclusion supported by any other details in this selection? If so, which ones? Do you agree with this conclusion? Why or why not?

EXPLORING OTHER SOURCES

In the library and/or on the Internet, find a poem or another short literary piece you like that describes and/or defines "home." Your instructor or the librarian may be able to suggest some sources to you. Share your literary piece with a small group.

VOCABULARY

profound: Deep; felt strongly (*pro-* means before; *-found-* refers to the bottom).
lore: Unwritten knowledge.

ᴀYNTHESIS ᴛHROUGH ᴡRITING

1. In your journal, reflect upon the following question. Did reading Saroyan's descriptions about home change your perspective about this concept in any way? If you have children or a spouse, what effect do they have on your perspective? Explain.

2. Write a personal essay defining what "home" means to you. Use details from your own life to support your conclusion(s). First make a cluster of all the things that home means to you. See the following sample illustration. Then use your cluster to help you organize your essay. Refer to additional writing strategies on page xix.

What "Home" Means to Me

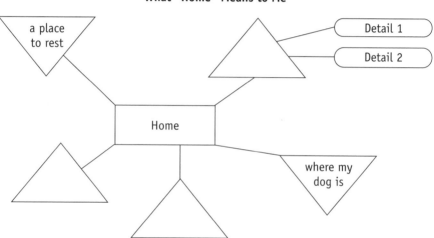

One More Adventure
Margaret Cousins

Growing old is not a time of life to which all people look forward. To some it means losing physical and mental capabilities. To others it means having to put up with gradually creeping wrinkles and other changes in appearance. The author of this selection looks at growing old a bit differently. She has learned to see it as an adventure, one that brings her new experiences, a different set of interests, and a greater appreciation of nature.

Margaret Cousins was born and raised in Texas. After graduating from the University of Texas at Austin, she moved to New York City where she became the managing editor of *McCall's* and *Good Housekeeping* magazines and the fiction editor of the *Ladies' Home Journal.* She is perhaps best known for her biographies for children, including *Ben Franklin of Old Philadelphia* and *The Story of Thomas Alva Edison.* She was awarded the George Washington Medal by the Freedom Foundation at Valley Forge.

Before You Read

Do you personally know of someone who has approached old age with a similar attitude? In your journal, describe that person.

 n my childhood, the subject of growing old rarely came up. We were too concerned with our immediate survival to spend time thinking about the future.

I grew up in a small town on the great Knox Prairie in western Texas the child of latter-day° pioneers. Both my grandfathers were homesteaders° whose families had gone west after Sherman marched to the sea and Lee surrendered at Appomattox.[1] My mother had been brought to Texas from Kentucky in a covered wagon at the age of five months, a journey from which her own mother never recovered. My father had left home at the age of fifteen to become a cowpuncher° and join the cattle drives headed north. Life was more difficult back then. It is hard for people today, who enjoy lengthened life expectancy, to realize the primitive state of medicine, surgery, immunology,° and the paucity° of resources for treating illness, which was commonplace in my youth. If my people considered the possibility of living to ripe old age, I think they would have been more likely to approach it with joy than courage. Courage was mentioned those days only when concerned with the ominous°—a funnel-shaped cloud or a rattlesnake.

VOCABULARY
latter-day: Belonging to recent times.
homesteaders: Those who settled on a piece of land and claimed it legally as their own.
cowpuncher: A cowboy.
immunology: The study of protection from disease by putting certain substances into the body (-*mun*- refers to changing).
paucity: A small number.
ominous: Relating to a bad omen or a bad sign for the future.

CULTURAL NOTES
[1]Appomattox is a town in central Virginia. William Sherman (1820–1891) was a general of the Union troops of the northern states during the Civil War. Robert E. Lee (1807–1870) was general in chief of the Confederate troops of the southern states during the same war.

I was fortunate enough to be born into a family whose members consistently stressed the basic values of a good life—morals, manners, respect for work and achievement, consideration for others, honor, truth, affection and love, discipline and self-reliance. I was consistently exposed to these and other philosophical principles, and my father had a profound determination about discipline and self-reliance in which I was thoroughly grounded with the aid of a peach limb. While I took a dim view of these matters at the time, I am eternally grateful for this grounding, for discipline may be more important at eighty than it was at eight.

Perhaps these beginnings account for the fact that I have never thought much about longevity.° I have always had friends of all ages, and one of my best friends as a child was an elderly gentleman who had been a captain in Hood's [2] brigade. He was a great storyteller and provided me with a bird's-eye view of the Civil War.[3]

When it was finally brought forcibly to my attention that I was growing old, I had neither the background, education, nor experience to cope with it. The corporation for which I had been working for several years retired me on the morning of my sixty-fifth birthday—the "automatic age," as specified in their pension° plan. I reacted with outrage. My record reflected profitability. I was working actively with a large number of accounts, several of which showed lively promise. I was scheduled to leave on a speaking tour. I could not believe that this great company, almost a hundred years old, could manage without me! If I had ever read the pension plan, I had forgotten what it said. But I reread it and it was plain—automatic age! After a few screams, cries, and hot tears, I accepted the pension and flounced° out to get another job. Needless to say, the corporation survived.

VOCABULARY

longevity: Having a long duration of life.

pension: An amount of money paid regularly to one who has retired (*pen-* refers to payment).

flounced: Moved in an exaggerated way to show displeasure.

CULTURAL NOTES

[2]John Bell Hood (1831–1879) commanded the Confederate troops of the southern states during the Civil War.

[3]The Civil War was fought in the United States between the north and the south from 1861 to 1865. It resulted in the freeing of the black slaves.

My new job provided me with a few years of fascinating experience in the workplace, but one day, when I was going along minding my own business, I was reminded of the unlikelihood of my becoming the first female Methuselah.[4] Hastening across Madison Avenue on 55th Street in New York City, at high noon, my left knee buckled involuntarily, without warning, and I fell sprawling in the middle of the street, just as the lights changed to green for onrushing traffic. I believe my life was saved by a bearded street person who rushed into the street, held up his hands to stop traffic, and literally dragged me to the curb, whereupon he disappeared. While this gallant if undignified rescue was in progress, I remember thinking woozily,° "Time to retire!" This instinct deepened when my doctor diagnosed the perfidious° knee ailment as rheumatoid arthritis,° which can only get worse.

The desire to maintain self-reliance encouraged me to carry out this decision to retire, made under stress severe enough to constitute° an omen.° To maintain my independence I felt that I must seek a simpler existence. For the first time, I experienced the necessity of courage as the fountainhead for old age. Courage persuaded me to examine the possibilities, make choices, devise new plans, and render accomplishment of them possible. Courage fueled optimism.

First I examined as many of the aspects of aging as I could ferret out.° One of the most consistent and depressing attitudes seemed to be resistance to change. This mind-set on the part of the elderly cropped up in all my studies. Old people simply fear the unfamiliar. They do not want anything to be different. They want everything to be the way it was.

Change, of course, is intrinsic.° There is no way to prevent it and no profit in fretting about it. It occurred me to me that the only way to cope with change was to join it. When I retired,

---

VOCABULARY

woozily: In a dazed or confused state.
perfidious: Faithless or disloyal (-*fid*- refers to faith).
rheumatoid arthritis: A disease involving swelling and stiffness of the joints.
constitute: Be part of.
omen: A sign of the good or evil to come.
ferret out: To drive out into the open.
intrinsic: From within; essential (*intri*- means inward). "There is no way to prevent it" is a clue.

CULTURAL NOTES

[4]Methuselah was a person who, according to the Bible, lived for 969 years.

then, at the behest° of my arthritis, I determined to change everything about my life. I decided to move to a place where I had never lived, where I had no contacts. I chose an old city with diverse cultures that had always attracted me, but which I visited only on holidays. I opted for an apartment in an old building, downtown, on the bank of a river, where there were few full-time residents. I decided to get rid of my car. Everything about my life underwent change. This took all my reserves of discipline and self-reliance, not to mention physical strength. But it accustomed me to change, sufficient to last a lifetime, and it challenged me to invent and build some sort of future for what must be euphemistically° known as my "declining years."

I can truthfully say that the last decade since my retirement has been one of the most exciting periods in my whole life, and I am profoundly grateful for the experience. Sudden access to unlimited time and declining demands of activities and energies provided me with a long-lost opportunity to review certain aspects of myself and my *modus operandi*.[5] A good many of these turned out to be mired° in the concrete of habit. I had grown so accustomed to my ways of thinking and acting and talking that I was looking backward instead of forward. I had become conservative, conventional, and stuffy.

The necessity for acquiring new occupations and making new friends drove me to discovering new possibilities. I became a volunteer, exploring church work, docentship,° public service, fund-raising for worthy causes, educational projects, literacy campaigns, animal rights, preservation and conservatism, local politics, storytelling, and even babysitting. An energetic, effective, enthusiastic world existed, which for sheer lack of time I had never experienced. I never said no to any feasible suggestion.

VOCABULARY

behest: Command.

euphemistically: Using a more pleasant or less direct word or phrase to take the place of an unpleasant or direct one (*eu-* means good; *-phemi-* means speech). The author's use of "declining years" instead of "old age" is a clue.

mired: Stuck.

docentship: The state of being a docent or a lecturer, often on a volunteer basis (*docen-* refers to teaching).

CULTURAL NOTES

[5]*Modus operandi* is Latin for a mode or way of operating.

Along with these things, which I found generally fascinating, I began to discover interests, about which most of my new friends were already aware—computers, word processors, audio, video, stereo, microwaves, cordless telephones, electronic marvels, modern music, postmodern art, minimal literature,° aerobic dancing,° and exercise, fitness, running shoes, nouvelle cuisine![6] I won't say I liked all these earmarks of emerging culture, but at least I learned they existed and had mass followings. Inevitable change is always more a beginning than an ending. Late in life I was gifted with one more adventure.

Of course, there is no gainsaying° the disturbances of old age—the stiffening joints, the declining faculties, the fading memories, the inescapable slowing down of every movement, the little flutters of panic, the unaccustomed fears. One's pride suffers at one's inability to stay the course. Hope wavers when it comes to exploration—the declining possibility of going and doing. Most devastating of all are the departures of the beloved ones, the boon companions, the long-term friends, the people who remember the same things we remember. Nothing recompenses° us for these deprivations—nothing—and only courage can hold us together . . .

But then—consider the morning light, streaked with gold; the sickle moon° dogged° by Venus, the night sky, full of stars. Think of wildflowers swarming down a rocky hillside, the taste of ripe peaches, the sound of music. Remember the wild surf, breaking six times to the horizon, the faces of children, the undeviating° loyalty of old dogs!

How could I get closer to this world? What could be more important? "World, World," wrote Edna St. Vincent Millay,[7] "I cannot get thee close enough." My sentiments exactly.

VOCABULARY
minimal literature: Literature that has a short message and uses a minimum of words.
aerobic dancing: Exercises done to music for the purpose of strengthening the heart and lungs.
gainsaying: Denying.
recompenses: Compensates; gives payment to make up for trouble, loss, or damage.
sickle moon: A moon that is shaped like a thin semicircle. It is being compared to a sickle, which
  is a semicircular blade attached to a handle.
dogged: Tracked or followed as if by a dog.
undeviating: Not moving away from the expected path or course (*un-* means not; *de-* means
  away from; *-via-* refers to a road).

CULTURAL NOTES
[6]*Nouvelle cuisine* is French for the most up-to-date dining or the very latest in foods.
[7]Edna St. Vincent Millay was an American poet and playwright who lived from 1892 to 1950.

QUESTIONS FOR REFLECTION/DISCUSSION

1. According to the author, she grew up in a family that stressed what she calls "the basic values of a good life" (p. 307). How do the values you grew up with compare with hers? Have your values changed in any way now that you are older? If you have a family of your own, what values do you stress with them? Discuss with a partner. Summarize the discussion in your journal.

2. What did the author do to find a simpler existence than the one she had been leading? Why do you think finding this kind of existence was important to her? How do you think your own life might change once you retire? Talk about it with a small group. Then write about it in your journal.

3. What do you admire most about the author? Can you think of ways the author might make her old age even better? What advice might you give her? What advice might you give your own children to help them adjust to their growing old?

EXPLORING OTHER SOURCES

Research the topic, "growing old." Use library resources and/or the Internet. Look into questions such as the following:

1. What problems do you think the elderly often face in the country in which you live? Are these problems dealt with adequately? Explain.

2. How are the problems of the elderly in the country in which you live different from the problems faced by the elderly in other parts of the world? In what ways are they alike?

3. We often hear about people "growing old gracefully." What does that mean? How does one go about growing old gracefully?

If you need help, ask your instructor or the librarian for assistance. Share what you learn with a small group. To search the Internet, point your browser to http://worldviews.wadsworth.com for links to information about the elderly.

SYNTHESIS THROUGH WRITING

1. In your journal, react to the author's attitude toward growing old. What did you learn from her that you would like to take with you into old age?

2. Select one of the questions you researched in the previous section, Exploring Other Sources, and develop an essay around it. Create your own graphic organizer. See other writing strategies on page xix, if necessary.

An Interview with
Arturo Madrid [excerpt]

Bill Moyers

In a society as diverse as the one in the United States, it is important that its citizens show respect for one another's cultures, languages, religions, opinions, and all those things that are held dear by each individual. That doesn't mean that all its citizens have to accept for themselves those things that others hold dear, but they are expected to protect the rights of others to be different. In the interview you are about to read, you will learn about what it was like for Arturo Madrid, a highly educated Latino, to deal with the stereotypical ideas that abound in the United States about people of his ethnic background. Even though his ancestors were living in America long before the British and the Europeans arrived, he still finds himself asked, "And where are you from?" as though he were an alien who does not really belong.

Arturo Madrid lives in Claremont, California, and is the president of the Tomás Rivera Center, which examines the effects of policies and practices on the Latin-American community. Although Bill Moyers' interview with him could have fit into a number of themes in this book, I chose to include it in this unit because, as you will soon see, Arturo Madrid's dream for a new world comes through in almost every word he utters, so great is his desire to see it come true.

Before You Read

Have you ever felt like a stranger in your own country, or do you know someone who has? If so, what does it feel like? Write about it in your journal.

 OYERS:[1] You've said that you've spent most of your adult life trying to explain who you were not. In what sense?

CULTURAL NOTES
[1]Bill Moyers is a television commentator and journalist.

MADRID: When people look at me and find out what my name is and what my profession is—somehow, I am no longer part of their mental set, that is, I'm not part of an American reality that they know. Surely, I must be from somewhere else—Latin America, Spain, wherever. So I have to explain that I'm American, and then I have to explain that my parents aren't first generation, and that my grandparents aren't first generation, and that in fact my ancestors have lived here for a long time. I have to explain that I'm not somebody from some other country who's immigrated to the United States. That's what I mean by explaining who I am not.

MOYERS: This wasn't a problem when you were a child because you grew up in New Mexico, surrounded by people with similar names who looked alike and talked alike.

MADRID: No, it wasn't until I left New Mexico and came in contact with that larger world, particularly with people whose historical experiences have never really connected them to the Mexican origin community, that I began to have to explain who I was and who I wasn't. Los Angeles was very interesting because people in Los Angeles who met me assumed either that I was a recent immigrant or that my parents were immigrants. That then began to involve me in explaining the history of New Mexico and the Southwest.

MOYERS: What did it say to you that so many people perceived of you, a native-born American, as an outsider?

MADRID: It was problematical for me because that had not been part of my experience. My parents were educated folks. My mother was both an appointed and elected public official in New Mexico. People who had names like mine and looked like me held professional and political appointments and were part of the larger world. So I did not suffer the experience that so many other people of Mexican origin or Latinos in general experienced in America of being "defined out." I knew I was part of the fabric of the society. I had come out of a community where we were part of that fabric, and so when this "defining out" began to be a problem for me, I struggled against it and tried to understand where that was coming from and how my experience related to that of Mexicans and other Hispanics in the U.S.

MOYERS: "Defining out"—that's an interesting phrase. What did it mean to you?

An Interview with Arturo Madrid   **305**

MADRID: It meant that by virtue of the fact° that my name was not Smith or Jones, my presence had no validity in American life, that what I had experienced and what my family and the people around me had experienced was marginal° to what took place in the larger society. We were not seen as part of the American nation but as an accretion° to the American nation. We were Mexicans, and, therefore, we had another historical reality, another national process that was not the American process. So in that sense, we were "defined out."

Now, there was another way I was defined out, which was not a cerebral° process but a visual process. When I looked at movies and television, I saw that the Latinos in those movies were not Americans, but Mexicans or Latin Americans. So my experiences and the people around me were not to be found in public life, and they were not to be found on TV or in the movies. In that sense, I was defined out of reality.

MOYERS: So the popular culture was not sending back to you reflections of your own experience. When did you begin to feel that you were "the other"?

MADRID: It happened early on in New Mexico, simply because although we were the predominant° population, we came in contact with places like Los Alamos. As I grew older, I saw a different life from the life that we were part of, and all of those things and the media, little by little, cumulatively° said we were different from the rest of the society. We were the other. That was most acute° for me in two places. One was school, where we had a sense of what that larger reality was, and the other one was church, because there were two kinds of churches, the American church and the Spanish church. Even though in some of the communities where my parents lived there was no Spanish church, and we went to the American church, still we knew that our rightful place was in the other church, not in the American church.

MOYERS: Why did you know that?

VOCABULARY
by virtue of the fact: By reason of; on the basis of.
marginal: Small in importance.
accretion: Here it means something added externally.
cerebral: Relating to the brain (*cere-* refers to the upper part of the head).
predominant: Being a main force or influence.
cumulatively: Increasing by adding to something again and again (*cumul-* means heap)
acute: Here it means intense (*acut-* means sharp).

MADRID: Because there was nobody else like us in that church, and because it was something you felt very much.

MOYERS: What happens to you when you're made to feel like you're the other?

MADRID: Two things happen. One is that you start putting up your defenses very quickly against being made to feel that you're not good enough, that you're different, that you're not part of that larger world. The second thing is, you start working very hard to incorporate yourself into that larger reality, to present yourself as well as you can, and in those areas where you're made to feel that you're not good enough, you make sure that you're not only good enough but even better. So, on the one hand, defensiveness comes into play, and on the other hand, you really work hard to stand out.

MOYERS: Somewhere you said that it makes you feel either like a sore thumb or invisible.

MADRID: Entering a space where you are not wanted or that you haven't occupied before puts you in a very difficult situation. Are you going to be seen and dealt with appropriately, or are you going to be invisible? Are you going to stick out, or are you just simply not going to be noticed, and your interests and your concerns not reflected? . . .

MOYERS: What do we do? You have said that if we're going to settle some of these issues, we're going to have to change the way we talk about them. What do you mean?

MADRID: Among other things, we have to start thinking and acting like Garrison Keillor[2] in the world of Lake Wobegon, where all the children are above average. We have to start thinking that it's possible for all kids to do very well, and that we could have good housing, good nutrition, and good legal protection for all the citizens in the society. People must feel that it is their society and that it is responsive to them. If you empower people to demand the same benefits and protections that everybody else has, then there's a chance they'll get them. You can do something about your situation as a community. There is the example of COPS, the community organization in San Antonio. They said, "Despite the fact that we're paying taxes, our garbage doesn't get picked up. We don't have a good

---

CULTURAL NOTES
[2]Garrison Keillor is the author of a series of satires about Lake Wobegon, a fictional town in Minnesota.

water system. The potholes in the streets are not fixed." You can organize around those things and make sure that they get addressed.

MOYERS: They organized, and they changed that.

MADRID: You can similarly say, "Schools need to be better for our children. Our children need to feel safe when they go to school. They need to be able to learn. We should have better teachers and better materials. We should demand more of the school." And you can actually go in and do that. You may not be able to do very much about the macro-problems,° but you can certainly address the issues within your community.

MOYERS: So we've got to stop saying that Hispanics are noncompetitive, Hispanics are passive, Hispanics are interested in immediate gratification°—that's what you mean by "changing the way we talk about problems."

MADRID: Yes. To my Latino community, I say, "You have to develop a public voice, and you have to use it. You have to bring knowledge and information to bear. You can't just complain, you have to act." To the larger community in the United States, I say, "This is part of an American reality. This is part of America's future. You have to make space, and when you do, you'll find a very responsive community, a very creative, dynamic, and hard-working community, ready to participate fully."

MOYERS: You talk about the future—since 1965, seventy-eight percent of all the immigrants coming to this country have come from Latin America, Asia, and the Caribbean. What do you think this says about our future?

MADRID: First of all, what it says about our present is that we have to start dealing with our population in a very different way than we have, historically. We can't write off the human resources any more. You can't just put twenty percent of the population on welfare. You can't put another thirty percent of the population on unemployment. Every person matters. As we get to be an older population, it's important that the younger population be a working population, a healthy population, and a learning population, so that it can sustain this society. If we don't assure that the new immigrants and the people we have historically excluded from the larger life of the society are

---

VOCABULARY

macro-problems: Large problems (*mac-* means large).
gratification: Pleasure or satisfaction (*grat-* means pleasurable or favorable).

empowered—become education, get good jobs, and learn to learn, so that they can be adapting to all the change that's going on—our future is not assured. People are no longer distant or alien° from each other. Almost every population group in the world can be found in some part of the United States. So we need to learn to live together and to respect differences.

MOYERS: Does this mean that there's finally a melting pot in our future? Or are we going to remain a boiling caldron° in which all of these factions are indissoluble?° Or, to change the analogy,° will we be like a great quilt of many patches?

MADRID: I like the quilt of many patches. It is not in our interests for it to be a caldron. We need to work together. We need to learn how to deal with that diversity° and to understand that the only constant we have today is change. If we understand those two things, we won't have that caldron boiling. Maybe we can get it down to a simmer. But if we really work at it, maybe we can change that metaphor° and not talk about a caldron but a "salad bowl," where there are many different ingredients. There are radishes and tomatoes and onions in there—but still and all, they come together, and form a whole, a salad.

MOYERS: The myth is that we have been accepting of immigrants, that we have welcomed them and protected them, and that we tolerate diversity and pluralism.° But the reality has not been that benign,° has it?

MADRID: It has not, particularly not for the Latino population, which has been denied many of the protections of American society. They've enjoyed some of the advantages and some of the benefits, but been denied some of the protections, especially legal protections. Some of the advantages that have been denied—and they're not so much advantages as rights—are good education, access to good housing, and good medical care.

VOCABULARY

alien: Belonging to another country or race; foreigner (al- means other).
caldron: A big pot or kettle used for boiling.
indissoluble: Incapable of being broken up (in- here means not).
analogy: Likeness through comparison.
diversity: A variety (di- means aside; -vers- means to turn).
metaphor: A comparison not using the words "like" or "as."
pluralism: People of different races, cultures, religions, political views living together in peace
    (plur- means many).
benign: Harmless (beni- means well).

Those things are terribly important. If you are not well rooted in the society, if you always feel that your roots are very, very superficial,° then any storm will knock them out. Any storm will make it very difficult for the plant to grow. This has happened time and time again to the Mexican-origin community.

MOYERS: There's a term for that in Spanish—

MADRID: Yes. A *flor de tierra*—that is, a flower that has very shallow roots. We're desert people, and in the desert, that's part of what happens. You have very spare plants with very shallow roots. Sometimes those plants don't last. We have to figure out ways of sending deeper roots into the soil and making it possible for people to function well in this society.

MOYERS: The story of your grandmother illustrates that possibility.

MADRID: Yes, at the beginning of the twentieth century, my grandmother and her family decided to leave their small mountain village in the Sangre de Cristo Mountains in northern New Mexico and move down to the Rio Grande Valley of New Mexico. My grandmother, being a very religious person, went to her pastor to ask his blessing as she moved her family to the valley. Her pastor said, "Well, of course, Doña Trinidad, but I want you to promise something to me before you leave. I want you to promise me that you're going to go to church when you get to the valley." And she said, "Of course I will—but why do you ask?" And he said, "Because in the valley, there is not a Spanish church, there's only an American church." And she said, "But I don't know what difference that would make. I speak English, I write English, I read English, and I would be able to worship there without any problem." And he said, "No, you don't understand. It's not that you couldn't worship there, it's that they might not welcome you into the fellowship, and that's why I want you to promise me that you're going to go to church. And furthermore," he said, "I want you to promise me that if they don't let you in the front door, that you go in the back door. And if you can't go in the back door, that you go in the side door. And if they don't let you in the door, then you come in through the window—but you must go in, and you must worship there."

VOCABULARY

superficial: On the surface; shallow (*super-* means above: *-fici-* means face). "If you are not well rooted in the society" is a clue.

That's in a sense what has happened to many of us in American society. We were excluded by social, economic, and other types of pressures. And so over the last twenty-five years—and even before then—we were pushing at the doors of the institutions of American society and saying we have to participate in this society. Some of us were able to come in through the front door with all our credentials. But most of us had to come in through back doors and through side doors, and many, many came through windows. What happened in many of those cases is that we ended up in the back rooms or the side rooms or in the lobby or in the niches, and we really didn't get to participate fully in the life of the society. Some have, most have not. So our struggle is to continue working to be accepted in that larger space of American institutions and to participate fully. When that happens, I think we can begin to change some of the other things that happen in society.

QUESTIONS FOR REFLECTION/DISCUSSION

1. Madrid feels that, even though he was born and raised in the United States, he felt "defined out," or marginalized. Why do you think he felt this way? Had he always felt this way? Explain. Do you think being marginalized is the reality for other Americans as well? Explain. Do television and the media also define people out? Have you ever felt defined out? If so, how did it make you feel? Discuss these questions first with a partner. Then join a small group for a similar discussion.

2. Does there seem to you to be a pattern in the way nondominant groups are treated by dominant groups? Do you see an "us versus them" kind of thinking as being central to this issue? Explain. How does this kind of thinking relate to the formation of stereotypes? According to Moyers, what stereotypes have affected the Latino-American population in particular? What do stereotypes have to do with nondominant groups being marginalized? What groups other than ethnic groups have been affected by similar stereotypes? How can stereotypical thinking be overcome? Consider both the persons who allow themselves to think this way and the victims of such thinking.

3. Do you agree with Madrid that part of the answer to the plight of Latin Americans and other nondominant groups can be found in Garrison Keillor's world of Lake Wobegon? Do you think the answer can be found basically in education? Explain. With which recommendations made by Madrid do you agree the most? Are there any with which you

disagree strongly? If so, which ones? Are there other changes that you think need to be made that Madrid doesn't talk about?

4. Madrid feels that the public schools need to do a better job for our children. Do you agree? If so, how can they improve, in your opinion? If you have school-aged children, how would you rate their schools? What role should schools play in a diverse society?

5. Which comparison do you think describes best the society you would prefer—the melting pot, the quilt of many patches, or the salad bowl? Explain. Which one would you least like? Why?

6. What do you think Madrid means by these words, "We have to figure out ways of sending deeper roots into the soil and making it possible for people to function well in this society" (p. 318)? How might this be done? Is one's first language and culture relevant to sending deeper roots into the soil? Explain.

7. What advice did the pastor of Madrid's grandmother give her? Do you think the advice was good? Why or why not? What would your advice have been had you been the pastor?

EXPLORING OTHER SOURCES

1. Research the history of two or more nondominant groups in the United States. Here are some examples:
Native Americans
African Americans
Hispanic Americans
Irish Americans
German Americans
Italian Americans
Japanese Americans
Korean Americans
Vietnamese Americans
Laotian Americans

Find out as much as you can about their problems in their new country, not only of the first generation, but of succeeding generations. Use library resources and/or the Internet. To search the Internet, go first to http://worldviews.wadsworth.com for links to other sources. Ask your instructor or the librarian for assistance if you need it. Do you see any basic differences between the treatments by the dominant society of groups such as the Irish Americans and the German Americans and those of groups such as African Americans and

Japanese Americans? If so, how do you explain the differences in treatment? Could the differences have anything with the idealized "melting pot" becoming a "boiling caldron"? Share what you learn with a small group.

2. Set up an interview of your own with someone who has had experiences similar to those of Madrid. Use Moyers' questions as a guide. At World Views Online you will find a sample interview and a "Guide to Interviewing." Record your interview and play part of it to a small group. Discuss the answers that were given.

ᏚYNTHESIS ᏗHROUGH ᎳRITING

1. Have you ever felt "invisible" in a group? How did it feel? What was the situation? Why do you think you felt or were made to feel that way?

2. Select one of the questions you researched in the previous section, Exploring Other Sources, and develop an essay around it. Create your own graphic organizer. See other writing strategies on page xix, if necessary.

3. Write an essay about your own vision of the future for the United States or another country with a diverse population. Create your own graphic organizer. For additional writing strategies, see page xix.

Shalom, Salaam, Peace[1]—Views of Three Leaders

William Jefferson Clinton
Yitzhak Rabin
Yasser Arafat

In this section are the short, but vibrant, speeches made by William Jefferson Clinton, President of the United States; Yitzhak Rabin, Prime Minister of Israel; and Yasser Arafat, Chairman of the Palestine Liberation Organization at the Middle East peace-signing ceremony on Monday, September 13, 1994 in Washington.

With this peace signing came the hope of the world that the antagonisms and revenge for past atrocities be replaced by peaceful

---

CULTURAL NOTES
[1]These three words all mean "peace" in Hebrew, Arabic, and English, respectively.

coexistence and mutual cooperation among these nations of the Middle East. The agreement was first negotiated secretly in the guest house of Norway's Foreign Ministry in the middle of the night on August 20, 1994. Several officials representing all sides, including Foreign Minister Peres of Israel, initialed documents concerning self-government for the Palestinians in the West Bank and Gaza Strip, which Israel had occupied since the Arab-Israeli War in 1967. It was, without a doubt, an historic moment, and champagne was passed all around.

Less than a month later, came the official signing at the White House and the unforgettable speeches that everyone hoped would be a major turning point for that troubled part of the world.

Unfortunately, Yitzhak Rabin's life ended tragically as a result of his fight for peace. He was killed on November 4, 1995, by a twenty-seven-year-old Jewish law student representing the religious right. Rabin was shot as he was leaving a pro-peace rally in Tel Aviv after giving his last speech. The world was left stunned by this shocking event. However, the Jewish people vowed to continue his struggle for peace.

Before You Read

What do you already know about the history of the relationship between the Palestinians and the Israelis prior to these events? Share your knowledge with a small group.

William Jefferson Clinton

*P*rime Minister Rabin, Chairman Arafat, Foreign Minister Peres, President Bush, distinguished guests, on behalf of the United States and Russia, co-sponsors of the Middle East peace process, welcome to this great occasion of history and hope.

Today we bear witness to an extraordinary act in one of history's defining dramas, a drama that began in a time of our ancestors when the word went forth from a sliver of land between the River Jordan and the Mediterranean Sea.

That hallowed° piece of earth, and land of life and revelation is the home to the memories and dreams of Jews, Muslims, and Christians throughout the world.

As we all know, devotion to that land has also been the source of conflict and bloodshed for too long.

VOCABULARY
hallowed: Made holy.

Throughout this century, bitterness between the Palestinian and Jewish people has robbed the entire region of its resources, its potential, and too many of its sons and daughters. The land has been so drenched in warfare and hatred that conflicting claims of history etched so deeply in the souls of the combatants there that many believe the past would always have the upper hand.

Then, 14 years ago, the past began to give way when at this place and upon this desk three men of great vision signed their names to the Camp David Accord.[2] Today, we honor the memories of Menachem Begin and Anwar Sadat and we salute the wise leadership of President Jimmy Carter.

Then, as now, we heard from those who said that conflict would come again soon. But the peace between Egypt and Israel has endured. Just so, this bold, new venture today, this brave gamble that the future can be better than the past must endure.

Two years ago in Madrid, another President took a major step on the road to peace by bringing Israel and all her neighbors together to launch direct negotiations, and today we also express our deep thanks for the skillful leadership of President George Bush.

Ever since Harry Truman[3] first recognized Israel, every American President, Democrat and Republican, has worked for peace between Israel and her neighbors.

Now the efforts of all who have labored before us bring us to this moment, a moment when we dare to pledge what for so long seemed difficult even to imagine: that the security of the Israeli people will be reconciled° with the hopes of the Palestinian people, and there will be more security and more hope for all.

Today, the leadership of Israel and the Palestine Liberation Organization will sign a declaration of principles on interim° Palestinian self-government. It charts a course toward reconciliation between two peoples who have both known the bitterness of exile.

VOCABULARY
reconciled: Brought together in agreement (re- means again; -concile- means to unite).
interim: Here it means temporary.

CULTURAL NOTES
[2]The Camp David Accord is the treaty signed on March 26, 1979, in Washington by Menachem Begin of Israel and Anwar Sadat of Egypt and witnessed by then United States President, Jimmy Carter. The treaty, which was originally drawn up at Camp David in Maryland, transferred the Sinai back to Egypt from Israel and called for the negotiation of Palestinian autonomy in the occupied West Bank and the Gaza Strip. However, little progress was made on the latter until after Sadat's assassination in 1981.
[3]Harry Truman was the 33rd president of the United States. He served from 1948 to 1952.

Shalom, Salaam, Peace—Views of Three Leaders   **315**

Now both pledge to put old sorrows and antagonisms behind them and to work for a shared future, shaped by the values of the Torah, the Koran and the Bible.[4]

Let us salute also today the government of Norway for its remarkable role in nurturing this agreement. But of all—above all, let us today pay tribute to the leaders who had the courage to lead their people toward peace, away from the scars of battle, the wounds and the losses of the past, toward a brighter tomorrow.

The world today thanks Prime Minister Rabin, Foreign Minister Peres and Chairman Arafat. Their tenacity° and vision has given us the promise of a new beginning.

What these leaders have done now must be done by others. Their achievement must be a catalyst° for progress in all aspects of the peace process. And those of us who support them must be there to help in all aspects, for the peace must render° the people who make it more secure.

A peace of the brave is within our reach. Throughout the Middle East, there is a great yearning for the quiet miracle of a normal life. We know a difficult road lies ahead. Every peace has its enemies, those who still prefer the easy habits of hatred to the hard labors of reconciliation.

But Prime Minister Rabin has reminded us that you do not have to make peace with your friends. And the Koran teaches that if the enemy inclines toward peace, do thou also incline toward peace.

Therefore, let us resolve that this new mutual recognition will be a continuing process in which the parties transform the very way they see and understand each other. Let the skeptics of this peace recall what once existed among these people.

There was a time when the traffic of ideas and commerce and pilgrims flowed uninterrupted among the cities of the Fertile Crescent.[5] In Spain, in the Middle East, Muslims and Jews once worked together to write brilliant chapters in the history of literature and science. All this can come to pass again.

VOCABULARY

tenacity: Holding on to something firmly (*ten-* means to hold).
catalyst: Something or someone that causes a change to occur but is not affected by that change.
render: To give what is due.

CULTURAL NOTES

[4]The Torah (the first five books of the Bible) is the sacred book of Judaism; the Koran is Islam's sacred book; and the Bible (in its entirety) is the sacred book of Christianity.
[5]The Fertile Crescent refers to the shape of the area that constitutes the pieces of land in question and all that is currently Israel.

Mr. Prime Minister, Mr. Chairman, I pledge the active support of the United States of America to the difficult work that lies ahead. The United States is committed to ensuring that the people who are affected by this agreement will be made more secure by it, and to leading the world in marshaling the resources necessary to implement the difficult details that will make real the principles to which you commit yourselves today.

Together, let us imagine what can be accomplished if all the energy and ability the Israelis and the Palestinians have invested into your struggle can now be channeled into cultivating the land and freshening the waters, into ending the boycotts and creating new industry, into building a land as bountiful and peaceful as it is holy.

Above all, let us dedicate ourselves today your region's next generation. In this entire assembly, no one is more important than the group of Arab and Israeli children who are seated here with us today. Mr. Prime Minister, Mr. Chairman, this day belongs to you.

And because of what you have done, tomorrow belongs to them. We must not leave them prey to the politics of extremism and despair, to those who would derail this process because they cannot overcome the fears and hatreds of the past.

We must not betray their future. For too long, the young of the Middle East have been caught in a web of hatred not of their own making. For too long, they have been taught from the chronicles° of war. Now, we can give them the chance to know the season of peace.

For them, we must realize the prophecy of Isaiah, that the cry of violence shall no more be heard in your land, nor rack nor ruin within your borders.

The children of Abraham, the descendants of Isaac and Ishmael,[6] have embarked° together on a bold journey. Together, today, with all our hearts and all our souls, we bid them Shalom, Salaam, Peace.

VOCABULARY

chronicles (krŏn' ĭ kəlz): Records that present events in the order in which they happened (chron- means over time)

embarked: Set forth.

CULTURAL NOTES

[6]Isaiah, Abraham, Isaac, and Ishmael are figures described in the Bible and elsewhere. Ishmael is of particular importance in that Muslims consider Arabs to be his descendants.

Yitzhak Rabin

President Clinton, the President of the United States, your excellencies, ladies and gentlemen.

This signing of the Israeli-Palestinian Declaration of Principles here today, it's not so easy, neither for myself as a soldier in Israel's war, nor for the people of Israel, nor for the Jewish people in the Diaspora[7] who are watching us now with great hope mixed with apprehension.

It is certainly not easy for the families of the victims of the wars, violence, terror, whose pain will never heal; for the many thousands who defended our lives with their own and have even sacrificed their lives for our own. For them, this ceremony has come too late.

Today, on the eve of an opportunity, opportunity for peace, and perhaps end of violence and wars, we remember each and every one of them with everlasting love.

We have come from Jerusalem, the ancient and eternal capital of the Jewish people. We have come from an anguished and grieving land. We have come from a people, a home, a family that has not known a single year, not a single month, in which mothers have not wept for their sons.

We have come to try and put an end to the hostilities so that our children, our children's children, will no longer experience the painful cost of war, violence and terror. We have come—we have come to secure their lives and to ease the sorrow and the painful memories of the past, to hope and pray for peace.

Let me say to you, the Palestinians, we are destined to live together on the same soil in the same land.

We, the soldiers who have returned from the battles stained with blood; we who have seen our relatives and friends killed before our eyes; we who have attended their funerals and cannot look into the eyes of their parents; we who have come from a land where parents bury their children; we who have fought against you, the Palestinians, we say to you today in a loud and a clear voice: Enough of blood and tears.

Enough! We have no desire for revenge; we have—we harbor no hatred toward you. We, like you, are people—people who

---

CULTURAL NOTES
[7]The Diaspora refers to the whole Jewish group living outside of Israel.

want to build a home, to plant a tree, to love, live side by side with you in dignity, in affinity,° as human beings, as free men.

We are today giving peace a chance and saying to you—and saying again to you—enough. Let us pray that a day will come when we all will say farewell to the arms.

We wish to open a new chapter in the sad book of our lives together, a chapter of mutual recognition, of good neighborliness, of mutual respect, of understanding. We hope to embark on a new era in the history of the Middle East.

Today, here in Washington at the White House, we will begin a new wakening in the relations between peoples, between parents tired of war, between children who will not know war.

President of the United States, ladies and gentlemen, our inner strength, our higher moral values have been derived for thousands of years from the Book of the Books, in one of which, Koheleth, [Ecclesiastes], we read, "To every thing there is a season and a time to every purpose under heaven."

"A time to be born and time to die, a time to kill and a time to heal, a time to weep and a time to laugh, a time to love and a time to hate, a time of war and a time of peace." Ladies and gentlemen, the time for peace has come.

In two days, the Jewish people will celebrate the beginning of a new year. I believe, I hope, I pray that a new year will bring a message of redemption° for all peoples: a good year for you, for all of you; a good year for Israelis and Palestinians; a good year for all the peoples of the Middle East; a good year for our American friends who so want peace and are helping to achieve it.

For Presidents and members of previous administrations, especially for you, President Clinton, and your staff, for all citizens of the world, may peace come to all your homes.

In the Jewish tradition, it is customary to conclude our prayers with the word *amen*—as you said "Amen." With your permission, men of peace, I shall conclude with words taken from the prayer recited by Jews daily, and whoever of you volunteer, I would ask the entire audience to join me in saying "Amen." Amen.

VOCABULARY
affinity: Close connection.
redemption: Here it means fulfillment.

Shalom, Shalom, Peace—Views of Three Leaders   **319**

Yasser Arafat

"In the name of God, the Most Merciful, the Compassionate. Mr. President, ladies and gentlemen, I would like to express our tremendous appreciation to President Clinton and to his Administration for sponsoring this historic event which the entire world has been waiting for.

Mr. President, I am taking this opportunity to assure you and to assure the great American people that we share your values for freedom, justice and human rights—values for which my people have been striving.

My people are hoping that this agreement which we are signing today marks the beginning of the end of a chapter of pain and suffering which has lasted throughout this century.

My people are hoping that this agreement which we are signing today will usher in an age of peace, coexistence and equal rights.

We are relying on your role, Mr. President, and on the role of all the countries which believe that without peace in the Middle East, peace in the world will not be complete.

Enforcing the agreement and moving toward the final settlement, after two years, to implement all aspects of U.N. Resolutions 242 and 338 in all of their aspects, and resolve all the issues of Jerusalem, the settlements, the refugees and the boundaries will be a Palestinian and an Israeli responsibility.

It is also the responsibility of the international community in its entirety to help the parties overcome the tremendous difficulties which are still standing in the way of reaching a final and comprehensive settlement.

Now as we stand on the threshold of this new historic era, let me address the people of Israel and their leaders, with whom we are meeting today for the first time, and let me assure them that the difficult decision we reached together was one that required great and exceptional courage.

We will need more courage and determination to continue the course of building coexistence and peace between us.

This is possible and it will happen with mutual determination and with the effort that will be made with all parties on all the tracks to establish the foundations of a just and comprehensive peace.

Our people do not consider that exercising the right to self-determination could violate the rights of their neighbors or infringe° on their security.

Rather, putting an end to their feelings of being wronged and of having suffered an historic injustice is the strongest guarantee to achieve coexistence and openness between our two peoples and future generations.

Our two peoples are awaiting today this historic hope, and they want to give peace a real chance. Such a shift will give us an opportunity to embark upon the process of economic, social and cultural growth and development, and we hope that international participation in that process will be extensive as it can be.

This shift will also provide an opportunity for all forms of cooperation on a broad scale and in all fields.

I thank you, Mr. President. We hope that our meeting will be a new beginning for our fruitful and effective relations between the American people and the Palestinian people.

I wish to thank the Russian Federation and President Boris Yeltsin. Our thanks also to Secretary Christopher[8] and Foreign Minister Kozyrev,[9] to the government of Norway and to the foreign minister of Norway for the positive part they played in bringing about this major achievement.

I extend greetings to all the Arab leaders, our brothers, and to all the world leaders who contributed to this achievement.

Ladies and gentlemen, the battle for peace is the most difficult battle of our lives. It deserves our utmost efforts because the land of peace, the land of peace yearns for a just and comprehensive peace. Thank you.

Mr. President, thank you, thank you, thank you."

VOCABULARY
infringe: Here it means violate or disregard (*fring-* refers to breaking).

CULTURAL NOTES
[8]Secretary Christopher is Warren Christopher, the secretary of state under William Clinton during his first term of office.
[9]Foreign Minister Kozyrev represented Russia when the original agreement was worked out in Norway.

QUESTIONS FOR REFLECTION /DISCUSSION

1. What has happened in the Middle East since the death of Yitzhak Rabin? To what extent has his vision of peace been achieved?

2. William Clinton claimed "that the security of the Israeli people will be reconciled with the hopes of the Palestinian people. . . ." (p. 323). What was he really saying? Do you agree? Why or why not?

3. When William Clinton thanked Prime Minister Rabin, Foreign Minister Peres, and Chairman Arafat, he stated that "Their tenacity and vision has given us the promise of a new beginning" (p. 324). Describe what this new beginning might look like.

4. William Clinton reminded us that "every peace has its enemies, those who still prefer the easy habits of hatred to the hard labors of reconciliation" (p. 324). What did he mean? To whom might he be referring? In what ways are the habits of hatred easy and the labors of reconciliation hard?

5. Was there any danger to the peace treaty in Yitzhak Rabin's words, "We have come from Jerusalem, the ancient and eternal capital of the Jewish people"? If so, explain what that danger was. Has the question of who owns Jerusalem been resolved? If so, how?

6. Explain the irony involved in Yitzhak Rabin's lament, "We who have come from a land where parents bury their children" (p. 326).

7. Yitzhak Rabin stated, "We, like you, are people—people who want to build a home, to plant a tree, to love, live side by side with you in dignity, in affinity, as human beings, as free men" (p. 326-327). What does this say about the commonalty of us all? Why is it important to remember this?

8. Yitzhak Rabin quoted the lines from Koheleth (Ecclesiastes) beginning with "To everything there is a season and a time to every purpose under heaven. . . ." Do you think there should be a "time to kill," "a time to hate," and "a time of war"? Do you think some use these as an excuse to kill, hate, and make war? Explain.

9. Yasser Arafat addresses the people of Israel with " . . . let me address the people of Israel and their leaders, with whom we are meeting today for the first time, and let me assure them that the difficult decision we reached together was one that required great and exceptional courage." In what ways did it require courage on the part of Yasser Arafat? In what ways did it require courage on the part of

Yitzhak Rabin? What do you think was at stake in each case? Discuss these questions with a small group. Share your group's conclusions with your class.

10. Which speech did you like best? Least? Explain.

EXPLORING OTHER SOURCES

1. In the library and/or on the Internet, find out as much as you can about the efforts for peace that led up to or helped pave the way for the 1994 Middle East peace-signing ceremony at which these three speeches were given. Share what you learn with a small group. To search the Internet, first go to http://worldviews.wadsworth.com for links to information on the Middle East situation prior to 1994.

2. Interview several people. Ask them about their reactions to what the results of the Middle East Peace agreement have been so far. If possible, try to include persons from the Middle East in your interviews. After each interview, take a few minutes to summarize in writing some of the answers you received. Share the more interesting ones with a small group. Here are a few questions you might ask:

Do you remember much about the agreement between the Israelis and the Palestinians that was signed by Yitzhak Rabin and Yasser Arafat in Washington in 1994? What do you remember about it?

Do you feel that the agreement was an important one? Why or why not?

What were the short-term results of this agreement?

What do you think the long-term results will be?

Overall, do you feel it will prove to have been effective?

In addition, check the sample interview and "Guide to Interviewing" on the Internet at http://worldviews.wadsworth.com.

3. William Clinton talked about a time in Spain and in the Middle East when Muslims and Jews once worked together to write "brilliant chapters in the history of literature and science." See especially Spain and the Middle East from the years 711–1492. Research this time period. Share what you learn with a small group.

4. In the library and/or on the Internet, see if you can find information about other conflicting groups who eventually found peace after hostile encounters. Was the peace permanent? Was there any backsliding? Describe the processes that brought the conflicting groups closer together.

SYNTHESIS THROUGH WRITING

1. In your journal, address the following. In your opinion, how can peace best be reached between factions such as the Israelis and the Palestinians? Explain your ideas in a well-developed paragraph.

2. Yasser Arafat called the battle for peace the "most difficult battle of our lives." In what ways might this be true on a one-to-one basis in our daily living? Write an essay discussing your views about conflict resolution. Refer to the writing strategies on page xix. Create your own graphic organizer to help you develop your paper.

3. Yasser Arafat said, ". . . the responsibility of the international community in its entirety to help the parties overcome the tremendous difficulties which are still standing in the way of reaching a final and comprehensive settlement." To what extent do you think a nation should help such parties in other parts of the world? Some people in the United States feel that its citizens should "mind their own business" and not get involved in other parts of the world, especially if the involvement will cost money and/or maybe even lives. Write an essay developing your ideas on this important issue. Create your own graphic organizer. Refer to the writing strategies on page xix for additional ideas.

4. Write a short, formal speech on a subject about which you feel strongly. It may be peace in the world, caring for our environment, drugs and their relationship to crime, for example. You may want to use one or more of the three speeches you just read as a model. Create your own graphic organizer to help you develop your speech.

   Read your speech to a small group or record it on a cassette tape for playback. Ask your group to make a list of the ideas they feel to be most important in your speech. They may need to hear the speech more than once. Then ask them what they think of your ideas. Do they agree with them? Why or why not? What do they think the strengths of your speech to be? Can they suggest any ways you can improve it? You may want to rewrite your speech based on what you learn. Eventually, you may want to give your speech to the whole class.

The Creative Process

James Baldwin

Throughout history, artists have provided us with glimpses into the human character and have given perspective to the events shaping the societies in which they live. Some of them have been revered by their own people; others have been reviled.

Perhaps James Baldwin's best-known work is a collection entitled *The Price of the Ticket*. It includes three book-length essays: *The Devil Finds Work, No Name in the Street,* and *The Fire Next Time.* Like Maya Angelou, James Baldwin describes the African-American experience. And, like Maya Angelou, he goes beyond that experience to explore the human psyche in general. Both reveal visions for a better world in their works selected for this volume. Read the following essay to discover exactly what James Baldwins' vision is.

Before You Read

Why do you think some artists are revered and others reviled during their lifetimes? What makes the difference? Discuss these questions with a small group or write about them in your journal.

 erhaps the primary distinction of the artist is that he must actively cultivate that state which most men, necessarily, must avoid: the state of being alone. That all men *are*, when the chips are down,° alone, is a banality°—a banality because it is very frequently stated, but very rarely, on the evidence, believed. Most of us are not compelled to linger with the knowledge of our aloneness, for it is a knowledge which can paralyze all action in this world. There are, forever, swamps to be drained, cities to be created, mines to be exploited, children to be fed: and none of these things can be done alone. But the conquest of the physical world is not man's only duty. He is also enjoined° to conquer the great wilderness of himself. The role of the artist, then, precisely, is to illuminate that darkness, blaze roads through that vast forest; so that we

---

VOCABULARY

chips are down: In this particular context, it is used as an idiomatic expression meaning "the final reality is soon to be made known." Literally chips are small disks representing money in a game such as poker. "Chips are down," means that the person putting them down on the table is ready to find out whether or not he or she has won.

banality: A common conclusion or assumption. ". . . because it is very frequently stated" is a clue.

enjoined: Directed.

will not, in all our doing, lose sight of its purpose, which is, after all, to make the world a more human dwelling place.

The state of being alone is not meant to bring to mind merely a rustic° musing° beside some silver lake. The aloneness of which I speak is much more like the aloneness of birth or death. It is like the fearful aloneness which one sees in the eyes of someone who is suffering, whom we cannot help. Or it is like the aloneness of love, that force and mystery which so many have extolled° and so many have cursed, but which no one has ever understood or ever really been able to control. I put the matter this way, not out of any desire to create pity for the artist—God forbid!—but to suggest how nearly, after all, is his state the state of everyone, and in an attempt to make vivid his endeavor. The states of birth, suffering, love, and death, are extreme states: extreme, universal, and inescapable. We all know this, but we would rather not know it. The artist is present to correct the delusions° to which we fall prey in our attempts to avoid this knowledge.

It is for this reason that all societies have battled with that incorrigible° disturber of the peace—the artist. I doubt that future societies will get on with him any better. The entire purpose of society is to create a bulwark° against the inner and the outer chaos, literally, in order to make life bearable and to keep the human race alive. And it is abolutely inevitable that when a tradition has been evolved, whatever the tradition is, that the people, in general, will suppose it to have existed from before the beginning of time and will be most unwilling and indeed unable to conceive of any changes in it. They do not know how they will live without those traditions which have given them their identity. Their reaction, when it is suggested that they can or that they must, is panic. And we see this panic, I think, everywhere in the world today, from the streets of our own New Orleans[1] to the grisly battleground in Algeria.[2] And a

---

VOCABULARY

rustic: Characteristic of the countryside; unsophisticated (*rus-* means country). ". . . beside some silver lake" is a clue.

musing: Meditation or deep thought.

extolled: Heaped with praise (*ex-* here means up; *-tol-* means to lift).

delusions: Beliefs that evidence proves false (*-lus-* comes from *-lud-* which means to play).

incorrigible: Not able to be corrected (*in-* here means not; *-corri-* means to correct).

bulwark: A structure that forms or serves as a wall.

CULTURAL NOTES

[1]New Orleans is a city in Louisiana.
[2]Algeria is a country in northwestern Africa.

higher level of consciousness among the people is the only hope we have, now or in the future, of minimizing the human damage.

The artist is distinguished from all the other responsible actors in society—the politicians, legislators, educators, scientists, et cetera—by the fact that he is his own test tube, his own laboratory, working according to very rigorous rules, however unstated these may be, and cannot allow any consideration to supersede° his responsibility to reveal all that he can possibly discover concerning the mystery of the human being. Society must accept some things as real: but he [the artist] must always know that the visible reality hides a deeper one, and that all our action and all our achievement rests on things unseen. A society must assume that it is stable, but the artist must know, and he must let us know, that there is nothing stable under heaven. One cannot possibly build a school, teach a child, or drive a car without taking some things for granted. The artist cannot and must not take anything for granted, but must drive to the heart of every answer and expose the question the answer hides.

I seem to be making extremely grandiloquent° claims for a breed of men and women historically despised while living and acclaimed when safely dead. But, in a way, the belated° honor which all societies tender their artists proves the reality of the point I am trying to make. I am really trying to make clear the nature of the artist's responsibility to his society. The peculiar nature of this responsibility is that he must never cease sparring° with it, for its sake and for his own. For the truth, in spite of appearances and all our hopes, is that everything is always changing and the measure of our maturity as nations and as men is how well prepared we are to meet these changes and, further, to use them for our health.

Now, anyone who has ever been compelled to think about it—anyone, for example, who has ever been in love—knows that the one face which one can never see is one's own face. One's lover or one's brother, or one's enemy—sees the face you wear, and this face can elicit° the most extraordinary reactions. We do the things we do, and feel what we feel, essentially

---

VOCABULARY
supersede: To take the place of (*super-* means above; *-sede-* means to sit).
grandiloquent: Overly grand or lofty (*-loqu-* means to speak).
belated: Tardy.
sparring: Here it means fighting verbally.
elicit: Bring out.

The Creative Process

because we must—we are responsible for our actions, but we rarely understand them. It goes without saying, I believe, that if we understood ourselves better, we would damage ourselves less. But the barrier between oneself and one's knowledge of oneself is high indeed. There are so many things one would rather not know! We become social creatures because we cannot live any other way. But in order to become social, there are a great many other things which we must not become, and we are frightened, all of us, of those forces within us which perpetually° menace° our precarious° security. Yet, the forces are there, we cannot will them away. All we can do is learn to live with them. And we cannot learn this unless we are willing to tell the truth about ourselves, and the truth about us is always at variance° with what we wish to be. The human effort is to bring these two realities into a relationship resembling reconciliation. The human beings whom we respect the most, after all—and sometimes fear the most—are those who are most deeply involved in this delicate and strenuous effort: for they have the unshakable authority which comes only from having looked on and endured and survived the worst. That nation is healthiest which has the least necessity to distrust or ostracize° or victimize these people—whom, as I say, we honor, once they are gone, because, somewhere in our hearts, we know that we cannot live without them.

The dangers of being an American artist are not greater than those of being an artist anywhere else in the world, but they are very particular. These dangers are produced by our history. They rest on the fact that in order to conquer this continent, the particular aloneness of which I speak—the aloneness in which one discovers that life is tragic, and, therefore, *therefore,* unutterably beautiful—could not be permitted. And that this prohibition° is typical of all emergent° nations will be proven, I have no doubt, in many ways during the next fifty years. This continent now is conquered, but our habits and our fears remain.

VOCABULARY

perpetually: Without interruption; constantly.
menace: Threaten.
precarious: Dangerously unstable.
variance: Variability or changeability (*va-* means to bend apart).
ostracize: To not accept or to shut out.
prohibition: Keeping something from happening (*pro-* means in front; *-hib-* means to hold).
   ". . . could not be permitted" in the previous sentence is a clue.
emergent: In the state of coming forth (*ex-* means out; *-merge-* means to dip).

And, in the same way that to become a social human being one modifies and suppresses and, ultimately, without great courage, lies to oneself about all one's interior, uncharted chaos, so have we, as a nation, modified and suppressed and lied about all the darker forces in our history. We know, in the case of the person, that whoever cannot tell himself the truth about his past is trapped in it, is immobilized in the prison of his undiscovered self. This is also true of nations. We know how a person, in such a paralysis, is unable to assess either his weaknesses or his strengths, and how frequently indeed he mistakes the one for the other. And this, I think, we do. We are the strongest nation in the western world, but this is not for the reasons that we think. It is because we have an opportunity which no other nation has of moving beyond the Old World concepts of race and class and caste, and create, finally, what we must have had in mind when we first began speaking of the New World. But the price for this is a long look backward whence° we came and an unflinching° assessment of the record. For an artist, the record of that journey is most clearly revealed in the personalities of the people the journey produced. Societies never know it, but the war of an artist with his society is a lover's war, and he does, at his best, what lovers do, which is to reveal the beloved to himself, and with that revelation, make freedom real.

QUESTIONS FOR REFLECTION/DISCUSSION

1. What does the author mean when he says, "Most of us are not compelled to linger with the knowledge of our aloneness, for it is a knowledge which can paralyze all action in this world" (p. 333)? How does this idea relate to the message of the essay?

2. The author states, "There are, forever, swamps to be drained, cities to be created, mines to be exploited, children to be fed: and none of these things can be done alone" (p. 333). What do you think of his list? Should swamps be drained, cities created, and mines exploited? What might modern-day environmentalists say about such activities? What cautions might such environmentalists give? How might you change or or add to the list to make it reflect your own values?

VOCABULARY
whence: From where.
unflinching: Firm; resolute.

3. What does the author feel the role of the artist should be? Do you agree or disagree? Why does he call the artist an "incorrigible disturber of the peace" (p. 334)?

4. Do you agree that the artist is ". . . distinguished from all the other responsible actors in society—the politicians, legislators, educators, scientists, et cetera—by the fact that he is his own test tube, his own laboratory . . . to reveal all that he can possibly discover concerning the mystery of the human being" (p. 335)? Why or why not?

5. To what extent is it true that artists are "despised while living and acclaimed when safely dead" (p. 335)? Can you think of examples from history that support this point of view? Think of the artists who were and/or are revered while still living? What do you think might make the difference? Discuss these questions with a small group. Share your ideas with your class.

6. The author feels that ". . . we [in the United States], as a nation, modified and suppressed and lied about all the darker forces in our history" (p. 337). Think of examples that support this opinion. Do some current politicians and others try to cover up the darker side of the past? Do some even think it "unpatriotic" to look at our darker side? If so, why might this be a dangerous thing to do? How does this issue relate to what the author is saying about artists? Discuss these questions with a small group.

7. What, in your opinion, is this author's vision for a new world?

 ## EXPLORING OTHER SOURCES

1. Find out as much as you can about artists who were "despised while living and acclaimed when safely dead." You might want to consider researching artists such as Van Gogh and/or several of the French Impressionists, in particular. What was there about them and/or their work that made them so despised? Why were they eventually acclaimed? Use library resources and/or the Internet. Ask your instructor or the librarian for assistance if you need it. Share what you learn with a small group. If you have access to photos of some of the art pieces done by the artists you selected, you may want to share these also with your group. To search the Internet, point your browser to http://worldviews.wadsworth.com for links to information about Van Gogh and about the French Impressionists.

2. Research events in the history of a country of your choice that you feel may have been distorted or ignored by history books, museums,

politicians, and so on. Your instructor or the librarian may be able to help you. Discuss these events with a small group. Why do you feel they may have been distorted or ignored? How should they be presented? Why? Discuss them with a small group.

SYNTHESIS THROUGH WRITING

1. In your journal, react to the message of this essay. To what extent do you agree with the author?

2. Write your own essay about artists and what you feel should be their place in our society. You may want to use James Baldwin's essay as a guide. Refer to the writing strategies on page xix if necessary. Create your own graphic organizer to help you develop your paper.

3. Develop an essay about one of the topics you researched in the previous section, Exploring Other Sources. Create your own graphic organizer. See additional writing strategies on page xix.

MAKING CONNECTIONS: IDEAS FOR DISCUSSION AND/OR COMPOSITION

1. Of all the visions for the future that you read about in this unit, which one do you think is the most important? Explain?

2. Do you see any similarities in the visions for the future that you read about in this unit? If so, what are they?

3. Look again at the poem by Wendell Berry on page 300. How does the poem relate to several of the readings in this unit?

4. Use the Internet to find additional information about the authors and/or topics in this unit that you find of particular interest. Go to World Views Online at http://worldviews.wadsworth.com for suggestions and links to other sites.

5. Which unit in this anthology did you find most meaningful? Why?

6. How do the units in this anthology relate to one another? Do you see any parallels in thoughts, feelings, or ideas? Do you see any direct disagreements in any of the views expressed?

7. Use the Internet to find additional information about the authors and/or topics in this unit that you find of particular interest.

Reading for Enrichment

Bill Moyers: A World of Ideas
by Bill Moyers
Doubleday, 1989

Bill Moyers interviews several contemporary figures, many of whom have keen visions of the future. "An Interview with Arturo Madrid" on page 312 comes from this collection.

The Dream Keeper and Other Poems
by Langston Hughes
Alfred A. Knopf, 1960

Langston Hughes tells us in this poetry collection not to be afraid to dream. He gives us encouragement and a belief that we can overcome whatever obstacles may present themselves.

Dwellings
by Linda Hogan
Norton, 1995

Linda Hogan, a Chickasaw poet, novelist, and environmentalist, emphasizes our duty to secure the future for our own and other species. In Native American tradition, she reminds us of the importance of our honoring the earth and all who live there.

Mohandas Gandhi
by George Woodcock
Viking Press, 1971

This biography discusses Gandhi's nonviolent opposition to oppression by the British, the dominant group in India at the time. It examines how passive resistance can change the world for the better.

On the Pulse of Morning
by Maya Angelou
Random House, 1993

This poem about the future of our existence on earth was read by poet Maya Angelou at the Inauguration of William Jefferson Clinton in 1993. It warns us to change our ways if we want to survive.

Part 1: Defining Your Terms

Part II: Refining Your Writing

Part I: Defining Your Terms

Part I of this reference guide will help you become familiar with some of the key terms and concepts you need to understand to become a more effective writer. Consult these pages if you are not sure what a conjunction or a direct object is or how to tell the difference between a phrase and a clause. As you go through Part I, you will find helpful cross-references telling you where to look for more information about a particular topic. Part II will address grammatical terms and concepts that will help sharpen your writing. So either sit down and review the basics all at once or flip back to this section if you are unsure of a term or a concept you encounter in Part II or in class.

THE PARTS OF SPEECH

To understand how to put words together to form a sentence, paragraph, essay, research paper, job application letter, resumé, e-mail message, or any other form of writing, you need to understand the different jobs that words do. When we classify words according to their various jobs, we are grouping them into categories known as the **parts of speech.**

There are eight parts of speech: **nouns, pronouns, verbs, adjectives, adverbs, prepositions, conjunctions,** and **interjections.**

Nouns

A **noun** is a word that names a person, place, thing, or idea.

PEOPLE	Sonia, guitarist, Langston Hughes, carpenters, teenager, sister, doctor
PLACES	St. Louis, apartment, mall, Bolivia, Mt. Washington, bedroom, Florida
THINGS	couch, Microsoft, chimpanzees, dumpling, Toyota Tercel, handbook
IDEAS	equality, honesty, Buddhism, homesickness, prejudice, democracy

PROPER NOUNS AND COMMON NOUNS

There are two basic types of nouns: **proper nouns** and **common nouns.** A **proper noun** names a specific person, place, thing, or idea. A **common noun** names a general category of person, place, thing, or idea, rather than a particular individual within a category. Note in the following examples that proper nouns are capitalized, but common nouns are not.

COMMON NOUNS	PROPER NOUNS
writer	Langston Hughes, Willa Cather, Charles Dickens
city	St. Louis, Detroit, Boston, Tokyo, Kingston, Mexico City
company	Microsoft, Nike, Disney, Federal Express, Sony
religion	Buddhism, Christianity, Judaism, Hinduism, Islam

COMPOUND NOUNS

A **compound noun** is a noun made up of two or more words. Some compound nouns are written with a space or a hyphen between the words (see p. 335). Others are spelled as one word.

SEPARATE WORDS	HYPHENATED WORDS	ONE WORD
ballet dancer	ex-husband	armchair
Native American	merry-go-round	minivan
station wagon	self-knowledge	playwright

If you are not sure how to spell a compound noun, check the dictionary. *The Newbury House Dictionary of American English* is a good dictionary to use. If the compound is not listed, spell it with a space between the words. Sometimes you have a choice about how to spell a compound, as long as you spell it consistently. For example: *teenager* or *teen-ager, vice-president* or *vice president, website* or *web site.*

Note: For more information on using nouns correctly, see pages 368–369.

Pronouns

A **pronoun** is a word that is used in place of one or more **nouns** (pp. 334–335). Pronouns are shortcuts that help you express your meaning without having to repeat the same noun over and over again. Compare these two sentences:

> Peter called Peter's wife and told Peter's wife that Peter would be home a little late because Peter had missed Peter's train.

> Peter called *his* wife and told *her* that *he* would be home a little late because *he* had missed *his* train.

In the following sentences, the arrows point from the pronouns to the nouns they replace, called their **antecedents**:

The <u>children</u> were playing in the mud, and *they* made an incredible mess.

The <u>dog</u> was barking and pawing at the door, so Isabella took *him* for a walk.

Notice that a pronoun may be **singular** (replacing one noun) or **plural** (more than one). A singular pronoun may also show the **gender** of the noun it is replacing: masculine (male), feminine (female), or neuter (none).

TYPES OF PRONOUNS
There are many different types of pronouns:

Personal Pronouns
Personal pronouns (*I, me, we, us, you, he, she, it, him, her, they, them*) are used to rename specific persons, places, things, or ideas that have been named earlier in the sentence or in a previous sentence.

> Lydia is starting kindergarten on Wednesday. *She* is very excited.

Possessive Pronouns
Possessive pronouns (*my, mine, our, ours, your, yours, his, her, hers, its, their, theirs*) are used to show ownership or relationship. Although they are typically called pronouns because they replace possessive nouns (*Jim's, Sarah's*), some possessive pronouns actually function as **adjectives** (p. 338) that modify, or describe, nouns.

> Eliza's younger brother, Ben, never wants *his* sister to play with *his* toys but always wants to play with *hers*.

Reflexive and Intensive Pronouns
Reflexive pronouns (*myself, ourselves, yourself, yourselves, himself, herself, itself, themselves*) are used when the subject and the object of an action are the same. (Something is "reflexive" if it refers back to itself.)

> Nick told *himself* that everything would turn out fine.

Note: Notice that some but not all of the reflexive pronouns are based on the possessive forms. The correct form is *himself* and *themselves*, not *hisself* and *theirselves*.

Relative Pronouns

Relative pronouns (*that, which, who, whom, whose*) are used to introduce certain kinds of **dependent clauses** (pp. 352–354). The relative pronoun refers, or relates, back to the noun (or sometimes another pronoun) that the clause is describing.

The <u>movie</u> *that* we saw last night was terrific.
The main character is a <u>writer</u> *who* befriends a troubled teenager.
The <u>movie</u>, *which* takes place in Brooklyn, is based on a short story.

Interrogative Pronouns

Interrogative pronouns (*who, whom, whose, which, what*) are used to begin questions. (All of these words can also function as relative pronouns.)

Who was that on the phone?
Which restaurant is better?

Indefinite Pronouns

Indefinite pronouns (*all, any, anybody, anyone, anything, both, each, either, everyone, many, neither, none, no one, somebody, someone,* and others) are used to refer to people, places, or things that are not specifically named.

Everyone agreed that the movie was too long.
Nobody really believes that O'Brien can win the election.

Demonstrative Pronouns

Demonstrative pronouns (*this, that, these, those*) points out or identifies a noun. They can be used by themselves to substitute for nouns or as **adjectives** (p. 338) that modify, or describe, nouns.

That is an amazing bicycle. [*That* points out the bicycle.]
Those crows are incredibly loud. [*Those* points out the crows.]

Note: For more information on using pronouns correctly, pages 365–366. For more information on subject-verb agreement problems with pronouns, see page 363.

Adjectives

An **adjective** is a word that modifies a **noun** (pp. 334–335) or **pronoun** (pp. 335–337). To *modify* a word means to describe it or make its meaning more specific. An adjective modifies a noun or pronoun by specifying *what kind, which one,* or *how many.* In the following chart, notice that the *adjectives* are in italics, and the **nouns** they modify are in boldface.

WHAT KIND?	WHICH ONE?	HOW MANY?
enormous **dog**	*that* **store**	*many* **applicants**
sunny **apartment**	*those* **parents**	*few* **problems**
purple **flowers**	*third* **stoplight**	*some* **questions**

Although an adjective usually comes before the word it modifies, it can sometimes come later in the sentence.

> The **subway** is always *hot* and *crowded.*

ARTICLES

The words *the, a,* and *an* are a special category of adjectives called **articles** that appear in front of certain kinds of nouns (or in front of an adjective modifying a noun). *The* is called a **definite article** because it is used to identify or define a specific noun—to show that you are talking about a particular one. *A* and *an* are called **indefinite articles** because they show that a noun is one of several possibilities or is one of a general category—it is not precisely defined. For example, if you asked your friend, "Is this the toy that Ethan broke?" you would be suggesting that Ethan broke only one toy (and you are trying to determine if the toy you are looking at is it). If your friend replied, "Well, that is *a* toy that Ethan broke," she would be suggesting that the toy you are looking at is only one of many that Ethan has broken.

The can be used with either singular or plural nouns. *A* and *an* are used only with singular nouns. *A* is used in front of words that begin with a consonant or consonant sound; *an* is used with words that begin with a vowel or vowel sound.

> *a* <u>h</u>allway, *an* <u>h</u>onest man, an HMO
>
> *a* <u>u</u>niform, *an* <u>u</u>nderground pipe, a UFO

Note: For more information on using adjectives correctly, see pages 366–367. For more information on using articles correctly, see page 369.

Verbs

A **verb** is a word that expresses an action or a state of being. The action expressed by a verb can be either physical (*run, float, breathe*) or mental (*study, believe, remember*).

TRANSITIVE AND INTRANSITIVE VERBS

Action verbs are classified as either **transitive** or **intransitive**, depending on whether or not they take a **direct object**. The **direct object** of a verb is a **noun** or **pronoun** that receives the action or shows its result (p. 347). A **transitive verb** expresses an action that needs a direct object to complete its meaning.

Paul *washed* the <u>dishes</u>.
Jennifer *understands* the <u>poem</u>.
Our softball team *won* the <u>game</u>.

An **intransitive verb** expresses an action that does not need a direct object to complete its meaning.

Clayton *giggled*.
Elizabeth *hesitated*.
I *apologized*.

Many verbs can be either transitive or intransitive, depending on how they are used.

The manager *closed* the <u>store</u> early tonight. [transitive]
Usually the store *closes* at 9 p.m. [intransitive]

LINKING VERBS

A verb that expresses a state of being rather than an action is called a **linking verb**. This type of verb connects the subject of the sentence to a noun or pronoun that renames, identifies, or explains the subject or with an adjective that describes it. The most common linking verb is *be* (in all its different forms). Other linking verbs are *appear, become, feel, grow, look, prove, remain, seem, smell, sound, stay, taste,* and *turn*.

Doug Wong *was* my <u>roommate</u> last year. [noun renames the subject]
At first she *seemed* <u>snobbish</u>. [adjective describes the subject]
Soon we *became* <u>friends</u>. [noun renames the subject]

MAIN VERBS AND HELPING VERBS

Often a verb is a single word, but sometimes it is part of a **verb phrase** (p. 349) that consists of a **main verb** plus one or more **helping verbs**.

There are twenty-three words that can serve as helping verbs. Fourteen of them—all the forms of the verbs *be*, *have*, and *do*—can also function as main verbs: *am, are, is, was, were, be, being, been, have, has, had, do, does, did*. In addition, there are nine other words that can function only as helping verbs: *may, might, must, can, could, would, should, shall, will*. A <u>main verb</u> can have up to three *helping verbs*.

Rashid *has* <u>studied</u> for six straight hours.
Alana *will be* <u>going</u> to Seattle this summer for her sister's wedding.
The children *should have been* <u>fed</u> by now.

Sometimes the <u>main verb</u> is separated from its *helping verbs* by other words in the sentence.

We *may* never <u>know</u> what really happened.
Jasmine *did* not <u>see</u> her backpack anywhere.
You *could* still <u>catch</u> your plane if you hurry.

Note: For more information on using verbs correctly, see page 364. For information on subject-verb agreement problems, see pages 362–363.

Adverbs

An **adverb** is a word that modifies a **verb** (pp. 339–340), **adjective** (p. 338), or other adverb. To *modify* a word means to describe it or make its meaning more specific. An adverb modifies a word by specifying *how, when, where,* or *to what extent* (*how long, how much*).

HOW?	Kelly *slowly* <u>climbed</u> the stairs. [adverb modifies verb]
WHEN?	Imani <u>left</u> the country *yesterday*. [adverb modifies verb]
WHERE?	I <u>go</u> to school *here*. [adverb modifies verb]
TO WHAT EXTENT?	Matt was *totally* <u>amazed</u>. [adverb modifying adjective] My cat eats *too* <u>fast</u>. [adverb modifies adverb]

Many adverbs are formed by adding *-ly* to an adjective. If the adjective already ends in *-y*, change the *-y* to *-i* and then add *-ly*. If the adjective ends in *-e*, drop the *-e*.

angry	→	angrily	quick	→	quickly
general	→	generally	skillful	→	skillfully
happy	→	happily	terrible	→	terribly

Keep in mind, however, that there are many common adverbs that do not end in *-ly*, such as *above, after, almost, away, before, below, ever, far, here, later, much, never, not, often, now, quite, really, so, somewhat, then, there, too, very,* and *well*.

Also keep in mind that although an *-ly* ending is a good clue that a word is an adverb, that ending does not always signal one. There are several adjectives that end in *-ly*, such as *daily, friendly, lonely,* and *only*. (If a word modifies a noun, it is an *adjective*. If it modifies a verb, it is an *adverb*.)

Many adverbs (such as *above, after, around, down,* and *up*) can also function as **prepositions** (pp. 341–343), depending on how they are used.

Note: For more information on determining whether a word is being used as an adverb or a preposition, see pages 342–343.

Prepositions

A **preposition** is a word that comes before a **noun** (pp. 334–335) or **pronoun** (pp. 335–337) to explain its relationship to some other word in the sentence. Often that relationship has to do with location, direction, time, or association.

Common Prepositions

about	behind	except	onto	to
above	below	for	out	toward
across	beneath	from	opposite	under
after	beside	in	out	underneath
against	between	inside	outside	unlike
along	beyond	into	over	until
among	by	like	past	up
around	concerning	near	regarding	upon
as	despite	of	since	with
at	down	off	through	within
before	during	on	throughout	without

The noun or pronoun that comes after the preposition is called the **object of the preposition**. The preposition, noun or pronoun, and any words in between combine to form a **prepositional phrase** (pp. 349–350). In each of the following sentences, the *preposition* is in italics, the <u>object of the preposition</u> is underlined, and the **prepositional phrase** is in parentheses:

James fell asleep (***during** the <u>concert</u>.*) [time]
A car skidded (***toward** <u>me</u>.*) [direction]
Isabella went rollerblading (***with** <u>Mark</u>.*) [association]
Your address book is (***on** the tall white <u>bookcase</u>.*) [location]

A sentence often contains more than one prepositional phrase. Also, the object of a prepositional phrase may consist of more than one noun or pronoun.

(*On* a hot <u>day</u>) (*in* <u>July</u>) we drove (*to* the <u>beach</u>) (*near* Rebecca's <u>house</u>) (*with* a <u>cooler</u> full *of* <u>sandwiches and watermelon</u>.)

Some prepositions can also function as **adverbs** (pp. 340–341) depending on how they are used. To act as a preposition, a word must be followed by a noun or pronoun to form a prepositional phrase. In the following sentences, notice how the same words can be used as different parts of speech. In the first sentence in which the word is used as prepositions, the <u>prepositional phrase</u> is underlined:

I looked _up the word_ in the dictionary. [preposition]
Lydia looked _up_ and noticed a tall man standing beside her. [adverb]

I am going home _after the next song_. [preposition]
I am going home _after_ I find my sister. [subordinating conjunction]

Note: For information on using prepositions correctly after certain verbs, see page 370.

Conjunctions

A **conjunction** connects other words or parts of sentences.

TYPES OF CONJUNCTIONS

There are four types of conjunctions: **coordinating conjunctions, correlative conjunctions, subordinating conjunctions, conjunctive adverbs.**

Coordinating Conjunctions

Coordinating conjunctions connect words or parts of sentences that are of equal importance. There are seven coordinating conjunctions: _and, but, or, nor, for, yet,_ and _so._ They are frequently used to combine **independent clauses**—groups of words that express a complete thought and can stand alone as sentences.

We bought a new bicycle _and_ helmet for Emily. [connects two words]
I cooked dinner, _so_ you do the dishes. [connects two independent clauses]

Correlative Conjunctions

Correlative conjunctions also connect words or parts of sentences that are equally important. Unlike coordinating conjunctions, however, they are always used in pairs that are separated by other words. There are five such pairs: _either . . . or, neither . . . nor, both . . . and, not only . . . but also,_ and _whether . . . or._

Both Ella _and_ Lucas thought the math assignment was easy.
You can _either_ sit in your stroller _or_ hold Mommy's hand.

Note: When you use correlative conjunctions, make sure that the linked elements are grammatically similar, or **parallel.** See page 367.

Subordinating Conjunctions

Subordinating conjunctions connect sentence elements that are unequal in importance. This kind of conjunction is used to link a **dependent clause** (pp. 352–354) to an independent clause. The subordinating conjunction introduces the dependent clause and shows its relationship to the main part of the sentence. In the following sentences, the subordinating conjunctions are underlined and the **dependent clauses** are in boldface:

> I was late picking up my son at daycare <u>because</u> **I hit terrible traffic.**

> <u>Even though</u> **she was nervous,** Miranda raised her hand to ask a question.

Notice that some subordinating conjunctions are two or three words that work together.

Common Subordinating Conjunctions

after	as soon as	rather than	though
although	as though	since	unless
as	because	so that	until
as if	before	than	when
as long as	even if	that	whenever

Conjunctive Adverbs

Conjunctive adverbs (sometimes called **adverbial conjunctions**) are transitional words that connect independent clauses when they are separated by semicolons rather than commas. The conjunctive adverb tells how the two ideas in the clauses are related.

> Sarah broke up with Mark; *however,* she wants to stay friends with him.

> I'm angry about my neighbor's overflowing dumpster; *in fact,* I've complained to the city board of health.

Most conjunctive adverbs should be followed by a comma.

Common Conjunctive Adverbs

accordingly	consequently	in addition	moreover	similarly
also	finally	indeed	nevertheless	still
anyway	for example	in fact	next	then
as a result	furthermore	instead	nonetheless	therefore
besides	however	meanwhile	otherwise	thus

Note: Be sure to use a semicolon rather than a comma before a conjunctive adverb. (Otherwise, you will create a type of **run-on sentence** called a **comma splice**.) Use a coordinating conjunction if you are separating independent clauses with a comma. For more information, see page 361.

Interjections

An **interjection** is a word used to express strong emotion, such as surprise, excitement, happiness, anger, pain, horror, disgust, or approval. An interjection often comes at the beginning of a sentence and is followed by an exclamation point or a comma.

Whoops! I didn't know you were in the shower.
Wow! I didn't know you had such a great voice!

Common Interjections

aha	hooray	phew	whoops
hey	oh	ugh	wow

THE PARTS OF A SENTENCE

A **sentence** is a group of words that expresses a complete thought. A sentence must contain both a **subject** and a **verb**. The **subject** of a sentence is a **noun** (pp. 334–335) or **pronoun** (pp. 335–337) that tells who or what the sentence is about. The **verb** (pp. 339–340) is the word or group of words that tells what the subject of the sentence is doing or what is being done to the subject. In each of the following sentences, the subject is underlined, and the *verb* is in italics. (Notice that a sentence begins with a capital letter and ends with a period, question mark, or exclamation point.)

<u>We</u> *took* the kids to the zoo on Saturday.
Did <u>everyone</u> *have* fun?
<u>Claire and Joe</u> *loved* the gorillas!

Note: If a group of words does not have both a subject and a verb, it is a **sentence fragment** rather than a sentence. See pages 358–361.

Subjects and Predicates

Another way to describe the structure of a sentence is to say that every sentence has a **subject** and a **predicate**. The **predicate** is the part of the sentence that says something about the **subject**. The **simple predicate** is the same thing as the verb. The **complete predicate** is the verb plus all the words that go with it.

We can also talk about the **simple subject** and the **complete subject** of a sentence. The **simple subject** is the main noun or pronoun that names the subject. The complete subject is that noun or pronoun plus all the words that go with it. In each of the following sentences, the complete subject is separated from the complete predicate by two lines. The <u>simple subject</u> is underlined, and the *simple predicate* (verb) is in italics:

COMPLETE SUBJECT	COMPLETE PREDICATE
Ian's five-piece blues <u>band</u> ||	*performs* every Friday at the Lizard Lounge.

COMPLETE SUBJECT	COMPLETE PREDICATE
Most of the <u>students</u> at my college ||	*are* well over the age of twenty-five.

COMPOUND SUBJECTS AND PREDICATES

A **compound subject** consists of two or more simple subjects that share the same verb and are joined by a **coordinating** (p. 343) or **correlative conjunction** (p. 343).

<u>Heidi and her children</u> *are moving* to New Hampshire on Wednesday.
<u>Either Danny or Matthew</u> *is sharing* a room with Brian.

A **compound predicate** consists of two or more verbs that share the same subject and are joined by a coordinating or correlative conjunction.

<u>My mother</u> *knocked* on the door *and asked* to come in.
<u>I</u> *heard* the knock *but pretended* to be asleep.

Note: In a compound predicate, do not use a comma before the conjunction joining the two verbs. However, in a **compound sentence**, which has two different subjects or a repeated subject, you do need a comma before the conjunction: "I heard the knock, but I pretended to be asleep." For more information on compound sentences, see page 356.

Complements

A **complement** is a word or group of words in the predicate that completes the meaning of the verb. There are several different kinds of complements: **direct objects**, **indirect objects**, and **subject complements**.

DIRECT OBJECTS

An **object** is a complement that does not refer to the subject. A **direct object** is a noun or pronoun that receives the action of a **transitive verb** (p. 349) or shows its result. (A **transitive verb** is an action verb that needs a direct object to complete its meaning.)

James *broke* his <u>leg</u>.
Abbey *visited* <u>him</u> at the hospital.

Note: A direct object is never part of a **prepositional phrase** (such as *at the hospital*). For more information on prepositional phrases and **objects of prepositions**, see pages 349–350.

INDIRECT OBJECTS

An **indirect object** is a noun or pronoun that comes before the direct object and tells to what (or whom) or for what (or whom) the action of the verb is done. In the following sentences, the <u>direct objects</u> are underlined and the **indirect objects** are in boldface:

Clayton *gave* **me** his old <u>computer</u>.
I *bought* my **mother** some <u>flowers</u>.

Notice that both of these sentences could be rewritten using the prepositions *to* or *for*. In the rewritten sentences, the noun or pronoun following the preposition is no longer an indirect object. Instead, it is the object of the preposition.

Clayton *gave* his old <u>computer</u> **to me**.
I *bought* some <u>flowers</u> **for my mother**.

Every sentence that includes a transitive verb must have a direct object, but not necessarily an indirect object. The direct object is needed to complete the meaning of the verb, but the indirect object is not. It would make no sense to say, "I bought" without specifying *what* you bought, but you could say "I bought some flowers" without specifying *for whom* you bought them.

Note: When either a direct or indirect object is a pronoun, it should always be in the **objective case** *(me, him, her, us, them).*

SUBJECT COMPLEMENTS

A **subject complement** is a noun, pronoun, or adjective that follows a **linking verb** (pp. 339–340) and renames, identifies, explains, or describes the subject. A **linking verb** is a verb that expresses a state of being rather than an action: *be, appear, become, feel, grow, look, prove, remain, seem, smell, sound, stay, taste,* and *turn.* (Many linking verbs can also function as action verbs, depending on how they are used.)

Predicate Nominatives and Predicate Adjectives

There are two kinds of subject complements: **predicate nominatives** and **predicate adjectives.**

A **predicate nominative** is a noun or pronoun that follows a linking verb and renames, identifies, or explains the subject.

<u>My father</u> *is* a high school music **teacher.**
<u>Babies</u> *become* **toddlers** so quickly.

A **predicate adjective** is an adjective that follows a linking verb and describes the subject.

Our <u>apartment</u> *is* so **dark.**
<u>The kids</u> *look* **hungry.**

PHRASES AND CLAUSES

A **sentence**—a group of words that expresses a complete thought—is like a community. Although a community is made up of individual people, it is also made up of larger units—families, households, and other interconnected groups. If you think of a sentence as a community, then the words in a sentence are like the individuals who live there. Groups of related words called **phrases** and **clauses** are like the families and other kinds of households that individuals create within that community.

Phrases

A **phrase** is a group of related words that is missing a **subject** (pp. 346–347), a **verb** (pp. 339–340), or both. (If a group of words contains both a subject and a verb, it is a **clause**, not a phrase.) A phrase performs a single function within a sentence.

There are several different types of phrases. The most important categories are: **verb phrases, prepositional phrases, verbal phrases,** and **appositive phrases.**

VERB PHRASES

A **verb phrase** is a group of words made up of a **main verb** and one or more **helping verbs** (or **auxiliary verbs**) that work together (p. 340). There are twenty-three words that can serve as helping verbs: all the forms of the verbs *be, have,* and *do* (which can also serve as main verbs) plus *may, might, must, can, could, would, should, shall,* and *will.* A main verb can have up to three helping verbs. In the following sentences, the whole **verb phrase** is in boldface and the <u>main verb</u> is underlined:

Lucinda **has been** <u>taking</u> swimming lessons this summer.
Charles **will be** <u>going</u> to college in the fall.
Stephen **should have been** <u>encouraged</u> more in school.

PREPOSITIONAL PHRASES

A **prepositional phrase** is a group of words that begins with a **preposition** (pp. 341–343) and ends with a **noun** (pp. 334–335) or **pronoun** (pp. 335–337). The noun or pronoun that follows the preposition is called the **object of the preposition.** In the following sentences, the whole **prepositional phrase** is in boldface, the *preposition* is in italics, and the <u>object of the preposition</u> is underlined:

Some exchange students ***from*** <u>Germany</u> visited our class.
Megan and Dan had dinner ***on*** **the** <u>porch</u>.
Owen told them ***about*** his new <u>job</u>.

Note: When a pronoun is the object of a preposition, it should always be in the **objective case** *(toward me, with him, for her, to us, at them, between you and me).*

A prepositional phrase usually **modifies,** or describes, another word in the sentence. When a prepositional phrase modifies a noun or pronoun, it is functioning as an **adjective** (p. 338). When a prepositional phrase modifies a verb, adjective, or adverb (pp. 340–341), it is functioning as an **adverb.** Occasionally a prepositional phrase functions as a noun, usually as the equivalent of the **direct** object (p. 347) in a sentence. Prepositional phrases that function as these different parts of speech are sometimes called **adjective, adverb,** or **noun phrases.**

Let's take another look at the previous examples. In the first sentence, the phrase *from Germany* is an adjective phrase because it modifies the noun *students* by telling which ones. In the second sentence, the phrase *on the porch* is an adverb phrase because it modifies the verb *had* by telling where. In the third sentence, the phrase *about his new job* is a noun phrase that functions as the direct object of the verb by specifying what Owen *told* to the **indirect object** (pp. 347–348) *them.*

VERBAL PHRASES

A **verbal** is a word that is formed from a verb but that functions as a different part of speech: a noun, adjective, or adverb. Verbals include **present participles** *(being, painting, taking, burning),* **past participles** *(been, painted, taken, burnt),* and **infinitives** *(to be, to paint, to take, to burn).*

A **verbal phrase** is a verbal plus any words that go with it. (It is *not* the same thing as a **verb phrase.**) There are three types of verbal phrases: **participial phrases, gerund phrases,** and **infinitive phrases.**

Participial Phrases

A **participial phrase** is a phrase that begins with a **present participle** or a **past participle.** A participial phrase always functions as an adjective phrase modifying a noun in the rest of the sentence. In the following examples, the **participial phrase** is in boldface, the <u>present or past participle</u> is underlined, and the *noun* modified by the phrase is in italics:

<u>Watching</u> **the cars speed by,** *Luis* waited to cross the street.

<u>Covered</u> **with mud,** the *dog* ran gleefully through the woods.

Note: For information on the correct placement of participial phrases to avoid dangling and misplaced modifiers, see pages 366–367.

Gerund Phrases

A **gerund phrase** is a phrase that begins with a **gerund** (a verb form with the -ing ending that functions as a noun). A gerund phrase functions as a noun phrase, acting as a **subject** (pp. 346–347), **direct object** (p. 347), **object of a preposition** (p. 349), or **predicate nominative** (p. 348).

Playing the saxophone *is* one of my favorite things to do. [subject of the verb *is*]
I *enjoy* **playing** the saxophone. [direct object of the verb *enjoy*]
I get so excited *about* **playing** the saxophone. [object of a preposition *about*]
My *hobby* is **playing** the saxophone. [predicate nominative renaming the noun *hobby*]

Infinitive Phrases

An **infinitive phrase** contains an **infinitive**—*to* plus the base form of a verb. An infinitive phrase can be an adjective, adverb, or noun phrase (serving as a subject, direct object, object of a preposition, or predicate nominative).

Andy *needs* **to find** a doctor. [noun phrase serves as the direct object of the verb *needs*]
You have the *right* **to remain** silent. [adjective phrase modifies the noun *right*]
Leah is too *old* **to drink** from a bottle. [adverb phrase modifies the adjective *old*]

APPOSITIVE PHRASES

An **appositive phrase** is a phrase that contains an **appositive**—a noun or pronoun that interrupts a sentence to rename or give additional information about another noun or pronoun. A single-word appositive or appositive phrase usually comes directly after the word it is identifying and is set off by commas or dashes from the rest of the sentence.

Megan Bisset, **my daughter's first-grade teacher,** is on maternity leave this spring.
Joyce Koslovsky, **our downstairs neighbor,** just got a new job.

Clauses

A **clause** is a group of words that contains at least one **subject** and one **verb**. (If a group of words does not contain both a subject and a verb, it is a **phrase**, not a clause.)

INDEPENDENT CLAUSES

There are two basic kinds of clauses: those that can stand alone as sentences and those that cannot. A clause that can stand alone as a sentence is called an **independent clause** (or a **main clause**). An independent clause expresses a complete thought, even though it is often linked to another clause. Every sentence must contain at least one independent clause. Both of the following sentences consist of one independent clause. The <u>subject</u> of each is underlined, and the *verb* is in italics.

> <u>Jack</u> *plays* basketball every Wednesday night.
>
> <u>Mary Beth</u> *applied* to law school.

DEPENDENT CLAUSES

A clause that cannot stand alone as a sentence is called a **dependent clause**. Even though it does have both a subject and a verb, a dependent clause does not express a complete thought because it begins with a word that makes it dependent on another idea. A dependent clause must be attached to an independent clause to form a complete sentence. A dependent clause is sometimes called a **subordinate clause.** (*Subordinate* means "lesser in rank.") A dependent clause can come at the beginning, the end, or sometimes the middle of the sentence.

> **If we don't get a dog**, my son will be heartbroken.
>
> Brian wants to drive to Florida **because he doesn't have the money to fly.**
>
> Charlene, **who lives two doors down from us**, sometimes babysits for my kids.

A dependent clause begins with a **dependent word** that connects it to the rest of the sentence. There are two main types of dependent words: **subordinating conjunctions** and **relative pronouns**. A **subordinating conjunction** is a linking word (or group of words) that shows the relationship between the dependent clause and the independent clause in a sentence. In the first two examples above, the dependent clauses begin with the subordinating conjunctions *if* and *because*. A **relative pronoun** is a word that refers, or relates, back to a **noun** (pp. 334–335) or **pronoun** (pp. 335–337) in the independent clause. In the third example above, the dependent clause begins with the relative pronoun *who*. In the following list, notice that the word *that* can function as both a **subordinating conjunction** and a **relative pronoun.**

Common Dependent Words

SUBORDINATING CONJUNCTIONS			RELATIVE PRONOUNS
after	even though	though	that
although	how	unless	which
as	if	until	who
as if	in order that	when	whom
as long as	provided that	whenever	whose
as soon as	rather than	where	
as though	since	wherever	
because	so that	whether	
before	than	while	
even if	that	why	

Like phrases, dependent clauses function within sentences as the equivalent of different parts of speech: **adjectives** (p. 338), **adverbs** (pp. 340–341), and **nouns**. Depending on their function, dependent clauses are often classified as **adjective clauses**, **adverb clauses**, or **noun clauses**.

Adjective Clauses

An **adjective clause** modifies, or describes, a noun or pronoun. An adjective clause usually begins with a relative pronoun *(that, which, who, whom,* or *whose)* or a **relative adverb** *(where* or *when)*. In each of the following sentences, the **adjective clause** is in boldface, the relative pronoun or adverb is underlined, and the *noun* or *pronoun* the clause modifies is in italics:

The *vacation* **that we're planning** is going to be fantastic.
We're going to *Galiano Island,* **which is located off the coast of Vancouver.**
The *hotel* **where we're staying** has horses and riding trails.

Note: Sometimes you can leave out the relative pronoun *that:* "The vacation we are planning is going to be fantastic."

Adverb Clauses

An **adverb clause** modifies, or describes, a verb, adjective, or adverb by specifying *how, when, where, why,* or *to what extent (how long, how much).* An adverb clause usually begins with a subordinating conjunction. In each of the following sentences, the **adverb clause** is in boldface, the <u>subordinating conjunction</u> is underlined, and the *verb, adjective,* or *adverb* the clause modifies is in italics:

Sue *moved* to Boston <u>**after**</u> **she got married.** [modifies the verb *moved* by telling when]

Zoe is *upset* <u>**that**</u> **her cat died.** [modifies the adjective *upset* by telling why]

My sister is two years *older* <u>**than**</u> **I am.** [modifies the adverb *older* by telling how much]

Noun Clauses

A **noun clause** functions in a sentence as the equivalent of a noun. A noun clause usually begins with one of the following introductory words: the subordinating conjunctions *how, that, when, where, whether,* or *why* or the pronouns *who, whoever, whom, whomever, what, whatever, which,* or *whichever.**

Whoever made this mess *needs* to clean it up! [subject of the verb *needs*]

You can give away my maternity clothes *to* **whomever you want.** [object of the preposition *to*]

Paul finally told Sasha **that he loved her.** [direct object of the verb *told*]

Note: In some noun clauses the subordinating conjunction *that* can be left out: "Paul told Sasha he loved her." Use caution, however, in making this omission. Some sentences are confusing without *that,* particularly those with the verbs *believe, conclude, declare,* and *find.*

TYPES OF SENTENCES

A **sentence** is a group of words that contains both a **subject** (pp. 346–347) and a **verb** (pp. 339–340) and expresses a complete thought.

---

* When the pronouns *who, whom,* and *which* introduce noun clauses, they are not truly functioning as relative pronouns because they are not referring back to a noun or pronoun that the clause is modifying. Similarly, although some people classify *whichever, whoever, whomever, what,* and *whatever* as relative pronouns, these words do not refer back to another word in the sentence.

Four Purposes

Sometimes sentences are classified according to their purpose. A **declarative sentence** makes a statement and ends in a period. An **imperative sentence** gives a command or makes a request and can end in either a period or an exclamation point. An **interrogative sentence** asks a question and ends in a question mark. An **exclamatory sentence** expresses a strong emotion and ends in an exclamation point.

Yasue is going to the movies tonight. [declarative]
Please do not go to the movies tonight. [imperative]
Is Yasue going to the movies tonight? [interrogative]
I cannot believe Yasue is going to the movies tonight! [exclamatory]

Note: In an imperative sentence, the subject is understood to be the pronoun *you*.

Four Structures

Sentences can also be classified according to their structure, or form. **Sentence structure** is determined by both the number and type of **clauses** (pp. 351–354) a sentence contains. A sentence must contain *at least* one **independent clause** (p. 352). However, it may contain more than one, and it may also contain one or more **dependent clauses** (pp. 352–354). Classified according to their structure, the four types of sentences are **simple, compound, complex,** and **compound-complex.**

SIMPLE SENTENCES

A **simple sentence** has one independent clause and no dependent clause. This kind of sentence may not always seem very simple because it may have a **compound subject** (p. 346), a **compound predicate** (pp. 346–347), or both. It may include lots of **phrases** (pp. 349–351). Yet as long as it has just one independent clause, it is a simple sentence. In each of the following examples, <u>the subject of the independent clause</u> is underlined, and the *verb* is in italics:

<u>Marcia</u> *goes* to medical school.
<u>Marcia</u> *lives* in Brooklyn *and commutes* on the subway to medical school in the Bronx.
<u>Marcia and John</u>, my best friend from high school, *have been married* for two years.

In the second example, the independent clause has a **compound subject**—two subjects that share the same verb—plus an **appositive phrase** (p. 351) and two prepositional phrases. Yet all of these examples are simple sentences.

COMPOUND SENTENCES

A **compound sentence** has two or more independent clauses and no dependent clauses. The two independent clauses can be joined by a comma and a coordinating conjunction (p. 343), a semicolon, or a semicolon and a conjunctive adverb (pp. 344–345). Each independent clause may have a compound subject, a compound predicate, or both. In the following examples, the <u>subjects</u> are underlined, and the *verbs* are in italics.

The <u>sky</u> suddenly *grew* dark, and the <u>trees</u> *began* to sway in the wind.
<u>Gorillas and chimpanzees</u> *are* apes; <u>baboons and mandrills</u> *are* monkeys.
<u>I</u> *would love* to go shopping with you; however, <u>I</u> *have* to study for a test and then *do* my laundry.

In the first example, the two independent clauses are joined by a comma plus the coordinating conjunction *and*. In the second example, the two clauses are joined by a semicolon, and both clauses have compound subjects. In the third example, the two clauses are joined by a semicolon plus the conjunctive adverb *however*, and the second clause has a compound predicate.

Note: For a list of coordinating conjunctions and conjunctive adverbs, see pages 343 and 344–345.

COMPLEX SENTENCES

A **complex sentence** has one independent clause and one or more dependent clauses. In the following examples, the **independent clauses** are in boldface, and the <u>dependent clauses</u> are underlined:

<u>After I spoke to my brother</u>, **I decided to call the doctor.**
<u>When I called the doctor</u>, **she said** <u>that I should come into the office right away.</u>

In the first example, one dependent clause is linked to one independent clause with the subordinating conjunction *after*. In the second example, two dependent clauses are linked to one independent clause with the subordinating conjunctions *when* and *that*.

Note: For a list of subordinating conjunctions and relative pronouns, see page 344 and page 337.

COMPOUND-COMPLEX SENTENCES

A **compound-complex sentence** has two or more independent clauses and one or more dependent clauses. The following example contains two independent clauses joined by the coordinating conjunction *yet*. The first independent clause is linked to one dependent clause with the subordinating conjunction *that*. The second independent clause is linked to two dependent clauses with the subordinating conjunctions *because* and *that*.

Roger knew that he was acting like a jerk, yet **he couldn't stop himself** because he was so worried that Justine might break up with him.

II: Refining Your Writing

Part II of this reference guide will help you pay attention to your particular grammar and usage needs. As you consult the various sections that address your particular concerns, you may encounter grammatical terms that you do not fully (or even partly) understand. Do not panic! Part II is full of cross-references to the definitions, explanations, and examples covered in Part I. Even if you have not sat down and reviewed those "grammar basics," you can easily flip back to Part I whenever you are unsure of a term or a concept that is mentioned in Part II.

CORRECTING SENTENCE FRAGMENTS
Understanding Why a Fragment Is Not a Sentence

A sentence is a group of words that has both a subject (pp. 346–347) and a verb (pp. 339–340) and expresses a complete thought. To be considered a sentence, a group of words must contain at least one independent clause (p. 352).

A sentence fragment is an incomplete sentence: a broken-off part of a sentence that is missing an important piece of information. Some fragments are missing a subject, a verb, or both. Others contain both a subject and a verb yet still do not express a complete thought because they rely on another sentence to make their point. In each of the following examples, the first part is a complete sentence, but the second part is a fragment:

> Yesterday my daughter came home from school. And immediately burst into tears. [missing a subject]

> I gave her a big hug. Wondering what could be the matter.
> [missing a subject and a verb]

A sentence fragment may look like a complete sentence because it begins with a capital letter and ends with a period, question mark, or exclamation point. A group of words is a fragment if it cannot stand on its own, if it depends on another sentence to complete its meaning. Although fragments are quite acceptable in everyday speech, and although they are often used in advertisements and even political speeches, you should avoid using them in formal writing.

Recognizing and Fixing Different Types of Fragment

Most sentence fragments are groups of related words—freestanding phrases (pp. 349–351) or clauses (pp. 351–354) that seem to be complete sentences. When you are editing or proofreading something you have written, it can be hard to spot your own fragments—unless you know what to look for. Here are some clues that a group of words might not be a complete sentence. If you notice one of these warning signs, you should take a closer look. Does the group of words have a subject? Does it have a verb? Does it express a complete thought?

CLUE #1. The group of words begins with a preposition (pp. 341–343), such as *to, from, for, in, on, at,* or *with.* Check to see if this group of words is the introduction to a complete sentence. If not, it is a freestanding prepositional phrase (pp. 349–350) that is missing both a subject and a verb. Usually, the best way to correct a prepositional phrase fragment is to connect it to the sentence that comes before or after it.

INCORRECT	⊘ Yesterday my daughter came home from school. *And burst into tears.* [missing a subject] I gave her a big hug. *Wondering what could be the matter.* [missing a subject and a verb]
CORRECT	Yesterday my daughter came home from school and burst into tears. Wondering what could be the matter, I gave her a big hug.

CLUE #2. The group of words begins with an *-ing* word but does not have a helping verb (p. 340) in front of it. Check to see if this group of words is the introduction to a complete sentence. If not, it is a freestanding participial phrase (p. 350) that is missing both a subject and a verb. You can fix this by connecting it to the sentence that comes before or after it. You can also turn it into a complete sentence by adding a subject and a helping verb (a form of the verb be).

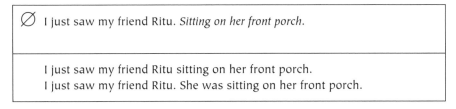

⊘ I just saw my friend Ritu. *Sitting on her front porch.*

I just saw my friend Ritu sitting on her front porch.
I just saw my friend Ritu. She was sitting on her front porch.

Note: For information on the correct placement of participial phrases to avoid dangling and misplaced modifiers, see pages 366–367.

CLUE #3. The group of words begins with an **infinitive** (*to* plus the base form of a verb.) Check to see if the infinitive is introducing a complete sentence. If not, the group of words is a freestanding infinitive phrase that is missing both a subject and a verb. Usually, the easiest way to correct an infinitive phrase fragment is to connect it to the previous sentence.

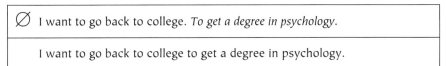

⊘ I want to go back to college. *To get a degree in psychology.*

I want to go back to college to get a degree in psychology.

CLUE #4. The group of words provides an example or explanation of something in the previous sentence. Check to see if this group of words is attached to a complete sentence or includes its own subject and verb. If not, it is a fragment. Pay particular attention if a group of words begins with a word or expression that signals that an example is about to be presented: *for example, for instance, such as, like, usually, particularly, typically,* or *especially.* To correct this type of fragment, either connect it to the previous sentence or turn it into a new sentence by adding a subject and verb.

 When she grows up, Esther wants to be a scientist. *A zoologist, biologist, or geologist, for example.*

When she grows up, Esther wants to be a scientist. She might become a zoologist, biologist, or a geologist.

CLUE #5. The group of words begins with a subordinating conjunction (p. 344), such as *because, although, if, when, unless,* or *after.* Check to see if this group of words is connected to an independent clause. If not, it is a freestanding dependent clause (pp. 352–354) pretending to be a sentence. Although this type of sentence fragment does have a subject and a verb, it does not express a complete thought. Usually, the best way to fix a dependent clause fragment is to connect it to the previous or following sentence. Another solution is to turn the clause into a sentence by getting rid of the subordinating conjunction.

FRAGMENT: Maya is studying sign language. *Because she wants to work with special needs children.*

CORRECTED OPTIONS:

Maya is studying sign language because she wants to work with special needs children.

Because she wants to work with special needs children, Maya is studying sign language.

Maya is studying sign language. She wants to work with special needs children.

COMMON SUBORDINATING CONJUNCTIONS			
after	as though	as	before
as soon as	that	because	than
rather than	whenever	so that	when
though	since	until	as long as
although	unless	as if	even if

Note: For a more complete list of subordinating conjunctions, see pages 344–345.

CLUE #6. The group of words begins with a coordinating conjunction (p. 343), such as *and, but, or,* or *yet.* Check to see if this group of words includes a subject. If not, it is the second half of a compound predicate (two or more verbs that share the same subject.) Usually, the best way to correct this kind of fragment is to connect it to the previous sentence (without a comma).

 Darnell got home from work. *And immediately checked his messages.*

Darnell got home from work and immediately checked his messages.

CORRECTING RUN-ON SENTENCES
Understanding What Makes a Sentence a Run-On

There are two types of run-on sentences. The first type, when two independent clauses (p. 352) are run together without any punctuation, is called a fused sentence.

FUSED SENTENCES:

I was born in Missouri I have lived in Massachusetts for ten years.

Nobody knows why he made that decision it was not a good one.

The second type of run-on, when two independent clauses are joined only by a comma, without a coordinating conjuction (p. 343), is called a comma splice. In each of the following examples, compare the run-on sentences with the corrected versions.

COMMA SPLICES:

Dogs are good companions, they can be trained to do many tasks.

She takes the bus every day, however, she doesn't enjoy it.

REVISING RUN-ONS

There are four techniques you can use to revise a run-on sentence. You will want to vary these techniques to avoid dull writing.

Technique #1—Use a comma and a coordinating conjunction to separate the two independent clauses.

 I was born in Missouri I have lived in Massachusetts for ten years.

I was born in Missouri, and I have lived in Massachusetts for ten years.

Technique #2 – Turn the independent clauses into separate sentences.

⊘ Nobody knows why he made that decision it was not a good one.
Nobody knows why he made that decision. It was not a good one.

Technique #3 – Separate the independent clauses with a semicolon.

⊘ Dogs are good companions, they can be trained to do many tasks.
Dogs are good companions; they can be trained to do many tasks.

Technique #4 – Add a subordinating conjunction (p. 344) to one of the clauses to make it dependent.

⊘ She takes the bus every day, however, she doesn't enjoy it.
Even though she takes the bus every day, she doesn't enjoy it.

CORRECTING PROBLEMS WITH SUBJECT-VERB AGREEMENT
General Points on Subject-Verb Agreement

Subjects and verbs must always agree. Once you have determined if the subject of the sentence is singular or plural, you must change your verbs to agree. It is not difficult to make subjects and verbs agree in simple sentences, but it is important to be careful when there are words between the subject and verb.

The **man** I met on the stairs **is** a doctor.

The **flowers** of South America **are** many and varied.

Their **disagreement** over where to buy new curtains **seems** foolish to me.

Agreement with Compound Subjects and Verbs

When sentences have compound subjects with *and,* the subject is generally considered plural and needs a plural verb. However, the two parts of the compound subject may refer to one thing or concept, and then require a singular verb. The **subjects** are bold, and their *verbs* are in italics.

Mary and her mom *travel* together often.

Search and rescue *is* his specialty.

Compound subjects with *each, every, neither,* or *either* require singular verbs. Try replacing the items after *each, every, neither,* or *either* with the word *one.* You will remember that the verb must be singular.

Each print and negative *has* to be catalogued.
Each one *has* to be catalogued.

Every ball and bat *belongs* to the sports center.
Every one *belongs* to the sports center.

Neither of the main dishes *contains* any meat.
Neither one *contains* any meat.

When a sentence has a compound subject with either/or or neither/nor, the verb agrees with the part of the subject that is closest to it.

Either the President or his **Cabinet Members** *have* an answer.
Neither the boys nor their **sister** *knows* where the dog is.

Agreement with Indefinite Pronouns and Quantity Words

Indefinite pronoun subjects require singular verbs.

Nobody *knows* who made the phone call.
Something *smells* funny in here.

Some quantity words use singular verbs, while others use plural verbs.

<u>Singular</u>	<u>Plural</u>
another	both
much	many
less	fewer
(a) little	(a) few
a great deal of	several
a large amount of	a large number of

Much <u>needs</u> to be done before the house can be sold.
About twenty people are on the committee. **Several** <u>are</u> lawyers.

Some quantity words can be used with both singular and plural verbs, depending on their antecedents.

all	no
any	none of
half of	other
a lot of	part of
more	some

All the luggage <u>is</u> lost.
All the runners <u>are</u> tired.

USING VERBS CORRECTLY
Verb Tenses

It is important to use appropriate tenses and standard forms of English verbs. English verbs (except for the verb *to be*) have five forms:

base form
-s form
-ing form
past form
past participle.

Since many verbs are irregular in English, be sure that you are using the correct form of the past or past participle.

> We went to the movies last weekend.
> She does not want any help.

- **Don't shift verb tenses abruptly** within paragraphs. When writing in the past tense, do not shift to future or present tense for no reason. If you have a reason to shift tenses, be sure that you signal the shift with transitional words or expressions.

> When we were young, we lived in the country. Today, we live in a suburb of a large city.

- **Past tenses** have specific uses; be certain to use them appropriately. The past perfect tense is used to show that one event occurred before another in the past. However, when there are sequencing words like *after* or *before*, use the simple past tense.

> When my mother arrived, I *had* already *cleaned* the house. (past perfect)
> After I vacuumed the bedrooms, I *did* the laundry. (simple past)

- **Present tenses** are used in a number of ways: to make generalizations; to talk about habits or repeated actions; to show future time in dependent clauses (beginning with *after, before, as soon as, if, until,* or *when*); or to talk about plays, films, or books.

> The *sun rises* in the East and sets in the West.
> I *have* dinner with my parents every weekend.
> Before she arrives, I *would like* to talk to you.
> The *movie is* a classic thriller that looks into the mind of madness.

- The **present perfect tense** is used to talk about actions that began in the past and continue in the present, and to talk about completed actions that occurred at an unknown or unspecified time in the past.

> I am sure I have met you before.
> She has been interested in biology for many years.

USING PRONOUNS CORRECTLY
Pronoun-Antecedent Agreement

Pronouns replace or refer to nouns (pp. 334–335) or indefinite pronouns (pp. 335–337). The noun that comes before a pronoun is called its antecedent; pronouns must agree with their antecedents. Be sure that pronouns have clear antecedents in sentences, and avoid confusing references.

 We put the stray dog in the yard next to the car and washed it.
(What was washed, the car or the dog?)

We wanted to wash the stray dog, so we put it in the yard.
OR
We put the stray dog in the yard while we washed the car.

Other Points about Pronouns

Be careful to use pronouns appropriately. When the antecedent is an indefinite pronoun, or is a word of unspecified gender, use a pronoun combination that is not gender specific.

An athlete should visualize his or her goal clearly before a competition.
Everyone must turn in his or her assignment before Monday.

Pronouns should agree with the nearest element of a compound antecedent connected by *or* or *nor*.

Either Martha *or* John will give us his opinion when we need one.
Neither the coach *nor* the players knew where their equipment was stored.

Pronouns must agree with collective nouns (class, committee, couple, family, team, etc.); usually, collective nouns take singular pronouns. However, when the collective noun refers to the members of a group who are acting as individuals, use a plural pronoun.

The committee scheduled its meeting for 10:00 a.m.
A family must consider the needs of all of its members.

BUT

The team cleaned out their lockers after the final game.
The judge polled the jury about their verdict.

In formal writing, use <u>you</u> only to refer directly to the reader.

In the chart below, you will see just how far profits have fallen. (correct)

Deciding on a career is difficult; you must consider many different factors.
(awkward)
Deciding on a career is difficult; there are many different factors to consider. (better)

Using the Correct Form of Pronouns

Decide which form of the pronoun is correct. Some antecedents will require subject pronouns; others will require object pronouns. Try separating the two pronouns and forming two independent sentences. This will tell you which form to use.

> ⊘ Leslie and me wanted to meet the professor after class.

Leslie wanted to meet the professor after class.
Me wanted to meet the professor after class. (incorrect)
I wanted to meet the professor after class. (correct)

> Leslie and I wanted to meet the professor after class.

Be sure to use the correct form of the possessive.

His car is new; hers is old.
The blue car is mine; the red one is yours.

CORRECTING MISPLACED AND DANGLING MODIFIERS

Modifiers are words or phrases that limit or describe other words and phrases.

Dangling Modifiers

Dangling modifiers are incorrect because they refer back to the wrong antecedent.

> ⊘ **Dancing and singing**, the restaurant had very talented entertainers.
> (The restaurant does not dance and sing.)
>
> The talented entertainers dance and sing at the restaurant.

> ⊘ **After finishing dinner**, the dirty dishes stayed on the table while we talked.
> (The dishes did not finish dinner.)
>
> After finishing dinner, we talked, and left the dirty dishes on the table.

Misplaced Modifiers

When used correctly, modifiers, especially limiting modifiers (even, just, merely, nearly, only, simply) are placed **next** to the word or phrase that they describe. **Misplaced modifiers** do not appear next to the word or phrase they describe.

> ⊘ We bought a hot dog from a man on the corner that tasted terrible.
> (The corner did not taste terrible; the hot dog did.)
>
> We bought a hot dog that tasted terrible from a man on the corner.

Be careful not to split infinitives by putting modifiers between **to** and the base form of the verb, which can cause clumsy and unclear sentences.

⊘ He explained how **to** carefully and patiently **assemble** the mechanism.
He carefully and patiently explained how **to assemble** the mechanism. OR He explained how **to assemble** the mechanism carefully and patiently.

USING PARALLELISM

Coherent writing requires the use of **parallel forms**. The most common use of parallelism occurs when your writing contains a series; each item in the series must have the same grammatical form.

⊘ She enjoys skating, reading, and to cook gourmet meals.
She enjoys skating, reading, and cooking gourmet meals.

Constructions that require parallelism

The most common constructions that require parallelism are correlative conjunctions (p. 343), and coordinating conjunctions (p. 343).

⊘ We can't decide whether to go back to Europe or visiting Asia this year.
We can't decide whether to go back to Europe or to visit Asia this year.

⊘ Living in a house is more expensive than to live in an apartment.
Living in a house is more expensive than living in an apartment.

Choosing the Right Words
Avoiding slang, jargon, clichés, and vague language

It is important to be direct in your writing. Use words that mean exactly what you need to say and be sure that they are appropriate to your purpose and audience.

- **Slang** is too informal for academic and professional writing. Words such as *kid* instead of *child*, or *cool* in place of *excellent* should be avoided.

- **Jargon** is usually too specialized. For example, language like *megabyte* and *logging on* should be used only if the audience is familiar with computer technology.

- Clichés such as *rags to riches, a word to the wise* make your writing predictable, less serious. Use a dictionary and a thesaurus to choose more exact words to convey your meaning.

Avoiding Wordiness

Communication is at its best when it is direct. Do not try to impress your audience or fill up space by using long, wordy sentences in your writing. Stick to your point and make it in as few words as possible. Compare:

> Her father has long been employed as a sanitation engineer. (wordy)
> Her father has worked as a janitor for many years. (concise)

Avoiding Sexist and Racist Language

- Do not use language that reinforces stereotypes about men and women and their roles in life. It is not safe to assume that certain professions, for example, are generally held by one gender or the other. Also, use generic nouns that do not specifically refer to male or female.

> The committee will elect a new chairman. (biased)
> The committee will elect a new chairperson. (neutral)

> For centuries, mankind has advanced and developed. (biased)
> For centuries, people have advanced and developed. (neutral)

- Be very careful not to use language that will offend because of racial or ethnic stereotypes, or which is clearly racist or bigoted. Test out your writing by asking yourself how you would feel if you were being talked about in the same way; if you do not like it, do not use it. If unsure, share your ideas with classmates or instructor.

WRITING CONCERNS FOR LANGUAGE MINORITY STUDENTS

Language minority students sometimes have special needs when writing formal English. This section covers some of the most frequent concerns; you may have other issues in your writing. Discuss them with your instructor.

Nouns and Articles

There are two types of nouns in English: *count* and *non-count*. Simply put, the English language separates nouns that can and cannot be counted.

Non-count nouns refer to physical substances which can only be measured but not counted (liquids like *milk*, small particles like *rice*, semi-solids like *mud*). Nouns that are not physical (*hate, information, news*) are also non-count nouns. Non-count nouns have only a singular form; count nouns can be singular or plural.

> She bought *seven apples* and *two sandwiches* for the picnic. (count)
> The *milk* spilled all over my notebook. (non-count)

Count nouns can be preceded by either definite or indefinite articles (p. 338). The indefinite article *(a/an)* refers to a noun in a general sense; it is often the first time the noun is mentioned in a writing or conversation. The definite article *(the)* is used to refer to a noun that has already been identified, or that is unique (a proper noun); the definite article can be used with either singular or plural count nouns.

> A new president is elected every four years.
> The president met with Congress to discuss the immigration laws.

Verbs Followed by Gerunds and Infinitives

Certain verbs require other verbs to follow them in either the gerund or infinitive form (pp. 350–351). The gerund is the *-ing* form of the verb; the infinitive is the *to* form. Some verbs can be followed by either form. The following verbs are followed by an infinitive:

> Example: I agree to finish my vegetables before I eat my dessert.

agree	decide	mean	refuse
ask	expect	need	wait
beg	fail	offer	want
bother	have	plan	wish
choose	hope	pretend	
claim	manage	promise	

These verbs are followed by gerunds:

> Example: I avoid eating snacks between meals.

appreciate	deny	imagine	recall
avoid	discuss	keep	resist
can't help	dislike	miss	risk
consider	enjoy	postpone	suggest
delay	finish	practice	tolerate

These verbs can be followed by either the infinitive or the gerund:

> Example: I begin to worry about my son if he is not home by 9:00.
> I begin worrying about my son after 9:00.

begin	hate	remember	try
continue	like	start	
forget	love	stop	

Two-Word Verbs

There are many verbs in English that are followed by prepositions. The best way for students to learn two-word verbs is to memorize them. Here is a list of the most common two-word verbs.

ask out	get away (with)	pick up	take care of
break down	get over	point out	take off
break up (with)	get up	put away	take out
bring up	go out (with)	put back	take over
burn down	go over	put off	think over
burn up	grow up	put on	throw away
call off	hand in	put out	throw out
call up	hand out	put together	try on
clean up	hang on	put up (with)	try out
come across	hang up	quiet down	turn down
cut up	help out	run across	turn in
do over	keep on	run into	turn on
drop in	keep up	run out (of)	turn out
drop off	leave out	see off	turn up
drop out (of)	look into	shut off	wake up
fill in	look over	speak to	wear out
fill out	look up	speak up	wrap up
fill up	make up	stay away (from)	
get along (with)	pick out	stay up	

Index